# Wealth Strategies for Your Business

# Wealth Strategies for Your Business

Over 500 strategies to increase profits and reduce costs

## TONY GRANGER

CENTURY
BUSINESS

Wealth Strategies for Your Business

First published in the United Kingdom by Century Ltd
Random House, 20 Vauxhall Bridge Road, London SW1V 2SA

Random House Australia (Pty) Limited
20 Alfred Street, Milsons Point, Sydney
New South Wales 2061, Australia

Random House New Zealand Limited
18 Poland Road, Glenfield
Auckland 10, New Zealand

Random House, South Africa (Pty) Limited
PO Box 337, Bergvlei, South Africa

Random House UK Limited Reg. No. 954009

Papers used by Random House UK Limited are natural, recyclable products
made from wood grown in sustainable forests. The manufacturing processes
conform to the environmental regulations of the country of origin.

ISBN 0 7126 7602 3

Typeset by SX Composing DTP, Rayleigh, Essex

Printed and bound in Great Britain by Mackays of Chatham plc,
Chatham, Kent

Companies, institutions and other organisations wishing to make bulk pur-
chases of any business books published by Random House should contact
their local bookstore or Random House direct:
Special Sales Director
Random House, 20 Vauxhall Bridge Road, London SW1V 2SA
Tel 0171-973 9000 Fax 0171-828 6681

# Acknowledgements

I am most grateful to my many friends for helping me with this book – for constructive criticism and comment, Johannes Jordaan and Nevin Weakley; for typing and helping with the research, Julie Backshall, without whose untiring help the production deadline would have been impractical; James O'Hare, David Abbey, Louise Drury and Geraldine Voysey for research and other assistance.

To the many hundreds of businesses which participated in our surveys – your information and advice was invaluable and this book would not have been realised without your input – thank you.

Finally, a special acknowledgement is due to Ross Hyett whose support and daily encouragement kept the literary juices flowing and to Elizabeth Hennessy of Random House, who had the faith.

\*\*\*\*\*\*

Acknowledgement is made to the following for permission to quote:

Arum Publishers for quotation from *The Book of Lists, the 90's Edition*, by David Wallechinskey and Amy Wallace.

Corgi Books for quotation from *The Wit and Wisdom of Forrest Gump*, by Winston Groom.

Strategy is: a scheme or principal idea through which an objective would be achieved.

David J. Luck and O.C. Ferrell
*Marketing Strategy and Plans*
2nd Ed, Prentice Hall, 1985

(1) The science of planning and directing large-scale military operations, specifically (as distinguished from tactics), of manoeuvring forces into the most advantageous position prior to actual engagement with the enemy. (2) A plan or action based on this. (3) Skills in managing or planning, especially by using stratagem.

*Webster's New World Dictionary*

A strategy describes the *direction* the organisation will pursue within its chosen environment and guides the allocation of resources. A strategy also provides the logic that integrates the parochial perspectives of functional departments and operating units and points them in the same direction.

George S. Day
*Strategic Market Planning:*
*The Pursuit of Competitive Advantage*
West, 1984

# Contents

# Preface

My objectives in writing this book were to develop workable strategies for owner-managed businesses to increase their profits and whilst doing so, to improve their efficiency through planned and focused structuring. By cutting out inefficiencies and business waste; by reducing costs; by following the 500+ success strategies mentioned, you can significantly add to the wealth of the business and the individuals in it.

A major consideration was the ability to find the problem or symptom and then to deal with it in a series of steps, developing a greater understanding and awareness of what could be done in a comprehensive and effective manner – in other words, to lay bare the situation and then to deal with it.

I wanted the business owner and serious business reader to think about the *consequences* of doing or not doing something. This action implies *knowledge* of what can or cannot be done, as well as information and knowledge which often tests the parameters of possibility.

Much has been written about the theory and principles behind modern business practice, yet there is, to date, very little cohesive information available about the inner workings of small businesses. This includes the practical mechanisms which the business owners can facilitate on an integrated basis across the full spectrum of the business's activities to reduce costs whilst increasing wealth. Sure, there are many books on taxation, management, pensions, employee benefits, motivation, goal setting, and the like, but a dearth when it comes to combining everything into effective strategies on which to model one's efficient governing of the business. Much takes place on what happens in the business; too little occurs on how to work *on the business* itself to build wealth.

Whenever I asked the question: 'Why are you in business?' I was usually met with the following retorts related to traditional thinking:

'To satisfy my customers.'
'To make a profit.'
'To provide employment – have something to do.'
'To add value . . .'

It came as no surprise that most people went into business for the wrong reasons. By asking yourself what you specifically wanted to achieve when you first went into business (your initial objectives – a better quality lifestyle, independence, higher earnings, having fun, and so on), you will agree that these are different from the stock answers above, which are more the *results* of being in a business, not the objectives from going into it in the first place.

When everything is said and done, most people are in business *to create wealth* – business wealth or personal wealth, whether as business owner or employee. In the final analysis you work and then (you hope) you retire. Everything you do and will do is geared towards this end objective. You may build up and sell many businesses to get there. You may even have failed more than once on your business journey. Your ultimate objective will be the same – you will use the business *to create wealth* for yourself (and possibly for those working for you); your employees will use the business to do the same.

The many *strategies* outlined in this book are ultimately about wealth building – keeping more of what you have; controlling more of what the business has to give away. They give you choices and actions to save the business money – money which is then converted into business owner and employee wealth creation.

Whilst mainly directed at sole traders, partnerships and limited companies, many of the strategies and principles outlined can be applied to bigger businesses with equal success – possibly on a larger scale when it comes to cost reduction and tax savings.

Businesses have learned one major thing over the past few recessionary years – the art of survival. It's not entirely a focus on profits, but one of managing cash flows, learning how to strike out obsolescence, reduce costs, squeeze that margin like never before. Business owners must get to grips with the *real issues* facing them as managers, whilst businesses today have every opportunity to create more wealth than ever before.

There are over three million small business owners in the UK, consisting of sole proprietors, shareholders and partners. Over 250,000 new businesses will start up in the UK this year, and 50,000 of them will fail. Many thousands of existing businesses will join their associates at the corporate graveyard in Cardiff. Yet much of this business trauma could be avoided with proper planning – and knowing the *consequences* of actions to be taken or not taken.

Business success is measured by results. How profitable and how resilient the business is; how adaptable it is to changing circumstances; and how the business ship is steered through often uncharted waters will be key determinants of this success.

Whatever the problem or inertia which may occur within a business, others have been there before with similar challenges. Their successes and failures have been documented and surveyed in order to pass on valuable and essential information to the reader. The author has spent over fifteen years in devising thousands of money-saving and wealth-building strategies, the key ones being detailed in this guide.

*The book is based on my understanding of current tax law and relevant legislation at the time of writing. The implementation of some of the strategies may require the reader to seek further professional advice, which should be considered, in any event, prior to the implementation of any strategies. Where investments are mentioned, the reader's attention is drawn to the fact that values may fluctuate up and down and that past performance is no guarantee of future success. Where loans are secured against property, there is always the risk of losing the property if loan payments are not maintained. Carefully consider your personal circumstances and those of the business before implementing any strategies as the author cannot be held responsible for any acts, errors or omissions (E & OE).*

*Figures used in calculations throughout the text refer to the 1995/96 tax year.*

Tony Granger
Harrogate, December 1995

The book is divided into three distinct parts:

*Part 1* deals with business financial strategies showing where cost savings can be made, setting achievable goals and getting the business into shape to deal with the future (Chapters 1–14).

*Part 2* details business tax-reducing strategies to save money, whilst using the existing tax system to best advantage to increase cash flows as well as profits (Chapters 15–23).

*Part 3* describes business wealth-creation strategies. Having made savings on costs and increased profitability, the best methods of wealth-creation are given. How to make the most of what you have; increasing it and not losing it (Chapters 24–31).

Each chapter begins with an overall objective, which is a main strategy. Mini-strategies are then given, which are numbered to provide easy access, and lead to the successful attainment of the chapter's objective. A key point summary is then given at the end of each chapter.

# Abbreviations

| | |
|---|---|
| 3i | Investors in Industry plc – the largest venture capital group in the UK, recently floated on the Stock Exchange |
| AA/FPCS | The Automobile Association's recommended fixed charge for mileage costs – fixed profit car scheme |
| ACT | Advance Corporation Tax, payable on profits in advance of dividend distributions, and deductible from mainstream tax |
| AIM | Alternative Investment Market |
| APP | Appropriate Personal Pension |
| AVC | Additional Voluntary (pension) Contributions made by employees at up to 15% of their taxable pay. The AVC must be part of the employer's main pension scheme |
| BUPA | Medical and hospital benefits provision company. Others are PPP and WPA, and Norwich |
| CAA 1990 | Capital Allowances Act 1990 |
| CCJs | County Court Judgments |
| CGT | Capital Gains Tax |
| CGTA | Capital Gains Tax Act 1979 |
| CIC | Critical Illness Cover, also known as 'dread disease' cover. Pays out a tax-free lump sum on diagnosis of a critical illness, such as cancer or stroke |
| Class NIC 1A | National Insurance Contributions payable by employers for company cars and fuel benefits |
| CPA | Compulsory Purchase Annuity made from a pension fund |
| CVA | Corporate Voluntary Arrangement |
| CV | Curriculum Vitae (work history) |
| CY | Current Year |
| DSS | Department for Social Security. Collects national insurance contributions (NIC) |
| DTI | Department of Trade and Industry |
| EIS | Enterprise Investment Scheme. The 'son' of the now discontinued Business Expansion Scheme |
| EPP | Executive Pension Plan. An employer-owned pension scheme for individuals with high funding levels |
| EPS | Earnings Per Share |
| ESOP | Employee Share Owner Participation scheme. Synonymous with an ESOT |
| ESOT | Employee Share Owner Trust |

| | |
|---|---|
| EU | European Union |
| EZT | Enterprise Zone Trust. Investments made in an EZT zone are usually 100% allowable against taxable income |
| FA | Finance Act |
| F (No.2)A | Finance (No.2) Act |
| FSAVC | Free-standing AVC with any pension provider |
| *FT* | *Financial Times* newspaper |
| FURBS | Funded Unapproved Retirement Benefit Schemes |
| GPPP | Group Personal Pension Plan |
| HR | Human Resources |
| HP | Hire Purchase |
| ICS | Investor Compensation Scheme |
| IHT | Inheritance Tax – Inheritance Tax Act 1984 |
| IRR | Internal Rate of Return |
| IT | Information Technology |
| IVA | Individual Voluntary Arrangement |
| LAPR | Life Assurance Premium Relief. Discontinued in 1984, but older policies may still benefit from it today |
| LTC | Long Term Care |
| LIBOR | London Inter-bank Offer Rate of interest |
| LINC | Local Investment Networking Company |
| LPG | Liquid Petroleum Gas |
| MBO/MBI | Management Buy Out/Management Buy In |
| MIRAS | Mortgage Interest Relief At Source. The tax relief on interest paid on a loan to purchase your main residence |
| NatWest | National Westminster Bank |
| NIC | National Insurance Contributions, collected by the DSS and the Inland Revenue for the DSS in certain instances |
| NRE | Net Relevant Earnings |
| OMO | Open Market Option for annuities |
| OPM | Other People's Money |
| P9D | Returns for lower-paid employees recording the value of benefits-in-kind |
| PAYE | Pay As You Earn – the tax collection system for Schedule E employees |
| PCP | Personal Contract Purchase for cars |
| PEFA | Private Equity Funding Association |
| PEPs | Personal Equity Plans – investments which grow tax free and suffer no capital gains tax |
| PET | Potentially Exempt Transfer for inheritance tax reductions. The asset must be held for seven years for full relief |
| PHI | Permanent Health Insurance. An insurance policy to protect your income if you become sick, injured or dis- |

|  |  |
|---|---|
| | abled |
| PLC | Public Limited Company |
| PIID | Returns for directors recording the value of benefits in kind |
| PPPs | Personal Pension Plans |
| PR | Public Relations |
| PRP | Profit-related Pay. A scheme designed to give tax-free income to employees |
| QFP | Qualified Financial Planner |
| s.226 | Retirement annuity plans were known as s.226 plans |
| Schedule D | The tax schedule for the self-employed and certain other classes of income |
| SERPS | State Earnings-Related Pension Scheme |
| SIB | Securities and Investment Board |
| SIPP | Self-invested Personal Pension Plan |
| SP | Inland Revenue Statement of Practice |
| ss | Sub sections of a particular act or regulation |
| SSAS | Small Self-Administered Scheme. An occupational pension scheme with no more than 12 members |
| SWOT analysis | Strengths, Weaknesses, Opportunities, Threats |
| TA 1988 | Income and Corporation Taxes Act 1988 |
| TCGA | Taxation of Chargeable Gains Act 1992 |
| TEC | Training and Enterprise Council. Provides training and business development grants for businesses |
| TESSA | Tax-Exempt Special Savings Account. Building Society investment giving tax-free income |
| TMA | Taxes Management Act 1970 |
| VAT | Value Added Tax. Collected by Customs and Excise |
| VCTs | Venture Capital Trusts. A tax-efficient higher risk investment introduced in June 1995 |

# PART 1

# Business Financial Strategies

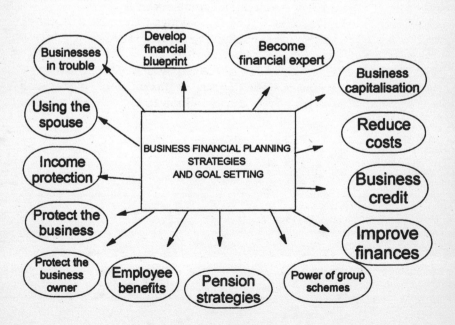

GETTING THE BUSINESS INTO FINANCIAL SHAPE

# CHAPTER 1

# Developing Your Business Financial Blueprint

*Most people aim at nothing and hit it with tremendous accuracy.*
**Making Your Business Really Fly seminar**

## Objective: Planning and goal setting for the business owner to achieve success in all facets of the business

When I first considered writing this book it was with the benefit of hindsight after helping countless businesses achieve their major definitive purpose – that of building wealth.

A poorly-constructed business is soon out of business. I was reminded of a Brian Tracy seminar when people were asked, 'If you won a million pounds today, what would you do with it?' One man responded by saying that he would go farming until all the money was gone. Some businesses will make it – many more will fail. Don't waste business oxygen on something which cannot succeed.

The problem with most businesses that fail is that they have not been properly structured from the very beginning. There has been very little long-term planning and certainly even less thought applied to *why* the owner was in business, or the employee worked for it. In other words, the singular lack of business *goals* and a major definitive

purpose can consign a business to the companies' graveyard in Cardiff
for ever.

---

### STRATEGY #1
### Proper planning is essential for success.
### Set your business goals

---

In 99 out of 100 cases, the only time I have seen a business plan is when
a business is forced to produce one to raise capital either by way of
loans or from private investors. It is only the rare exception which produces a business plan to set its strategic targets for the future.

If you are going to 'plan your work and work your plan', then you
need to set out your business goals *in writing*.

On a separate sheet of paper, write out as many *business goals* as
possible.

Now, *prioritise* these in order of importance.

---

### STRATEGY #2
### Set out your personal goals for the future

---

What do you want to do with your life? What do you want to achieve
for you and your family? What is your primary objective in life? There
have been many books written on goal setting – all brim-full of good
ideas on how to go about it.

The crux appears to be that everyone has a different perception of
life's needs, wants and opportunities. Often we have 'blockers' which
stand in our way of setting and achieving goals – because we feel a particular goal is unattainable, it raises a fear of failure, so we don't attempt
it in the first place. So, what one great thing would you *dare* to dream
if you knew you could not fail?

Write it down. This will in time become your major definitive purpose in life. Put your dream up on the wall where it faces you every day
and focuses your attention every time you look at it. All entrepreneurs
have plenty of vision. What many of them lack is focus. *Focus* is the
direction and 'bulls-eye' of your innate attention. Focusing in on the
task at hand will help to eliminate distraction, and you will be able to
concentrate on your major planning objectives.

Take the case of a top salesman faced with a half a million pound
target from his company. The previous best he had ever achieved was
£300,000, working at full pace. He had the clients but never enough
time, and a half-million pound sales target for the year was, he

considered, unattainable. He would never reach it.

This type of problem is common when viewed as a whole. However, if broken down and visualised as 'bite-sized' chunks, with proper planning and focus, the task – £500,000 worth of sales – could be attainable. In this case, the planning sequence would go as follows: £500,000 divided by 48 weeks (everyone deserves a holiday!) and again divided by five working days is £2,083 per day. The average size sale per client is £1,000, so our super-salesman must see about two clients a day.

He knows if he does business with an average of two clients every working day, he will reach his target. To get two clients, he needs many more prospects, so organisation and planning is geared to prospecting and producing possible clients for sales. Using a telesales team to make his appointments, he begins the journeys towards *his* personal goals (family security, wealth-building, exceptional lifestyle) which in turn form the basis for his business goals.

---

## STRATEGY #3
## Combine personal with business goals for maximum effect

---

Have you ever thought why so many employees say, 'I hate this job - I only do it because of the security,' or 'It's a roof over my head,' or whatever? Very few people seem to have job satisfaction where they love what they do and feel happy doing it.

There are many reasons for these feelings. You could write books on how badly people feel about their jobs. One of the biggest reasons is because there is no harmony between their jobs and their personal goals. Wouldn't it be fantastic if everyone enjoyed what they did and experienced their just rewards for doing it? Unfortunately, we live in an imperfect world, and often the things we want elude us – for some, for ever. However, those who do set personal and business (or work) goals, and are able to harmonise them (or reconcile them) to establish their major definitive purpose in life, are well on their way to focused enrichment.

Let's get down to the 'nitty gritty' – developing a blueprint for success.

By now, you should have your goals established. It's time to develop your 'mission statement' and then your business plan with key result areas and actions to take you forward. Working within a defined structure, with focus, will give you a sense of direction and peace of mind you never had before.

## STRATEGY #4
## Complete your mission statement

The mission statement is the business's goal(s) encapsulated into a few short paragraphs. The greatest companies in the world all have a mission statement – it is the core focus for what the business is about. I have been into many businesses to conduct benefit audits and business reviews and it never ceases to amaze me how few have a mission statement.

A simple example would be:

> The business aims to produce and sell a quality product whilst providing exceptional service to its customers, at an affordable price.
>
> In doing this, the business will maintain the development of a happy and contented work force, produce profits for its shareholders through increasing share values and dividends, and share profits with its work force through profit related pay.
>
> The business will increase its market share by 2%, thus maintaining its position as the leading company in the widget sector.

Here, the business has subtly combined the twin focus areas for business owners (shareholders) and employees of wealth-building through profit sharing.

Ask yourself – why are you in business? Why do you work? Why risk your capital in the business? Remember, there are very few philanthropic entrepreneurs. People work to make money and create personal wealth; businesses exist to make money for their business owners and to create wealth for them. Other so-called reasons are nice to know about (in business to create jobs for other people; in business to give me something to do, etc) but not necessarily true – the real reason is to make money, and lots of it!

## STRATEGY #5
## Make your business make money – your strategies

An obvious strategy is to make a profit. Profits are the results of income exceeding expenditure. Yet profits alone are not the only area to be considered. For tax reasons, some businesses will contrive to make a loss –

but they will still be in business. Others will make a loss through poor trading or bad business decisions, but their reserves will carry them through.

The strategies in this book will indicate areas for making a profit, but will also show you how to massage cash flow, reduce costs (the biggest killer of profits is costs), and build wealth through taking profits out of the business in ways other than merely taking a dividend or increasing a salary.

---

## STRATEGY #6
## Create your strategic plan for the business

---

Most business owners are familiar with what a business plan looks like and what it is meant to do. If you are not, then ask your local bank manager for a sample plan, or call in at your local LINC or Business Link or TEC offices (Training and Enterprise Councils) and get a copy.

The business plan is laid out in sections. These sections differ as to format, depending on what the business plan is to be used for. If one has been done for raising money, it will be heavily weighted towards influencing a lender, with plenty of forecasts and cash flows, methods of repayment and so on. A business plan which is marketing oriented (more of a sales and marketing plan) will be differently tempered to cater for these needs.

The type of business plan which we are looking for here is one to be used for *strategic planning*. Cash flows, capital requirements and marketing analysis will all be part of such a plan. If you can't do it yourself, call in an expert (usually a business management consultant) who can. Up to 50% of the costs can be met by the DTI. It's well worth the money, considering it will be your blueprint for years to come.

### Component parts of a strategic plan

1. Mission statement.
2. Business goals with measurable standards – (i) assumptions; (ii) key result areas.
3. Description of the business and what it does.
4. Management team and CVs.
5. Ownership structure including shareholder, share capital and working capital positions.
6. Present position of the business. Accounts for the year end and management accounts.
7. Cash flow forecasts for up to five years.
8. Profitability forecasts.

9. Marketing strategy including sensitivity analysis on competitors and market niche.
10. Sales strategies.
11. Production strategies.
12. Expenditure analysis and strategies for cost reduction.
13. Pay, payroll, remuneration and employee benefit strategies.
14. Capital requirements and business funding.
15. Training.
16. Succession planning, business protection, shareholder coverages.
17. Monitoring, review and feedback.

The above are the main areas around which your strategically- focused planning will take place. You may, of course, add sections to it or delete those of no relevance to your business.

---

## STRATEGY #7
## Save time by having an expert develop your plan with you or for you

---

There are a number of extremely good business planners around. Perhaps your first stop is your accountant – certainly you will need correct figures and forecasts for your plan. If you have an in-house capability, get your management team to come up with a blueprint for success. If not, management consultants, the TECs, etc, can assist the smaller business which is probably the sector requiring the most help.

If unhappy, get a second opinion, or a third opinion.

Be prepared to pay the price.

---

## STRATEGY #8
## If failing in business, withdraw to protect your personal wealth

---

Your business plan may show that your chosen course of action will not succeed; or that some ingredient is missing and the business will fail.

There may come a time when it is better to get out rather than stay in. If this is the case, then consider options and strategies for a phased or planned withdrawal if you have to. There is absolutely no point in compounding matters and putting your personal wealth at greater risk.

## STRATEGY #9
## Always pay yourself first

Those in business (especially small ones) usually learn this lesson the hard way. If the business is in a formative phase (starting up) or in decline (not making it), then the usual action is to try to hang on for as long as possible, massaging your scarce resources. Paying employees when the business is short of cash is both a moral and emotive area, and can cause a big drain on the business owner. *Always* pay yourself first. If, unfortunately, you cannot afford to pay the employees, discuss it with them. Most will wait for a month or two; others will temporarily accept a reduction; others will simply leave.

Although you may take a reduction (along with your employees), you should always ensure that you do not run down your private financial reserves as it will be difficult to get started again if you have to. Also, the stresses on health, family life and marital relationships worsen when financial aggravation enters the picture. Make sure that you do not neglect yourself financially – pay yourself first. If you go out of business, there is no business and no employment for others.

## STRATEGY #10
## Do a SWOT analysis to focus on
## developmental areas

SWOT – **S**trengths, **W**eaknesses, **O**pportunities and **T**hreats.

What are your strengths? What are your weaknesses? Consider not only yours, but also those of the business. Where do your opportunities lie and what threats stand in your way to success? Knowing these is to know yourself.

Often your goals and objectives will grow from identifiable strengths and opportunities. Some opportunities may come from dealing with those weaker areas requiring developmental strategies.

## STRATEGY #11
## Learn from those who are successful and then do what they do

There is no point in reinventing the wheel. If someone else has successfully accomplished a task or successfully developed a business, then it is important to learn from them. Seeking out role models to emulate will focus the entrepreneur on successful habits and processes, rather than those stereotypes which have failed. Study the failures as well, however, to learn where they have gone wrong and, more importantly, *why* they went wrong.

Research your particular industry sector and business sector. Discover who the successful people are and what they did and still do to be high achievers. Successful people will respond positively if asked. Read books (such as Stephen Covey's *The 7 Habits of Highly Effective People*) and continually think and focus on *how* to realise your business dreams for success.

Developing strategies gives you the 'how to' – goal setting gives you the *desire*. Decide what you want for your business, your family, your employees, the business environment and for yourself.

Learning from those who have gone before you will help you avoid unnecessary and costly mistakes. Business statistics on business failures (there are hundreds of thousands each year) pinpoint lack of planning and structure, poor management, lack of business expertise and lack of capital or undercapitalisation as the major causes. To this list I would add not knowing the consequences of certain actions and also the lack of information generally on how to run a business successfully.

## STRATEGY #12
## Make sure that the business is properly capitalised

With the best will in the world, a plant will not grow without water and sunlight, a motor vehicle will not run without fuel, and businesses cannot function without adequate working capital.

A number of bank managers told me that on average those seeking capital are usually asking for 50% too little. In other words, they felt that at least *double* the capital asked for was actually required. Entrepreneurs seem to think that if smaller amounts are asked for, they will be easier to get. In fact, the reverse is often the case. Larger loans are more profitable to lenders, and bankers would rather a business was properly funded in the first place or not at all.

There are many perfectly good and sound businesses which simply run out of working capital and come to a standstill – like a motor car which has run out of petrol. One of the most important strategies for you is to ensure adequate funding for the business.

---

### STRATEGY #13
### To develop a successful business, get the best team to help you

---

Business owners are policy makers. They are allowed to, and encouraged to, dream. From them flows the vision for the business. The management and employees implement the policy decisions and 'draw down' the focus.

Surrounding yourself with a good management team with solid track records is an important ingredient for business success. They will help you save costs, increase profits, expand the business turnover, cope with constant change in the business environment and provide management expertise to take the business forward.

Above all, you and the management team will be able to develop the *right strategies* for your business circumstances, through undertaking reviews on where the business is now and where it wants to be; ascertaining what may go wrong through incorrect or insufficient strategies (or none at all) so that all eventualities may be considered; and setting measurable and attainable goals.

To assist every business owner, partner, director, manager and employee to develop their personal and business success, this book contains over 500 useful strategies.

## Key points summary

- This chapter gives the reader the incentive to set personal as well as business goals for future success. Goals must be attainable and measurable.

- All businesses should have a 'mission statement' which is designed to focus the people in the business on its major definition purpose.

- Steps in the creation of a strategic plan for the business are given, as well as basic strategies for success, including proper capitalisation and the use of experts.

# CHAPTER 2

# Becoming Your Own Financial Expert

*Chiefly the mould of a man's fortune is in his own hands.*
**Francis Bacon (1561–1626) Essays: 'Of Fortune'**

**Objective: Obtain the full picture about your business whilst developing your own financial expertise**

If you are ever going to take control of your own financial future, you must become aware of the parameters of your planning opportunities. In other words, if you don't know what is out there and available to you, how can you plan to make effective use of it, or discard it as not being relevant to your objectives?

How do you know that the 'expert' advice which you receive from others, many of them professionally qualified, is in fact appropriate, or that your advisers have the necessary knowledge?

That is *the* major problem experienced by people wanting to properly structure their personal and business affairs. Unsure of whether they are getting the best advice or not, they either act or do not act. Sometimes it is a case of damned if you do and damned if you don't.

> ## STRATEGY #14
> ## Make sure you have all the necessary
> ## information available to ensure success

If you only have limited information available to you, and you take decisions based on that information, then the consequences could be disastrous. In addition, if you know what the possible consequences are of taking certain actions or not taking them, then you can plan accordingly.

A number of examples spring to mind. We did a study of risk awareness on financial products amongst our clients some years ago. It is common practice, when advising clients on which investments are most suitable for them, to ascertain how risk-averse or risk-preferent they are before advising them.

In the mind of the financial adviser is the full spectrum of investments from money under the mattress to the most speculative equity investments. He will rate these on a scale of one to ten with 'one' being the most safe and cautious to 'ten' being the most risky and speculative. He will ask his client where on the risk line he would consider himself to be. The client, for example, says 'five'.

In his mind the financial adviser sees a medium risk investment structure with, say, gilts and managed funds. However, in his or her mind, the client may be considering some of the investment in the building society, the balance in National Savings. In essence, they are poles apart. Why? The answer is lack of information and ignorance as to what is available and why it is risk-rated in the way it is. Our actual tests showed the financial adviser with full knowledge rarely deviated from the mean, whereas the client with limited knowledge and understanding of the products was often *over 50%* either side of the mean. The 'mean' is the middle point on the scale of measurement. Deviation either side of this middle point indicates that the standard is not being met.

Years later the client may say that he was a medium risk taker and enquire as to why he was placed in the wrong investment portfolio by the financial adviser when equity markets fell, when all he wanted was a fixed deposit in the building society. The financial adviser would have been clearly at fault for not ascertaining the true requirements of the client or for not educating him properly before advising him. In fact, at that time, the SIB (the supreme regulator, the Securities and Investment Board) stated that the greatest levels of complaint were those received from investors placed in the wrong type of investments for them, according to their risk preferences and personal circumstances.

Take the tragic cases of hundreds of thousands of people with houses repossessed and businesses liquidated throughout the late 1980s and 1990s. At the time of writing, over 4,000 homes are still being repossessed a week, with more than half a million homeowners six months or more in arrears with mortgage payments. Bankruptcies, liquidations and redundancies have all added to the toll of broken families, suicides and stress-related illnesses. The real tragedy is that not enough information was available to enable people to take into account the *consequences* of losing a home, business or family. Much of what actually happened could have been avoided and still can be.

How many homeowners thought that the mortgage guarantee indemnity premium was there to protect *them* – not the lender? How many voluntarily handed in the keys to their homes thinking, 'Well, we made a loss, but that's the end of it'? They did not realise that they were also liable for the losses suffered by the lender, and had no power over the give-away sales prices their previous homes fetched. These people ended up in deep financial trouble and with high levels of stress.

It is essential to have as much information available as possible to make the correct decisions which will ensure business success. Not having sufficient information on which to base business decisions could result in the wrong decisions being made.

---

### STRATEGY #15
### Develop your understanding of the big picture first

---

Much of the above could have been avoided with adequate planning and knowledge. More importantly, knowing what financial tools are available and having knowledge of the overall picture are crucial. For example, skilled debt negotiators (see Chapter 14) could have saved your house or your business. You do not need to go bankrupt if an IVA (Individual Voluntary Arrangement) may save you (or a CVA – Corporate Voluntary Arrangement for your business), all you need is the knowledge.

Becoming your own financial expert is not necessarily becoming an expert on all matters. It is knowing what to do and whom to approach for appropriate structuring and planning – and often taking more than one opinion. Not all advice is free. Be prepared to pay a small sum now for greater wealth-building and savings later.

## STRATEGY #16
## Get yourself a qualified financial planner

Most wealth-builders have professional advisers. These are usually people operating in isolation from one another, often offering an overlap of services, and may include a solicitor, an accountant, an insurance broker or agent or independent financial adviser, or a bank manager or stockbroker. It is usually up to the client to bring these 'experts' together or to interpret their individual recommendations.

If you feel unable to co-ordinate everything yourself, then engage a qualified financial planner to do so. For example, a fellow of the Institute of Financial Planning would be ideal.

## STRATEGY #17
## Obtain a written report on where you are and where you want to be

Either ask each adviser for a written report, or have your qualified financial planner construct one using information from each of your professional advisers.

This then becomes your knowledge base. You are now ideally positioned to become an expert on yourself, and you can get whatever additional information you need from your personal financial planning advisers.

You will then have expert financial information in the following areas:

| | |
|---|---|
| Solicitor | Will, trusts, contracts, legal planning, tax planning. |
| Accountant | Tax planning, remuneration and deductions planning, business planning. |
| Stockbroker | Investments and portfolio planning. |
| Insurance broker | Insurance and pension policies, some investment plans, mortgages. |
| Bank manager | Banking arrangements, loans, general advice, bank investments. |
| Qualified financial planner | Personal financial plan. |

---
**STRATEGY #18**

**If a business owner, consider a corporate report on the present position and future of the business**

---

In the same way that you have considered personal financial planning, you should become an expert on all aspects of your business. Once you know where you are (or, in fact, where others think you are) you can then plan for a corporate future of wealth-building.

---
**STRATEGY #19**

**The quickest way to become your own financial expert is to get experts to keep you informed – so do so now**

---

Most people give the excuse of not having enough time to read. Yet others get up at 6 am and read articles on business and motivation for an hour before going to work.

Regular briefings, audio and video tapes, articles and layman's literature in your chosen area can go a long way to providing the understanding required to utilise the expert's information fully.

A mentor or strategy planning business consultant to bounce ideas off is also invaluable. It's not only a matter of being able to read a balance sheet which is important to a businessman, but how to read the signs within the business and from its employees. These are essential for future direction planning.

---
**STRATEGY #20**

**Learn to understand the numbers**

---

Anyone who owns or manages a business must be able to understand basic accounting and be able to read financial statements and management accounts. Without this essential knowledge and skill, you can't possibly determine exactly what is going on in the business, and how to plan for the future. A full knowledge of accounting is not required, just a comprehensive knowledge of basic bookkeeping. I am reminded of the story of the Wall Street stockbroker who put together many successful deals, often referring to a sheet of paper kept secretly locked in his wall safe. Everyone wondered how he did it. On his death, management opened his safe to see what the secret was. On the sheet of paper was written, 'Remember debits on the left, credits on the right.'

The following example is most revealing on where to concentrate business effort and energy.

| | Base £ | Change % | Result £ |
|---|---|---|---|
| Price of product | 100 | 5% increase | 105 |
| Sales volume | 100 | 5% increase | 105 |
| **Total revenue** | **10,000** | | **11,025** |
| Variable costs | 6,000 | 5% decrease | 5,700 |
| Gross margin | 4,000 | | 5,325 |
| Fixed costs | 3,000 | 5% decrease | 2,850 |
| **Net profit** | **1,000** | **147.5% increase** | **2,475** |

Small changes in certain areas – a small increase of 5% in sales and price, and a small decrease of 5% in costs – can have a substantial effect on net profit. In this case, the increase is 147.5%!

Your understanding of the *numbers* is therefore crucial to your future success or failure.

Don't be afraid to implement your strategies. Learn the business from the figures upwards. Become your own financial expert.

## Key points summary

- You must know the parameters of your planning opportunities.

- Gather together all relevant information so that you have enough data to make important decisions.

- Use experts to help you and keep you informed.

- Compile a corporate report on the present position of the business and its future objectives.

- Learn the numbers – this is essential in planning and understanding the business.

CHAPTER 3

# Borrowing Money – Financial Control Strategies

*The only time you can't raise finance is when you need it.*
**A Law of Finance**

**Objective: Ensuring that the business is properly capitalised and remains so**

This chapter is not about the theory of finance or the principles of corporate finance – about which many excellent books have been written – but is concerned with the various types of finance available and the best places to find it. It is about how, when the banks and lending institutions seem to be against you, you will still be able to raise capital from other sources. You will also learn how to give a different slant to business plans requiring debt financing (loans) as opposed to equity capital from investors.

> ## STRATEGY #21
> ## Determine which part of the business growth cycle your business is in

Businesses have four distinct phases of growth. Each phase has a differently-structured need for capital, depending on the financial and business risks involved. It is therefore important to determine whether the business is in a start-up phase, a growth phase, a maturity phase or is in decline.

The following table indicates generally-acceptable factors inherent in each phase:

|  | START-UP | GROWTH | MATURE | DECLINE |
|---|---|---|---|---|
| Business risk | very high | high | medium | low |
| Financial risk | very low | low | medium | high |
| Funding source | venture capital | equity investors for growth | retained earnings plus debt | debt |
| Dividend policy | nil | nominal | high | maximum |
| Growth prospects | very high | high | medium to low | negative |
| Price/earnings multiple | very high | high | medium | low |
| Current profitability – earnings per share | nominal | low | high | low and declining |
| Share price | grows rapidly but volatile | growing but volatile | stable with low volatility | declining and increasing in volatility |
| Cash inflows | negative | medium | high | low |
| Cash outflows | very high | high | low | increase due to fixed costs |

There is a difference between business risk and financial risk. Where the business risk is very high (start-up), then the financial risk should be kept as low as possible. Only risk-preferent equity investors will be attracted, because they expect a high capital gain. Dividends would certainly not be paid because of the negative cash inflows to the business. Traditionally these types of venture capital investors will wish to realise their gains within three to five years, and again invest in higher risk businesses. Different equity investors, who will still expect a capital gain, but at a lower growth rate, will then be attracted to such a growth company.

*Start-up* companies will not gain from using debt financing and should preferably be funded by equity. Debt will increase the risk of defaulting on loans which will reduce value for investors. The *likelihood* of defaulting (even for small loans) in a start-up business is also much greater. Start-ups, by definition, will have little or no cash inflows, and servicing loan debt could lead to financial distress.

*Growth companies* should see increased sales volumes with a shift to emphasis on increasing market share. Overall business risk reduces with low financial risk, but is still high because of rapid sales growth. Equity funding should be continued to keep financial risk low. New equity investors will replace venture capitalists. This is often the period to consider a flotation for funding. The business will be investing inwardly during this phase and dividends will be nominal. Investors are still looking for capital growth, reflected in the growth in earnings per share (EPS).

*Mature companies* will see high, stable sales with reasonable profit margins. Business risk levels will reduce and the market could see increasing price competition. Financial risk, through debt financing, can now be increased. Positive cash flows allow the debt to be reasonably serviced. If debt funding is used, more cash is available to pay dividends to investors at a higher rate. Future growth prospects are considered lower, and increased dividends on higher-valued shares will be attractive to investors who will now expect less from capital growth. Assets are now fully employed with stable cash inflows and higher levels of profitability. The need for reinvestment reduces, the business has high positive cash flows, and is in a position to raise debt financing.

*Companies in decline* will experience lower cash inflows as demand for the product falls, and static cash outflows, if properly managed. Although business risk is low, there is a place for high financial risk debt financing. Negative future growth prospects can be linked to a high dividend paying policy, especially if debt financing is introduced for reinvestment. The share price should steadily decline, but higher dividends (effectively repayments of capital), should keep investors reasonably happy. This type of business should pay particular attention to cost reduction strategies, especially in the area of fixed costs, by changing to a variable costs basis and short-term contracts. Borrowings would be structured against realisable assets of the business, but lenders will of course be cautious when dealing with a business in decline. A declining business may seek to diversify or be acquired, giving it a second lease of life.

Financial strategy should therefore be carefully tailored to the appropriate development phase of a business. The correct funding of the business will have a major impact on the investors and their preferences for risk and return, so it is important to have a proper understanding of the type of capital or financing required by the business.

## STRATEGY #22
## Determine whether the business requires debt financing or equity financing

There should always be an inverse correlation between business risk and financial risk.

Decrease of business risk – increase of financial risk.
Increase of business risk – decrease of financial risk.

There are two main sources of external funding: equity capital and debt financing.

## Equity capital

Shareholders, having made an equity investment, cannot demand a return of their investment from the company. Shares may grow in value and produce a capital gain and a flow of income in the way of dividends but there are no guarantees and the company decides whether to pay a dividend or to reinvest the cash in the business. The shareholders are owners in the company but often have less rights than its creditors, only being paid on liquidation after all other claims have been settled in full.

Shareholders may hold *ordinary* shares or *preference* shares. Preference shares have a fixed level of dividends and holders rank before ordinary shareholders for repayment if the company is wound up. Preference shares, although equity in name, can sometimes be classed as debt because of their nature.

## Debt financing

This is usually by way of loans, or other similar financial investments. Debt is repayable as to the capital amount and interest is payable for the use of the capital borrowed. Those making debt available are legal creditors of the borrower, and also prescribe the terms and conditions of the debt, such as defaulting on payments. Usually corporate or personal guarantees are taken as security for the debt – in most cases today a first charge against assets. The lender will try to limit its risk with onerous obligations.

If given a choice of capital provision, what should the business opt for? The company may feel that debt funding is higher risk than equity; the investor may feel that equity is higher risk; the lender will see debt as low risk. Every party will have a different view of risk depending on the circumstances.

Debt funding will always be cheaper for a company than equity funding. Equity funding is more expensive and the existing owners of the company will have to give up part of their ownership to new shareholders. If new shares are issued, there could be a dilution in value for existing shareholders.

Tax law allows for interest on debt financing to be tax deductible to the company, thus cheapening its cost even further.

One should not undertake an equity risk for the returns offered from debt financing. In other words, the return on equity (in capital growth value of shares and dividends plus, if appropriate, director's fees), should always be significantly higher than the return on debt financing (interest payable). The ultimate distinction between debt financing and equity financing is that debt is repayable, equity is not. Equity financing has a higher risk profile for the investor (he could lose his investment), but a lower risk profile for the company (it need not be repaid and there are fewer restrictions on its usage) than debt financing (which must be repaid).

The effect on the business is that it receives the capital resources it requires. It *must* service debt, whereas it *may* service shareholders (dividends). Depending on the phase of the business growth cycle of the company, debt financing can bring enormous *benefits* for equity shareholders, by freeing up cash for dividends. It also prevents direct dilution of the shares by further share issues. As the repayment of future debt is a long-term liability, the net worth of the company will obviously be less in the long run if things remain static but, all being well, the business will use debt financing for future growth, which should offset this.

---

## STRATEGY #23
## Be prepared to give up equity to raise capital

---

Many companies (especially family-owned businesses) refuse to give up equity. In that case, their only funding will come from debt instruments. This is a fundamental position which needs to be considered early on in the process.

## STRATEGY #24
### If the company has to give up equity, consider selling shares to the employees for leveraged tax deductible capital and interest

The company sets up an ESOT (Employee Share Owner Trust) to purchase shares in the company for the employees – at least 10% of the shares. Financing raised for the funding of the trust is tax deductible for *capital* as well as interest. This is one way to introduce cheaper working capital into the business.

## STRATEGY #25
### Wherever possible, when giving guarantees, separate personal assets from business ones

It's not always possible, but try to avoid giving security against your personal assets, such as your house. If the business fails (or even if it does not and the bank calls in a loan) you could lose your home.

## STRATEGY #26
### Determine how much capital needs to be raised by the business, and why

Many businesses remain undercapitalised because they did not ask for enough capital in the first place. Some think it's easier to ask for a smaller amount, as the bank is more likely to grant smaller funds than larger ones. The opposite is true. The banker or lender wants the assurance that the business will succeed and will treat undercapitalisation as poor judgment on the part of management.

The new capital could be used for a variety of reasons or objectives such as:

- new business opportunity
- purchase of new plant and machinery
- purchase of business property
- working capital for business expansion
- new product development costs
- tooling up of a production process
- taking out other investors or loans (repayments)

- business acquisitions
- management buy outs/buy ins
- starting up a new business.

---

### STRATEGY #27
### Add the costs of raising capital to the amount required

---

Venture capital is usually the most expensive. Actual costs in cash outflow could be as much as 20%+ a year in management charges, preference share dividends, and fees. Bank financing is usually the cheapest – LIBOR plus 1.5% to 4%+ depending on the risk profile. The cost of raising private investor capital such as EIS (Enterprise Investment Scheme) could be up to 10% initially and 1.5% to 5% per annum.

The cost of a flotation usually ranges from about £80,000 on the AIM to over £1 million for certain companies seeking a full stock exchange listing.

One company was charged £350,000 in fees for raising £750,000. Because of the high fees, the capital wasn't enough, putting further pressure on the business and its shareholders.

---

### STRATEGY #28
### Look inward before going for external funding

---

Consider whether the business can supply the funding itself, and whether this is a feasible option within given cost constraints. Where do businesses *source* their funds? A typical statement of *source and application* of funds is usually published with the profit and loss account and balance sheet of a company. Funds could come from:

- an increase in share capital
- an increase in retained profits
- an increase in depreciation provision (profit set aside to meet the cost of replacement of fixed assets).

Whilst retained profits are a likely source, as well as new equity (shareholders' capital), there are other areas of the business able to provide finance, or which can be used for the provision of finance:

- loans from directors' pension funds

- employees purchasing shares (ESOT)
- sale and lease back of fixed assets
- factoring of debtors to improve cash flows
- invoice discounting to improve cash flows
- cost reduction exercises – negotiated discounts.

By improving cash flows, cash is freed up to use for other purposes. However, this may not be enough. The business may be trying to solve its long-term funding problem with short-term funding solutions. It is inevitable that the one will eventually catch up with the other. If retained profits and shareholders' capital are insufficient or non-existent, then the business must look to external sources of funding.

---

## STRATEGY #29
## If internal funding is insufficient or not appropriate, go for external funding sources

---

Business owners have many options within the two main categories of equity funding or debt financing.

## Equity Funding

1.    New capital from *existing* shareholders.
2.    New capital from *new* shareholders.

New shareholders could be venture capitalist institutions (such as 3i) or private venture capitalists, often known as 'business angels'. Some investors are passive, wanting only to make the investment and then to wait for a capital gain; others wish to be more active in the business, becoming non-executive or even executive directors and 'following their money'. Those investors are found through a variety of sources, such as Venture Capital Report, the Capital Exchange, the IFP Taxsaver Portfolio and others. Many investors are from personal contacts, familiar with the business. Other companies may wish to take up an equity stake.

LINC, Business Link and the TECs have a wide network of investors, as do Midland Bank and NatWest Bank, amongst others.

## Loan or Debt Financing

The following are common forms of raising loan or debt financing:

1.    Short, medium or long-term loans from banks and other lenders,

including private individual lenders.
2.      Shareholders and directors making loans to the business.
3.      A mixture of financial instruments from the capital markets including secured debt, unsecured debt, junior and subordinated debt, convertibles (loan stocks), convertibles (preference shares), corporate bonds and PEPs etc.
4.      Loans made on the security of debtors (factoring).
5.      Loans made on the security of shareholders' capital (at present £2 for £1 invested).
6.      Mortgage loans using property as a security.
7.      Loans made by companies.

The above are the main sources of external debt funding. Each has its own risk profile and rate of return. The less the risk, the cheaper the financing.

## Hybrid Situations

Some joint venture investors may supply a mix of equity as well as loan finance. Equity is usually 30% to 49%, with a return of 25% of net profits and an option to sell shares after three years and a definite sale of shares at five years. Loan terms are generally favourable at LIBOR plus 1% to 3%.

## Grants

There is a wide scope for the application of grants funded through various Enterprise agencies, TECs, the EU and through the Department of Trade and Industry (DTI). These are available for start-ups through to business expansion and other consultancy work, marketing, export initiatives and other areas.
   Larger businesses will use the full range of equity and debt financing applications, including stock exchange listings to raise capital. However the smaller business will, in most cases, use the following:

## Equity

1.      Existing shareholders for new funds.
2.      New investors seeking tax reliefs under the Enterprise Investment Scheme (EIS). An investor (1995/96) gets 20% off his actual tax bill on individual investments of up to £100,000 in any one tax year (£20,000 tax relief on an investment of £100,000).
3.      Investors seeking to roll over a capital gains tax liability who may invest the gain in an unquoted company and defer tax payable at up to 40%. This investment is unlimited.

4.    Venture capitalists, more particularly 'business angel' type investors who have a high level of risk preference.
5.    Personal contacts who invest because they know the business owner and his/her business.

## Debt financing

1.    Increased overdraft for working capital purposes from a high street bank.
2.    Loans from a high street bank or secondary lender over a fixed period at an agreed rate, based on the business plan of the business.
3.    Government guaranteed loan scheme – up to 85% is guaranteed by the government on loans of up to £250,000 are now possible.

## Grants

Grants are available from a variety of sources. This is 'free money' which need not be repaid and if the business qualifies for grants, then take them.

---

### STRATEGY #30
### Make sure your company qualifies under the Enterprise Investment Scheme (EIS) initiative (and for CGT Reinvestment Relief)

---

If your business qualifies (booklets are available from the DTI and Inland Revenue), then obtain interim approval *now* from the Inland Revenue. This will enable investors to get tax relief (if they qualify) on their investments in your company. Combined EIS and CGT (capital gains tax) investments could give 60% tax reliefs. Qualification is mainly assessed on being a trading company, in a trade which qualifies. The Enterprise Investment Scheme and capital gains tax qualifying companies have broadly similar criteria.

---

### STRATEGY #31
### If a sole trader or in a partnership, then obtain capital individually

---

Sole traders and partnerships are at a distinct disadvantage to companies. They have nothing to offer investors as they cannot give off equity – unless the incoming investor becomes a partner. Only new *partners* can buy into a partnership. Interest payments on loans taken out to do this are deductible to the partner.

Loans are possible, but usually have to be backed by personal guarantees or security against personal assets.

Professional practices, such as solicitors, accountants or doctors, can take up unsecured loans, as long as they take out an endowment policy or a pension as a repayment vehicle (the lump sum portion from the pension scheme being used to repay the loan). Special schemes cater for these types of loans, available only from specialist lenders.

---

### STRATEGY #32
### If you need larger funding, consider incorporating

---

By becoming a company, sole traders and some partnerships may have more options for funding than if they remained a sole trader or partnership (as outlined in Strategy #31). This is particularly the case with investors providing equity capital who will get shares in a company, which is impossible otherwise. Only unquoted qualifying companies may accept capital gains tax reinvestments, for example.

---

### STRATEGY #33
### Construct a business plan for equity investment or loan (debt) financing

---

Having determined how much capital you need to raise, and for what purpose, you now need to construct the ideal business plan to turn your business dreams into reality.

Funding (or the lack of it) either succeeds or fails depending on how strong your business plan is, and how well presented it is. Presentation is everything. Cumbersome business plans with no clear direction will go nowhere very fast. Business plans which are clear, unambiguous and well laid out with an executive summary position at the beginning, will at least get to first base. Most business plans are fairly standard. In fact, for £65 you can purchase software capable of providing a good end-product. Alternatively, your accountant or a specialist management consultant can do one.

Others able to offer advice on business plans include LINC, Business Link, the Capital Exchange, PEFA – the Private Equity Funding Association – or your bank. Both Midland Bank and Lloyds Bank have pro forma specimen business plans which you can use. The emphasis of the business plan will be different for equity investments (giving details of what private investors can expect) as opposed to one for debt financing (giving details for loans required, with repayment possibilities and interest servicing).

In any event, a business plan will enable the business to state its objectives and to plot its future growth path and is necessary as a blueprint for developing the business (see Chapter 2).

The *essential components* of a good business plan should include the following:

- colourful front cover
- summary of proposals and requirements
- details of the management team and their CVs
- description of the business, its products (brochures if possible) and trading history
- reasons why the capital is required and how it will be used – financing requirements
- what do investors get for their investment, or lenders for their financing?
- accounts as up to date as possible. Financial performance of the business
- cash flow forecasts for at least three years, preferably five years; profit forecasts; balance sheet
- competitive advantages and opportunities
- the target market and market 'sensitivity' analysis
- marketing and selling
- goals of management, strategy and action timetable
- the prospects for the business.

The 'executive' *summary* at the beginning of the plan should be about one or two pages in length, highlighting the key points in the plan:

- a brief introduction to the business
- the market for goods or services
- the business potential
- current growth position
- forecast of profit figures
- abbreviated cash flows for at least three years
- finance or investment required
- prospects for the investor/lender, including exit routes for the investor or lender

Include the fact (if so) that a Keyman policy (or policies) has been effected for the amount invested or borrowed.

## A business plan summary

The following example is taken from our case files, and is reproduced with the permission of the company. This company raised the first £40,000 of its £150,000 investment requirement within days of presentation of its business plan to unknown investors. In addition, the plan (with minor changes) was used to secure Government Loan Guarantee Scheme financing to complete its funding requirements.

### THE CLEVER MAP COMPANY LIMITED
#### *The Executive Summary*

This business plan has been produced by the management of the Clever Map Company and reflects both the present and future status and goals of the company. This plan is not an offer to purchase shares, nor is it a prospectus. It is merely an informative document.

The Clever Map Company was set up with the sole purpose of producing maps that are both innovative and informative with the attention to detail which is unrivalled.

> The Clever Map Company is seeking to raise £150,000 (one hundred and fifty thousand pounds sterling) by way of equity.

The company is seeking new capital to fund its identified expansion programme to capitalise on new and existing market potential in the increasing range of its innovative maps; and to ensure the company's rapid growth.

The company has four major products ready to launch and seeks sufficient funds to employ the key sales staff necessary to ensure that its sales targets are met.

In particular the company has obtained the contract to produce The Imperial Hotels Guide to London. This will be a monthly product given away free to every guest of the Imperial Hotel chain in London. This chain of hotels situated mainly in the Bloomsbury area of London fills 120,000 beds a month. The guide will generate approximately £40,000 of advertising revenue per month at approximately 50% gross margin.

The company also has plans to launch a monthly give-away map in association with *Time Out*; a National Speed Trap Map in association with the AA and a London Driver's Survival Map which combines the successful Back Street Map, London

Parking Map and the London Speed Trap Map.

The Clever Map Company is offering 30% of the equity in the company to investors by way of issuing new shares in the business.

The company has received interim approval from the Inland Revenue that it qualifies as an Enterprise Investment Scheme (EIS) company under the qualifying regulations. Investors may therefore qualify for tax relief on their investments into the company.

The company also qualifies for those investors seeking CGT rollover reinvestment relief.

The Business Plan envisages repayment of the interest on the loan on a monthly basis and of the capital sum 24 months after its advance.

The company has effected a Keyman Life and Critical Illness insurance policy on Mr Rupert Saunders, the Managing Director, for the full amount of investor's equity to be raised.

---

## STRATEGY #34
## Invest in a strong management team

---

Whilst lenders will look closely at your figures, they are in fact more interested in who is running the business. Essentially, lenders and investors invest in the management team of the business. You may need to strengthen your team – on paper, at least – by bringing in additional expertise. This need not be full-time employees – expert or specialist part-timers will do.

---

## STRATEGY #35
## Display strong market potential, particularly for niche markets for your products or services

---

Investors and lenders want to know that you will be around in the future – as well as your business.

Funding development or expansion capital in a niche market or low competition markets will mean that the product or service stands more than an even chance of success. Give the market *potential* for your target market.

---

### STRATEGY #36
### Include a marketing and competition 'sensitivity' analysis in your plan

---

Some business owners avoid this issue, because they fear the possibility of no investment, or investment in competitors, if they disclose the true picture of the marketplace. Nothing could be further from the truth – displaying an awareness of the marketplace and its competitors, highlighting the potential of the business, will indicate to investors and lenders that every aspect has been considered.

---

### STRATEGY #37
### Approach your bank manager or lender with the business plan

---

Banks offer overdrafts and loans. They also offer the guaranteed loan scheme, where the government guarantees up to 85% of the loan.

You may wish to practise on another bank (to get your presentation right). Your own bank knows you and the business. This could be a good thing or a bad thing, depending upon your circumstances and relationship with the bank manager.

Many bank managers can only approve smaller loans, and may have to refer you elsewhere. One thing is for sure – by not giving your own bank the opportunity to pitch for the business, you could sour later relationships.

#### How to present yourself

- Be practised. Have the information at your fingertips
- Look conventional
- Bring out the important parts of your plan – don't waffle
- Get to the decision-makers
- Answer all questions clearly and listen carefully
- Research and present additional information well
- Prepare yourself for criticism. Your plan *will* be critically examined
- The process is one of negotiation – so be prepared for this
- Ask for the right amount. If you go in too high, you can always come down
- Consider carefully proposals for security against personal, non-business assets

• Be prepared to invest yourself. The lenders want to see personal sacrifice

---
**STRATEGY #38**
## Know what the bank manager looks for, and be prepared
---

Bank managers use a system for loan assessment. Whilst some will have their own, the following is standard:

## The PARSRS System

*P: Person*    The person behind the proposal. The areas covered are character, competence and capacity. This includes personal background, qualifications, experience and determination to succeed.

*A: Amount*    The amount, purpose of the loan and its effect on the business. The manager will want to look at the type of loan required (overdraft for short-term funding, loans for longer periods); cash flows and detailed expenditure and income; how much the business owners are putting in and whether additional working capital requirements to fund growth are included.

*R: Repayment*    How will the bank be repaid? There must be a source of repayment, from profits or the sale of an asset. Possibly a funding vehicle (endowment type) is appropriate. The bank manager will look at past business performance (if any), projected figures and underlying assumptions. Budgets for expenditure and cash flow forecasts showing the day-to-day cash/bank position of the business need to be shown. Costing, pricing and contingency plans for if there is a setback will need to be seen.

*S: Security*    The degree of risk is considered next and the security required. The bank will first look to the business owner before taking third party security. Security should be easy to value, readily available and possibly connected to the purpose of the loan.

*R: Remuneration*    The fees the bank can expect from setting up the loan arrangement. Interest and commission rates will also be negotiated.

*S: Services*    Other services the bank can offer you.

The bank, if satisfied, will then send you a written facility letter stating:

- what you are being offered by way of loan or overdraft
- what the bank wants as security
- what management accounting information it requires
- the cost of arranging the loan and interest and commission charges.

---

### STRATEGY #39
### Shop around for your bank loans for the best deal

---

Always include your present bankers in your round of presentations. However, go to different banks with your proposition. Some may turn you down; others may make you an offer. Use the criticism from the 'no gos' to improve your business plan. Your presentation skills will also improve the more you have to make the presentation of your plan to lenders.

---

### STRATEGY #40
### Your best strategy is to prepare a business plan when you don't need it

---

It will always be best to negotiate your future borrowing position when you are in a position of strength. The weaker the business gets, the less likely a lender will be interested. You will also get better terms if in a commanding position. Prepare your business plan *now* in order to obtain advance approval for future facilities.

---

### STRATEGY #41
## Use commercial finance experts to source your funds – but beware the up-front fee 'rip offs'

---

Using professional fund raisers can save you a lot of time. They know their way around the system and which lenders to approach for your business requirements. The usual change is about £500 up-front for 'administration' and a fee based on successful raising of the money – usually 2%.

Only use reputable capital raisers with a successful track record. No one works for nothing today, so be prepared to pay a small fee to get things going. It also shows commitment on your part.

There are also professional grant raisers whose extensive knowledge of the system is invaluable. They usually charge an up-front fee plus a percentage of the amount raised.

Venture capital brokers will also charge an up-front fee plus a percentage of the amount raised. For example, Venture Capital Report will do a five-page assessment of your business for £350 (+VAT) and a success fee of 2.5% plus £1,000 on any capital raised from private investors. It is well worth it because your business not only appears in their magazine, but also the *FT* and *Investors Chronicle*, as well as on the Internet.

---

### STRATEGY #42
## Control the funding process – don't let it control you

---

Be in control of your funding destiny. Carefully examine all propositions in the best interests of the shareholders and the business.

Make sure that you 'learn the numbers'. This means an appraisal and understanding of the financial statements of the business.

It is important also to have a financial yardstick to measure the results of the business. By learning which ratios to apply in your analysis, you will develop a much deeper understanding of the business.

*Liquidity ratios*, for example, determine if a company can meet its short-term liabilities:

$$\text{Current ratio} = \frac{\text{current assets}}{\text{current liabilities}}$$

$$\text{Quick ratio} = \frac{\text{current assets minus stock}}{\text{current liabilities}}$$

They both indicate if the company could survive if all the creditors wanted their money at once. The quick ratio is also known as the 'acid test', and is useful if the business holds stock for a length of time or sells on credit. Increased liquidity ratios indicate a safer position. In the following example the higher figure in 1995 indicates that the business has a better liquidity position than in 1994:

**1994**                                  **1995**

$\frac{1500\text{-}800}{600} = 1.17$          $\frac{1425\text{-}600}{400} = 2.06$

The above type of ratio is one of many. There are comprehensive books written on the analysis and interpretation of accounts and ratio analysis. *These are the most important areas:*

- Liquidity ratios
- Capital structure ratios
- Activity and efficiency ratios
- Profitability ratios, including a return on the owner's equity
- Capital gearing ratios.

Some are geared towards investigating liquidity, others to investigating performance. Whilst not perfect, ratio analysis does give a general indication of trends in the business, such as increasing need requirements for new capitalisation. See Chapter 28 where ratio analysis for investors is discussed in greater detail.

---

## STRATEGY #43
## Use business financing strategies to build business wealth

---

Using equity and debt financing to capitalise or recapitalise the business is an important step towards wealth accumulation in share values as well as profitability by way of dividend flow and employee benefit provision. Corporate finance for the borrower is a key strategy dealing with financial objectives and decisions. One of these is to maximise shareholders' and business owners' worth. This is how the bank sees the provision of corporate finance for its customers.

Give the lenders and investors a good chance to build your wealth!

## <u>Key points summary</u>

- Establishing where the business is in the business growth cycle will help to determine what type of funding it requires – debt or equity.

- Determining the capital needs requirements of the business, the costs of raising capital, and where to find it is given.

- The importance of a properly-structured business plan with an executive summary and how to present it to investors and lenders is described in depth.

- Developing financial control strategies, including ratio analysis is given.

- Using financial strategies to build business wealth summarises the chapter.

# CHAPTER 4

# Effective Cost Reduction Strategies

> *Whenever someone says, 'I am here to help you,' hold on to your wallet.*
> **Winston Groom *The Wit and Wisdom of Forrest Gump***

**Objective: To save thousands of pounds through making costs savings now and regularly thereafter**

Managing a business's costs is an essential discipline. Costs are divided into two main categories – fixed costs and variable costs. All too often a business becomes unprofitable, and even fails, because it is unable to control its costs. Yet, this need not happen if cost and credit control strategies are employed and if ongoing cost management is a constant focus.

To increase its profitability a business usually focuses on increasing its sales. Yet, if costs are rising rapidly and sales are constant or increasing more slowly, then the gross profit margin will shrink. It may only require small decreases in costs and small increases in sales to make a significant difference to business profitability.

The following example (adapted from Strategy #20) will best

illustrate the scenario that it only requires small changes to create bigger profits.

Tom Eardley is in business producing micro-processors which are sold on to the manufacturers of computer equipment. The price of each unit is £100, and he will sell 100 units at this price. His production capacity allows him to increase (by 5%) the number of units produced, and he has a market for his sales. He is able to create some costs savings, and he also elects to increase his price per unit by 5%.

The following is the result of these changes:

| | Base £ | Change % | Result £ |
|---|---|---|---|
| Price of product | 100 | 5% increase | 105 |
| Sales volume | 100 | 5% increase | 105 |
| **Total revenue** | **10,000** | | **11,025** |
| Variable costs | 6,000 | 5% decrease | 5,700 |
| Gross margin | 4,000 | | 5,325 |
| Fixed costs | 3,000 | 5% decrease | 2,850 |
| **Net profit** | **1,000** | **146.5% increase** | **2,475** |

Changing any one of these variables by even a small percentage (price, sales volume, variable costs, fixed costs) will produce an effect on net profits. The message is – it's not only price manipulation (the most common one) but also cost control and management which can produce a result.

## STRATEGY #44
## Determine exactly what your fixed and variable costs are

*Fixed costs* are those costs, known in advance, which will not change (or should not change) over a given period. These are usually costs seen to be essential to the running of the business. However, they may not be *vital* to the business. There is a difference in what is vital and what is essential or non-essential to a business. When it is said that these costs will not change, it is rather the fact of their existence which is difficult to change, as opposed to their monetary value. So, even though the item is fixed, allow for inflationary and other increases in fixed costs as a matter of course – such as the rent increasing. A fixed cost is an expense or overhead which does not vary with the level of production.

*Variable costs* are those costs over which the business has no, or little, control – except for the ultimate sanction of not incurring the cost in the first place. These could be variable as to the amount (the quantum) as well as to the price you pay for the item, and may also be variable in terms of usage of the costed item. A variable cost is an expense or overhead which can vary with the level of production.

The following list, which is not exhaustive, will give some idea of what are generally classified as fixed and variable costs.

| Fixed costs/Expenses (occur regardless of whether the asset is active or not) | Variable costs/Expenses (depend on the rate of output) |
|---|---|
| Salaries and wages | Bonuses |
| Employee benefits | Raw materials |
| National Insurance contributions | Sales commissions |
| Property taxes | Labour costs |
| Utilities | Maintenance costs |
|   – Gas | Utilities if used in the process |
|   – Electricity | Overheads |
|   – Water |   – Sales and marketing expenses |
| Leases/HP |   – Professional fees |
|   – Cars | Dividends (on outflow) |
|   – Insurance | |
|   – Maintenance contracts | |
|   – Office | |
|   – Computers | |
|   – Telecommunications | |
| Office cleaning | |
| Machinery | |
| Plant | |
| Warehousing | |
| Interest payment on capital | |
| Interest payments on loans | |
| Audit and accounting charges | |
| Equipment purchases | |
| Loan repayments | |
| Taxation | |
| VAT | |
| Office and administration | |
| Postage | |
| Print and stationery | |
| Rent | |
| Travel | |
| Bank charges | |
| Service charges | |
| Telephone/fax | |
| Other overheads | |

Costs and expenses may often fall into either category, depending upon their usage. Generally, though, the rule is that if the cost has to be expended irrespective of the sales or production process, then it will be fixed – it has to be paid regardless of the success or otherwise of the business. Variable costs will generally depend on the level of usage of the asset or service. The above lists may not fall strictly into balance sheet definitions, but are merely given as outflows of the business.

CASH FLOW = REVENUE - FIXED COSTS - VARIABLE COSTS

The less the costs, the less the deductions from revenue or sales and the greater the cash flow. The following strategies are designed to reduce costs and expenditure and increase cash flow and profitability.

In our example, if we merely decreased fixed and variable costs by 5%, and did not increase sales or the price per unit then an increase in net profit of 16.5% is the result.

|  | Base £ | Change % | Result £ |
| --- | --- | --- | --- |
| Price of product | 100 | 0% increase | 100 |
| Sales volume | 100 | 0% increase | 100 |
| **Total revenue** | **10,000** |  | **10,000** |
| Variable costs | 6,000 | 5% decrease | 5,985 |
| Gross margin | 4,000 |  | 4,015 |
| Fixed costs | 3,000 | 5% decrease | 2,850 |
| **Net profit** | **1,000** | **16.5% increase** | **1,165** |

---

### STRATEGY #45
### Once you have determined the expense and cost outflows of the business, examine each item for potential savings

---

Questions to ask are:

- Does the cost or expense need to be made?
- Can it be done more cheaply?
- How will this affect the cash flow and profits of the business?
- What is necessary, essential or vital to the business?
- Must the expenditure or cost be done away with altogether, or can the expenditure process be better managed? By delaying expenditure or negotiating better terms, this may have the same cash flow implications for the business on the whole.

- What are the identifiable areas of *wastage* which can be eliminated?

All too often, businesses concentrate mainly on increasing sales. Yet, better *profitability* may be achieved if sales remain constant and expenditure is reduced. Sales may even reduce and cost savings can still increase profits.

---

### STRATEGY #46
### Look at the small repeat items for cost savings, by avoiding duplication

---

One business saved literally thousands of pounds by centrally administering its subscriptions to newspapers, magazines and periodicals. On examination, it was found that many of the same magazines were purchased by all the managers in the same building – annual cost £22,000. By having a smaller number with a distribution sheet for readers, the annual cost shrank to £2,600 – a saving of £19,400.

---

### STRATEGY #47
### Avoid the 'knee jerk' reaction to cost savings

---

If the message is, 'Save costs,' the knee jerk reaction is often to make the mistake of cutting down in areas which are associated with the sales process or other *revenue producing* parts of the business. Training is usually the first expenditure to be cut, closely followed by Marketing. Sales commissions may be reduced resulting in a correspondingly reduced incentive to perform. And, of course, one of the biggest temptations is to cut down on personnel.

There is nothing wrong in having a 'leaner-meaner' organisation, but the cost cutting must be focused on the correct areas.

---

### STRATEGY #48
### Avoid always reacting to the 'painful bits' first

---

The business is not performing as it should. Large bills keep coming in, sales are down and cash flows are severely affected. Business pain is felt at management level, and the immediate reaction is to get rid of the problems most closely connected with the business as quickly as possible. This could result in the wrong decisions being taken – decisions which may have a long-lasting and sometimes terminal effect on the business. You may delay the ordering of essential new plant and machinery, cut down on the year's sales promotion and marketing or whatever. Failure to identify the true issues and then to focus on them could be costly in the long run.

---

## STRATEGY #49
## Draw up an action list with target cost reduction areas

---

Take as an example Bonpound plc.

| Area | Present expenditure £000 | Target savings £000 | Remedy/action to achieve the savings |
|---|---|---|---|
| **Fixed costs** | | | |
| Salaries, wages | 2,000 | 250 (12.5%) | Profit related pay; down-size employees by 30% |
| Employee benefits | 200 | 20 (10%) | Rebroke, change pension fund |
| NIC | 220 | 11 (5%) | NIC avoidance schemes |
| Property taxes | 50 | 2.5 (5%) | Renegotiate |
| Utilities | 150 | 15 (10%) | Renegotiate |
| Office administration | 40 | 2 (5%) | Merge functions inter-dept |
| Leases | 90 | 9 (10%) | Review and rebroke |
| Cars | 200 | 20 (10%) | Down-size status |
| Cleaning | 35 | 3.5 (10%) | Change cleaners |
| Interest payments | 100 | 10 (10%) | Re-schedule |
| Audit, accounting | 25 | 2.5 (10%) | Negotiate |
| Machinery, plant | 300 | 15 (5%) | Negotiate better funding |
| Warehousing | 85 | 15 (18%) | Restructure for space savings |
| Equipment purchases | 75 | 15 (20%) | Leave non-essential purchases |
| Subscriptions | 22 | 19.4 (88%) | Centralise subscriptions and circulate |
| Loan repayments | 50 | 0 | No change now |
| Taxation | 200 | 20 (10%) | Tax saving schemes/measures |
| VAT | 60 | 3 (5%) | VAT strategies for savings |

| | | | |
|---|---|---|---|
| Postage | 13 | 3 (23%) | Check usage. More 2nd class |
| Print/stationery | 27 | 5.4 (20%) | Renegotiate/change printers |
| Rent | 80 | 0 | No change now. Possible later |
| Bank charges | 6 | 2 (33%) | Bank check and renegotiate |
| Service charges | 10 | 1 (10%) | Renegotiate |
| Telephone/fax | 16 | 3.2 (20%) | Change system supplier |
| Insurance | 80 | 16 (20%) | Rebroke |
| Computers | 110 | 30 (27%) | Renegotiate |
| **Sub totals** | **4,244** | **493.5** | |
| | | | |
| ***Variable costs*** | | | |
| Bonuses | 200 | 20 (10%) | NIC avoidance only |
| Commissions | 150 | 0 | No change |
| Raw materials | 3,570 | 178.5 (5%) | Better buying/renegotiate |
| Labour costs | 815 | 40.75 (5%) | Natural wastage |
| Maintenance costs | 60 | 0.94 (1.6%) | Renegotiate |
| Legal costs | 60 | 6 (10%) | Change supplier; renegotiate |
| Marketing | 150 | 7.5 (5%) | Defer one programme |
| Sales expenses | 80 | 1.6 (2%) | Buy cheaper advertising |
| Dividends | 200 | 20 (10%) | Reduce |
| Professional fees | 30 | 3 (10%) | Renegotiate |
| Travel | 400 | 200 (50%) | Cut out unnecessary flights |
| **Sub-totals** | **5,715** | **478.29** | |
| **Totals** | **9,959** | **971.79 (approx 10%)** | **Target savings** |

Bonpound plc should make projected target savings of 10% of its fixed and variable costs expenditures. Each expenditure item has been examined for cost savings as well as the impact on the business. In effect, very little has changed, as savings are either due to effective renegotiation strategies with suppliers, or by doing away with non-essential expenditures. In addition, tax planning techniques (see Part 2) have a role to play.

Don't let inertia dictate your business expenditures – do something about it.

## STRATEGY #50
## Use your cost reduction strategies to overcome business obsolescence

The time spent in re-examination of the business's costs can equally well be spent in examining for areas of obsolescence in all things. For example, employee benefits products may become obsolete over time and better value can be obtained through reassessment and rebroking. Similarly, if the business is used to paying for goods and services over a long period of time, then costs will automatically rise with inflation – so subtle, you hardly know it's been happening. The same is true with pricing maintenance, cleaning and service charges, as well as rent and warehousing increases – often way beyond inflation. The following rules may help you:

- Draw up a list of suppliers and the contract person for each category
- Note what you are paying for, and how you are paying for it
- Open up lines of communication to establish whether there is a better deal to be had and at what price
- Negotiate better terms for your business
- Establish whether a trade-off is possible, for example under the corporate barter system. You could get printing, travel, warehousing, staff incentives, capital equipment purchases and so on, on barter. This could save on cash flow if you qualify. (See Chapter 25.)

Cost savings mean more wealth for the business.

## STRATEGY #51
## To save your time, make use of specialist cost reduction experts

Cost reduction is an art as well as a science. The pressure on businesses during the late 1980s and well into the 1990s has resulted in a major growth industry in experts developing cost reduction techniques in all cost and expense areas. This ranges from the supply of tea and coffee to workers, to reducing the cost of utilities, such as gas, electricity and water, business rates and so on. Usually the deal from the expert is a percentage of the savings made. In other words, your business is in a win-win situation – the expert only gets paid if reductions are made.

Some savings 'splits' are as high as 50:50.

---

## STRATEGY #52
## Use the cost reduction expert to compile a report on savings areas

---

The report generated is an invaluable tool in that a fresh pair of eyes is giving your business's cost structure 'the once over'.

One company was spending £80,000 a year (1,000 employees using up to four beverages a day) at 30p per cup from vending machines. By changing suppliers, this cost was more than halved. Yet coffees and teas are generally thought of as low-cost items.

The following are the most common areas where cost reduction specialists can be gainfully used.

### Energy management

Gas supply
Electricity tariff and supply
Electric motors and heat conducting
Boiler efficiency (gas, oil, LPG)
Water and sewage supply

### Business management

Property rates
Telecommunications systems and equipment
International telephone calls and mobiles
Postal equipment (franking machines and existing leases)
Onerous leases
Next-day deliveries
Office equipment
Printing and stationery
Maintenance contracts
Business insurance
Fleet (cars)
Employee benefits
Audit fees
Office cleaning
Cleaning products
Computer supplies
Business incentives
Coffee/tea/soft drinks

Savings of as much as 50% a year can be made in certain areas.

---

### STRATEGY #53
### Obtain cost savings for bank charges

---

There are literally thousands of redundant bank managers who have set themselves up in business to check companies' past bank charges and, if necessary, to negotiate better ones for the future.

It is a known fact that some banks have been overcharging on fees and interest charges – often for years. Sophisticated computer software has been developed which back-tracks on these charges and produces a statement of what you should have paid. The former bank managers know the system inside out and will be quick to spot any over-charging or discrepancies. Most work on a success fee (a percentage of savings), so your business has nothing to lose by having an expert examine your charges. Companies have been known to recover £50,000 and more from banks by employing this service.

---

### STRATEGY #54
### Use tax saving techniques to reduce costs and cash outflows

---

You can do anything legal to save tax. (See Part 2.) However, many people fear the taxman, the VAT man and the DSS official and, by avoiding claiming what is theirs by right, are doing themselves a disservice.

For example, every profitable business should have a profit-related pay (PRP) scheme. Over two million employees are on different ones in the UK at this time. This has the effect of returning part of pay tax-free to the employee and can be done on a PAYE basis. The business, about to experience a substantial cost in salary increases, substitutes profit-related pay for the salary increase. Result – the Inland Revenue funds the increase. The business is no worse off in terms of cash outflow, and the employee has more pay because he or she pays less tax.

There are also ways of reducing the effect of NIC which can add 10.2% to the employee's wage bill and the same again on employee benefits and company cars (NIC 1A). A manipulation on how the benefit is paid, or how the company car is given to and used by the employee, can save the business thousands of pounds. This area is more fully covered later in this book. Other tax saving areas include maximum use of capital allowances and the better structuring of employee benefits. Tax saved is cash flow increased.

# STRATEGY #55
# When reducing costs, always lead from the top down, not the bottom up

Think of the message which the management is giving to the workers. Those managers who are seen to be participating in the same cost reductions as the ones expected of the employees will help to keep up morale and have a positive influence on the business.

If the chairman of the company is willing to drive a smaller car, he should have few problems in introducing car fleet savings to the business across the board. If generally reducing the payroll and making redundancies, avoid giving the directors large salary increases and other benefits. Work on the business, not in it, if you are a business owner. If, by reducing overall costs and making savings, the owners and directors increase their wealth, try to temper things by giving something back to the workers – even if only profit-related pay, or low-costed group scheme arrangements.

# STRATEGY #56
# Involve the work force in cost reduction processes

If someone else suggests it, the chances are that he/she is best able to play a part in its implementation. This can be best accomplished through:

- Suggestion box for cost savings and efficiency improvements.
- Awards for suggestions which are implemented. One company gives a percentage of savings made to the employee making the suggestion.
- Reduction of personal use of business assets. This ranges from telephone calls to using the business as your own personal print and copy shop.
- Call for cost reduction ideas. Employees working in smaller, job-related areas usually know what is wastage and costs money. A large percentage of savings can be made solely through having the workers *recognise* these areas and report them back to management. Tax-free suggestion awards may be made to employees, where their ideas are implemented.

---

### STRATEGY #57
### Pay and payroll is usually the biggest expense area of any business. Deal with cost reductions in this area

---

This is probably the most emotive area. Managers are known to suffer stress-related illnesses and most are ill-equipped to deal with personnel in this way. Employee 'down-sizing' can be an expensive business, especially if redundancy payments have to be made. The following suggestions may be helpful if costs are to be saved through employees leaving the business.

## 1. The 'soft' approach

- Natural wastage target is set.
- A hold is placed on further employment except for essential staff; or
- A voluntary redundancy programme is offered, usually with generous terms; or
- An overall reduction in salary is offered as a temporary measure to help the business overcome its cash flow difficulties; or
- Job re-scheduling takes place. Perhaps the employee can be more usefully employed elsewhere. Often it is the *job itself* which becomes redundant, not the employee in the job.
- Redundancy counselling is made available to employees and their partners.
- Employees are shifted from Schedule E (employment) to Schedule D (self-employed), offering services to the company from home.

## 2. The 'hard' approach

- Redundancy targets are set and employees are dismissed; and
- Redundancy counselling is made available.

## 3. The 'cash for equity' approach

- Employees are invited to take up equity in the business, through an employee share trust, thus providing working capital for the business and retaining their jobs. This method should also improve the motivation and efficiency of the business. The first ESOPS/ESOTS arrangement in the UK was Roadchef. There are now thousands of approved employee share owner trust or participation schemes in existence.

Down-sizing the work force is never easy. Most employers usually look to other areas of cost savings first, before embarking on this route.

---

**STRATEGY #58**

**The cost of computerisation can take 100% or more of your profits. Carefully analyse your computer hardware and software requirements**

---

Computer hardware companies are in business to sell more and more computers. Likewise, with software companies. In fact, what you buy today is usually already out of date. It is too easy to be fooled into keeping up-to-date with new technology, rather than fully maximising the use of what you already have.

The person wielding the most power in your business will be, without doubt, the IT manager. Nearly everyone else does not understand information technology and what the requirements are. Sadly (although they won't admit to it), the IT manager in your business is probably equally out of date and responds most readily to market requests for new sales.

If the truth were known, what you already have is probably only about 2% or less utilised (for what you purchased it for).

IT strategists have shown that the problem is more associated with trying to get the hardware and software to fit the need requirements of the business, rather than the other way around.

Literally millions can be spent on new computer technology which will either become out of date or not have the necessary future capacity for your needs. What is required is a firm of computer assessment and IT analysts properly able to assess the capability of what a firm already has and how best to use it, without incurring mega-pounds in costs. This strategy alone can save your profits for years to come.

---

**STRATEGY #59**

**Get the best deals for company cars – cash, HP or lease – and save the business thousands**

---

The summary below gives the best buying position for company cars and their usage.

The main choices are between paying cash, buying on hire purchase, personal contract purchase, lease purchase and lease hire. One rule is: never buy a car over a period of more than three years. Below 36 months, you are ahead; beyond that, the HP company is. Much will depend on what the cash resources of the individual or the business are, and whether the business is VAT registered or not.

I am indebted to Fleet Management Services Limited of Shrewsbury for taking me through the car financing maze. Taking each of the options in turn:

## Cash

Although this method ties up capital unnecessarily, those paying cash will own the car outright. Companies must show the purchase as an asset but will get 25% writing down allowances and resulting tax reliefs. Note that writing down allowances only apply to cars costing £12,000 or less at present. More expensive vehicles will lose out on a proportion of these capital allowances.

There are no cash flows or VAT advantages by paying cash.

## Hire purchase

This method is a popular way to purchase a car, but there could be large monthly payments and interest rates may vary. An initial deposit is made and then the loan is repaid in fixed monthly instalments. The car becomes the owner's with the final instalment. Any loans taken out will be secured against the car. VAT is recoverable on running costs for VAT registered payers. There are also writing down allowances, similar to those for cash purchases.

## Lease purchase

If a business user wishes to end up owning the car, then lease purchase has significant cash flow advantages. The car is owned by the finance company until the end of the term. The business owner pays reduced rentals but agrees to buy the car outright at the end of the lease period for a cash payment.

Monthly payments are generally lower and there are tax allowances on the interest element of the monthly payments. However, both the car and the loan are shown as an asset and liability on the company's balance sheet.

## Lease hire

This method has greater cash flow advantages as well as VAT advantages, following the relaxation of the VAT rules from 1 August 1995, making monthly lease costs even lower.

The car is hired over an agreed period, with full maintenance cover. This can be included in the monthly payments. All risks are carried by the company hiring out the car.

Lease hire has multiple benefits. The leasing company can reclaim all VAT on the purchase of the vehicle, whilst if the business is VAT registered, it can claim VAT back on the rentals. The saving in VAT is usually reflected in lower rentals. VAT is recoverable at 100% for business use; 50% for private usage.

The car does not appear on the balance sheet as an asset as this is an operational lease. Monthly rentals are low if VAT registered, but can be much higher if not.

## Personal Contract Purchase (PCP)

This is more suitable for non-VAT registered businesses or individuals. The low monthly payments are the big attraction for this method.

There are cash flow advantages, but a lump sum is payable as an initial deposit – usually about 30%. The value of the car at the end of the period is worked out and deducted. You then fund the rest in lower monthly instalments. In reality you are only funding the depreciation of the car, not the whole cost of the car.

At the end of the period, you can hand the car back with nothing to pay, buy it for the agreed sum or take up the scheme on another car. If used in the business, the usual costs of running and maintaining the car will then be an allowable expense. Similar to HP, you should be able to write off capital allowances if you intend to keep the car.

## Personal loans/business loans

It is possible to take out personal or business loans from a bank to purchase the car. If so, the deductibility rules may allow a writing down capital allowance of 25% per annum, as opposed to an annual deduction of interest owing to the bank. It would be better for the business to borrow the money from the bank 'generally' and then to purchase the car. Interest payable should be deductible, and writing down allowances will apply for the car.

Personal or business borrowings usually have lower interest rates than HP or lease interest rates.

The way in which the car is purchased could result in big cash savings for the business, when taking into account capital allowances, VAT reclaims and whether the car is an asset in the business or not. Always shop around or get expert advice on what to do. Cars and fleet costs are a heavy burden for any business, being one of the greatest expenditure items. There are, however, 'bulk deals' to be made which could be taken advantage of, all in all saving the business thousands of pounds.

---

### STRATEGY #60
### Company car usage, tax and insurance strategies

---

The company car is a major cost issue for any business. Not only does the business usually fund the cost of purchase or hire or lease, but it also pays for insurance, maintenance, running costs and taxes for the use of the car.

Successive chancellors of the exchequer have homed in on the company car for rich pickings over the years. Any private usage is heavily taxed, both by the Inland Revenue and by the DSS for National Insurance Contributions (1A), and also in some instances for loss of VAT relief for private usage, if applicable.

The tax attractiveness of the company car has been steadily eroded over the years. Employees would ask if it is still an attractive benefit. It may pay an employee to take cash from the employer and make his or her own arrangements.

The advantages to the employee of having a company car, however, are many, and the upside will usually outweigh the downside. For example, there is no cost or financial risk on repairs, depreciation or payments. The fleet manager usually has most of the aggravation, should anything go wrong. If the position of the employee changes, then possibly a change of car will also follow.

If the employee takes cash instead of a company car, then he may be financially better off, and can have increased freedom of choice in what kind of car is run and how the extra cash is spent.

The employer providing a company car could be facing the following annual costs at present:

- Annual lease charges
- Road taxes and licences
- Fuel costs
- Servicing
- Repairs
- Breakdown service membership (AA, RAC, etc)
- Insurance
- Loan interest
- Capital payments and deposits
- Employer's NIC on benefits
- VAT adjustments on fuel and fuel scale charges
- Extra salary to fund some of the above items.

Tax relief is available through capital allowances and deductible business expenses.

Car provision can be a complex area which requires evaluation of many inputs, including looking at the broader remuneration planning aspects.

Other areas to consider could be increased salaries, reimbursement of expenses for business mileage and the provision of cheap or interest-free loans for car purchase. The employer will also consider the position of down-grading cars, switching to the employees' own cars and the replacement of company cars at greater intervals, buying second-hand cars and so on.

A number of firms of accountants as well as fleet providers have software which can 'model' various scenarios for different outcomes and thus indicate the best course of action for any particular circumstances.

The following *mini-strategies* may prove helpful to those with *employer cars* (not only company cars).

1. Consider financial modelling to ascertain the best tax and financial incentive position for your business and its car-user employees.

2. Consider remuneration packaging whereby the employee chooses how much of his package is spent on the car benefit, and how much on other benefits.

3. Make it mandatory for each 'company' car user to carry a logbook to record business and personal mileage.

4. Use the logbook to calculate exact NIC 1A as well as business mileage fixed cost allowances and business mileage/usage reimbursement costs.

5. Use the logbook to calculate whether usage of the car is below 2,500 miles a year (where non-usage penalties apply) or above 18,000 miles a year where usage deductions apply. If mileage is low, then get it into the safe zone.

6. If the business is registered for VAT, then choose a financing method where VAT is reclaimable.

7. If private usage can be 'covered' by the employee, then valuable allowances and reliefs will not be lost. Consider making beneficial loans to employees (at present loans of £5,000 or less can be made with no questions asked) or bringing in tax saving schemes, such as profit-related pay, where the level of 'free pay' can cover some of the tax loss.

8. Consider down-sizing fleet costs to the capital allowance levels – at present £12,000. Possibly the individual could subsidise costs (with loans) down to lower levels.

9. Consider paying an agreed (with the Inland Revenue) fixed cost allowance to employees for business mileage allowances as opposed to the business mileage reimbursive method. This way, extra could be provided to cover the cost of private mileage.

10. Shop around for the best car insurance deals. Even if employees are paying for their own cars, they will be better off under a bulk buy group car insurance deal. For those employees driving less than 18,000 business miles a year, there is a possibility of reducing the taxable benefit by up to 20%.

Employers can now offer interest-free beneficial loans of up to £5,000 to employees without giving rise to a taxable benefit.

Employees may now contribute up to £5,000 towards the purchase of their company car. By doing this, the employee can legitimately reduce the cost to be taken into account when calculating the taxable benefit for using the car privately.

By using the beneficial loan to pay off part of the purchase price of the new car, the employee gets significant benefits. There should, however, also be a contractual agreement between the employer and employee that on the sale of the car, pro rata proceeds go to the employee, who then uses this to repay the loan. If a portion of the loan is written off, it would be a taxable benefit in the employee's hands.

**Example:** Monica is an advertising executive. She has a company BMW 3 Series car: purchase cost £16,000. Residual value after three years is £9,500. She borrows £5,000 from the company and uses it against the purchase price of her new car. The results of this combination are as follows:

|                            | Business mileage | | |
|                            | Below 2,500 | 2,500–18,000 | Above 18,000 |
|----------------------------|-------------|--------------|--------------|
| Benefit tax percentage     | 35%         | 23.33%       | 11.67%       |
| **Without loan/contribution** |          |              |              |
| Annual benefit             | 5,600       | 3,733        | 1,867        |
| x 3 years                  | 16,800      | 11,199       | 5,601        |
| **With loan/contribution** |             |              |              |
| Annual benefit             | 3,850       | 2,567        | 1,284        |
| x 3 years                  | 11,550      | 7,700        | 3,850        |
| **Loan write-off**         |             |              |              |
| Amount                     | 2,031       | 2,031        | 2,031        |
| **Total taxable benefits** | 13,581      | 9,731        | 5,881        |
| **Reduction in benefit**   | 3,219       | 1,468        | –            |

*Source: Bentley Jennison*

Businesses can save tens of thousands of pounds through structured cost reduction programmes. Cost savings mean that more cash is available for wealth creation in the long run.

## Key points summary

- The understanding of small decreases in costs substantially improving net profits is outlined.

- Determine exactly what the business's fixed and variable costs are.

- Target costs for savings, showing how these are to be made.

- Don't over-react, but use a structured cost saving process to save time and money.

- Use cost reduction experts to help you – at no cost to the business.

- Costs saved enhance the wealth-creation programme of the business.

# CHAPTER 5

# Obtain and Maintain Your Business Credit

*Let us all be happy, and live within our
means, even if we have to borrer the money
to do it with.*
**Artemus Ward (1834–1867)** *Science and
Natural History*

## Objective: How to obtain business credit and keep it, whilst developing good credit management systems

Poor credit management can cost the business up to hundreds of thousands of pounds as a percentage of lost turnover and bad debts and could even lead to business failure if not properly controlled.

In a survey of three major research studies (Trade Indemnity plc) undertaken in 1993 amongst a total of 900 companies in the mechanical engineering, packaging and chemicals sectors (with turnover ranging from £0.5 million to over £50 million), the percentage of turnover written off as bad debts was up to 2% and more for 6% of mechanical engineering companies, 8% of chemical companies and 12% of packaging companies.

The *impact* of bad debt on the companies in the survey translated on average as follows:

| Bad debt | Engineering | Packaging | Chemicals |
|---|---|---|---|
| Written off by company | 0.7% | 1.1% | 0.5% of turnover |
| £ lost by company | £27,700 | £180,000 | £90,000 |
| Industry loss | £230 million | £200 million | £140 million |

Put in another way, if the company is losing money through poor credit practices, the shareholders are losing wealth. It is as important for the business to *retain* its cash as it is to make it in the first place.

This chapter deals with two sides of the same coin:

1. Obtaining and keeping business credit and repairing poor credit profiles; and

2. Developing good credit management habits and systems.

In many ways, the business striving for its own best credit management systems must first get its own house in order. It must develop a profile whereby credit suppliers will deal with the business on favourable terms.

## 1. OBTAINING CREDIT AND MAINTAINING IT

Credit is really a short-term loan given by one business to another.

---

### STRATEGY #61
### Obtain a credit reference on your own business first

---

This will give you an idea of your state of credit-worthiness. Anyone else accessing credit referencing agencies should get similar information. Once you know precisely what the situation is, then you can develop further strategies to deal with it.

The main credit reference agencies are: Dun & Bradstreet, Infocheck, ICC, CCN, Equifax, Infolink and Graydon.

If the credit reference is poor, then there are various steps which can be taken to improve the position.

## STRATEGY #62
## Correcting a poor credit position

Much depends on what the circumstances surrounding the poor credit position are. For example, being consistently late with paying suppliers could be rectified by developing a new credit history of speeding up payments.

Defaulting on interest payments (due to cash flow difficulties) can be rectified by paying arrears and developing a new credit profile – but this does take time.

Legal actions, such as county court judgments (CCJs) can be removed by settling the debt and placing this fact on record – or contested when they arise, so that legal processes are spun out for longer periods.

Whatever the problem, there will be a solution to it. It is really only serious default arising through bankruptcy or liquidation which may seriously affect the same company's lines of credit, or even a new company but with the same principles.

### How to correct a poor credit position

1. Develop good credit habits

   - pay bills on time or within time
   - only give credit sparingly
   - have proper credit management systems
   - don't exceed credit limits
   - pay bills when due
   - pay bills or loans off early
   - remain creditworthy

2. Obtain trade references.

3. Communicate your new good credit record to suppliers, together with trade references.

4. Ask for a banker's report on the state and strength of the business. Send it to credit suppliers.

5. Make sure your accounts are published (at Companies House) and are up to date. Many businesses call for the latest accounts before offering credit facilities, or even doing business with another company.

6. Provide credit reference agency status reports and sales ledger records to suppliers.

7.  Ensure that contacts within the industry only have positive things to say about your business.

8.  Get credit insurance for your business and your suppliers.

9.  Trade with cash for a period, gradually winning the confidence of the supplier, until credit terms are acceptable.

10. Establish from suppliers which credit reference agencies they use. Contact these to ensure that you will qualify first, before asking for credit. Remember, your file will note who has contacted the credit reference agency, and this information is available to anyone else who does so. If others have subsequently turned your business down for credit, then new suppliers will also do so.

11. Arrange for a bond to be lodged for the benefit of suppliers against your business's performance. (Performance guarantee or trade bond.)

12. Build the best possible picture for your business – work on the business to get the best balance sheet and profit and loss account.

---

### STRATEGY #63
## Get as much business credit lined up as you can

---

If you qualify for it, then arrange it. You may never use it, but it will always be there if you need it. Establish credit references and terms with your target suppliers well in advance of any usage.

---

### STRATEGY #64
## Never bank with only one bank

---

Business banking with one bank can lead to financial disaster, especially when things go wrong for your business. The worse the situation gets, the less inclined your bank will be to help the business.

Always have *at least* one other business account with another bank, showing positive cash positions only. You never know when you may need the second bank – if only for a positive credit reference in the future.

## STRATEGY #65
## Always have credit insurance. This is essential

Credit insurance will pay for bad debts. If the supplier knows that your business is covered for credit insurance, you are far more likely to get the credit you need. Without credit insurance, a major bad debt could put the business under. Have the business assessed for credit insurance to see if it qualifies. No business wants to deal with another where it cannot effect credit insurance. The risks are just too great.

## STRATEGY #66
## Ensure that the business complies with the legalities when arranging credit

The Consumer Credit Act 1974 applies to credit arrangements for up to £15,000. There is no limit if a private borrower is over-charged for credit. The 1974 Act applies to all loans and credit arrangements except those made by banks, exempted lenders and companies with capital of over £250 million that provide a 'highly specialised banking service'. If the debtor is a company and the credit is over the £15,000 limit and no other banking legislation applies, then contract law applies.

Make sure that proper agreements are drawn up, stipulating the terms and provisions as well as those for security. Often, when a supplier gives your business credit, the supplier finances this through a finance house, or factors his debtors.

## STRATEGY #67
## Become a good payer – creditors have better memories than debtors

Lenders have found that good payers continue to be good payers. Bad payers continue to remain as bad payers. No one likes to chase others for monies owed to them. It is important for credit referencing purposes that your history has you or your business as a good payer.

A good credit rating is worth its weight in gold – you never know when you might need it. So develop clever credit habits.

---
### STRATEGY #68
## Delay paying what you owe within the parameters of your good credit habits
---

This may sound like a contradiction in terms but you also have an obligation to conserve and retain cash in the business for as long as possible. You could consider not paying bills until asked to. You could introduce a paying schedule where cheques are only made out once a month. You could simply adopt delaying tactics, such as 'your cheque is in the post' or it's 'with our accounts department for processing' or 'we never received the invoice – send another'. However, these tactics may lose your supply of future credit. Possibly one of the best routes is to establish your own payment schedule – send a cheque for a third of the amount owing, with a note stating the balance will be paid the following month, or whatever. So long as there is evidence of some payment, you will usually not be bothered.

Remember – most successful small businesses have to stoop to delaying payment to their suppliers at some time during their development.

## 2. DEVELOPING GOOD CREDIT MANAGEMENT SYSTEMS

Making sales is one thing; getting no money in from all of your hard work is another. Poor credit management, like poor cash flow management, can cause the business to fail. The whole question of credit management brings into focus how well you can *manage the debt* equation of the business.

Most businesses owe the Inland Revenue something – few realise that if the Inland Revenue are not paid within 21 days, then statutory demands and bankruptcy positions follow fairly quickly. Even if the company has a positive net worth, if a claim from any creditor is for £750 or more, they can begin proceedings. Take the case of the following partnership:

| Assets | £ |
|---|---|
| Interest on freehold property | 50,000 |
| Book debt | 3,000 |
| Bank balance | 2,000 |
| **Liabilities** | |
| Inland Revenue overdue | 15,000 |
| Net worth | 40,000 |

Even though there is a positive net worth, the Inland Revenue can bankrupt this business. In fact, any substantial creditor can. Credit management is therefore vital, not only to preserve and retain business and individual wealth, but also to speed up cash flows – the life blood of the business.

**STRATEGY #69**
**Combine credit control objectives with business objectives**

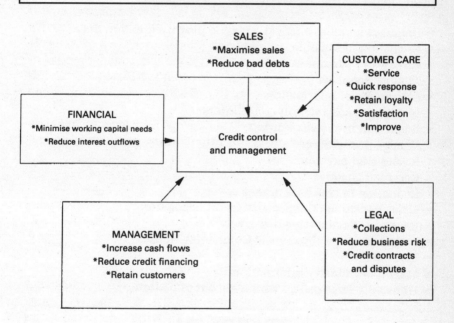

The credit management department of any business must be friendly but firm. Apart from the sales team, usually the credit managers are the only persons in regular contact with the client or customer. In many ways, this internal department fulfils the functions of public relations and customer communication. The business will seek to retain customers, not lose them, and customer care is an important and rewarding function. To be effective, credit management should be used as follows:

- As a positive element in customer service
- With as much emphasis placed on it as sales
- To maintain the right balance between the customer relationship and systems and procedures

Remember, an effective credit management and control team can save the business thousands of pounds.

---

### STRATEGY #70
## Spot the early warning signals for a defaulting creditor

---

If one or more of the following events occurs, then immediately tighten up your credit management controls.

- Disputed invoices – this is a classic ploy used to buy time
- Formation of separate companies
- Changes in personnel
- Moving premises
- Late financial information
- Inability to keep within credit limits
- Reduction in supplies/orders
- Change in suppliers
- Round sum payments
- Returned cheques
- Reduction in credit insurance cover
- Using consultants, especially credit negotiators
- Bank reports reporting negatively
- Failure to lodge accounts at Companies House
- Part payments
- Market or industry information
- Unusually large orders which are out of pattern

---

### STRATEGY #71
## Watch out for payments beyond the due dates

---

Most businesses seem to buy themselves additional time, if the Trade Indemnity plc survey is anything to go by. The following table shows the days beyond the due dates over typical payment periods for UK customers in the 1993 survey.

| Time/Days late | % of respondents |
| --- | --- |
| 0 | 2% (on time) |
| 1–10 | 22% |
| 11–20 | 35% |
| 21–30 | 25% |
| 31–40 | 6% |
| 41–50 | 5% |
| over 50 | 5% |

Patterns were broadly similar for export customers, except that 11% paid on time.

The longer the payment is due, the more financial stress is caused to the company. It has to basically subsidise late payments and incur bank debt to do so.

Our own survey (1,000 smaller companies, June 1995) showed the measures to which companies were prepared to go to get the cash from the creditor into the bank. These ranged from:

- Discounts to pay early (3%–15%)
- Part payments up front
- Penalty interest if late payers – at up to 2% per month
- No credit terms given – payment up-front and credit arranged or the company arranges its own financing
- Early negotiation with creditor to get paid

---

## STRATEGY #72
## Use discounts as a powerful incentive and penalties as a powerful disincentive for creditor

---

Our survey showed that most firms were prepared to offer substantial discounts for early settlement. The average was about 5%, but this was often on a sliding scale, with, for example, 15% discount for payment within seven days and only 5–10% for payment after 28 days.

Conversely, by stretching payables the creditor may incur ill-will as well as losing the discount. In addition very late payments incur penalty interest charges. It may be cheaper for the creditor company to factor its debtors, i.e. get a factoring company to pay on time to get the discount and offset this against factoring charges.

## STRATEGY #73
## Learn the five main steps of credit management

1. Establish normal terms of sale. Decide the length of the payment period and the size of any cash discounts.
2. Decide the form of contract with your customer – as proof of indebtedness. Does the buyer merely sign a receipt, or is there a contract, promissory note, letter of credit, or trade acceptance?
3. Assess creditworthiness of the customer. Take up bank and trade references, do credit reference checks, call for accounts and financial statements, check with other creditors.
4. Decide on how much credit to extend and set limits. *The job of the credit manager is not to minimise the number of bad debts, but to maximise profits*, i.e. increase the customer's credit limit as long as the probability of payment times the expected profit is *greater* than the probability of default times the cost of goods.
5. Collect the money owed when it becomes due. You need to be firm, but not to offend (in case the customer has a genuine delay). Keep track of payments and take steps against reluctant payers.

## STRATEGY #74
## Set meaningful targets for credit management control

It is useful to know what payments for sales are outstanding on a *daily* basis rather than waiting for, say, 90 days to find this out. Relate bad debts as a percentage of the business's sales, not as a benchmark against the industry average. If comparisons need to be made, compare rather with the previous year, than the previous month. It is useful to know the cash collections each week/month/year.

Credit management attitudes need changing. Whilst eight out of ten financial managers claimed that standard procedures were adhered to for credit management, only one in three managers set performance targets for their departments. Fifty per cent of financial managers 'don't worry' about major customers paying late, and only one in three are 'concerned' before payment by major customers is 60 day overdue.

This is further shown up by what the top performing companies do against the worst performers.

## Worst performers

- Very little investment in personnel and training, with less responsibility delegated to the credit manager.
- Reactive approach is only acting as a last resort.
- Too much reliance on industry grapevine and trade references, and then only for new customers.
- Terms and conditions 'generous' and tend to be more lenient and 'flexible' with late payments.
- React later to non-payment and then resort to threats.

## Top performers

- Invest in credit management personnel and training. Responsibility delegated to credit managers. Integrated approach with business objectives.
- Proactive and preventative approach.
- Full evaluation of creditworthiness of new *and* established customers.
- Prompt accurate invoicing.
- Use of external as well as internal credit information.
- Do not exceed limits and systems.
- Monitor closely and react early to late payments.

Targets can be set using the top performers' successful profile.

---

# STRATEGY #75
# Manage the credit control function effectively

---

The following is typical of percentage time spent on credit management activities:

- 15% on gathering information on creditworthiness
- 15% on analysing and evaluating customer's creditworthiness
- 30% on day-to-day monitoring of accounts and cash flow
- 40% on chasing overdue accounts

The following should be established on a regular basis:

- Written contract with all customers.
- Visits to customers.
- Number of applications for credit refused in last month.
- Value of orders waiting for credit approval.

- How soon after the due date are creditors chased?
- What is the business's outstanding creditor days? (When are payments made on average; is it getting better or worse, and by how much?)
- The number of debts referred for collection and how many legal actions are pending.
- Is there regular communication with one of your competitors? Credit controllers?

Effective credit management can not only save the business money, but reduce the cost of sales through fewer bad debts. Through the correct assessment of creditworthiness, prudent credit limits, proper payment arrangements and follow-up on overdue accounts, prompt billing and an accurate sales ledger, the credit management function can contribute substantially to the business.

It won't do so, without the proper *systems*, vital to this function.

## Key points summary

- Methods of obtaining (and keeping) business credit are discussed.

- Credit repair strategies follow with advice on how to build up a good credit profile for the business.

- Effective credit management strategies designed to improve the cash flow of the business are given.

- Credit management should be fully integrated with business objectives.

CHAPTER 6

---

# 29 Ways to Improve Your Business's Finances

*Cash flow is king.*
**Small Business Forum, 1995**

**Objective: To improve significantly the overall financial position
of the business**

In the same way that blood must circulate around the body to sustain
life, sufficient cash or liquidity is necessary to sustain the life of the
business. Modern business theory concentrates on profitability of the
business as the major success determinant. However, in these times, I
would suggest that adequate and continuous cash flow is the most
important determinant for businesses succeeding – and staying in business.

The following strategies will help you to improve your business's
finances, whilst maintaining its cash flows.

## STRATEGY #76
## Determine the current financial position of the business

Successful businesses usually have some form of monthly management accounts. In addition to this, you may need to develop your own software programme of cash in (income and capital) and cash out (expenditure).

Plan around your fixed costs and variable costs, establishing the latest dates for payment in each case. The cash flow analysis prepared for your business plan is a good starting point.

Get used to the idea of regular cash flow management and *focus* on it. Too many businesses have failed because they could not manage their finances or anticipate income shortfalls. Wary banks, lenders, suppliers on credit and creditors would rather 'pull the rug' on an ailing business or one with 'temporary difficulties' than give extra time (or help with cash flow management).

Heard the one about the bank which 'starts up' financing more small businesses than any other? It advertises this fact regularly. A little-thought-about fact is that the same bank often withdraws its financial support from similar small businesses just as easily as it offers it. The ones who gained the most during the UK recession were company receivers and insolvency practitioners. Yet, for many of these businesses, liquidation could have been avoided with proper cash flow management.

## STRATEGY #77
## Become a money miser

The secret technique of massaging cash flow is to become a money miser. This means later payment rules for you, early payment rules for everyone who owes you.

Whilst small businesses complain to the government about late payments affecting their cash flows (and putting them out of business), the factor of self-preservation means that your business can't afford to pay early, unless it is cash rich or getting a large discount for doing so. Pay late and keep your cash as long as reasonably possible.

---

### STRATEGY #78
### Make part-payments over a period of time, rather than large lump sum payments at once

---

It is becoming fairly common practice to massage your cash flows by spreading your payments unilaterally 'in reduction of the amount owing'.

Paying debts and creditors this way certainly gives you *more* time – keeping your money in the bank account for as long as possible. Even much larger businesses are adopting this practice – in the interests of cash flow.

Importantly, this practice is unlikely to affect your credit rating as you are not stopping payment altogether. You can always speed up the frequency of payments if need be.

This unilateral extension of supplier credit or debt can buy you at least 90 to 120 days of extra time. Remember – you are still paying, but much more slowly.

---

### STRATEGY #79
### Always operate more than one business bank account – with separate banks

---

A big problem facing businesses struggling with cash flows is to rely on one bank (usually out of loyalty – and often misguided) for all of their banking business. Usually it is also the same bank where you have your overdraft. Big mistake.

If the bank knows you are in trouble, or that their loans or overdrafts are at risk, they have the discretion to help themselves from your account to satisfy your liabilities to the bank. This is notwithstanding the fact that your major contract has come in, a payment has been made into your bank account for the business, and now you wish to earmark the cash received for projects or payments other than the bank. Believe me – it happens often.

Your strategy is to keep your overdraft with one bank (and some income flow), but make another bank your main recipient for income. In time, this strategy may prove invaluable should you require further bank finance and you have built up a good name with the second bank. If you do take bank finance from a second lender, again open up an account with a different bank to receive large lump sum payments.

## STRATEGY #80
## Get expert help if necessary to improve your cash flows

I was so impressed with work done for a couple of my corporate clients (with cash flow trouble) by a company specialising in designing, negotiating and managing cash flows for clients, that now I do not hesitate to recommend them. They have undoubtedly kept these businesses alive at a crucial time for them – both businesses were recommended by their accountants to go into receivership. Due to our timely intervention, both are now fit and flourishing.

In the same way as you wouldn't expect a GP to remove your brain tumour, don't expect a non-expert to solve your problem when clearly you need alternative, expert advice. Don't give away your business unnecessarily. Get in an expert to advise you. Cash flow is everything. Without proper management of cash flows, the business starves.

## STRATEGY #81
## Negotiate a better deal with suppliers of finance

Do not be afraid to ask. If you do not ask, you do not get. Finance suppliers are certainly not going to contact you and say, 'It's time for a new, lower rate'!

The key strategy here is *negotiation* with banks and creditors for a better deal – particularly if you are a long-standing customer. No one wants to lose your business. Others are getting the better deals – why should you be denied?

## STRATEGY #82
## Get training in effective negotiation techniques

A number of courses are offered on successful negotiating techniques – some of them by bank managers. Get yourself on to one of these courses, or buy books on negotiation.

If the above is not possible, use an expert third party negotiator to do the job for you. Many are cost reduction specialists and they earn their fees as a percentage of what they save you.

---

## STRATEGY #83
## If money is owed to your business, get it back early

---

In particular, there may be refunds owing by the Inland Revenue, Customs and Excise (VAT) and the DSS.

The Inland Revenue is quick to charge you interest on overdue payments *owing*, but slow to pay you interest (if at all) for hanging on to your money, or to refund money it may owe you.

As it is, the Inland Revenue and other tax collectors can be said to be partners in your business, regularly taking up to 35% or more (in taxes) of your cash flow. What's more, they expect to be paid first. If you don't pay them, they can put you out of business. If they don't pay you what they owe, they can put you out of business.

So, do your best to negotiate an early repayment if possible. There has recently been some relaxation in the rules for the collection of VAT to assist cash flow in small businesses. However, don't expect such generosity from the Inland Revenue. Their interest clock runs immediately if you owe, but not if you are the owed.

---

## STRATEGY #84
## Get back overpaid interest

---

Banks have been known to overcharge their business clients. In fact, recently there has been a court case where it was held that a bank had *unfairly* overcharged its client for many years and it was forced to give a fairer rate to that client. The fact is that smaller businesses have very little negotiating power with banks and are usually charged over the odds for loans and overdrafts. Larger businesses usually achieve better-rated loans, often 2% less than their smaller counterparts.

If you feel that overcharging has occurred in the past with interest payments and charges, then have it investigated. 'Bankcheck' software programmes can assist you with this. Also, ex-bankers (some of the 200,000 plus bank staff made redundant over the past five years) who know their way around the banking system, can investigate your bank accounts as well as negotiate better deals. They take a percentage of the savings made for you.

## STRATEGY #85
## If you can't negotiate a better deal, move your whole banking arrangement to a bank which can accommodate you

Where a bank refuses to extend overdrafts, or give loans and negotiate, your best strategy is to move to another bank. We frequently do this for clients requiring expansion or working capital and are able to renegotiate better deals for them.

For example, a client owning a number of cash rich butcher shops wanted to set up a new distribution warehouse. After examining his position, it was apparent he did not require long-term financing because of the high level cash flows to the business. He needed a shorter-term larger overdraft, which his existing bank refused to give him, plus a short-term loan. So, we moved his whole account to another bank. *In addition*, he had given security over personal property to the previous bank as well as personal guarantees. Part of the new deal was that these were removed as payments decreased beyond a certain point.

## STRATEGY #86
## Try not to pledge personal assets against bank debt

Commercially, the lender often won't lend unless the business owners personally guarantee loans with charges against their homes. Excessive debt levels usually require this as a mandatory feature of lending.

If this applied to you, but now your business has improved to a stronger position, renegotiate your guarantee position away from you personally back to the business's balance sheet. If reserves or capital lie in the business, then arrange for a special deposit guarantee investment to be made, removing your personal guarantees.

Try to separate the assets, debts and fortunes of the business from you personally. If you lose your business, you don't want to lose your house and family as well.

If you are a sole proprietor, think about incorporating to limit your liability.

---

**STRATEGY #87**
**Free up your cash flow**

---

Cash flow is king. Without it, the business starves. There are many actions which can be considered to help a business improve its cash flow. Some businesses have 'idle' assets which could be geared towards injecting more cash into the business, or used to generally improve liquidity.

These are:

- factoring of accounts. Usually up to 80% of the outstanding accounts (debtors) can be paid to the business and collected by the 'factor'.
- invoice discounting. Similar in many ways to factoring.
- discounts for early payment may get the cash in quicker.
- changing or managing debtor periods to have money owed paid sooner.
- extending credit periods so that the business pays creditors later.
- renegotiate car and equipment leases for a better deal. HPs and leases over three years mean that the lender is making it – you're losing it.
- lease-backs on property and motor vehicles.
- renegotiation of onerous leases. I know a company specialising in this area which regularly saves clients thousands of pounds.
- borrowing from directors' pension funds. In effect, your directors' pension fund is the business's own bank – at least you don't have to go 'cap in hand' to get access to much-needed cash – so long as the reason is commercial.
- geared working capital schemes. By using ESOPS (Employee Share Owner Participation Scheme), money borrowed from a bank to fund the ESOPS is tax deductible to the business. The ESOPS buys shares from the company. The company has cash for working capital. It has actually achieved tax deductible working capital!
- directors' loan accounts should be paid commercial interest to keep their cash in the business.
- cheaper bank funding to replace other expensive funding. Shop around.
- see if you qualify for government loans and grants. For example, the DTI and the TECs will subsidise certain activities up to 50%. This is money saved by you. Every business should appoint a grant and loan person to continually advise them. Activities such as manufacturing for export would be well supported.
- raising new capital from investors can substantially improve

liquidity in the business.

The above list is not exhaustive but should at least provide a starting point for many businesses.

---

## STRATEGY #88
## Save cash through cost reduction programmes

---

There is a deal to be made with almost any supplier to your business. This is especially the case with utilities companies (gas, water, electricity) but also any supplier. Why? Competition is the answer. The more competitive everyone gets, the better it is for you.

Cost reduction strategies can save you thousands of pounds and are covered in Chapter 4.

---

## STRATEGY #89
## Better investing of the business's profits

---

Where does your business invest its retained reserves (profits from previous accounting periods which have not been distributed to shareholders plus other cash)?

It never ceases to amaze me that businesses will leave their cash in low-interest bearing accounts for extremely long periods. Instead of getting their money to work even harder for them, it lies fallow, gathering nothing more than dust, in a current account.

At present gross offshore bank accounts can achieve three to four times more in interest than an ordinary current account in the UK.

Many businesses play the money markets with their corporate cash or treasury accounts, but some should consider growth investments as well – particularly if the money is not earmarked for anything specific.

---

## STRATEGY #90
## Freeing up idle or frozen money

---

The biggest source of idle money lies in directors' loan accounts or partners' capital accounts. I came across a Yorkshire business the other day where one of the director's loan accounts was over £200,000 with no interest being paid. The money had gradually accumulated over a long period of time, and the business was extremely profitable. Guess what?

The owner of the business had actually *sold* the business two years previously! When asked why he had left his money in the business (not even as equity), his retort was that he had built up the business and felt he should 'leave it there'.

That same £200,000, if invested *personally* ten years previously, could have been worth over £430,000 if invested at only 8% per annum.

Your strategy is a director's loan account redemption scheme. This plan means that the director's loan account is replaced with low-cost bank financing. Interest paid is tax deductible to the business. Your capital is released to be invested outside the business in a growth investment to increase your personal wealth. If the business needs additional future capital, your new investment could always support this.

Alternatively, get the business to pay interest at a reasonable rate for borrowing your money.

---

## STRATEGY #91
## Conduct employee benefit efficiency programmes

---

This action will show you how to reduce costs *and* improve employee benefits in what is the most expensive area for any business – pay, payroll and the provision of employee benefits, protection and health benefits. See Chapter 4 for the full strategy programme.

---

## STRATEGY #92
## Reduce the cost of working capital

---

If your working capital is provided through expensive bank and other financing, then look to other areas which may be less expensive and easier to arrange (in some cases).

You could introduce new equity capital into the business and repay the bank.

Alternatively, you could use your valuable employees to arrange working capital. This method involves the setting up of an employee share trust. The trust borrows money from the bank (capital is tax deductible) and this is backed by the company. Either the trust or the company can pay the interest on the loan.

The trust (ESOPS or ESOT) then uses the cash to buy shares. This can be from shareholders (who then lend the money to the company) or directly from the company itself. The company now has cash which it uses, in part repaying existing loans with the bank.

This gearing exercise can occur as often as you wish. The secret here is that your *capital* borrowed is *tax deductible* to the business, one of the few arrangements where it can be (pension funding and EZT investments are the others). The interest paid is also tax deductible. The cost of your working capital is therefore *reduced* by the tax savings (25%–35% usually) on the money. For example, if the capital borrowed is £100,000:

| | | |
|---|---|---|
| a. | Bank finance of £100,000 at 12%: | £12,000 |
| | Interest deductible item at 25% | (3,000) |
| | Cost of capital | £9,000 |
| | | |
| b. | Bank finance of £100,000 at 12% to trust: | £12,000 |
| | Interest deductible item at 25% | (3,000) |
| | Capital deductible item at 25% | |
| | (£100,000 × 25%) | (25,000) |
| | Cost of capital | -(£16,000) |
| | | -(16%) |

Employees will have the option of purchasing shares from the trust. If they do not do so within seven years then the tax relief on the capital is withdrawn. However, your business would have had highly-geared cheaper working capital for many years.

Over 2.5 million employees are now on ESOPS. See Chapter 23 for more details.

---

### STRATEGY #93
### Plug all the holes – or watch cash haemorrhage from your business

---

Cash and cash flow management are *the* most important aspects for any business to consider.

Your strategy is to build a profile on *how* cash leaves the business, and in what form: for example, loose office equipment purchasing arrangements by staff, personal telephone calls, use of company property for personal matters, wastage in production and manufacturing, not using tax reduction strategies and so on. If you focus your mind on where savings can be made, you will achieve them. Build a picture of everything from paying insurance to the type of company cars you buy.

By not controlling cash flow properly, you could ruin your business.

It does not only apply to money leaving the business – it could also be irreplaceable assets or opportunities. For example, I advise a number of law firms in the conduct of financial services. Take the case of a firm arranging probate for a client's heirs, paying out substantial cheques to beneficiaries. What do these beneficiaries do? They walk over the road and deposit their investment in the nearest building society. The law firm could have acted as investment advisers or referred the beneficiary for independent financial advice, earning *new fees* for doing so. Result of not doing so – haemorrhage of cash resources.

---

### STRATEGY #94
### Introduce profit-related pay to reduce income tax

---

Any business can have an approved Inland Revenue profit-related pay scheme (PRP). Once registered, employees can get part of their pay tax free. This is the lower of either 20% of pay or £4,000 at present. So, a higher rated taxpayer can get a tax deduction of up to £1,600, a basic rate taxpayer one of up to £1,000.

Some businesses use PRP to give salary increases (it costs the business no more to do so); some reduce pay and substitute PRP to make up the difference. The government, though, wishes to see PRP in its purest form – giving employees the incentive to share in the success of the business. Over 1.5 million employees are now on PRP – which can be paid monthly through an adjustment in tax codings.

This is one of the most effective ways to help build personal wealth for employees at little extra cost (only audit charges) to the business. See Chapter 19 for more details.

---

### STRATEGY #95
### Find the cheapest sources of finance for the business

---

Examine all possible sources of finance, their terms and their costs, including:

- bank finance
- using pension fund loans
- shareholders for equity sales
- new investors through the Enterprise Investment Scheme (EIS)
- property lease backs
- factoring and invoice discounting
- property and asset sales

- profit-related pay strategies
- directors' loan accounts
- ESOPS/ESOTS capital injections
- new credit
- new deals with suppliers
- better cash flows through savings and cost reduction
- corporate bonds, debentures

You will no doubt think of others. The list is not exhaustive by any means. Finance is a commodity and therefore if the same terms (or better terms) are offered, take the best deal. Find out just how far banks, creditors and suppliers will go. Communicate and make contact to do so.

---

### STRATEGY #96
### Get even better deals by buying in bulk or through barter

---

By combining with other businesses wanting the same things, you can buy commodities, services and products more cheaply by buying in bulk. I have been arranging bulk-buy insurance and employee benefits for clients for many years.

Join the local Chamber of Commerce, trade associations, credit unions, affinity groups etc to achieve better purchasing through bulk-buying power. The Federation of Small Businesses is typical of an organisation which should command bulk-buying at low prices. Even the NHS (the largest employer in Europe) has a special department to arrange bulk-buy cheaper deals ranging from holidays and travel to discounts at department stores.

There are one or two similar groups operating in this way for smaller businesses. They have negotiated bulk-purchase packages for small businesses and save anything up to 50% in this way.

You could also join a barter organisation, such as the Capital Barter Corporation, to increase incremental trade and services. This saves on cash flow, and you can have anything, from accounting and legal services to holidays in the sun, on barter.

---

### STRATEGY #97
### Negotiate lowest charges and commissions

---

Don't accept anything at face value. Although everyone has a price below which they *won't* do business, usually you can get a reduction of fees, charges and commissions simply by asking.

If you don't ask, you don't get.

Reductions may range from, say, 10% at the local sports shop to 30% from your consultants to the business. *Always* negotiate the price of the deal *before* you do it. Trying afterwards is a waste of time. For good ongoing relations, though, try to achieve a 'win-win' position. Let the other person believe he has won by giving you the negotiated deal. If you went in at, say, 30% off and came out with 20% off, it's a good deal!

---

## STRATEGY #98
## Repair your credit holes

---

If your balance sheet has holes in it, then you need credit repair strategies (see Chapter 5 for details).

The better your accounts are (up to date) and the better your balance sheet appears, the better they will influence investors, suppliers and credit agencies into dealing with you.

In some extreme cases it may mean 'running down' one business and starting another; in other cases it may mean the removal of CCJs and other methods of credit repair.

Get a credit reference report on *your own company* or business to see how others see you, before doing anything. Once changes are made, have the change *added* to the credit reference report, or the old information deleted. You have the legal right to do this.

---

## STRATEGY #99
## Use OPM if you can – try to limit your own risk

---

OPM is 'other people's money'. Use other people's money rather than your own – unless you are mega-wealthy and not wanting to give away any equity.

Using the bank's money to best effect, or raising grants for business projects, or low-cost (sometimes) government guaranteed loans is infinitely preferable for most business owners – so long as they don't have to give too much away. Even then, the cheapest money is that which you don't have to pay back – so equity capital from private or other investors may be a good bet.

Even the most effective use of tax allowances is using OPM – in this case the government's money is best utilised by the business owner.

---

## STRATEGY #100
## Establish tight business controls to manage your cash flows

---

The concept of debt management is as important as managing a business towards profits. You need to establish tight cash flow controls with a monthly tracking and accounts management system. Once you have established your controls, you need to tell everyone what they are and how they will work, and more importantly, *why* they are being introduced.

In the final analysis, the better the business does, the better the wealth-building opportunities for all the people in the business.

---

## STRATEGY #101
## Create business development programmes to sell more to your customers

---

Don't forget *increased sales* and turnover also do much (if not the most) to increase the positive financial position of the business.

You need to critically examine ways in which to improve the business's performance. See Chapter 24 for more details on how to increase sales, keep clients, increase clients and customers.

---

## STRATEGY #102
## The best things in life are free – find out what they are

---

You don't even have to pay for some things – they are free! This ranges from new banking facilities to no credit card fees.

Free offers – buy one, get one free, are all the rage. Possibly the best 'freebie' on offer is constructive business and financial advice to guide the business owner through the maze to the promised land. Well, almost free, as I almost forgot – there is no free lunch! Some people are prepared to work on a success or a commission basis related to success. So you will have no upfront charges (which is free) but may have to pay for results (which is not free, but there again, the pleasure of gaining a successful result means you may not mind paying for it).

---

## STRATEGY #103
## Consider the most tax efficient ways for cash to leave the business

---

If the business can get tax reliefs, allowances, rebates and lower-costed charges, then it should consider all of these aspects.

Is it more effective to pay dividends or bonuses? To pay extra salaries or have employee benefits? These are just some of the areas to consider. If it benefits the business in some way to adopt a different paying-out strategy then it is commercially correct to examine these areas.

Most of these strategies are covered in Part 2 of this book.

---

## STRATEGY #104
## Recognise the need for different approaches and strategies depending on the problem

---

Your strategies and approaches, methods of communication and conduct will differ, depending upon the state of your business and what you are seeking to accomplish. For example, if you have cash in the bank, you are dealing from a position of strength. If your business is in trouble, you are dealing from a position of weakness. Whichever one it is, remember in the final analysis success or failure is decided on results.

Dealing with large institutions hide-bound by their own internal rules requires a different strategy (patient negotiation) from dealing with a supplier desperate for your business (quick responses). You must recognise these areas and be prepared to call in an expert to help you if need be.

### Key points summary

- Most of these 29 ways of improving the finances of the business are related to recognising the problem of restricted cash flows and then knowing what to do about it – either by yourself or with expert help.

- Ways to improve the financial position through managing cash flows and credit, as well as increasing sales, are considered.

- This chapter covers negotiations with suppliers, creditors, bankers, the tax authorities and the like. It also considers ways of increasing cash by reducing tax, repairing credit holes and investing the business's money.

CHAPTER 7

---

# Unleash the Power of Group Schemes

*There can be no economy where there is no efficiency.*
**Benjamin Disraeli (1804–1881) to constituents, 3 Oct 1868**

**Objective: To show the enormous cost savings and benefit enhancements through buying benefits in bulk**

Group scheme-costed benefits can save you up to fifteen times what you would normally spend on health protection, private medical and other benefits. If you don't know about these benefits and cost savings, it's because your broker hasn't told you about them. Usually very low commission-bearing products experience low sales, and this is a case in point. Extremely good value for the client in every way, poor value for the broker unless he adds a fee to your premium.

Don't stop reading because your business is very small – even 'one man bands' can achieve group-costed rates if they know where to look!

---

### STRATEGY #105
## If you want to increase profits, ascertain if your business qualifies for group-costed savings

---

Everyone has either heard of a group scheme arrangement, or knows someone who is a member of one. The overall impression of a group scheme is that it is the sort of arrangement only found in really large organisations where there are many hundreds or thousands of employees, but group schemes can work as effectively for small groups as they do for larger ones. To obtain quotations for your business, you will need to supply the following information:

- number of people in the group who will require the benefit
- a breakdown of males/females
- ages and dates of birth
- salaries or earnings for each person
- occupations or titles and tasks
- location or place of work
- the level(s) of cover required: this is usually given as a percentage of salary
- the term – e.g. to age 65
- your type of business. What is the structure of the business (company, partnership, sole proprietor with employees)?

The more people going into the group scheme, the better for the group as a whole. The more younger people in the group, the cheaper the premium.

A 'group' can be as few as one person (some product providers have minimums of five or ten) but there may be minimum premiums applying for very small groups.

Obtain quotations from group scheme providers.

---

### STRATEGY #106
## For very small groups where minimum premiums apply, ask for more cover

---

In large groups, sheer weight of numbers enables the employer to attain a bargaining position of some strength – the more people belonging to, or making use of, the scheme, the cheaper it is for everyone, and the better the benefits for each participant.

Smaller sized employers and business owners with very little bargaining power amongst product providers have traditionally not enjoyed the benefits of group scheme arrangements in the same way that the larger business entity has. As a result, most employee benefit schemes for the smaller business have been largely individualistic as well as costly. The levels of benefits have been low in comparison to large group schemes and certainly more expensive.

However, smaller businesses can take comfort in the many changes in attitude and underwriting procedures over the past few years.

Group rates for smaller entities may be more expensive than very large group scheme rates, but will still be cheaper than individually-costed rates. If a minimum premium applies, then ask the provider for an uplift of cover, so that you get what you pay for.

---

### STRATEGY #107
### Alternatively, if a very small business, join an affinity group scheme for cheaper benefits

---

A recent phenomenon has been the introduction of the affinity group scheme. Take 100 self-employed data processor operators, or 50 sole proprietors in corner shops. They operate their own businesses, but are too disparate a group to have a voice in group purchase arrangements or to gain from bulk buying, unless brought together for this purpose. In fact, *employer* groupings were unheard of until fairly recently. One or two brokers can now offer benefits on a group affinity basis as follows:

### TYPICAL AFFINITY GROUP SCHEME COSTINGS

| | Ages 18–60 | | |
|---|---|---|---|
| | Level 1 | Level 2 | Level 3 |
| Life cover | £10,000 | £10,000 | £40,000 |
| Critical illness cover | £5,000 | £15,000 | £40,000 |
| Permanent total disability cover | £10,000 | £20,000 | £40,000 |
| **Monthly premium** | **£10** | **£20** | **£40** |

These rates would apply to anyone aged 18–60, who is employed or self-employed, and their spouses. Some employers looking for low-costed packaged benefits (even where the employee pays) may be tempted by this package of benefits. Clubs and associations can offer a package like this to their members. No evidence of health is required for groups of ten or more.

One or more of the benefits may apply to you. For example, an insured in Level 2 suffers a heart attack and claims £15,000 critical illness benefit. The condition prevents him from ever working again and so a further £20,000 may be claimed as a permanent total disability benefit. The remaining life cover reduces to £5,000 since the original critical illness benefit is regarded as an advance or accelerated payment of the life cover. The remaining £5,000 will be paid out if death occurs before age 60. Thus the total possible benefit at this level is £40,000.

---

## STRATEGY #108
## Use group affinity scheme benefits to top up your existing coverages

---

If you have existing coverages, top them up with your employer's group scheme benefits, or join an affinity scheme for your top-up. First, though, check to see if your *existing* coverages (even if individually-costed) can be topped up. Do the comparison – you could save hundreds of pounds.

---

## STRATEGY #109
## Alternatively, use group or affinity scheme benefits to provide a base-line and top up

---

Although the purists will have you calculating insurance and other benefit requirements to the exact penny, my belief is that most people can never have enough cover. I have yet to hear from a recent widow who got too much, but there are plenty who state they never got enough. So, top up wherever possible.

---

## STRATEGY #110
## If in poor health, try to get on to a group or affinity scheme

---

Because the group is actually a pool of people coming together to share their risks of calamity, the actuaries work out the probability of a claim for each group. Based on their claims experience, they will offer a premium. Most will offer 'free of evidence of health' levels of cover where you can join a scheme without having to prove good health.

As long as you are within the scheme guidelines, you will be covered.

Some schemes will want to apply to *all* employees or at least 80–90% of employees must join it. This enables the insurer to guarantee a spread of risk. It is because of this principle that someone who may not normally qualify for cover is now able to get it – a very valuable benefit indeed.

I have known of uninsurable people going to work for an employer not for job prospects, but solely to get group protection benefits. If you can't normally get cover, it doesn't take much to realise the peace of mind and appreciation of being able to do so.

---

## STRATEGY #111
## If uninsurable, and you require shareholder or partner protection cover, go the group route

---

Use the power of the group (all of your employees) to get your necessary coverages. You may offer employees, say 1 × annual salary and you (and other shareholders or partners) opt for 4 × annual salary or more.

Some or all of your coverage may be assigned or used to cover the terms of your shareholder or partner protection agreement (see Chapter 11).

---

## STRATEGY #112
## Don't be fooled by low coverages – go for the maximum. Get up to 18 times salary covered

---

There is a common belief that the maximum amount of group life cover is set at 4 × annual salary. In fact, the rules for death-in-service benefits state that you can have 4 × *final salary* calculated on your expected salary at retirement date. That could work out as up to 18 × *present annual* salary. All that happens is that on death before retirement your lump sum death benefit tax-free payout is calculated on your salary or earnings at that time. Any excess is used to pay additional annuity benefits to your spouse, children or dependants.

Group cover is inexpensive – make the most of it.

## STRATEGY #113
## Set up a trust for your group scheme life cover benefits to avoid inheritance taxes and income taxes for your beneficiaries

If your cover is paid to your estate, you may be liable for inheritance taxes, payable at 40% (after the nil rate band has been deducted).

*Either*
- ensure that benefits are paid in trust for your beneficiaries. Some schemes may not cater for this – check it out. You would usually leave a side-letter for the company or trustees to pay out to your nominated beneficiaries.

*Or*
- set up an offshore trust for the purpose of receiving your group life or death-in-service benefits. By doing this, you can make use of the 'Dead Settlor' Rule under *section 547* of the Income Taxes Act 1988.

As you, the settlor (founder) of the trust are no longer alive, there is no one to hang a tax charge on to. This means that your beneficiaries can receive tax-free income from the trust investments forever under present legislation. They would also avoid IHT and CGT under present rules.

## STRATEGY #114
## If divorced, tell the trustees of your group scheme benefits

If divorced, you no longer have a spouse. You don't have a widow either, if you die. If benefits are payable to 'widow' or 'surviving spouse' then they may not devolve according to your wishes. You may wish an ex-spouse to benefit, especially if you are liable for maintenance. The maintenance order does not necessarily end when *you* die. If maintenance is payable to an ex-spouse until he or she remarries or dies, then *your estate* is liable for payments and an amount will be capitalised from your assets to provide for this.

This is the case *even* if you have a new spouse and dependants. They share second, after the former spouse with the maintenance order has been satisfied.

---

## STRATEGY #115
### Where group schemes for partnerships are entered into, make sure they are properly underwritten

---

Inland Revenue rules are framed in such a way that a partnership group scheme, underwritten on a group basis, will pay out the first claim usually tax free. Second and subsequent claims may well be taxable.

To overcome this, have each partner individually own his share of the group scheme policy. You can still get group-costed rates for partnerships, but ensure that current Inland Revenue practice is catered for.

---

## STRATEGY #116
### Comparing group scheme and individually-rated costs

---

The following are the *main* categories of group scheme *core* benefits:

- Group pension scheme
- Group life cover (or death-in-service benefits)
- Group permanent health insurance (PHI)
- Group critical illness cover (CIC)
- Group medical and dental cover (PMI)
- Group long-term care cover (LTC)

Other benefits which can be arranged for employees on a group basis include:

- Group mortgage arrangements
- Group general insurance for cars and household contents
- Group wills for employees and spouses/partners

Group schemes mean power buying in bulk. Either your group is large enough (like a large employer) or your business is banded together with other businesses by a broker to get a 'bulk-buy' at discounted rates – as with the affinity group scheme.

The true value of how the group scheme arrangements are most cost-effective is when they are compared to the best the market can offer for individually-costed benefits. Two examples are given below.

Our company example has 30 employees, males and females, in the age range 18–60. Normal retirement age is 65. Salaries range from

£5,700 to £39,000 per annum. Only protection benefits are compared.

The last column shows the total of *individual* premiums for this group if all employees are in good health and all are non-smokers. Group benefits paid for by the company are tax deductible; those paid individually are not. However, for the sake of simplicity, the individuals' total will not be grossed up to allow for tax – all we will consider is base cost.

## COMPARISON OF GROUP AND INDIVIDUAL BENEFITS COSTS (30 PEOPLE)

| Benefits | Group premium per person per month | Total group premium p.a. | Average individual premium per person per month | Total of best individual premiums |
|---|---|---|---|---|
| Life cover (2 × salary) | £2.34 | £1,124 (£843 after tax) | £9.67 | £3,480 |
| Critical Illness Cover (2 × salary) | £3.50 | £1,682 (£1,261 after tax) | £15.56 | £5,600 |
| PHI (75% of salary after 6 months' waiting period) | £3.00 | £1,503 (£1,127 after tax) | £11.67 | £4,200 |
| Totals | £8.84 | £3,231 (after tax) | £36.90 | £13,280 |

This example includes employees age 18 as well as up to age 60. At the older ages, premiums could be 10–15 times greater than the *averages* given above. The group was relatively small so the example shows the power of the group scheme purchasing effect. In this case, overall, the company group scheme was over four times more effectively costed than if the individuals had to do it themselves.

The bigger the business, the greater is this divergence.

Take an even smaller example (both examples are taken from our actual case files) of the managing director of a small eight-employee computer software company and compare these benefits (the MD is a male, married, two children, 46 years old and earns £58,000 p.a.):

## COMPARISON OF GROUP AND INDIVIDUAL COSTS
## (VERY SMALL COMPANY)

| Benefit | Cover | Group scheme rate | Individually costed rate |
|---|---|---|---|
| Life assurance | £174,000 | £18 p.m. | £89 p.m. |
| PHI | £3,625 p.m. | £9 p.m. | £69 p.m. |
| Private medical insurance | pays all expenses - whole family | £51 p.m. | £97 p.m. |

The figures speak for themselves. You and your employees are better off under group-costed arrangements.

---

### STRATEGY #117
### If already in group schemes, get them reviewed to overcome the cost of obsolescence

---

You could be paying too much for existing arrangements. Financial services products and benefits are like any other commodity. They have a life cycle, and over time become obsolete. This means you are paying too much for something which is out of date. Every prudent business-man should be on the look-out for areas of obsolescence, and be prepared to make changes for the sake of economy.

With the introduction of modern underwriting techniques and increased competition, one can now get *better value* for the *same* expenditure. This is translated into cheaper costs for the same amount of benefit, or more benefits for the same cost.

Example: Group life premium and cover changes 1985 and 1995: 2 × annual salary coverage for 30 employees. (Similar ages and group pro-file.)

|  | 1985 | 1995 |
|---|---|---|
| **Group premium** | £3,125 p.a. | £2,625 p.a. |

Saving, ten years later, for the above benefits: £500 p.a.
*Source:* own files.

Treat all group scheme benefits like you would your car insurance. Most people instruct their brokers to obtain the best-rated coverages for them each year. Why not do the same with group scheme benefits on a regular basis? Businesses can achieve savings for their coverages –

especially if the group schemes have been in existence for some time.

A review is also an opportunity to consider integrated and flexible benefit planning for directors and employees.

If your business has the power to buy benefits in bulk, on a group scheme basis – then use it.

## Key points summary

- Whether the business is large or small, it can achieve considerable savings through purchasing group-costed benefits.

- Further savings can be made through rebroking obsolete benefits – or benefit enhancements made.

- By having a range of group employee benefits, individual employees need to spend less, and therefore have more disposable income.

# CHAPTER 8

# Planning Your Best Pension Strategies

*An annuity is a very serious business.*
**Mrs Dashwood in *Sense and Sensibility* by
Jane Austen (1775–1817)**

**Objective: To plan pension strategies now for best value for your
money in retirement**

This chapter covers the understanding of pension provision from the
point of view of the business setting up a pension fund and making contributions to it, and also from the point of view of the director,
employee, partner and sole trader ultimately enjoying its benefits.

Whilst there should be interaction from the two parties around the
provision of adequate pension funding, often a divergence occurs when
the objectives of the business differ from that of the individual. The
requirements of the individual for a maximum pension in retirement
may not be adequately met by the business making the provision.
Sometimes it will be woefully inadequate, and will require intensive
additional funding from the individual.

This need to maximise pension benefits by individuals will come at
the same time as the business is battling to cope with the additional
costs of funding, particularly for occupational pension schemes,

following landmark court decisions in the EU. The resultant pressures could well force business into a critical examination of their current funding practices, including the investment performance and cost structures of their funds.

The tax treatment of pensions is given in Chapter 20, and retirement planning strategies in Chapter 31, involving the final export of personal wealth from the business. Pension funding is not only one of the most tax-efficient investment mediums available to store wealth, but also complements the business objectives of recruiting and retaining staff and discharging its obligations in a moral (and legal) sense to employees.

The complexity of pensions and the different types available for various business groupings commands a full study in itself – what this chapter seeks to do is to develop various strategies to get the best value out of pension provision – for both the business and the individual.

## PENSION STRATEGIES

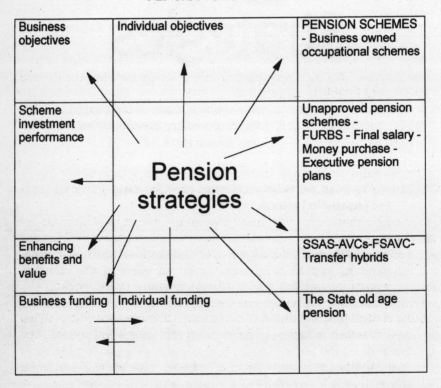

| Business objectives | Individual objectives | PENSION SCHEMES - Business owned occupational schemes |
|---|---|---|
| Scheme investment performance | **Pension strategies** | Unapproved pension schemes - FURBS - Final salary - Money purchase - Executive pension plans |
| Enhancing benefits and value | | SSAS-AVCs-FSAVC-Transfer hybrids |
| Business funding | Individual funding | The State old age pension |

---

**STRATEGY #118**
**Develop an understanding of the various perspectives in pension provision**

---

## The employer's point of view

- Believes that the business is under pressure to provide adequate retirement benefits for directors and employees.
- Must take into account the costs of pension provision. Some occupational pension schemes face up to 50% or more in increased costs with equalisation of pension ages, poor investment performance of some schemes and the using up of surpluses which have bolstered schemes to date.
- Will usually try to fund pension schemes at the lowest possible levels to save on costs.
- Wishes to provide settled conditions of employment and employee benefits to recruit and retain staff.
- Is possibly more concerned with pension protection issues at present. These include safeguarding the pension scheme assets and limiting the liability of transfers.
- Is concerned over pensions law reform issues which could involve the businesses in rapidly rising costs. These issues include the following:

  - strict rules on trustees, including investment policy
  - loans and financial assistance to sponsoring companies to be prohibited (April 1997)
  - annual solvency tests and minimum solvency standards of schemes
  - scheme liabilities revalued on a 'cash equivalent' basis
  - full valuations every three years and a certificate in each other year
  - increased funding to maintain scheme solvency levels. Schedule of contributions eventually to maintain 100% solvency levels
  - legislation to override existing scheme rules, in a winding up, so each member receives a minimum 'cash equivalent' of accrued rights
  - establishment of a compensation scheme with levies on pension funds
  - pensions increases to be funded (for increases) by at least the LPI each year (Limited Price Index to a maximum of 5%). This affects money purchase schemes and appropriate personal pensions as well

&middot; strict rules on dealing with pension scheme surpluses.

- The employer will believe that pension provision is adequate for employees. If the employee requires more pension benefits, he or she should fund it themselves.
- Company policy will dictate the needs of the company, and pension provision will be part of that policy.
- Business owners will use pension schemes to maximise *their* wealth personally.
- Business owners will use pension schemes as tax shelters.
- Business owners will include director and/or employee pension schemes in their tax planning initiatives.
- In respect of employees generally, it is doubtful whether significant increases to pension funding will be made by the business – except in the case of final salary schemes, where actuarial funding determinations are made.
- Business will, in fact, consider alternatives to final salary schemes to reduce escalating future costs.

## The Employees' Point of View

- Believe that business will provide *adequate* retirement provision.
- Believe that employers won't let them down. They are in the pension scheme, so it 'must be all right'.
- Are generally ignorant of their pension benefits, with a low knowledge of what their pension benefits actually are.
- Have a general inertia in respect of pension issues so fail to provide adequately for themselves. These factors include:

  &middot; the belief that the employer is providing adequately
  &middot; little or no idea of the funding possibilities available such as AVCs or FSAVCs (additional voluntary contributions)
  &middot; a belief that the State old age pension will be an adequate supplement. (Single person's OAP 1995/96 is £59.15 p.w. Married couple's OAP 1995/96 is £94.45 p.w.)
  &middot; ignorance of the consequences of an inadequate pension in retirement
  &middot; government restrictions on adequate funding (contributions are restricted)
  &middot; lack of power to influence employer funding
  &middot; lack of additional cash to do anything about additional funding
  &middot; realising that many people will outlive their pensions 'value' with people living longer and pensions not keeping up with inflation. The age group which is expanding fastest is the over-75 group. People are worried about outliving their money.

In most cases, the objectives and perceptions of the employer or business owner are miles away from those of employees.

## The self-employed's point of view

Here, one would expect a mix of business owners' perceptions and those of employees. The self-employed or partners in businesses have the *means* (they control business policy) but often suffer from the *inertia* as ascribed to employees.

Very few (who can) contribute at maximum funding levels to ensure adequate pension benefits in retirement. Of the UK adult population, 12.1% have personal pension schemes (about twice as many men as women). Many schemes are in existence only to contract out of SERPS, and have no other funding provision.

Yet, it is the self-employed who have the greatest measure of flexibility to fund for pension purposes (if they have the money). In addition, pension funding will provide the best tax-free growth investments and tax shelters for taking money out of the business.

---

### STRATEGY #119
### Develop an understanding of the types of pension schemes available

---

Job mobility has meant that people who were formerly employed may now be self-employed and vice versa. Pension transfers may have occurred from one fund to another, or the pensions may simply remain 'frozen' or paid up with accrued and protected benefits.

It is therefore important to have a basic understanding of the structure of the main types of schemes described in the schematic table showing pension strategies on page 98.

There are basically two main types of pension schemes: final salary schemes and money purchase schemes; and all schemes are a variation of these.

- *Employer owned* – occupational pension schemes (approved); group schemes and executive pension plans (EPP)
- *Employer owned* – unapproved pension schemes (FURBS)
- *Employer owned small self-administered schemes* (SSAS)
- *Individually owned* – personal pension plans (PPP); old style retirement annuities (RAs); group personal pension plans (GPPP); transfer policies – Section 32 buy outs

Taking each type in turn:

## A. Employer owned occupational pension schemes

- approved by the Inland Revenue
- large employers will have either group final salary or money purchase schemes
- smaller employers will have executive pension plans (EPPs) or SSAS arrangements, the latter having less than 12 members
- normal retirement date is between 50 and 75
- a member is entitled to a pension and a tax-free lump sum at retirement age

*Pension*

i)      pre 1987      ⅔ × final remuneration after 10 years' service
ii)     post 1989    ⅔ × final remuneration after 20 years' service
(for lesser periods, fractions apply)

*Lump sum – (tax-free)*

i)      pre 1987      1.5 × final remuneration after 20 years' service
ii)     post 1989    2.25 × initial annual rate of pension before commutation (includes the value of AVCs and FSAVCs)

*Final remuneration* is determined according to various formulae and by the rules of the fund and may include the value of employee benefits.

i)      pre 1987      no cash limit
ii)     post 1989    limited to earnings cap which is (1995/96) £78,600

(One cannot have a pension of more than ⅔ of final remuneration. The final remuneration is limited to £78,600. Therefore the maximum allowable pension is ⅔ × £78,600 = £52,400.)

Usually schemes are contributory. The employer and the employee contribute a percentage of salary to the scheme. Some schemes are non-contributory – the employee makes no contributions.

Employees may make additional voluntary contributions (AVCs) to the main scheme or free-standing AVCs to their own plans from independent pension providers (but which follow the main scheme rules) of up to 15% of capped remuneration.

Early retirement (ill-health) reduced pension benefits are available, as well as death benefits.

Retained benefits from previous employers must be aggregated for the ⅔ pension provision, but not for post 1987 lump sum benefits or pre 1987 onwards for dependants' benefits.

*Final salary* schemes are distinguishable from *money purchase arrangements* by their methods of funding.

- Final salary schemes are known as defined benefit schemes. The level of funding is actuarially determined and the employer has no real control over costs. The certainty is a pension calculated with reference to years' service × final remuneration.
- Money purchase schemes are known as defined contribution schemes. The employer knows exactly the cost of contributions, but the end fund amount is not known exactly until retirement date. The employer may have to consider additional funding to meet pension requirements at this time.

*Executive pension plans* have an accelerated funding programme depending mainly on the member's age and years left to retirement.

## B. Employer owned unapproved schemes

The most common is the FURBS – funded unapproved retirement benefit scheme.

- Usually provided as a top-up to existing pension arrangements for executives.
- Benefits are unlimited and do not affect normal pension arrangements from approved schemes.
- Schemes may be funded or unfunded.
- The tax treatment is different from approved schemes – investment income and capital gains are taxable, income tax is payable by the employee either on the contributions or on the benefits; the lump sum is tax-free if funded; taxable if unfunded.
- Corporation tax relief is only available once the employee pays his income tax.
- Death-in-service benefits are fully assessable to income tax.

## C. Small self-administered schemes (SSAS)

- For company controlling directors or partners and selected employees, but it must have *less* than 12 members.
- Special rules apply to prevent directors from abusing SSASs in respect of contribution levels, investments undertaken and other areas.
- The SSAS must not be invested solely in insurance policies and there are also borrowing restrictions on its funds as well as on loans to the employer (up to 50% of assets after two years but until then, only 25% per year).
- The SSAS can hold commercial property, shares in a private company and shares in its sponsoring company (5% of assets).
- The pension benefits payable are calculated as for other employer

owned occupational pension schemes.

## D. Individually owned pension schemes

- Personal pension schemes (PPP) have been available since July 1988. In that year, the last Section 226 retirement annuity contracts were sold – but the type of PPP scheme is similar in many ways to old-style retirement annuities.
- Pension contributions are made on the money purchase principle and accumulate tax-free to produce a fund which provides, in turn, a tax-free lump sum and taxable pension (see Chapter 31).
- Retirement age is from 50 to 75.
- Contributions can only be made from taxable income or 'net relevant earnings'.
- Net relevant earnings are capped at £78,600 in the 1995/96 tax year, on which contributions are based.
- The self-employed and employees not contributing to an occupational pension scheme (unless the latter only provides a lump sum benefit on death-in-service or pensions for spouses and/or dependants; or is used to contract out of SERPS) may contribute to a personal pension plan (an appropriate personal pension).
- Contributions attract tax relief at higher rates of tax.
- The fund generated pays out a tax-free lump sum (25% of the fund), the balance being used to purchase an annuity (pension).
- Group personal pensions are a group arrangement for individually owned personal pension plans, specially tailored to save costs, but exactly the same in all other respects to PPPs.
- A Section 32 buy out pension policy accepts transfers from other pension schemes and is also funded on a money purchase basis.
- The funding basis for personal pension plans 1995/96 is given below:

### PERSONAL PENSION CONTRIBUTION LEVELS 1995/96

| Age at 6 April 1995 | % limit of net relevant earnings |
|---|---|
| 35 or under | 17.5 |
| 36–45 | 20 |
| 46–50 | 25 |
| 51–55 | 30 |
| 56–60 | 35 |
| 61 and over | 40 |

This percentage is subject to maximum earnings of £78,600.

There are many other rules and regulations and plenty of legislation to digest in respect of pension schemes. However, the above will give a general understanding of which types of pension schemes apply under different employment and ownership situations.

The following strategies will assist the business, as well as the individuals within the business, in their respective wealth creation endeavours:

## PENSION STRATEGIES FOR THE BUSINESS

---

## STRATEGY #120
## Review the business's present pension scheme position

---

It is important to review the overall position of the pension fund in respect of costs, expected benefits, contribution levels and availability to employees. Decisions may have to be made to change from one type of scheme to another (such as final salary to money purchase or group personal pension schemes) to examine alternative methods of funding and other areas, such as investment performance and other benefits.

---

## STRATEGY #121
## Get a copy of your scheme rules

---

To get to where you want to be, you must know where you are. The following check list will give you a broad enough picture of the benefit value of the business's pension fund and the business's funding liability at present. If more than one pension fund is in existence, then complete your own internal audit for each.

**Name of fund:**

**Fund managers:**

**Trustees of fund:**

**Type of fund:**   final salary/money purchase/group personal pension scheme/SSAS/executive personal pension scheme/hybrid arrangement

**Numbers in fund:**

**Number receiving pensions:**

**Employer contributions:**        £        **1996/97**

         or        %

**Employee contributions:**        £        **1996/97**

         or        %

**Employer contributions as a % of payroll:**     %

**Additional employee contributions allowed: AVC/FSAVC**

**Death-in-service benefits:**

**Widows' benefits:**

**Widowers' benefits:**

**Orphans/dependants' benefits:**

**Retirement age:**        **males:**        **females:**

**Contracted in or out of SERPS:**     **in:**        **out:**

**Investment performance of fund: this year**

                                   **5 years**

                                   **10 years**

**Quartile sector of fund performance:**     upper/middle  upper/middle lower/lower

**Pension formulae:**

**Definition of final salary:**

**Pension fraction:**     40ths, 60ths, 80ths, 120ths

**Lump sum fraction/%:**

(or) pension as a % of final salary:

Present value of fund: £

Additional information:

---

### STRATEGY #122
## Determine what sort of pension fund the business would like and can afford (even if you have one already)

---

Now that you know what sort of pension fund you presently have, what would you *like* the business to have, within given cost and contribution parameters?

The best starting point is to determine how much the business can afford to pay for its pension funding. There is no point in going for a deluxe model which is going to break the bank. Equally there is little point in having a pension fund which is derisory.

As a general rule:

- If unlimited resources are available: final salary scheme
- If adequate but capped resources are available: money purchase scheme
- If resources are limited or sporadic: group personal pension scheme
- If small business with directors or partners: SSAS
- If small business with directors and employees: EPP
- Sole traders: PPP, or self-invested PPP (SIPP).

---

### STRATEGY #123
## If your pension fund contributions are killing your business, consider changing the scheme for a cheaper one

---

There are two main types of pension funding – the final salary schemes which fund for an end benefit; and money purchase schemes which have a defined contribution, the end benefit being unknown.

Final salary schemes account for the bulk of occupational pension schemes and are basically an open cheque book. Businesses find it difficult to control their costs, being at the whim of actuarial decisions on how much contribution money is required each year.

It will come as no surprise that at least one life office (Scottish Mutual) has reported that over 60% of their final salary schemes have been changed to money purchase schemes or other arrangements. Another life office (NPI) will allow you to change schemes with full reinstatement to your old scheme within a year if you make a mistake.

Money purchase schemes have a set and agreed contribution rate where contributions build up a pension fund. You know how much goes in but not exactly how much is available in your fund at retirement date – until you actually get there.

Final salary schemes are thus *more certain* (they will provide a percentage of salary times the number of years' service at retirement); however, they can be *more costly*.

The lowest-costed group scheme is the group personal pension (GPPP) which is similar in structure to a money purchase scheme. Contributions are made into individual retirement plans by either employer or employee or both.

---

## STRATEGY #124
## Set your pension cost parameters

---

Employers set their pension costs usually as a fixed sum, which is actuarially determined, or by a percentage of payroll. The range for the latter is between 1% and 15% of pay, depending upon the circumstances of the business and its employee benefits policies. Each year, the business reviews its performance and either increases, decreases or pays nothing (especially if the fund is in surplus) for the next year.

---

## STRATEGY #125
## Use the Inland Revenue to fund your pension scheme

---

Pension contributions are tax deductible to the business as well as to the individual making contributions at their highest rates of tax.

Increasing pension contributions therefore reduce the tax bill of the business or individual. In addition, no National Insurance contributions (10.2% for employers in 1995/96) are payable on pension contributions, nor is the value of a contribution which is paid into an approved scheme taxed in the hands of the individual.

Pensions therefore make excellent tax shelters. The Inland Revenue enables *employees* to make grossed-up pension contributions which *include* their tax relief (the self-employed claim theirs off their tax return) whilst *employers reduce* the cost of their contributions through tax deductions.

---

### STRATEGY #126
### Directors can get even bigger reliefs for pension contributions. Employed spouses can also qualify for larger reliefs

---

Although contribution levels were reduced in 1994, directors of companies (and their employed spouses – see Chapter 13) can make contributions two to four times greater than the self-employed by contributing into an Executive Personal Plan (EPP), or a SSAS (Small Self-Administered Scheme).

### NORMAL RETIREMENT DATE AT AGE 65

|  | Age | Contribution as % of salary | |
|---|---|---|---|
|  |  | m | f |
| EPP | 40 | 34.39% | 34.22% |
| EPP | 50 | 48.03% | 47.79% |
| EPP | 60 | 55.18% | 54.90% |
| SSAS | 40 | 72.33% | 87.36% |
| SSAS | 50 | 67.85% | 81.95% |
| SSAS | 60 | 43.88% | 53.00% |
| Self-employed | 40 | 20% | 20% |
| Self-employed | 50 | 25% | 25% |
| Self-employed | 60 | 35% | 35% |

---

### STRATEGY #127
### If changing your pension fund or scheme, get professional advice first

---

Cost is only one of the determinants which a business looks at when considering its pension fund options.

Other considerations would include:

- Real value retirement benefits

- Tax-free and tax-effective wealth-creation medium for business owners and employees
- A substitute for other benefits such as share options
- An asset which may be protected from creditors (of the business or employee)
- Using the pension fund for loans to expand the business. This is particularly the case in smaller businesses with director-only schemes. Loans can be made by the pension fund to the business for commercial purposes.
- An increased measure of wealth for the business. Although the value of the pension fund is 'off balance sheet' it is often reflected in the value of a business. Director-only pension funds are a more valuable 'business asset' because of the ability to provide loans to the company.
- Moral, social and 'feel good' factors will certainly play a part in whether a business provides a pension scheme for its workers or not.

Because there are so many different aspects to consider, always obtain professional advice before taking any action.

---

### STRATEGY #128
### If the pension fund's investment performance is poor, then move funds fast

---

One thing everyone understands is investment performance. A pension fund with good, consistent investment performance at expected levels will mean that less costs (from not having to make additional contributions to compensate for poor performance) can be expected from the business in the longer term.

A poor-performing pension fund's investments can cost the business dearly. A 1% *loss* of investment performance in *one year* can result in the fund losing the compounding effect on that amount – it could diminish the fund *value* by up to 20% over an 18-year period.

To establish how the pension fund has been performing, it must be viewed relative to other funds in the *same* sector. It must also take into account instructions on fund investments. Most pension funds are cautiously invested, giving lower performance figures, and perhaps changes to investment strategy should occur.

---

## STRATEGY #129
## Change the investment strategy or change the fund managers

---

Pension funds involve long-term investments. There should therefore be an investment portfolio allowing for long-term growth. Many investment strategies set ten years ago or more may well be obsolete now, but inertia in the investment review process allows the situation to continue. Don't be caught in the 'investment inertia trap'. Do something about it. The fund managers will be only too pleased to tell you how well they have done.

---

## STRATEGY #130
## Always aim for the best in investment performance. Don't be satisfied with mediocre returns

---

The following table (from the Bacon and Woodrow *Pensions Pocket Book 1995*) shows pooled pension fund performance. This table sets out the median returns achieved by the UK Pooled Pension Funds participating in the CAPS survey over cumulative periods ending 31 March 1994.

### POOLED PENSION FUND PERFORMANCE

| Annualised returns | 1 Yr % | 2 Yrs % | 3 Yrs % | 4 Yrs % | 5 Yrs % | 6 Yrs % | 7 Yrs % | 8 Yrs % | 9 Yrs % | 10 Yrs % |
|---|---|---|---|---|---|---|---|---|---|---|
| UK Equity | 16.5 | 21 | 14.6 | 13.3 | 12.4 | 13.8 | 10.7 | 13 | 15.5 | 16.3 |
| Overseas | 25.5 | 25.6 | 17.1 | 11.7 | 11.8 | 13.9 | 8.6 | 10.8 | 12.6 | 13.5 |
| North America | 3.3 | 16.1 | 14.5 | 12.6 | 13.9 | 14.3 | 9.1 | 9.1 | 8.9 | 11.2 |
| Europe | 25.9 | 22.2 | 16.9 | 8.2 | 14 | 16.1 | 8.7 | 8.9 | – | – |
| Japan | 26.3 | 31.2 | 11.8 | 8.8 | 3.3 | 6.5 | 6.2 | 11.9 | 15.1 | 12.8 |
| Pacific Basin (excl. Japan) | **46.3** | **41.2** | **31.9** | **21.6** | **23.8** | 25.5 | 19.5 | **25.7** | **19.8** | 17.5 |
| Fixed interest | 10.2 | 16.1 | 15 | 16.8 | 12.6 | 11.4 | 11.3 | 10.9 | 12.6 | 12.1 |
| Index linked | 6 | 14.9 | 10.7 | 11.2 | 9.4 | 10.4 | 8.9 | 9.9 | 8.9 | 8.9 |
| Property | 20.4 | 2.3 | 4.3 | -6.6 | 8.4 | **29.4** | 20 | 8.5 | 9.6 | 10.4 |
| Cash | 5.7 | 7.3 | 8.7 | 10.3 | 11.2 | 11.2 | 10.9 | 10.9 | 11.1 | 11.1 |
| Non-Property Mixed | 16.1 | 20.5 | 15 | 13.3 | 13.1 | 13.4 | 10 | 11.3 | 13.9 | 14 |
| Mixed with Property | 17.2 | 21.1 | 15 | 13.1 | 12 | 13.3 | 10.5 | 11.7 | 13.9 | 14.2 |

*Note:* The best performing sector over each period is highlighted in **bold** typeface.

*Source:* CAPS Survey of UK Pooled Pension Funds (Quarter ended 31/03/94).

The following table shows pension fund investment performance for various years to 31 March in each case.

### PENSION FUND INVESTMENT PERFORMANCE FOR YEARS TO 31 MARCH

| Total Fund | 9th Decile | Lower Quartile | Median | Upper Quartile | %<br>1st Decile |
|---|---|---|---|---|---|
| 1984/85 | 12.7 | 14.1 | 15.5 | 17.4 | 19.4 |
| 1985/86 | 25.3 | 28 | 30.6 | 33.3 | 35.5 |
| 1986/87 | 18.6 | 20.4 | 22.3 | 24.5 | 26.8 |
| 1987/88 | -11.1 | -8.8 | -6.7 | -4.7 | -2.6 |
| 1988/89 | 18.2 | 19.7 | 21.2 | 22.9 | 24.9 |
| 1989/90 | 5.6 | 7.3 | 9.4 | 11.6 | 13.4 |
| 1990/91 | 5.1 | 6.9 | 8.7 | 10.4 | 12.1 |
| 1991/92 | 1.2 | 2.7 | 4.3 | 5.7 | 6.7 |
| 1992/93 | 22.2 | 24 | 25.9 | 28 | 30 |
| 1993/94 | 14.8 | 16.1 | 17.5 | 19.2 | 20.6 |

*Source:* Bacon and Woodrow *Pensions Pocket Book*.

## PENSION STRATEGIES FOR INDIVIDUALS WITHIN THE BUSINESS

Your pension scheme will be the most tax-efficient investment which you can make towards your long-term wealth-building goals. It will therefore be one of the most valuable assets in your wealth portfolio.

Sadly, though, out of the 60,000 people who retire each month in the UK, only about 10% will have accumulated enough to retire on satisfactorily.

The following strategies will assist you in making the crucial decisions necessary to achieve your retirement planning goals – as painlessly as possible. Strategies will cover the employed as well as the self-employed.

---

## STRATEGY #131
### Set your retirement funding goals

---

Forget what the majority of financial advisers tell you. Usually their advice is driven by tax deduction considerations. You would have been advised to save for retirement at up to the maximum contributions levels allowed for pension funding. Because contributions are usually designed to build up a fund worth a maximum of ⅔ of your final salary (which most people won't attain in any event, because they don't have enough years' service with one employer) it follows that the best you could achieve from this approach is income in retirement of ⅔ of your pre-retirement income. Even with the State pension, most people find it difficult to service massive income reductions at retirement – especially if they wish to maintain existing lifestyle standards.

Your strategy is therefore to opt for the 'money benefits' approach – aim to retire on what you were finally earning – or slightly less if your major liabilities are paid off, such as the mortgage. To do this you need to *combine* your pension funding with other investments, such as PEPs or unit trusts, to make up the balance, bringing your retirement funding up to 100% of your needs requirements.

---

## STRATEGY #132
## Set your retirement date

---

Your employer may have a compulsory normal retirement date, usually between 60 and 65 for men and women.

Some pension scheme rules allow you to take early retirement, but there are financial penalties for doing so.

If self-employed, you can choose a retirement date between the ages of 50 and 75.

---

## STRATEGY #133
## Determine how much pension to fund for

---

You need to set yourself a funding target. You can either:

1.  Take today's salary and escalate it forward with expected salary increases and inflation until you have a figure at your retirement age. Then a fund value is determined which will provide your target pension benefits at that time; OR
2.  Simply decide what percentage of current salary you would like at retirement, and fund for that figure in today's terms.

*Example:* (1) Ian has a salary of £25,000 now. He wishes to retire in 20 years' time. Inflation is expected to be 3% p.a. Salary increases over the period are expected to be 3.5% p.a. (average).

Using the above information:

Salary in 20 years' time will be £88,091 p.a. One can now work out what size a pension fund must be for either a ⅔ pension or a 100% pension.

a. Fund required then for *⅔ salary*: £600,000.
b. Fund required to *replace income 100%*: £900,000.

In order to achieve these different funding levels, Ian will have to make annual payments for the next 20 years, which will be invested at an average of 10% growth per annum. Ian has two choices on how to contribute to each type of fund. He can keep his annual contributions level or he can escalate them by, say, 5% per annum. The following examples show how much should be funded each year to achieve either a ⅔ fund or a 100% fund objective.

a. *⅔ fund:* annual investment at 10% for 20 years: £9,550 p.a. for ⅔ fund (level funding); £6,695 p.a. escalating at 5% each year for 20 years.
b. *100% fund:* annual investment at 10% for 20 years: £14,300 p.a. for a full 100% fund (level funding); £10,040 p.a. escalating at 5%.

---

### STRATEGY #134
### To reach your target retirement fund (for 100% income in retirement), choose an investment spread of pension fund and other growth investments

---

If you can afford it, to build up to maximum in retirement, you would ideally contribute what you are entitled to within the tax allowances for pension contributions, the balance of your investment programme to come from other growth investments such as PEPs, unit trusts or investment trusts.

---

### STRATEGY #135
### Choose pensions with low charging structures and superior investment performance

---

Excessive charges reduce what's left for you to live off in retirement. Charges have been known to eat up 30% or more of your fund's worth – high-charging pension providers are to be avoided at all costs.

Likewise with historic low investment performers. Lower

investment performance means *less for you* at retirement date.

---

## STRATEGY #136
## If self-employed, or employed but not on a pension scheme, choose a personal pension plan

---

In fact, you don't have much choice in the matter. It's the only type of
pension plan available to you. You must be 18 or over and have 'net
relevant earnings' (taxable earnings). The Inland Revenue will allow
you to contribute *only* a fixed percentage of your net relevant earnings,
depending on your age. There is no differentiation between men and
women. The contribution levels are as follows:

| Age at 6 April 1995 | Personal Pension | Retirement Annuities* |
|---|---|---|
| 35 or under | 17.5% | 17.5% |
| 36–45 | 20% | 17.5% |
| 46–50 | 25% | 17.5% |
| 51–55 | 30% | 20% |
| 56–60 | 35% | 22.5% |
| 61 and over | 40% | 27.5% |

*New retirement annuities cannot be bought any more, but you may be
contributing to an existing one.

You cannot pay any other income into a personal pension plan – it must
be 'net relevant earnings'. Dividends or income from other investments
cannot be used to fund a personal pension plan.

---

## STRATEGY #137
## Keep within the allowable funding limits or face tax penalties

---

You may inadvertently overfund your personal pension plan by paying
in too much, believing your contributions to be within the limits.
   At the very least, these excess payments will be returned to you with
or without interest. The Inland Revenue could tax you and apply penalties, especially if you had tax relief on the contribution in the first place.
   If you thought the government encouraged maximum *benefit* pension

funding (as opposed to tax-related contributed funding) – it does not.

---

### STRATEGY #138
### If employed, contribute up to 15% legally into an AVC or FSAVC

---

You may contribute up to 15% of your salary or remuneration into an AVC (additional voluntary contributions linked to the employer's main fund) or into an FSAVC (a free-standing AVC from any pension provider). The amount contributed is tax deductible to you.

Whilst you cannot take a lump sum (only a pension), the AVC/FSAVC does increase the value of the main fund, which in turn will give a larger lump sum tax-free from that source.

---

### STRATEGY #139
### Don't wait – do it now – the cost of delay of one single year can seriously affect your wealth.

---

The cost to the individual in the loss of eventual fund benefits by delaying further provision (making contributions) by one year, at various ages, is as follows:

Delay age 21 to 22 = 15% loss
Delay age 31 to 32 = 15% loss
Delay age 41 to 42 = 16% loss
Delay age 51 to 52 = 18% loss
Delay age 61 to 62 = 38% loss

---

### STRATEGY #140
### Use profit-related pay to give employees additional money for pension contributions – get the tax reduction twice

---

If they have not done so already, businesses should set up an approved profit-related pay (PRP) scheme. This enables the employee to receive part of pay tax-free. The formula used is 20% of pay, or £4,000 of the actual PRP received in the year, whichever is the lesser. By combining

PRP with additional pension contributions, one can achieve a gearing effect on the same money.

For example:

Mary Dillon, aged 45, earns £25,000 taxable income p.a.

| | |
|---|---|
| Net taxable earnings | £25,000 |
| less PRP | £4,000 |
| gross taxable income | **£31,000** |
| less pension contributions at 15% | £5,250 |
| net taxable income | **£25,750** |

There is a saving in tax of £3,700 for an outlay of £5,250 (32%). This may be made and claimed each year. Net cost is therefore £1,550 of the pension contribution – the Inland Revenue has paid 70% of your contribution through profit-related pay which, over 15 years annually, equates to a massive pension.

---

### STRATEGY #141
### If divorced, carefully plan your pension funding strategy to avoid the loss of too much income in retirement

---

Pension law reform (1995) has meant that divorcing couples split pension rights and values at retirement (not at the time of divorce). This will cause all manner of problems for both parties, including the monitoring of pensions over long periods of time. Careful planning is required to ensure maximum pension income in retirement. *In addition*, a divorced former spouse has no widow's or widower's benefits payable, unless arrangements are made in advance with the pension fund trustees to nominate the former spouse for such benefits.

---

### STRATEGY #142
### Get additional tax reliefs and increased pension funding through 'carry back' and 'carry forward' provisions using personal pension plans

---

If you are self-employed or employed (but have no membership of an employer's pension scheme) or you have more than one source of income which qualifies as net relevant earnings, then any unused tax relief can be applied from previous years.

If you have not utilised your maximum contributions each year, you may *carry forward* unused reliefs for up to six years. This enables you to make additional pension contributions for that or those tax years above the maximum percentage allowable for that year. The earliest year to commence the process in 1995/96 is 1989/90.

'Carry back' enables members to have part or all of a contribution counted as being paid in the *previous* tax year, provided there is unused relief for that year. If there are no net relevant earnings in the previous year, you may go back another year. Employer contributions may not be carried back. By using previously unused reliefs, contributions to pensions can be greatly increased. This assists those who have not had the money in the past by being able to contribute when they do have it.

---

### STRATEGY #143
## Contract out of SERPS if it is in your interests to do so

---

SERPS is the State Earnings Related Pension Scheme. The government has been trying to wean people off this second-tier state pension for some years, by offering to pay a proportion of NIC contributions into an approved pension scheme. Gradually this incentive has decreased (the contracting-out rebate) and is, at present, 4.8% of band earnings (1.8% for the employee and 3% for the employers) until April 1997 for contracting-out final salary schemes.

In addition, as an alternative to a company scheme, employees may contract out individually into an appropriate personal pension (APP) or a free standing additional voluntary contribution scheme (FSAVC). Full NIC (National Insurance Contributions) is still paid by the employer and employee, but the DSS (Department of Social Security) contributes a rebate back to the Personal Pension Plan or FSAVC. From April 1993 the DSS will pay 1% of band earnings to an appropriate personal pension plan if over age 50. To this amount (for APPs only, not FSAVCs) another amount is added which is equivalent to the tax relief at the basic rate on the employee's share of the rebate.

These 'maximum contribution' benefits payable by an APP or FSAVC do *not* count against Inland Revenue maximum limits, nor employer and employees' maximum contributions.

It is unknown whether you would be better off by contracting out or not. Some years ago the Prudential began contracting its clients back in wherever possible, as they obviously thought clients would be better off back in SERPS.

However, this may be an opportunity not to rely on the State pension system, by building up your own pensions with some government help.

At present, those in the population who are not contracted out of SERPS number nearly eight million people (3.5 million men; 4.3 million women). This is 16.9% of the total adult UK population. (*Source:* Bacon and Woodrow [1992 survey] *Pensions Pocket Book 1995.*)

---

### STRATEGY #144
### Reduce other employee benefits, increase pension funding for a happier, longer retirement

---

A benefit is of no use unless you can actually use it. Some benefits, like the company car (taxed as a benefit in kind) are in fact wasting assets. They do not add value to your personal wealth. By electing for a cheaper car, savings can be made by the employer which can be used to boost pension funds and other savings plans. (See Chapter 9.) As the employee gets older, the need to boost pension funding is greater, and the need for status symbols may lessen.

---

### STRATEGY #145
### Get ready *now* for retirement later – even if ten years or more away

---

Too many people wake up to the fact that retirement planning should have been commenced at least ten years before retirement date. From that time, one should begin a 'Retirement Countdown Planning Programme', maximising savings and pension funding wherever possible. One or two years before retirement is too late - there is no time to build up sufficient funding or to get your wealth-building strategies into gear. Over 60,000 people retire *each month* in the UK and less than 10% will have adequate income in retirement. As people live longer, their incomes in retirement will decline in real terms, unless indexed-linked for inflation. Begin planning now, involving your employer in your plans if possible.

### Key points summary

• Pension funding is a major wealth-building investment in a tax-efficient environment.

- Understanding is required, not only of the different objectives and perspectives of employers and employees, but also of the different types of pension scheme available.

- Investment performance, charges, expenses and contributions are key determinants of the success of the pension fund and must be closely watched and changes made if appropriate.

- Employer and employee strategies to maximise wealth creation through pensions are given.

CHAPTER 9

# Remuneration and Employee Benefit Strategies

> There are few ways in which a man can be
> more innocently employed than in getting
> money.
> Samuel Johnson (1709–1784) in Boswell's
> *Life of Johnson*

**Objective: To save costs whilst significantly enhancing benefits.
To integrate benefit structures with employee needs'
requirements**

It has been said that salaries and employee benefits are the most expensive ongoing cost of any business. The provision of employee benefits can easily add another 50% or more to your salary bill. On top of that can be added another 10.2% for the business's National Insurance contributions (NIC). (10% in 1996/97.)

Although some cost savings are possible through the tax deductibility of salaries and employee benefits, few companies generally have an annual cost savings review process, and most blindly continue to pay in the future what they have always paid in the past. The biggest trap to fall into is to pay a high premium for something which is *obsolete* or of limited use to only a few people. It is a fact of life that employee benefits and services do become obsolete on a continuous basis.

In fact, this review process can save your business thousands, if not hundreds of thousands, of pounds in the long run.

---

## STRATEGY #146
## Decide on the remuneration and pay policy of the business

---

Whether your business offers employee benefits or not, you should have a definable policy of what it is prepared to offer or not to offer. At this level of strategic planning, most businesses will adopt a policy of remuneration close to the median for similar businesses in the same sector. This could vary widely depending on competitive forces of supply and demand for labour coupled with the business planners' own ideas of how much the business is prepared to give and for what reasons.

- Some businesses have a policy of equal benefits for all directors and employees on a pro rata basis.
- Many businesses give more to directors and senior managers and less to ordinary employees.
- Some businesses pay salaries only, with little or no employee benefits for employees.

There are two main principles to consider:

- The remuneration 'spend' principle. How much is the business prepared to pay? How much can the business afford to pay?
- The business 'benevolence' principle. Does the business see itself as a caring employer or not? If so, how flexible in approach is it prepared to be?

Some employee benefits need not cost the business anything but, by providing the structure for employees to be part of a 'bulk buy', can save employees hundreds of pounds and still appear to be caring and benevolent.

The greatest problem is that either the business has an historical and long-established existing remuneration policy which it does not wish to tamper with, or the human resources director is too close to the action (usually 'fire fighting') to do any meaningful planning.

---

### STRATEGY #147
## Get up to 50% of the costs of strategic planning paid for

---

The DTI and the regional TECs have a sponsored consultancy policy whereby consultancy reviews can be part paid for under their business growth initiatives. Your local or regional TECs can advise you on what is applicable in your area.

---

### STRATEGY #148
## Decide, before your business does anything, how much it is prepared to pay for employee and director benefits

---

The cost measurement is usually related back to basic pay, and given as a percentage of salary. For example, if salary is £40,000 per annum and 25% of that is available for employee benefits, then the total package is 125% of salary. The employee would have a salary (100%) plus 25% worth of employee benefits. These employee benefits could range from the provision of a company car to pension and health benefits.

If the total salary bill of the business was £1 million, then £250,000 would be available for additional benefits, if employee benefits account for 25% of payroll.

This could be broken down further as follows:

|  |  | Salary | Amount for benefits |
|---|---|---|---|
| Director | A | £40,000 | £10,000 |
|  | B | £35,000 | £8,750 |
|  | C | £35,000 | £8,750 |
| Manager | D | £28,000 | £7,000 |
|  | E | £28,000 | £7,000 |
|  | F | £26,000 | £6,500 |
| Employee | G | £10,500 | £2,625 |
|  | H | £7,800 | £1,950 |
|  | I | £5,500 | £1,375 |
| Total |  | £215,800 (100%) | £53,950 (25%) |

In order to manage its cash flows and budgeting requirements, the business now knows exactly how much to spend. To this should be added the business's NI contributions on salary and those benefits attracting NIC.

---

## STRATEGY #149
## Work out your remuneration costs each year allowing for increases in salary

---

This is a necessary budgeting exercise in any event. If the business is doing badly, work out your percentage deductions for the year.

---

## STRATEGY #150
## Decide whether your remuneration policy is flexible or rigid

---

Flexible means that the director or employee has *more* choice. This does not necessarily mean total choice.

For example, a business may stipulate that *all* employees will be on certain *core benefits*, such as a pension scheme, death-in-service benefits and a permanent health insurance (PHI) scheme.

The balance of their 'benefit cost allocation' may then be applied to other employee benefits (or salary) of most value to them.

Alternatively, the employee may be given total flexibility to design his or her own remuneration package within the given cost parameters. In both of the above cases, the employee should work closely with an independent financial adviser or financial planner to construct the most optimum package.

This approach has certain advantages and disadvantages:

### Advantages for the employee

- Better opportunity to build personal wealth.
- Able to change with changing personal circumstances.
- Greater control over personal financial planning.
- Making optimum use of the business's cash to fund personal benefits requirements and use of benefits. Some may consider a 'benefit' offered by the business to have no use to them and therefore to be a waste of money which could be better utilised elsewhere. A benefit is not a benefit unless able to be used.

## Disadvantages for the employee

- Losing out possibly on the effects of 'bulk buying' of employee benefits. Individual costs could be up to 15 times higher than group scheme costed benefits. It is better for the employee to include group scheme benefits in his or her portfolio of benefits.
- If ignorant or without adequate advice for personal financial planning, the employee could make crucial mistakes affecting his or her long-term wealth-building.
- Losing out on tax reliefs which the business may get, but not the employee. Extra salary also attracts tax at higher rates, meaning less is available to buy benefits.
- Losing out of company contributions, for example, to pension funds.

## Advantages to the business

- More satisfied employees, providing a 'feel good' factor as employees have more control and responsibility in building their own packages.
- A neutral position on tax deductibility and cash flow.
- Allowing employees greater choice in the construction of their remuneration packages overcomes the competitive and morale-sapping in-fighting of one employee of a similar status being seen to have a better deal than another. This is particularly the case with newer employees earning more than older ones.
- Limits the costs of employee benefits within defined parameters.

## Disadvantages to the business

- Employees may wish to leave schemes which have been set up for specific numbers. This could affect the costing of the schemes.
- Perceived higher levels of administration.
- Difficulties in changing from traditional arrangements to flexible arrangements.
- Too many people on different schemes and arrangements could again cause problems in administration and control.
- The degree of flexibility may be too great. The levels of flexibility may have to be limited.
- Monitoring the different arrangements may be more difficult.
- More employees requiring planning advice will be time- consuming.

The general trend is towards a more flexible approach in the structuring of employee benefits packages. Called the 'cafeteria system', the employee has certain core benefits and *also* the opportunity to have certain flexible benefits within a defined range. Often, he or she will opt for less of one benefit (say a reduced value company car) and apply the savings to another benefit (say increased pension funding).

Businesses operating remuneration policies within defined parameters can achieve the best of both worlds – a contented work force with some flexible options.

---

## STRATEGY #151
## Select the types of benefits to be offered by the business at various levels

---

Whilst the following list is not exhaustive, it does give plenty of scope for selection purposes.

### Savings

Pension fund
Additional voluntary contributions (AVC/FSAVC)
Share schemes

### Protection

Death-in-service benefits/group life scheme
Directors'/partners' shareholder protection

### Health Protection and Sick Pay

Permanent health insurance (PHI)
Critical illness cover (CIC)
Health checks and monitoring
Private medical insurance (PMI) – such as BUPA
Disability cover
Sick pay

### General

Company car
Fuel allowances
Mobile telephones
Annual level entitlement/thirteenth cheque
Profit-related pay (PRP)
Wills as employee benefit

Company loan to £5,000
Nursery and day care
Gym and leisure block membership
Business incentives – travel and holidays
Legal and tax advice as employee benefit
General insurance – bulk purchase – for cars, household contents
Spouse and partner benefits
Bonus diversion and NIC savings schemes
Share option and share schemes
ESOPS/ESOTS (employee shareowner participation schemes)

## Wealth building

Approved and unapproved funds, such as FURBS
Subsidise mortgages and loans
Subsidise school fees
Personal financial planning reports and advice

Once you have selected the *core benefits* which everyone will have (if this is your strategy), then made available the range of further flexible benefits, as part of your benefit planning, it is now appropriate to confirm your views with those of the employees.

---

### STRATEGY #152
### Conduct an employee survey to test your planning objectives

---

This is a delicate area, and businesses must beware of giving hopeful expectation. Some businesses avoid doing this survey because they feel it may have an adverse effect on morale if suggestions are forthcoming but later rejected.

It should be carefully handled under the guise of a 'general review' in line with market forces. However, you will find it most revealing in remuneration structuring and benefit planning in the years to come. For example, our own surveys have shown a shift away from traditional benefits towards personal wealth-building, with a far higher requirement for health related benefits over the years. Assistance with the mortgage is usually in the top three on employees' 'want lists'.

Possibly having an independent survey conducted is the most appropriate way of achieving this.

---

## STRATEGY #153
## Conduct a corporate benefit audit (or total review) of what you have and how much it costs

---

It is most important that the business has a full corporate benefit audit conducted in order to ascertain:

- what employee benefits it has
- whether these existing benefits are considered obsolete or not
- what the value of the benefits is to the employee
- what the costs of the benefits are to the business
- what the costs of the benefits are to the employees individually

By showing the present benefits position of the business and its costs, compared with its objectives and likely furture position and costs, it is likely that considerable savings can be made as well as an *enhancement* of benefits.

This is illustrated by the following:

Xerxes Limited is a manufacturing company with 80 employees and was formed 16 years ago. Following a corporate benefit audit, the following changes and recommendations were made:

| Existing position | | New position | Cost |
|---|---|---|---|
| *Benefits* | *Cost p.a. (premiums)* | *Changes* | *Premiums* |
| Pension scheme. | £105,600 | Improved widows' and childrens' benefits. | £105,600 |
| Lower quartile investment performer for 10 years. | | Shift indicated to better performers. | |
| Death-in-service (group life) 2 x annual salary | £4,700 | Improved to 3 x annual salary. No additional cost. | £4,495 |
| Permanent health insurance 50% of salary less state benefit. | £5,270 | Uplifted to 75% of salary less state benefits. Struck out obsolete scheme. | £4,008 |
| Private Medical Insurance, 50% of tariff, company liable for balance. Employee and family. | £53,840 | Shift to new PMI provider. 100% of tariff and company has no further liabilities. Employee plus family. | £48,000 |
| Commercial insurance on fixtures/buildings and cars. Premiums escalating p.a. | £29,100 | Complete review for better deal. | £25,800 |
| Company car scheme NIC 1A additions. | £31,200 | Complete review and logbook for each participant. Fleet shift to different basis. | £22,750 |

| | | | |
|---|---|---|---|
| Shareholders' protection £100,000 cover each (1982). No Keyman. Shareholders' agreement. Buy and sell type (obsolete). | £4,650 | Uplift to truer values £450,000 each. No premium payments in first year. Includes Keyman. Change to Double Option Agreement; introduce flexible provisions plus Keyman plus disability. | £8,200 |
| No authorisation advice and servicing for employees. | | Introduce authorisation plus '0800' contact number. Ensures each employee has access to independent financial advice. | £800 |
| No group critical illness cover for employees. No additional voluntary pension arrangements. | | Recommended introduction at 2 × annual salary. Recommended introduction from employees at own cost. Includes 1% enhancement of benefit. | £4,485 |
| No employee benefit management service | | Recommend introduction of this service to monitor costs and make suggestions for saving and enhancement annually. (Financial management tool.) | £4,200 |
| % spent on employee benefits p.a. as a % of payroll. | 16.7% | % spent on employee benefits p.a. *plus* additional benefits *plus* authorisation *plus managing* the employee benefits as a % of payroll. | 16.19% |

The above percentages relate directly to employee benefits as a cost to the business and do not include the *savings* for commercial insurance, nor the shareholder protection/Keyman uplifts and policy increases.

It *does* show overall improvements in the *value* of the business benefits.

As you can see, considerable *savings* have been made, the employee benefit position has been rationalised for optimum effect, and existing benefits upgraded. In addition, the way is now open to introduce new benefits within the defined cost parameters.

---

## STRATEGY #154
## Get rid of old, obsolete benefit structures and replace them with new ones

---

The principle of overcoming obsolescence should be uppermost in most financial and human resources directors' minds. Why? No one likes to pay for obsolescence. Why pay profit pounds for a benefit which is past its sell-by-date? You wouldn't manufacture or indeed purchase commodities which are not up-to-date and competitive, so why put up with increasing costs and decreasing employee benefit returns?

Why do employee benefits become obsolete? Well, in the first place, over the years underwriting procedures and benefits costings have changed. Pound for pound you get better value for benefits today. In other words, an employee benefit has become just another commodity and should attract little or no loyalty value to keep it if redundant. New, better products have emerged over the last few years, making a corporate benefit review almost mandatory for most businesses.

Take the case of critical illness cover (CIC). This pays out a lump sum on *diagnosis* of a critical illness such as heart attack, stroke, cancer, kidney failure, major organ failure and a host of other disabilities such as Alzheimer's disease. Yet ten years ago, it was relatively unknown as an individual product and has only been introduced into the UK as a group scheme product over the last three or four years. A lump sum of 2 × annual salary in a group of 30 employees on a group-costed basis costs only about £3 per month each. The chances of an employee age 40 developing a critical illness before retirement age at age 65 is up to eight times that of dying before age 65. Important coverage? You bet it is. Yet few businesses have it.

The way benefits for employees are introduced to the business has usually been very ad hoc. Usually a financial adviser or broker suggests a product or service, and the business takes it on. Over the years, you can end up with a mish-mash of employee benefits. There is nothing wrong with this – the business merely reacted to demand forces when it had the financial capability to do so. Yet it belies the fact that properly thought-out structuring within defined cost and benefit parameters has not taken place.

## STRATEGY #155
## Immediately review your most costly benefit – pension funding

Getting a second opinion need not cost you much, if anything. A 1% loss in investment performance over, say, 18 years compounds to over a *20% loss* in expected fund value. Many companies put up with lower-quartile pension fund investment performances for many years and do nothing about it.

You don't need to perform at number one – just aim for the upper quartile performance – the grouping of investments within your fund in the upper quarter of investment performance. Quartiles look like this:

**UPPER**

**MIDDLE UPPER**

**MIDDLE LOWER**

**LOWER**

Ask yourself where you would like your fund to be performing. The answer is self-evident. The problem is that if your fund is not performing well, then, at some stage, the business may have to *increase* its contributions, thereby affecting profitability.

---

### STRATEGY #156
## Rebroke or get quotes on your other employee benefits

---

As with pension schemes, other benefit structures such as group schemes could be found better and cheaper elsewhere. However, you will never know unless you do something about it. You have nothing to lose (except profits if you don't do it).

For example, a new client had in place the following group arrangements, which were rebroked for a better deal:

| Benefit | Existing annual cost (1982) | Amount | New annual cost (1995) | New amount |
|---|---|---|---|---|
| Group life cover | £2,760 | 2 × annual salary | £2,200 | 3 × annual salary |
| PHI | £3,500 | 66% of salary | £2,700 | 75% of salary |
| Private medical | £3,200 | Private hospital (company paid excess cost) | £2,500 | Full tariff payable |
| Dental cover | £22 per person | Employee only | £8 per person | Family |

As you can see, considerable savings were made, with an uplift in benefits.

## STRATEGY #157
## If your broker can't help you, move to one who can

The popular 'defence' for staying with existing brokers is that they have been with you for some time. But they are not doing you any favours. Ask yourself why your existing brokers haven't come up with similar strategies. Get a second opinion.

Many brokers are not interested simply on the basis of the measure of reward. Commissions payable on group health and protection benefits average out at about 4% per annum. The amount of work involved for a couple of hundred pounds' commission does not make it worth their while (in their opinion) for small to medium-sized businesses. Yet for the client, the cost savings and benefit enhancements can be significant. In other words, a good deal for the client, a bad deal for the broker. Be prepared to pay an 'installation fee' on smaller schemes.

## STRATEGY #158
## Provide the link between the business benefits and the employee's personal requirements

If the benefits in the business are 'wrong' or out of kilter with the personal financial planning requirements of the individual, or if benefits are old and obsolete and out of date, or if the benefit provided is of no use or benefit to the employee, then the business is throwing good money after bad.

In the final analysis, the benefits structure of the business is to provide or complement the personal benefit requirement and structure of the individual employee. He or she works to retire and works to build wealth.

Changing times and more flexible structures mean that the business is now able to move away from the traditional 'here's your package – take it or leave it' approach, to a more business-to-employee integrated approach. The human resources (HR) director can now spend more time on planning, rather than advising and counselling – jobs he or she is probably not qualified for.

## Previous position

Board sets policy
HR director implements policy
↓
Employee given a range of rigid benefits
Employee assisted by HR director
↓
Employee makes up the difference in benefits required himself,
often with no advice

## New position

Board sets policy
HR director plans and structures then implements
according to individual requirements
↓
Employee given some rigid, some flexible benefits
↓
Employee designs own package
assisted and advised by financial planner
↓
Financial planner advises the business and consults
on problem areas or implementation

The more integrated approach saves the company and the employee
money. What the employee does not get from the business has to be
made up *personally* at greater cost (up to 15 times more) with less disposable income to build wealth.

---

### STRATEGY #159
### Provide an authorisation service and 'hot line'

---

Whilst the HR director and other company officials may advise their
own employees generally on their own benefit structures, they may not
do so specifically (even on the company's benefits) unless authorised to
do so by one of the regulators. *To give unauthorised financial advice is
treated most seriously and carries a gaol sentence.* In addition, the company official is not covered by the ICS – the Investors' Compensation
Scheme.

Requests from employees of 'Should I take the pension scheme lump
sum?' or, 'Should I contribute to the AVC scheme?' should always be
met with the response, 'Take independent financial advice.'

Similarly, if not covered by the Consumer Credit Act 1974, then don't advise the employee to pay off his Visa card with a welfare loan, for example.

Some independent financial advisers and others offer an 'authorisation service' where the employee has immediate and direct access to authorised advice. This costs from as little as £10 p.a. per employee and it is well worth not getting the aggravation which you don't want.

Also, make sure you have tax deductible directors' and officers' liability coverages in place in your business.

---

## STRATEGY #160
## Review the whole – avoid the 'piecemeal' approach to save thousands of pounds

---

Combining the policies of review to overhaul the benefit structures of the business – even if you are a rigid traditionalist – with the policy of integration between the business and the employee, will go a long way to meeting the objectives of the business in saving costs and increasing profits.

It will also go a long way to improve the wealth-building of employees and business owners. Some may see this approach as a radical departure from accepted practice; others will see it as commercial common sense.

### Key points summary

- A general review of what benefits the business offers and how much these benefits cost can save the business thousands of pounds.

- One should recognise and strike out obsolete structures, and now be in a position to integrate the business benefit structures fully with the employees' need requirements.

- Don't give specific advice if you are not authorised and don't take specific advice from those not authorised or competent to give it.

# CHAPTER 10

# Protecting the Business – Insuring the Keyman

*97% of all businesses have no Keyman cover.*
Swiss-Re Survey

## Objective: Obtain low cost, effective Keyperson protection strategies for life cover and disability cover

Why cover the desk, but not the man or woman behind it?

Ask any businessman if he has employer liability and office contents insurance and over 95% will agree that they have. Ask if key people are covered so that if anything happens to one or more of them, the business is covered against the financial effects of the loss and only 3% of businesses will have done so. Why? What is easier to replace – a desk or a trained employee? It's all a question of priorities and, if not viewed as important, could even spell financial ruin for the business.

Businesses are, after all, about people. People are the life blood of the business and, without them – and this includes you – there is no business. If the business suffers a financial loss or closure, then the impact is felt all the way down the line. So much so that one can say that business protection is also family protection.

The example which follows can be said to be fairly typical of how quickly disaster can strike, and its far-reaching consequences.

After a successful ten-year stint with Burcom plc as their chief engineer, Bob Lake decided it was time to open up his own business servicing telecommunications companies by replacing obsolete equipment. Bob's dream was to build up a profitable business to provide for his eventual retirement provision when sold. Over the years, he had built up hundreds of useful contacts in the trade and knew he would make a success of it once he got going.

With a small business start-up loan and a remortgage from his house, Bob soon built up a thriving and enterprising business. By the end of Year five he was employing 80 people and enjoying an annual turnover of £5 million. He and his wife Sarah enjoyed the kind of lifestyle which comes with success: a £300,000 home, take-home salary of £60,000 and private education for the three children. Aged 49, Bob began thinking of expanding the business and decided that bank finance was the best route to take. Bob's credit was good, privatisation meant more work was forthcoming and the future looked very rosy indeed.

Within six months of Bob's 49th birthday, there was no business. Eighty people had lost their jobs, the bank was in the process of repossessing his beautiful home, his children had left their private schools and Sarah was job-hunting – a difficult proposition at the age of 46 with no experience of full-time employment for over 20 years. Bob had been killed in a car accident, coming back from addressing a Rotary meeting late one night. The drunken driver slewed across the carriageway and ploughed head-on into Bob's new BMW. It's a thing about drunks – they always seem to survive. Bob didn't.

This is a true story. Some months later, Sarah's story featured in the *Sunday Times* – she was destitute, the family had been split up, the home and security were gone, the children were staying with relatives and she was advertising for help as she couldn't find a job.

I wrote an article at the time entitled, 'It will never happen to me', which I circulated widely amongst clients and friends – so profound was the effect of this human disaster on me. Although the loss of a loved one has incalculable value, the loss of the business and break-up of the family could have been avoided for as little as £150 per month at the time. That's right – £150.

Bob was a Keyman – key to the survival to his business and key to the survival of his family. The business couldn't survive without him – he *was* the business. Once he went, his business connections were lost forever, the bank relied on him to cover its loan exposures and creditors gave credit to the business because he was at its helm. Bob had very little life assurance and no critical illness cover. In his case, £1 million worth of ten-year term assurance could have satisfied immediate creditors and provided *time* to appoint someone new to take over the business. The cost – £150 per month – was about one quarter of what the lowest-paid employee was paid in the business.

Because of the structure of this particular business – a sole trader – Bob's 80 employees had a statutory redundancy claim against his estate – money which had to be paid *before* anything went to his dependants.

---

## STRATEGY #161
## Determine who the key people in your business are and their financial value

---

Even the biggest companies protect their key employees against business financial loss – often for millions of pounds. You don't need to be a business owner to be a Keyperson – it could be a valuable person in your organisation such as the Head of Production or Design or, more commonly, highly-valued salesmen, who fulfil this function.

Some financial losses are absorbable by the business. Others need to be specifically covered by Keyman insurance, after assessing the commercial risk.

The following table can assist you in determining *who* are the key people to the business and the financial implications of their loss to the business.

| Name | 1 | 2 | 3 |
|---|---|---|---|
| 1. Effect on profits: | £ | £ | £ |
| 2. Cost of replacement: | | | |
|     Locum | | | |
|     Advertising | | | |
|     Employment costs | | | |
| 3. Cost of replacing know-how: | | | |
| 4. Benefit costs: | | | |
|     Pensions | | | |
|     Annuities | | | |
|     Dependants' benefits | | | |
| 5. Lost contracts costs: | | | |
| 6. Work in progress lost (value): | | | |
| 7. Employee contractual payments: | | | |
| 8. Loan account in business: | | | |
| 9. Shares repurchase: | | | |
| 10. Intrinsic value of employee: | | | |
| 11. Other: | | | |
| **Total value of key employee:** | | | |

Each item in the table can be defined as follows:

1. *Effect on profits:*
The financial loss experienced by the business, affecting profits, good-will, or turnover, if the Key employee died or became incapacitated.

2. *Cost of replacement:*
The costs of finding and hiring a new employee. If using an agency: up to 17% of annual salary.

3. *Cost of replacing know-how:*
Placing a value on the knowledge base of the employee and the effect of this loss of experience on the business. Include here costs of retraining, promotion of others, etc.

4. *Benefit costs:*
What the business has to pay out to an estate or dependants. (Claims may result in increased premiums or higher funding required.)
    If no employee benefits, the business may wish to pay a dependant's annuity or lump sums.

5. *Lost contracts costs:*
The Keyperson could have brought in a new contract or be working on an existing one, which is lost to the business. The value of that contract, or similar.

6. *Work in progress lost:*
As above, but for the value of work in progress lost. Time value. Include consequential future possible losses, such as professional indemnity run-off.

7. *Employee contractual payments:*
Lump sums, salary balance owing to the employee on termination of employment. Include here the cost of still having to pay an incapacitated employee who is replaced.

8. *Loan account in business:*
Value of directors' loan accounts in the business to be repaid on death, etc. Include partners' capital accounts.

9. *Shares repurchase:*
Cash to buy back shares in the absence of a shareholder's agreement.

10. *Intrinsic value of employee:*
Human value of the Keyperson – financial knock-on effect on the

business; cost of boosting morale.

11. *Other:*
Includes here, if a business owner, the cost of keeping the business going, if this is desirable. Include all business liabilities and exposures, loans, guarantees offered and other debts or potential debts.

*Total value of key employees:*
Values of all factors taken into consideration for Keyman cover purposes.

## Key points summary

• Ascertain exactly who is a Keyperson and why.

• Determine the financial value of the Keyperson and whether Keyperson cover is required or not,

---

### STRATEGY #162
### Determine the financial aspects of Keyman loss – finding the correct level of cover

---

The previous strategy allowed for subjectivity and sensitivity in determining the effect of human loss on the business. We will now consider a few less subjective approaches, acceptable to the Inland Revenue.

You can value a Keyperson for life assurance and disability or critical illness cover in a number of different ways. The figure given will then be your sum assured or level of cover. Don't forget to index coverages for inflation and natural business growth.

There are four methods to determine this sum:-

| | |
|---|---|
| Method 1 | Actual liability cover (Strategy #161) |
| Method 2 | 10 times salary of Keyperson |
| Method 3 | 2 times gross profits × % impact |
| Method 4 | 4 times net profits × % impact |

*Example:* Determine the range of coverage required, assuming a Keyperson with an annual salary of £30,000 and a company with gross profits of £250,000, net profits of £75,000. Actual liabilities are £175,000. The Keyperson has an impact % of 30% on profits. Coverages would then be in the range:

1. £175,000
2. £300,000

    3. £500,000 × 30% = £150,000
    4. £300,000 × 30% = £90,000

The Keyperson coverage range is £90,000 to £300,000 in this case. With a view to certainly covering (1) at £175,000, the company will probably choose a figure between that and £300,000. This level of coverage should satisfy the Inland Revenue when allowing premiums as a deduction to the business. (Under the 'reasonable amount' test.)

    Summarise your action plan as shown:

| Keyperson | (1) | (2) | (3) |
|---|---|---|---|
| Method 1: | £ | £ | £ |
| Method 2: | £ | £ | £ |
| Method 3: | £ | £ | £ |
| Method 4: | £ | £ | £ |
| Choice £ | | | |

## Key points summary

- Working out the sum assured for Keyman coverages.

- Within the Inland Revenue 'reasonable amount' test for premium deductibility.

---

### STRATEGY #163
### Determine which of the three different types of Keyman coverages you will need

---

There are three main types of Keyperson coverage available to be considered. Businesses usually consider Keyperson life cover (which is really death cover!), but more are including health protection coverages and disability cover.

    Problems for the business often arise when a Keyperson (or any employee for that matter) becomes incapacitated and expects to be supported by the business, which has the additional costs of replacing that person whilst the business income is probably failing.

    Take, for example, the case of Henry Miller. Henry graduated from Oxford with a first-class law degree and soon found articles with a practice of four partners and 25 staff. Within ten years Henry had himself become a partner, along with two others in the firm, and was responsible for £300,000 worth of fees a year. In addition, he had built up his capital account in the firm's books to £220,000. The firm, which now numbered six partners and 72 employees, was on an upward spiral, Henry in particular bringing in lucrative trade union business.

At the age of 43, Henry, due to stress from pressure of work, suffered a series of strokes. Unfortunately, he was not covered for critical illness cover (neither personally nor through the firm) – a policy which would have paid a lump sum on diagnosis of his condition, nor was there any income protection for disability in place (such as PHI).

The problems were:

1. Henry didn't die, but survived, unable to work.
2. The firm has to replace him as a fee earner, but has a moral obligation to support him.
3. The firm has to find two incomes (one for Henry, one for his replacement), but only has one fee stream. It cannot do this indefinitely (especially supporting Henry's high level of earnings).
4. Henry would want access to his capital account which the firm uses for working capital. This would place an intolerable burden on the firm.

What the firm should have had was:

- Critical illness Keyman cover.
- Permanent health insurance Keyman cover.

The above protection policies would have preserved Henry's income and provided replacement financing for his successor, whilst preserving Henry's capital account.

Were Henry to succumb to his condition and die, then, in the absence of suitable clauses in the firm's partnership agreement, his heirs would have *an immediate call for cash* (under the 1890 Partnership Act – note the position is *not* the same for shareholders in a company whose heirs cannot make this sort of demand).

In this case the problems would be:

1. Payment of the large capital account to Henry's heirs and dependants (the firm is presently using it for working capital) on his death.
2. Replacing Henry's fee income.
3. Losing his valuable know-how and contacts. The general effects of the loss of Henry on the firm.
4. Possible forced dissolution of the firm.
5. Responsibility for the ongoing professional indemnity claims liability, which Henry, as a partner, leaves as a contingent liability in the firm.

These problems would have been prevented by:

* Partnership Keyman life cover.
* Restructuring of partnership agreements.
* Possible combination Keyman and partnership agreements to save on costs (see Strategy #181).

As a result:

* The firm replaces the capital account with life assurance proceeds.
* Henry's heirs get *immediate* payment of value for his shares of the business.
* The firm is able to provide a financial cushion until Henry is replaced.
* The firm need not dissolve.
* Seventy-two staff and five partners keep their jobs.

You may think that professionally-qualified advisers would not allow their own situations to develop as above – but recently this situation (where no cover was in place) happened to a practice with eight accountants' partners and a staff of 45 in the north of England. One partner became critically ill and later died. The firm had no business agreements and heirs of the deceased further demanded payment of his share of the practice. The firm, heavily affected by the recession, couldn't pay and ended up by dissolving the partnership. It could all have been avoided by a £250 per month premium payment in this case. Skimping on the small issues – and thinking, 'It will never happen to me' – can spell disaster for any business.

## Key points summary

* There are three main types of conventional Keyman cover:
  · life cover
  · critical illness (and disability) cover
  · permanent health insurance (PHI) (and disability) cover

* There is a further type of disability cover – Keyman business expenses cover which is unconventional (see Strategy #196) in that it covers *all* business expenses.

* If a Keyman suffers a 'living death' and is critically ill (and incapable of earning), there could be major consequences for the business, family and medical expenses needs. You need *more* income, not less.

* Find out immediately what strategies your business has in place for Keyman protection.

## MONEY SAVING STRATEGIES FOR KEYPERSON PROVISION

> ### STRATEGY #164
> ### Select the right kind of policy

You have a choice between different variations of term assurance or whole of life cover.

If for a short period – up to five years – then select term cover. For longer periods, select *renewable term* (you can continue with the same cover, an increased premium and no medicals); or *convertible term* (the option to convert term to whole of life).

For even longer periods, use *term* or *whole of life maximum cover*, the latter being similar to an 'open-ended term policy'.

> ### STRATEGY #165
> ### Make your Keyman policy tax deductible

Term policies of five years or less, with a reasonable sum assured, which are not renewable nor convertible, and where the life assured has no substantial interest in the business (between 0% and 5%) will make the *premiums* payable tax deductible.

An alternative is to use *pension term* policies in small businesses, owned by the partners or shareholders, and providing key person coverage *outside* the business. You can have up to 5% of your personal pension premium for this.

> ### STRATEGY #166
> ### Make your Keyman policy proceeds tax-free

All *term* policies owned by a company have their proceeds taxable.

Whole of life policies owned by a company have tax-free proceeds, but the policy *gain*, which is the difference between the surrender value and premiums paid, is taxable.

Term policies held *outside* the business, usually in trust, by the shareholders or partners, will have *tax-free* proceeds. Your strategy would be to arrange the Keyman cover outside the business, and to lend the proceeds to the business by way of directors' or partners' loan account.

This is more appropriate for smaller businesses, rather than larger ones (such as PLCs) where you opt for term policies *longer* than five years, or which are renewable or convertible, or where the Keyperson owns a substantial stake in the business.

---

### STRATEGY #167
### Save the business thousands in tax by keeping the policy outside the business

---

If the company owns a term policy, the proceeds are taxable. To achieve true coverage, you then need to *increase* the sum assured by between 25% and 35% to provide for tax payable.

Proceeds on *term* policies are *taxable* whether the premium is tax deductible or not. The *solution* is to have the policy in trust outside the company, especially if longer than a five year term, renewable or convertible. Premiums come from increased salary paid by the business. Salary is tax deductible to the business. Although National Insurance contributions are payable in the increased salary, this cost is less than the cost of any taxable proceeds. Increased salary also incurs increased pension funding as the salary on which pension contributions are based is higher.

---

### STRATEGY #168
### To ensure premiums are tax deductible, get it in writing from the Inland Revenue

---

If the company-owned term policy qualifies for premium tax deductions, get it in writing from the Inland Revenue. This only applies to a term policy of five years or less, which satisfies the conditions. Company owned whole of life premiums are *never* tax deductible.

---

### STRATEGY #169
### Never have a Keyperson policy with an investment element to save up to 50% of premium costs

---

Only use term policies, or *maximum* cover whole of life policies. The latter give the flexibility of open-ended term policies, with a minimum investment element. Some are even *cheaper* than longer term policies.

*However*, watch out for *policy reviews*, especially after ten years, when your premiums could be reviewed upwards. As no one knows when death will occur, the ultimate protection vehicle is term for life or a low-cost maximum whole of life policy.

---

### STRATEGY #170
### Top up existing coverages regularly

---

If the business is expanding rapidly, don't be caught short. Regular policy reviews (say, every two years) are important.

Some policies can be *indexed* to increase cover at the inflation rate, or at selected rates of up to 10% per annum.

---

### STRATEGY #171
### Save on policy fees by combining Keyperson policies with shareholder or partnership policies

---

Where the option is used to have the Keyperson *outside* the business in trust, you can *combine* shareholder or partner protection to save on costs.

If there are, say, three shareholders requiring both Keyperson *and* shareholder cover, instead of six policies (three Keyman and three shareholder policies), the same objectives can be achieved with three policies. A *combination* Keyperson and double option agreement is essential if this strategy is followed. (See Strategy #181.)

Combining can save the business thousands in costs including policy costs.

---

### STRATEGY #172
### Don't let cancer kill your business

---

Life cover Keyperson options are only one element of the coverages required.

The business should also examine critical illness cover and disability cover as additional options. Both can also be used in the combination double option agreement *outside* the business, if required.

## Key points summary

- Choose the right policy.

- SAVE tax.

- Get premiums deductible.

- Combine Keyperson and shareholders'/partner protection *outside the business*.

- Don't forget critical illness and disability cover.

- Keyman coverages are there to protect profits and to enable business continuation to occur. Failure to do so may put wealth-building through the business in a precarious state.

- The various strategies show how to obtain the best coverages and to save money in doing so.

CHAPTER 11

# Shareholder and Partner Agreements

*Together, we can do more.*
Life Office Slogan 1985

**Objective: To develop structured succession planning for the business, including a ready market for shares on death or retirement**

The following scenario is fairly typical for businesses which allow *outside forces* to dictate how they leave business assets on the death, certainly, and possibly also the serious disability, of a business owner. This is the same situation as an individual dying intestate (without having made a will) and can have catastrophic consequences for the business, other shareholders or partners and employees.

Our first example deals with John Claxton from Fairknox, a limited company. John was the majority shareholder holding 80% of the shares; his wife, Mary, held 5%; and two senior managers held the balance of 15% between them. The company employed 80 people and enjoyed an annual turnover of £2 million. The business manufactured motor vehicle components in competitive conditions. It had a bank overdraft of £350,000, John having signed as personal guarantor with the bank to secure this loan, with his house offered as collateral security. On his death, John intended to leave his shares, valued at £750,000 to Mary. There were no shareholder agreements in place, and although the senior managers would have liked a greater stake, John's attitude was very much that of keeping it in the family.

John died.

Whilst typical of many businesses, the consequences of his death could have been avoided. Firstly, the bank, exceedingly nervous with its exposure, immediately called in the loan as a precautionary measure. Because there was no succession planning, the management and direction of the company rapidly degenerated into chaos, with employees leaving, taking customers with them.

Other customers became apprehensive as their sources of supply dried up and began sourcing new suppliers. Mary was totally unprepared for having to cope with John's death and gave no thought to the business which was now hers. She had no financial experience and little business expertise. The once valuable asset – the business – was rapidly deteriorating before her eyes and she felt powerless to do anything about it.

In fact the last will and testament of John Claxton of Fairknox Limited, a once proud and prosperous company employing 80 people and thereby supporting over 240 dependants of employees, might just as well have said something like this:

# LAST WILL AND TESTAMENT

## of

## JOHN CLAXTON of FAIRKNOX LIMITED

I, John Claxton, being of sound mind, hereby bequeath my business assets as follows:

1. To the Inland Revenue I leave 25% of my company. I wish HM Customs and Excise to be included also for any claims on the company.

2. To my partner in the business, National Westminster Bank, I immediately bequeath the sum of £350,000 plus accumulated interest.

3. To any receivers called in to administer what remains of my business, I leave at least £100,000 in fees, which may escalate considerably as more and more time is spent in seeking a buyer or selling off assets.

4. To my creditors, who supported the cash flows of the business, I leave 10 pence in the pound on all amounts owing to them.

5. To my competitors, I give them first choice over my best employees and company contracts.

6. The balance of my employees, to whom I am deeply grateful for their many years of faithful service, I leave the State the opportunity to support them where I have left off.

7. The balance of my business assets I leave to my wife, Mary, who selflessly helped and supported me whilst I built the business. This will unfortunately not be very much as my shares' value could be negligible.

*In addition*, should Mary predecease me, then her share will pass to my children. In that case, I further bequeath 40% of that value to the Capital Taxes Office.

8. Should my company be unable to meet its debts, I leave and bequeath my family home to the bank.

9. As pallbearers, I nominate Messrs Dun and Bradstreet, and it is my wish that my company's remains be interred at the corporate graveyard in Cardiff.

10. As executors and administrators of my corporate estate, I nominate an extremely expensive firm of receivers and/or liquidators. Only the best will do for my company.

Given under my hand at London on this 1st day of March 1996.

Signed: *J Claxton*                              Witnesses: *2 senior managers*

What went wrong? How did a successful company with a prosperous future allow itself to die intestate?

The smaller the company, the more vulnerable it is. The greater the concentration of shareholdings in one person, the bigger the need for adequate succession planning. That is not to say that it doesn't happen to big companies – it can, and it does.

Shareholders (even passive ones) have no rights to call for value from a company in trouble. In fact, they will *always* be last to get any value – known as a distribution dividend, if there is one. The fact of the matter is that unquoted company shares are generally unmarketable and all the more so if anything happens to the company.

*Partnerships* are even more vulnerable. On the death of a partner, in the absence of any agreements, the 1890 Partnership Act takes over by default. This means that the heirs of a deceased partner have an immediate call for cash for the value of the deceased partner's share. This could spell serious financial trouble for the surviving partners. The other consequences would be as for a company if the partnership failed to survive.

Perhaps the most vulnerable is the sole proprietor. His business usually dies with him. *In addition*, his employees would have a statutory redundancy claim against his estate. In other words, his employees 'inherit' something *before* his family and heirs.

Adequate *succession planning* is therefore *vital* for all businesses, large and small.

The following strategies will guide you along the correct commercial paths in making a proper 'will' for your business.

---

### STRATEGY #173
### Read Chapter 10 on business protection

---

Providing adequate cash at the right time gives the business financial 'breathing space' whilst it sorts out and implements succession planning objectives. Keyman cover is a vital element here.

---

### STRATEGY #174
### Develop your succession planning objectives

---

The following list may assist you:

- If anything happens to you, such as death or incapacity, what are your plans for the business?
- If misfortune befalls *other* shareholders or partners, what would you like to happen?
  - shares pass to their heirs
  - shares pass to you
  - shares pass to management and/or employees
  - business buys back shares
  - business is sold
  - shares pass to surviving shareholders or partners, with cash paid to heirs
- Who can run the business effectively? Are people earmarked, or must someone be brought in to do so?
- What happens on retirement?
  - business is sold
  - MBO/MBI (managers buy the business)
  - employees buy the business
  - new shareholders
  - business ceases

## STRATEGY #175
## If a sole proprietor, insure for estate liquidity

Because *you* are the business, you need to protect your estate and heirs. Business liabilities and debts – including salaries owing – could come from your estate.

Alternatively, consider incorporation (forming a company) to protect your personal wealth.

## STRATEGY #176
## If a sole proprietor, have a Buy and Sell agreement with another sole proprietor

Unfortunately, the value of your business dies with you – unless it can be sold for reasonable value *after* your death.

The strategy is to find someone with a similar business in the same position as you. Enter into a Buy and Sell agreement for the other party to purchase your business on your death or even retirement. The parties insure each other to provide the *cash* to make this sale possible. Examples are, say, a pharmacist in one town entering into this arrangement with a pharmacist in another.

With a Buy and Sell agreement A *must* purchase from B.

## STRATEGY #177
## If there are shareholders or partners then consider a 'double option' agreement between the parties

A double option or cross option agreement overcomes the problem of *finding cash* to purchase the deceased's shares and at the same time gives shares to those who want them (the survivors) and provides *cash* for those who require this (the heirs of the deceased).

It is also a useful, flexible device to *control* who gets what. Because it is an agreement between the parties, there should be a smooth transaction on death, or even disability.

The parties usually insure one another (or take out a life policy and assign it to a trust), with the sum assured paying out to the survivors. The heirs have the *option* to call for cash from the survivors, and the survivors have the *option* to call for the deceased's shares. Whoever triggers the option must expect the other party to perform. If neither party acts, then the status quo remains with the heirs keeping the shares, the survivors the cash.

This type of agreement is one of sale *after* death and *may* happen – if the option from either side is activated. Consequently the shares fall outside the inheritance tax net.

A Buy and Sell agreement is similar, but is regarded as a contract for pre-sale and may lose business property reliefs on death and incur IHT liabilities. Here, the parties *must* act and exchange shares for cash.

---

### STRATEGY #178
### Examine existing Buy and Sell agreements

---

If you have a Buy and Sell agreement in place, then perhaps a double option agreement will be more effective or tax efficient for you. Each type of agreement has its place. However, the future loss of business property reliefs for Buy and Sell agreements has caused a switch to double option agreements over the years, where business property relief on death is not lost.

---

### STRATEGY #179
### Check existing levels of cover to ensure full coverage

---

Older, existing agreements may be out of date, as well as levels of coverage. The agreement should have a clause allowing for updating as the value of the business changes.

---

### STRATEGY #180
### Check types of coverage to cover all angles

---

Life cover is the most popular. However, incapacity, disability or critical illness may have the same effect on a business as death. Modern agreements may incorporate a clause allowing the incapacitated shareholder or partner to *buy back* his shares after recovering from a heart attack or other critical illness. Many life policies incorporate disability coverages and should be considered. On average, you have, at age 40, a one in eight chance of suffering a critical illness before age 65 rather than of dying.

## STRATEGY #181
### For maximum flexibility, include Keyman cover above the line with shareholder or partner cover

Usually the business takes out the Keyman policy, pays the premium (which may be deductible – see Chapter 10) and the *business* receives the policy proceeds. These will be taxable *in full* if a term policy, tax-free if a whole of life (although any *gain* is taxable – this is the difference between the premiums paid and the surrender value).

The shareholders or partners effect the shareholder protection policies on each other's or their own lives and pay the premiums. These premiums are *usually* (unless pension term policies) not tax deductible for the premiums, but the proceeds are tax-free.

For maximum efficiency *and* flexibility, combine the two sets of coverages. If three shareholders have, say, £100,000 shareholder protection cover and *also* £100,000 Keyman cover, there will be six policies with six separate policy charges. Combining reduces these charges by 50%.

**Previous position**


**New position**

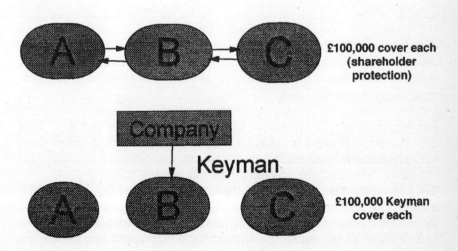

Assume C dies:

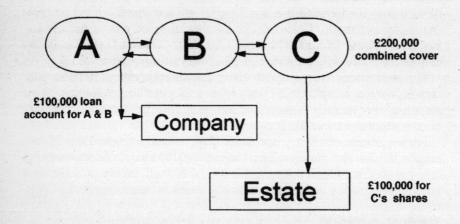

A and B receive £200,000. Of this, £100,000 goes to C's estate to purchase C's shares. The Keyman cover remains, as £100,000 tax-free cash, in the hands of A and B. They can then evaluate the position of the business after the loss of C and:

- pay cash into the business by way of directors' or partners' loan accounts. (Loan accounts can be withdrawn at any time. Cash entering the business in this way is *not* taxable.)
- keep the cash if the business does not need it.
- pay more of the cash to C's estate or dependants.

Each business must assess its own position. The combination Keyman and shareholder/partner protection arrangement can be *included* in the double option or Buy and Sell agreement.

# STRATEGY #182
## Include ESOTs, employees and managers in your succession planning

The parties to the shareholders' sales agreement may be diverse, or as one-sided as you see fit. Some shareholders may wish to buy but not to sell on death of a party to the agreement – or vice versa.

An excellent method of creating marketability of your shares is to have the trustees of your ESOT (Employee Share Ownership Trust) take out a Keyman life policy on your life. When you die, the cash proceeds pass to the trustees, who *buy your shares* from your estate. In this way, a sales process is set up for the shares to pass to employees and managers.

The company can fund the ESOTs trust. This funding is tax deductible to the company. The trust then pays the premiums on the policy.

# STRATEGY #183
## Use the above strategy to fund the purchase of your shares on retirement

Capital passes to the trust, which is tax deductible, from the company or borrowings. The trustees buy shares from the shareholders.

Marketability in shares is created.

# STRATEGY #184
## Your best strategy is to phase your sale of shares

Sales of shares to the ESOT's trust need not all be at once. They can be phased over a number of years. This allows the seller the opportunity to use annual CGT exemptions. Roll-over reinvestment relief is also available.

---

## STRATEGY #185
## Get tax deductible coverages for shareholder protection

---

Shareholders or partners qualifying for personal pension plans are allowed by law to have 5% of their allowable pension contribution to purchase tax deductible term assurance cover. They need not take out a pension, if they do not wish to do so.

The cost of cover is then significantly reduced – by up to 40%, using this method. However, you must have net relevant earnings for pension term cover. Term is generally cheapest, but may be inflexible as it ends at retirement age.

For example:

Male, age next birthday: 40
Net relevant earnings: £40,000
20% allowable contribution to pension: £8,000
less 5% for pension term: £2,000
(15% for pension contribution): £6,000

£2,000 p.a. buys £550,000 term cover to age 65.
Net cost £1,200 p.a. for a 40% taxpayer.
If a female, then £1m worth of cover may be purchased at this age.

Having read this chapter, you should have:

- developed succession planning for your business
- ensured that the correct agreements are in place
- arranged adequate protection and coverages for the business in the most flexible and tax-efficient way

## Key points summary

- A properly structured shareholders' or partners' agreement is like a will for the business.

- Protect the business and business owners whilst creating instant marketability of shares.

- Cost-saving premium strategies make your protection planning an inexpensive exercise.

# CHAPTER 12

# Choosing the Best Income Protection Plans

*It costs a lot of money to die comfortably.*
Samuel Butler (1835-1902) **Note Books**

**Objective: To provide adequate income protection for sickness, injury or disability, at the best possible price, to protect business profits**

The government is seriously damaging your wealth. What the State fails to cover can now fall on your business as an additional cost. Where the State has previously covered a significant portion of invalidity and injury benefits for employees, as the State winds down its responsibility for these coverages, businesses are now rapidly becoming a dumping ground for medical and sick pay expenses.

The statistics are alarming: over the past 15 years, the number of claimants has risen by nearly one million, from 600,000 in 1978/79 to nearly 1.5 million in 1993/94 – a rise of 150% at a cost of £1.6 billion a year. Only about 12% of the working population is covered through individual or group PHI. Over 75% of UK firms do not offer PHI as a part of their benefit package. The DSS statistics for 1993 showed that 182,000 people between the ages of 20 and 64 were unable to work through ill health for between six months and one year. About 470,000 people were off work between one year and three years, and 757,000 had been unable to work for more than three years.

In fact, one in five working people could be off work for three months or more (*source:* Unum research 1995). You are much more likely to claim against a permanent health insurance policy than to die (before you do so). A family man aged 45 is 15 times more likely to be off work for six months than he is to die in the next 12 months. Indeed, the chances of a middle-aged individual at work becoming disabled for six months or more are five times greater than the likelihood of him or her dying before the age of 65.

The State is trying to reverse an upward trend of £6.1 billion payouts and costs spent on those claiming sickness and invalidity benefit in 1995, rising to an expected £9.8 billion in the year 2000. Through drastic cost-cutting, the State is hoping to reduce this expenditure to around the £2 billion per annum mark.

On 13 April 1995, the old style tax-free invalidity benefits payable to those employees injured, sick or disabled so that they cannot perform their *own* occupations was replaced by a new style *incapacity benefit*. (In a recent Swiss RE (UK) survey, the level of awareness of changes in the system was less than 15% amongst the general public.)

This has the following implications for *all* businesses.

- The new incapacity benefit will affect higher earners the most. They will experience up to and over an 80% reduction in what was previously available.
- The new incapacity benefit is taxable after the first 28 weeks. People who previously looked to replacing *net* incomes must now replace *gross* incomes.
- There are *new* medical tests to determine whether you incapacitated or not. You are if you score 15 points or more from a 14-step check list.
- To discourage claims, your own GP *cannot* conduct the test – it must be done by a State-appointed independent doctor.
- You could also be means-tested and not qualify for certain benefits.
- The *definition* of incapacity is no longer the inability to perform your *own* occupation – but *any* occupation. If sick or injured for one type of work, but not another, you don't qualify. The State would rather have you claiming unemployment benefit and income support than claim incapacity benefits.

Statutory sick pay is the amount which your business must pay to an employee for the statutory period of 28 weeks. For the 95/96 tax year this is £52.50 per week. Thereafter, the employee is either still paid by the business, or qualifies for the much lower State Incapacity Benefit, or lives on income from a permanent health insurance policy (PHI) if he or she has one.

To keep sick, non-productive employees on the payroll can be an expensive matter.

The statistical chances of an employee becoming ill, injured or disabled and so unable to work are as follows:

Age 20–64, any given period, per employer

| Number of employees | Off work for six months | Off work for one year | Off work for one year+ |
|---|---|---|---|
| 10 | 1 in 30 | 1 in 37 | 1 in 43 |
| 20 | 1 in 15 | 1 in 18.5 | 1 in 22 |
| 50 | 1 in 6 | 1 in 7.7 | 1 in 8.3 |
| 100 | 1 in 3 | 1 in 3.7 | 1 in 4.3 |
| 300 | 1.05 | 1 in 1.25 | 1 in 1.4 |
| 500 | 1.75 | 1.34 | 1.14 |
| 1,000 | 3.5 | 2.68 | 2.29 |

*Source:* Unum Database 1995.

These are average figures, and obviously vary greatly between sectors of employment and different industries and occupations.

The implications are even greater at management and executive level. To support non-productive senior executives can be *very* expensive for any business. Even though private sick pay policies (PHI) may be in existence, they only cover (usually) 75% of salary less the State Incapacity Benefit. Yet everyone knows that to live on 25% less income is extremely difficult.

Unum, the PHI insurer, has the following claims statistics as its most 'popular' PHI claims for 1995 (in descending order of number of claims per category):

- Cardio – heart, stroke
- Skeletomuscular – back pain
- Cancers and tumours
- Mental, stress, fits
- Arthritis

Men are more likely than women to have extended periods off work. Unum further states that its payout periods on average are:

- up to 1 year – one-third of people claiming
- 1–5 years – almost two-thirds of people claiming
- over 10 years – negligible amount of people claiming

Companies could conceivably carry a (moral) salary burden for at least one year and most likely longer.

The State is definitely attempting to shift the burden of incapacity pay to the private sector. As the years go by, businesses will be *forced* into adopting more aggressive sick pay policies. Why should they do this? Many businesses treat employees merely as replaceable commodities, that's why. Some certainly have a policy to get rid of non-productive employees as quickly as possible. Pay and payroll *costs* are usually the most expensive items in any business's books.

Why then would any business wish to establish a sick pay policy of supporting employees when off sick, injured or disabled?

- To keep valuable employees the business may otherwise lose
- Cost of retraining new employees
- Cost of replacing old employees
- Work-force morale and the 'feel good' factor within the business
- Moral obligations
- It can afford to do so
- Provides 'settled conditions of employment'

The following strategies will assist the business in saving costs whilst getting the best value for money.

---

## STRATEGY #186
## Define your sick pay policy – keep 'em or lose 'em

---

The first step in the process is to know where you want to be in the future. This also indicates to the work-force the type of employer you are.

Surveys of employees requesting their views on which employee benefits are most required or desired by them, usually have income protection (PHI) and sick pay salary continuance either at the top or near the top of the list. Naturally, preferences vary from business to business and also regionally. Up-to-date information may be obtained from IDS and other pay and remuneration monitors.

Establish the *objectives* of the business. What is it you hope to achieve? What coverages do you already have? Are there any gaps to be filled or made up? Are existing coverages adequate?

Businesses may find the following terminology useful – the whole area of medical and health protection can be difficult to understand.

## Permanent Health Insurance (PHI)

This provides *income replacement*, usually up to 75% of salary (less the State incapacity and other benefits). Some businesses have up to 90% of net pay. The average coverages appear to be around the 66% of salary mark.

The usual definitions will provide for income to be paid in the event of sickness, injury or disability occurring within the definitions. This will usually be for 'own' occupation as opposed to the State's more liberal interpretation of 'any occupation'. So, if you break a leg in a car accident and are off work for longer than the deferred period (usually 4 weeks to 104 weeks) then a health insurer will pay the *income only* (no lump sum) at the insured rate.

Rates vary from, say, £3 per person per month for a 75% of salary group scheme to individually-costed cover which could be 15 times that amount or more.

## Critical Illness Cover

This pays out a lump sum on *diagnosis* of a critical illness, such as heart condition, stroke, paraplegia, cancer, kidney failure and a host of others such as Alzheimer's disease and Multiple Sclerosis. Complementary to PHI, it can pay out in certain areas not covered by PHI. For example, the onset of cancer may mean hospital treatment, but not necessarily being off work. PHI won't pay out, but critical illness cover will.

Rates vary from, say, £2.60 per person per month for a 2 × annual salary lump sum on a group scheme, to individually-costed cover which is much greater. Many businesses now incorporate this benefit to overlap with PHI. Over the last three years, more critical illness cover has been purchased by individuals than PHI coverages, which shows the shift in attitude of the buying population towards this type of coverage.

## Private Medical Cover

This type of cover pays for actual hospitalisation and other medical costs, and is the alternative to the National Health Service. Companies which spring to mind are BUPA, PPP, WPA, Norwich and others.

Premium rates can be on a cheaper group basis or the more expensive individually-costed basis.

## Long-term Care (LTC) Cover

Provides an income to pay for long-term nursing care, usually until death. Although not common with businesses, some PHI/critical illness policies incorporate a useful LTC option which carries on after retirement – but at today's premium rate.

What then will be most appropriate for your business? Often a tailor-made scheme is best. You can incorporate as many or as few of the features required as you wish.

---

**STRATEGY #187**
## Decide whether sick pay, income continuation is necessary

---

Following your review decide if:

- the firm will cover sickness pay and benefits itself
- the firm will not pay and will leave the employee relying on the State's lower benefits
- the firm will take out sickness insurance coverages

---

**STRATEGY #188**
## Decide when the firm will make arrangements for sick pay

---

If the business wishes to do what it can for employees, then timing is important. Our example is Robert Pudnick, a 47-year-old married man, whose wife is not working; they have two child dependants. He earns £25,000 p.a. and has take home pay of £18,455 (1995/96). The difference between what the State will pay and what the PHI payments will cover are given in the following table:

| Salary | Statutory sick pay period 28 weeks | Incapacity Benefits 28–52 weeks | Incapacity Benefits 53 weeks+ |
|---|---|---|---|
| £25,000 | £52.50 p.w. (£1,470) | £79.40 p.w. (£1,905.60) | £112.90 p.w. (£5,870.80 p.a.) |
| 100% | 6% | 8% | 23% p.a. |
| £25,000 | Sick leave: full pay 4 weeks–13 weeks | PHI benefits are 75% of salary less State Incapacity Benefits | |
| 100% | (say) deferred period | £18,750 less State Incapacity Benefits above | |

The best Robert can expect from the State is 8% of salary for the first year, rising to 23% of salary after one year – if he qualifies. The PHI coverage with the State benefit should cover 75% of salary. He has to hope the business will top this up.

Deferred periods have a lot to do with cost. The *longer* the deferred period (the period where you wait whilst sickness or disability is confirmed) the cheaper the premiums and vice versa.

---

## STRATEGY #189
## To save premium costs, select a longer deferred period

---

The business can choose when privately funded benefits become payable. By deferring the payment of benefits you can choose a cheaper premium and have sufficient time to establish if the claimant will recover or not.

Premium savings over deferred periods are:

| Deferred period | Premium cost per month | |
|---|---|---|
| 4 weeks | £[a] – | £[b]69 |
| 13 weeks | £219.07 | £40.72 |
| 26 weeks | £174.92 | £33.23 |
| 52 weeks | £159.56 | £26.09 |
| 104 weeks | £138.44 | £22.01 |

*Source:* Unum

[a]Group scheme 19 employees PHI 75% of salary less State Incapacity Benefits: payable to age 65. Salary £30,000 average. Class 1 occupations. Non-smokers.

The range for group rates is from £219.07 per month, or £11.53 each person, at a 13-week waiting period, to £138.44 per month, or £7.29 each person at 104 weeks waiting period.

[b]Individually-costed benefits, male 40 next birthday, PHI benefits payable to age 65. Salary of £30,000. Benefit 75% of salary less State Incapacity Benefits. Best rates, any provider. Class 1 occupation. Non-smoker. The range for individual rates is £69 at four weeks waiting period to £22.01 for a waiting period of 104 weeks.

---

### STRATEGY #190
### Always choose a group scheme rate for cheaper PHI premiums

---

Believe it or not, you can have a group scheme of one person! The power of group schemes is further developed in Chapter 7.

For example:

Group PHI at 75% of salary less State Incapacity Benefit. Thirty employees, age range 18–60. Earnings range £5,700–£39,900. Retirement age 65. Deferred period four weeks. *Premium per person: £3 per month.* This is tax deductible to the business.

Compare this with the following best non-smoker rates for the same benefits, but individually-costed:

Male, age next birthday 18, salary of £10,000: £11.29 per month.

Female, age next birthday 25, salary of £18,000: £37.66 per month.

Male, age next birthday 55, salary of £35,000: £184.00 per month.

The above benefits apply to 75% of salary. This shows the power of buying group scheme costed benefits over individually-costed benefits.

---

### STRATEGY #191
### At least provide the group scheme facility even if your business won't pay the premium

---

Even if employees pay for the PHI benefit themselves, by allowing the company to own the scheme, the employer is providing useful cost savings benefits for the employees. This helps the 'feel good' factor in the business.

---

### STRATEGY #192
### Use the business to create tax deductions for PHI premiums

---

If the employee pays for private PHI, the premium is not tax deductible. The first 12 months of the benefits received by the employee is tax-free. Thereafter it is taxable. (1996/97 benefits are all now tax-free.)

Where the *company* pays the premium on the PHI policy owned by it, the *premiums* are tax deductible. The benefits received are taxable in the hands of the employee, with *no* 12-month tax-free period. However, the benefits payable by the company to the employee are tax deductible to the company. Remember, lower-costed group rated premiums are significantly cheaper than individually-costed ones. Weigh this aspect against the tax saved for individually-owned benefits.

---

### STRATEGY #193
### Use the business to get cover for those who normally may not get it

---

The group scheme can be used not only to *reduce* the overall cost of cover, but also to make sure that people who may not qualify for health reasons can now get cover.

Each group scheme will have a level of 'free cover' below which no medical examinations are required. Some individuals (often senior, older executives) can take advantage of this. Not only will they get cover, but *also* it will be at premium levels *well* below what they might usually pay individually.

The following example will illustrate this. A firm of accountants with 12 partners and 140 staff has a group PHI plan.

*Total premium* for 75% of cover, less the State Incapacity Benefits for the group of 152 people: £2,400 p.a. *(£1.32 per month each person).*

*Total premium* for the 12 partners only: £1,440 p.a. *(£10 per person per month).*

Crazy isn't it! Same firm, same level of benefits, but separating out the younger ages (the employees) from the older ones (the partners) has this effect. It would actually have been 7.5 times cheaper for the partners to have remained in the larger group *and* to allow their employees to get really inexpensive PHI income continuance benefits.

Incidentally, *partners* receiving PHI benefits through the firm's group policy can receive the first 12 months' income tax-free.

---

## STRATEGY #194
## Shop around to save on PHI and other health and protection benefits costs

---

The 4% commission payable on low-costed protection group scheme arrangements rarely excites the average broker to go out of his way to get the best deal for the client. Insist on a range of competitive quotes. Be prepared to possibly pay an 'installation' fee.

Proper structuring and tailor-making of your scheme could save the business thousands in costs, charges and future administration.

---

## STRATEGY #195
## Protect the income of your whole work force for less than 50% of the cost of employing a cleaner each year

---

There are two schools of thought – use your own money (the business's money) to carry those off sick, or injured and away from work; or use OPM.

OPM is 'other people's money': in this case, the PHI and critical illness cover product provider's money. The annual cost is minuscule compared with having to fund salaries for one in every 15 employees who may be off sick or injured/incapacitated from work for six months or more, each year.

Like the cleaner's salary, the PHI premium is also tax deductible.

---

## STRATEGY #196
## Protect the business's cash flows and profits – buy Keyman PHI

---

What if Digby Pocock, the managing director of a large firm, was paralysed in a car accident? Digby is the person responsible for over 80% of the income of the firm. He has organised the contracts and he makes things happen. Finding another Digby will take time – at least 12 months. Income may slowly dry up, but bills still have to be paid. Rent, salaries, utilities, tax, VAT, supplies – the list is endless. You can bet it also grows and rarely reduces.

Digby also needs 100% of his income to live on, and in fact needs more, now that extra nursing care is required. He has a mortgage, children to educate, maintenance to pay a former spouse – and to get 25% less in sickness benefits from the company just doesn't suit his present lifestyle. The State is even less sympathetic: its incapacity benefit payment would be 83% less than what he earns.

Big problem – keeping the business going as well as yourself (or supporting essential key players as best you can).

The best the company can expect is about 2.5 to 3 times Digby's salary if Keyperson disability and PHI cover is obtained from a life insurer. The Lloyds market, however, can offer full coverage of *all* business expenses, including 100% or more of salary. The reason is that this type of cover is underwritten in 'general insurance' and not 'life insurance'. The Lloyds of London coverages can pay out income and/or a lump sum, e.g. £20,000 income per month and a lump sum of £1 million for the Keyperson total disability.

---

## STRATEGY #197
### Set your coverage requirements. Mix and match between life offices and the Lloyds of London market

---

The ideal combination would be:

Group scheme PHI: protects the work-force's income
Keyman PHI: protects the business's income and cash flows
Individual PHI: protects the individual's income especially if the business does nothing

The State's Incapacity Benefits are a last resort after strict qualifying criteria – and then they produce a pittance anyway. Don't rely on them.

---

## STRATEGY #198
### If your company won't do it, and you can't afford to do it – join someone else's scheme

---

Many trade unions, societies, associations, and other affinity groups may operate group schemes for their members. Use their scheme as a base benefit and then top up privately.

## STRATEGY #199
## Get your spouse covered for income protection
## – even if he or she doesn't even have any
## income

Some group schemes and many private PHI schemes are available to *give* spouses an income on sickness, injury or long-term disability. This also applies to critical illness cover for spouses and children which is often *free*.

The loss of a spouse through incapacity in the home or helping in the business can have a serious knock-on effect on *your* income. You may need to employ full-time nurses, child carers or other personal attendants.

## STRATEGY #200
## Check your policy terms carefully – especially
## the 'own' occupation changing to 'any'
## occupation clauses

Of the PHI providers surveyed by us, 85% had contracts which allowed for the definition of 'sickness, ill health, injury or other disability' which precludes you from carrying out your 'own' occupation. This means you can't do the job for which you trained and the policy should pay out. If the definition was 'own or *any* occupation', then the policy only pays out if you can't do *any* reasonable or similar occupation.

The State changed its definition of incapacity to 'any' occupation in April 1995, for benefit claimants. Don't let the private insurers catch you out – read the small print.

## STRATEGY #201
## You can have a group PHI scheme with only one
## member

Some insurers won't consider groups of less than ten people. Others will start off with only one, but will probably have a minimum premium. If a minimum premium applies, ask for more cover - after all, you are paying for it.

---

**STRATEGY #202**
## Critically examine health, medical and similar schemes, not only PHI arrangements

---

The general principles which have been applied to the above income protection and continuance schemes can also be applied to other benefit schemes, such as critical illness cover, medical expenses cover and private healthcare arrangements.

## Key points summary

- There is a clear need for a review of existing arrangements to see if they can be obtained at less cost with enhanced benefits.

- The business can help the cash flow of the employee by allowing itself to be used for low-costed group schemes – savings of up to 15 times or more are achievable individually.

- The State won't help you – it's winding down its commitments in this area. So do not neglect the protection of your income.

- This chapter is important because disability and income protection plans have a small cost compared to the effect on profits if having to pay for an employee who is no longer contributing to the business's performance and success.

- Unprotected businesses can fail. The best form of offence is defence, so keep the business going with adequate protection coverages. This is another way of protecting your investment in the business.

CHAPTER 13

# Using Your Spouse in the Business

*Money is like muck, not good except it be spread.*
Francis Bacon (1561–1626) ***Essays***: 'Of Seditions and Troubles'

**Objective: Spread income between additional taxpayers to create huge savings in taxes. Get your housekeeping tax deductible**

Employing your spouse in your business can literally save you thousands of pounds. Whilst the following strategies are more appropriate and more likely to be used in smaller businesses, there is no reason why your spouse cannot play a financial wealth-building role for the family coffers in larger businesses. In fact, if larger employers are willing to employ your spouse as well as yourself, the benefits accruing could be as good, particularly with flexible benefit programmes.

The Inland Revenue will want to ascertain that your spouse does actually do some work in the business, so don't treat this action as of no consequence. Spouses can assist with many duties, such as secretarial, typing, marketing, reception, conference organising, filing, bookkeeping, customer dealing and general management duties.

---

### STRATEGY #203
### Give your spouse an employment contract

---

An employment contract will dictate the terms of employment. This will include salary, hours to be worked each week, holiday entitlement, duties of employment and so on. The employment contract should be of an employee for services and duties to be rendered and not merely one of services. Complete the necessary PAYE and NIC forms and ensure that your accountant is aware of the position.

The employment contract is useful to establish the legality of employment. For example, if the business is wound up and you cannot pay your spouse at that time, then the Department of Employment can satisfy the spouse's claims for salary foregone, usually for two to three months' pay, or a percentage of that amount.

---

### STRATEGY #204
### Employ your spouse to get the housekeeping tax deductible

---

Salaries paid to spouses are tax deductible to the business. Housekeeping paid to a spouse from after-tax income is not tax deductible to you although your salary, if a company employee, from the business is deductible. Note that drawings for the self-employed are not tax deductible. However, your spouse is entitled to at least a personal allowance, which will further reduce your tax bill. The personal allowance in the 1995/96 tax year is £3,525, which means that the first £3,525 is not taxable.

Tom Wragge previously paid his wife housekeeping of £1,000 per month (£12,000 p.a.). The after-tax cost of £12,000 to him as a 40% higher rate taxpayer is £12,000 grossed up by 40%, i.e. £20,000. He now employs her in the business, paying her £12,000 p.a. The net cost savings on the same money is substantial.

# 1. Where Tom gives Mary housekeeping from after-tax income

| Previous position 1995/96 | Tom £ | Mary £ |
| --- | --- | --- |
| Drawings/salary | 40,000 | 0 |
| Personal allowance | 3,525 | 0 |
| **Taxable amount** | **36,475** | |
| Tax | 10,785 | 0 |
| **Net after tax** | **25,690** | |
| Housekeeping | 12,000 | |
| **Balance** | **13,690** | **12,000** |
| Disposable income | 17,215 | 12,000 |

## 2. Where Tom employs Mary, there are big income tax savings to be made

| Previous position 1995/96 | Tom £ | Mary £ |
| --- | --- | --- |
| Drawings/salary | 28,000 | 12,000 |
| Personal allowances | 3,525 | 3,525 |
| **Taxable amount** | **24,475** | **8,475** |
| Tax | 5,985 | 1,959 |
| **Net after tax** | **18,490** | **6,516** |
| Disposable income | 22,015 | 10,041 |
| Housekeeping adjustment | (1,959) | 1,959 |
| | 20,056 | 12,000 |

*Total income tax savings: £2,841*

Thus, by employing your spouse in the business, you can have enough savings for a great holiday!

---

### STRATEGY #205
### Save on National Insurance contributions if possible

---

Many directors or business owners employ their spouses on an income *below* the level where National Insurance is applied. In the 1995/96 tax year, National Insurance contributions (NIC) are not payable (by either the employer or employee) on earnings below £3,067 per annum. These figures apply whether contracted in or out of SERPS (the State Earnings Related Pension Scheme). Thus the spouse may play a valuable part in transferring income and benefits from the business in a cost effective manner.

If you choose to pay your spouse only under the NIC level, i.e. *under* £59 per week or £255 per month, £3,067 per annum, then:

- No NIC is payable on this amount
- No income tax is payable on this amount (as this is under the personal allowance of £3,525 in 1995/96)
- In addition *you* save (if a 40% tax payer and diverting income or reducing your own income) over £1,200 in additional taxes *plus* NIC savings of at least £312, i.e. a total over £1,500!

---

### STRATEGY #206
### If tax savings outweigh NIC savings, then pay your spouse more

---

In our previous example, where Tom Wragge employed his wife, Mary, in the business, considerable tax savings were made. The National Insurance computation for Class 1 NIC would look like this:

|  | Salary | Business pays NIC | Employee Pays (Tom) | (Mary) |
|---|---|---|---|---|
| 1. Tom on salary/drawings | £40,000 | at 10.2% £4,080 | Class 1 (£39.28 p.w.) £2,042.56 p.a. | Class 1 – – |
| 2a. Tom on salary-drawings of | £28,000 | £2,856 | (£39,28 p.w.) £2,042.56 p.a. | – |
| 2b. Mary on salary of | £12,000 | £1,224 | – | (£18.36 p.w.) |
| Total | £40,000 | £4,080 | £2,042.56 | £954.72 |

By paying Mary a salary of £12,000 and reducing his drawings from £40,000 to £28,000, the *business* will still pay the *same* level of NIC (at 10.2% in 1995/96) i.e. a total of £4,080.

However, from a *personal* NIC payment point of view, Tom's stays the same at £2,042 but Mary must *now pay* Class 1 NIC of £954 for the year.

However, the couple are *still ahead* on overall tax savings of (£2,841-£954) £1,887.

There are further strategies which may reduce the NIC bill for Mary.

# STRATEGY #207
## Pay your spouse below the NIC level for 51 weeks and give a bonus in the 52nd week

Employing your spouse must be commercially justifiable to the Inland Revenue. You may structure a remuneration package any way you wish, bearing in mind this principle of commerciality.

The following elements could be included in a remuneration package.

- Salary
- Bonus scheme
- Benefits in kind
- Reimbursement of expenses
- Profit-related pay
- Share incentive arrangements

If the spouse package was:

| | |
|---|---|
| Salary | £3,067 p.a. |
| Bonus | £8,933 (payable in last week of tax year) |
| Total | £12,000 |

Income tax is the same. However, NIC is calculated on a weekly basis and only as income arises; so NIC will only arise in the last week of the tax year and will be capped at the maximum payable for that week, i.e. £39.38. The salary of £3,067 per annum is under the NIC limit, so no NIC is payable on that. The bonus will attract personal NIC of £39.28. This is a savings of £915.44. The NIC payable by the business is the same, i.e. 10.2% on the salary and bonus.

*Check the current position with your accountant or professional advisers before you act, as the situation may have changed from the time of writing.*

```
┌─────────────────────────────────────────────────────────┐
│                     STRATEGY #208                         │
│     Use the spouse and other family members in            │
│       the business to create additional tax               │
│                     allowances                            │
└─────────────────────────────────────────────────────────┘
```

The main aspect to bear in mind is that the remuneration of anyone must be on a commercial basis. There is no reason why your spouse and other family members cannot be gainfully employed in the business – even on a part-time basis.

Each family member has a personal allowance. Only income received over that limit is subject to tax.

So, Tom and Mary have three children, all at school. The business has taken off in a major way and there is plenty of additional help required, ranging from stuffing envelopes to answering the telephone and dealing with customers. One of the children is at college and needs vacation work to help pay the college fees. This is an ideal way to get those fees *tax deductible and tax-free*! By creating a multiplicity of taxpayers, you can create big savings, divert your money where you want it to go and build your business at the same time.

| | Salary | Personal allowance | Taxable amount | Tax | NIC Class 1 | Employer NIC |
|---|---|---|---|---|---|---|
| Tom – salary/drawings (before) | 40,000 | 3,525 | 36,475 | 10,785 | 2,042 | 4,080 |
| Tom – salary/drawings | 28,000 | 3,525 | 24,475 | 5,985 | 2,042 | 2,856 |
| Mary – salary | 4,366 | 3,525 | 841 | 168 | 191 | 131 |
| Jason (18) – salary vacation | 3,067 | 3,525 | 0 | 0 | 0 | 0 |
| Elizabeth (17) – salary – part-time | 3,067 | 3,525 | 0 | 0 | 0 | 0 |
| Michael (15) – salary – part-time | 1,500 | 3,525 | 0 | 0 | 0 | 0 |
| Totals | 40,000 | 17,625 | 25,316 | 6,153 | 2,233 | 2,987 |

Net tax savings on £40,000:     (£10,785-£6,153) = £4,632
Net NIC savings:     (£6,122-£5,220) = £902
**Total savings:  £5,534**

Using your family in the business as a means of using all legal allowances due to you and them, has in this case created a saving of over £5,000, or 14% – money going into your pockets, not the State's.

In this case, the children can help towards college fees, as well as paying for their keep. Commerciality can happen both ways you know!

---

## STRATEGY #209
### Transfer the married couple's allowance for greater tax effectiveness, if appropriate

---

If the low paid spouse is the husband, then remember that you can now fully transfer the married couple's allowance between the husband and the wife, especially where the wife is a higher rate taxpayer, and the husband is not.

---

## STRATEGY #210
### Make use of profit-related pay to boost income

---

Your spouse can belong to a profit-related pay scheme (PRP). This can boost the amount of tax-free income accruing. The scheme must be approved by the Inland Revenue. You can get up to £4,000 of your income tax-free under current legislation. For higher rate taxpayers, this is a tax saving of £1,600; for basic rate taxpayers, £1,000 saving in tax. The tax-free amount is up to a limit of the lower of 20% of pay or £4,000.

---

## STRATEGY #211
### Give your spouse a tax deductible pension

---

The spouse need not be reliant solely on his or her partner for income after retirement.

In the 1995/96 tax year a spouse can be employed and earn up to £3,067 p.a. tax and N.I. free. This advantage can be 'geared' by the business pensioning these tax-free earnings. The level of pension funding is substantial – as much as twice the salary level or more.

| Female retiring at 60, salary £3,067 p.a. | | |
| --- | --- | --- |
| Present age | Annual current funding allowed | |
| 30 | £1,012 | 33% |
| 45 | £2,330 | 76% |
| 55 | £7,452 | 243% |

Employees able to benefit from this type of funding are:

- All limited company employees
- All employees of partnerships
- All employees of sole traders

The pension scheme for working spouses is most tax efficient. Premiums are a tax deduction to the business, contributions are invested in a fund which suffers no tax, and a tax-free cash lump sum is produced as well as a taxable pension.

The working spouse is entitled to make pension contributions. Using an Executive Pension Plan, the employee can contribute a substantial amount of earnings. This used to be as much as 100% of salary or more, but new rates have reduced the contribution amount recently. However, this remains an important savings area, which gives the spouse a pension and tax-free lump sum at retirement.

---

### STRATEGY #212
### Use the working spouse pension scheme to take maximum advantage of personal allowances

---

You can only make (or have made for you) pension contributions if you have what is called 'net relevant earnings', usually income from employment. If the main breadwinner spouse employs (or the business does so) the non-working spouse, the spouse is paid under the NIC limit and a pension contribution is made for the spouse, then the net effect is as follows:

|  | Mr A | Mrs A | Mr B | Mrs B |
|---|---|---|---|---|
| Gross earnings | £40,000 | Nil | £36,933 | £3,067 |
| Pension premium for spouse | £0 | £0 | £2,330 | £0 |
| Tax payable | £10,785 | £0 | £9,906 | £0 |
| Net income | £29,215 | £0 | £24,697 | £3,067 |
| Combined income | £29,215 | | £27,764 | |
| Total benefit (income and pension investment) | £29,215 | | £30,094 | |

The above pension contribution, if maintained annually for 20 years, could accumulate a pension fund of about £147,000 at an average interest rate of 10%. This could provide a (taxable) pension of about £15,000 p.a. Again, the utilisation of personal allowances and tax deductible pension contributions can be structured in such a way as to create savings whilst not affecting cash flows too much.

---

### STRATEGY #213
### Obtain additional tax-free benefits if your spouse earns under £8,500 p.a.

---

When the spouse earns under £8,500 per annum, including the value of any benefits, and is not a director, then favourable taxation rules apply to fringe benefits such as tax-free child care, car, mortgage subsidy, school fees assistance and similar benefits.

It is important that these fringe benefits flow from the employment of the employee and not from the relationship or shareholding of a higher earning or director spouse, otherwise those benefits may be included and taxed in the hands of the higher earning or director spouse.

Remuneration packages should be carefully structured to avoid the payment of fringe benefit (or benefits in kind) taxation.

---

### STRATEGY #214
### If the business is a partnership, make your spouse a partner

---

Where the business is a partnership, the spouse could be given an entitlement to a share in the business profits, normally treated as earned income, and to a private retirement plan.

The maximum contributions to a personal pension plan are: (1995/96)

| Age at 6 April 1995 | Contributions as a % of net relevant earnings |
|---|---|
| 35 or under | 17.5% |
| 36 to 45 | 20% |
| 46 to 50 | 25% |
| 51 to 55 | 30% |
| 56 to 60 | 35% |
| 61 and over | 40% |

Thus if you are age 47 and have pensionable earnings of £12,000 p.a., you can contribute 25% (£3,000) a year into your personal pension plan – and have it tax deductible to you. Discuss partnership tactics with your accountant – your spouse may be better off on a salary instead.

The spouse need not be an active partner – he or she could be a 'sleeping partner'. This is also attractive for retirement reliefs, which can be doubled by using the spouse.

---

### STRATEGY #215
### Use 5% of your contribution allowance to purchase tax deductible pension term life assurance

---

If your contribution level is 25%, then 5% can buy you pension term cover, whilst the balance of 20% buys you pension contributions. This is the only way in which individuals can obtain *tax deductible life cover which is tax-free.*

---

### STRATEGY #216
### Use the spouse to build wealth in and outside the business

---

The whole idea is to keep more of what you make. Payments can be channelled more tax effectively to boost your net spendable income, whilst at the same time creating wealth-building programmes. Pension planning for the spouse is just one of these areas. Reducing tax and getting the housekeeping, school fees and mortgage payments 'tax-free' or tax deductible as earned income offset against personal allowances is another.

Be careful to pay the spouse no more than the job is worth. Any disallowed spouse's wages will be taxed in the other spouse's hands as a disallowed business expense. Draw up a proper contract of employment, detailing the spouse's duties and salary. If in a partnership, make sure you have a properly drawn up partnership agreement. A partner spouse will share in profits, and does not have to prove 'activity' like an employee spouse.

If a partnership, note that if the spouse's share of the annual profits is between £6,640 and £22,880 (1995/96) then this is charged to Class 4 National Insurance contributions at 7.3%, but with a maximum of £1,185.52 payable.

The spouse may play a valuable role in transferring income and benefits from the business in a cost effective manner.

---

### STRATEGY #217
### Set up your own small business to employ your spouse

---

If you are employed or not in a position for your main business to employ your spouse, then consider setting up a business from home, so that you can employ your spouse. The same strategies would then apply.

## Key points summary

- Employ your spouse or enter into a partnership arrangement to dilute your tax payable, creating a new taxpayer to utilise personal allowances and other deductible benefits, such as pension contributions.

- Use an employment contract and, if a partnership, a partnership agreement.

- Using the spouse in the business is a major route towards combined wealth-building – but it must be a commercial proposition. The savings made can be diverted to long-term investment accumulation.

# CHAPTER 14

# Businesses in Trouble

*I think that Capitalism, wisely managed, can probably be made more efficient for attaining economic ends than any alternative system yet in sight, but that in itself it is in many ways extremely objectionable.*
**J M Keynes (1883–1946) *The End of Laisser-Faire***

**Objective: Strategies for dealing with businesses, which are: getting into financial trouble; or already in financial trouble; and for protecting assets from creditors**

At any one time in the UK today there are literally thousands of businesses in the business oxygen intensive care unit. Some require major surgery to save them; others require a degree of specialist surgery to get them on the path to full recovery – and others will die.

No one knows exactly how many businesses start up and then fail, or how many existing businesses fail in the UK in any one year. One yardstick of measurement is the level of registrations and deregistrations for VAT which occur each year. Another is to monitor the levels of corporate insolvencies each year (but this would then exclude statistics for non-company small businesses and partnerships). Statistics for both are included in recent years, but the problem is obviously compounded by the unknown businesses which have quietly faded away.

The VAT registrations and deregistrations were further affected by increasing thresholds (in 1993 and 1994) as well as adjustments to encourage eligible traders to apply for exemption from registration in 1992, and these have been taken into account in compiling the tables. These estimates were the first to be produced from the Central Statistical Office's new register – the Inter-Departmental Business Register. It is important to remember that the figures do *not* relate to the births and deaths of businesses – others may be trading but at reduced levels of business – some may be trading but at reduced levels of business below the VAT registration threshold. However, the statistics do give an insight into general business trends and give some idea of the extent of the problem (note that many smaller businesses may not be reflected in these figures as no official statistics exist for them).

*Source:* Statistical press release P/95/542 dated 15 August 1995 and prepared by the Government Statistical Service for the Department of Trade and Industry.

## VAT REGISTRATIONS AND DEREGISTRATIONS: 1992, 1993, 1994

| United Kingdom | Thousands | | |
|---|---|---|---|
| | **1992** | **1993** | **1994** |
| Start-up stock (of businesses) | 1,628 | 1,589 | 1,567 |
| Registrations | 187 | 191 | 190 |
| Deregistrations | 226 | 213 | 185 |
| Net change | -39 | -22 | 5 |
| End-year stock (of businesses) | 1,589 | 1,567 | 1,572 |

During 1994 there were 190,000 registrations and 185,000 deregistrations, resulting in a net increase of some 5,000 VAT registered businesses (0.3% of the stock of 1.6 million businesses at the start of the year).

This compares with a decrease of 22,000 businesses in 1993, when there were virtually the same number of registrations but 28,000 more deregistrations.

## NET CHANGE IN THE NUMBER OF BUSINESSES BY SECTOR: END 1991–END 1994

| United Kingdom | Thousands | | | | |
|---|---|---|---|---|---|
| Sector | End 1991 stock | 1992 net change | 1993 net change | 1994 net change | End 1994 stock |
| Agriculture | 169.2 | -1.6 | -0.4 | -0.7 | 166.5 |
| Production | 150.5 | -4 | -5 | -0.7 | 140.8 |
| Construction | 253.6 | -22 | -15.4 | -7.2 | 209 |
| Transport | 70.1 | -2.8 | -2.2 | 0.3 | 65.4 |
| Wholesale | 121.7 | 0.5 | -2.9 | -1.6 | 117.7 |
| Retail | 245.6 | -7.8 | -8.5 | 8.1 | 237.4 |
| Finance etc | 158.2 | 2.4 | 2.7 | 2.9 | 166.2 |
| Catering | 122.1 | -2.3 | -1.7 | -0.8 | 117.3 |
| Motor Trader | 77.4 | -2.6 | -2 | -1.0 | 71.8 |
| Other services | 259.5 | 1.1 | 13.4 | 21.7 | 295.7 |
| **United Kingdom** | **1,627.9** | **-39.1** | **-22** | **21** | **1,587.8** |

The only *increases* in any sectors over the three-year period were businesses in finance and 'other services' – all the other sectors experienced a *net decrease* in business.

The following figures for corporate insolvencies are taken from *Insolvency – the General Annual Report 1994*, from the Department of Trade and Industry (ISBN 0115153950).

## CORPORATE INSOLVENCY 1989 TO 1994

| Type of insolvency | 1989 | 1990 | 1991 | 1992 | 1993 | 1994 |
|---|---|---|---|---|---|---|
| | Company insolvencies – England and Wales | | | | | |
| Total | 10,456 | 15,051 | 21,827 | 24,425 | 20,825 | 16,728 |
| Compulsory liquidations | 4,020 | 5,977 | 8,368 | 9,734 | 8,361 | 6,597 |
| Creditors voluntary liquidations | 6,436 | 9,074 | 13,459 | 14,691 | 12,464 | 10,131 |
| Receiverships | 1,706 | 4,318 | 7,515 | 8,324 | 5,362 | 3,877 |
| Administrator appointments | 135 | 211 | 206 | 179 | 112 | 159 |
| Voluntary arrangements | 43 | 58 | 137 | 76 | 134 | 264 |
| Members voluntary liquidations | 3,966 | 4,092 | 3,719 | 3,523 | 2,962 | 2,818 |

| Company Insolvencies – Scotland | | | | | | |
|---|---|---|---|---|---|---|
| Total | 428 | 470 | 616 | 670 | 551 | 444 |
| Company liquidations | 229 | 251 | 304 | 310 | 286 | 242 |
| Creditors voluntary arrangement | 199 | 219 | 312 | 360 | 265 | 202 |
| Members voluntary liquidations | 241 | 234 | 253 | 215 | 151 | 111 |

Note that some companies were subject to more than one form of proceeding.

## BANKRUPTCIES AND COMPANY LIQUIDATIONS: ANALYSIS BY INDUSTRY 1994

| Industry classification | | England and Wales | | | Scotland | | |
|---|---|---|---|---|---|---|---|
| | Bankruptcies | Company liquidations | | | Company liquidations | | |
| | | Total | Compulsory liquidations | Creditors voluntary liquidations | Total | Compulsory liquidations | Creditors voluntary liquidations |
| Agriculture and horticulture | 231 | 166 | 50 | 116 | 3 | 1 | 2 |
| Manufacturing: | | | | | | | |
| Food, drink and tobacco | 33 | 142 | 31 | 111 | 3 | 2 | 1 |
| Chemicals | 23 | 108 | 11 | 97 | 3 | 3 | 0 |
| Metals and engineering | 523 | 932 | 402 | 530 | 45 | 18 | 27 |
| Textiles and clothing | 95 | 736 | 189 | 547 | 10 | 6 | 4 |
| Timber, furniture, etc | 176 | 252 | 57 | 195 | 2 | 1 | 1 |
| Paper, printing and publishing | 142 | 579 | 162 | 417 | 14 | 5 | 9 |
| Other manufacturing | 133 | 859 | 168 | 691 | 12 | 3 | 9 |
| Construction | 3,362 | 2,401 | 1,439 | 962 | 94 | 50 | 44 |
| Transport and communication | 1,402 | 774 | 406 | 368 | 18 | 8 | 10 |
| Wholesaling: | | | | | | | |
| Food, drink and tobacco | 94 | 244 | 60 | 184 | 6 | 3 | 3 |
| Motor vehicles | 28 | 112 | 23 | 89 | 1 | 1 | 0 |
| Other wholesaling | 160 | 638 | 185 | 453 | 10 | 5 | 5 |
| Retailing: | | | | | | | |
| Food | 981 | 299 | 118 | 181 | 11 | 8 | 3 |

| | | | | | | | |
|---|---|---|---|---|---|---|---|
| Motor vehicles (including filling stations) | 343 | 226 | 83 | 143 | 6 | 1 | 5 |
| Other retailing | 1,615 | 1,186 | 464 | 722 | 38 | 24 | 14 |
| Financial institutions | 241 | 259 | 71 | 188 | 8 | 5 | 3 |
| Business services | 1,537 | 1,807 | 1,222 | 585 | 76 | 41 | 35 |
| Hotels and catering | 2,102 | 777 | 396 | 381 | 11 | 9 | 2 |
| All other industries and businesses | 1,893 | 4,231 | 1,060 | 3,171 | 73 | 48 | 25 |
| Employees | 2,279 | – | – | – | – | – | – |
| No occupation and unemployed | 3,696 | – | – | – | – | – | – |
| Directors and promoters of companies | 628 | – | – | – | – | – | – |
| Occupation unknown | 3,917 | – | – | – | – | – | – |
| Total | 25,634 | 16,728 | 6,597 | 10,131 | 444 | 242 | 202 |

The following *reasons* for business failure could also be a measure of early warning signals to business owners to do something about it before it is too late.

1. *Undercapitalisation*, or not having enough capital is the major reason for business failure. This applies to new as well as existing businesses. Often the vehicle is there (the business), it has a journey to go on (plenty of potential business), but it has run out of petrol (no cash resources to run the business). It needs business oxygen or capital to continue.

2. *Poor business resilience*, or not continuously playing the 'what if?' scenario. Business resilience is the ability to withstand calamity in any form happening to the business. What if suppliers don't deliver? What if the bank forecloses on a loan? What if the contract falls through? What if the contracts manager dies?

The business must continually assess its weaknesses and prepare for their eventualities. Too often, it is exactly this unawareness of where the business should be resilient that takes it by surprise and causes its demise.

3. *Poor and bad management*, usually from inexperienced people in business, is a contributory factor to business failure. 'The business was plain managed into the ground.' This is often the case when the business owner is absent or has too many outside interests. Business management training is essential. The problem sometimes stems from

the fact that someone who was once a successful *employee* in someone else's business, now starts up in business on his own account. The transition from employee to business owner is often not successful. I have witnessed at least one case where former employees were invited to participate as business owners and to introduce capital into the business. The problem was that they still thought like employees, enjoyed the security of having been an employee, but were not prepared to take business risks and business decisions. The cultural shock was too difficult for the employee to make the change to employer (or business owner) comfortably and failure occurred.

A major problem in business society today has been the large rewards given to non-performing or loss-producing business management and directors. It is as if those managers are not really linked to the success or failure of the business at all.

Management can be properly trained to succeed – a quality company will spend at least 2% of its turnover on annual training.

4. *Mismanagement of business cash flows* is now given as one of the top five reasons for business failure. Previously, this has been seen as more of a *function* of the business (the recording of inflows and outflows of cash), but now it is recognised as a major determinant of success or failure.

Proper planning relating to cash flow management is vital. Become mean with your business money – only pay out what you have to, when you have to. Successful massaging of cash flows from month to month can mean the difference between success and failure. To succeed here, you must 'know the numbers' (how accounting and financial management work) and have proper tracking systems in place so that you know what the financial position of the business is on a daily and monthly basis.

Sub-categories of cash flow management, the mismanagement of which leads to business failure, are:

- *giving too much credit.* This stretches your business resources, as the business ends up financing creditors.
- *not getting in the debtors.* These are people or other businesses who owe your business money. Not getting paid creates bad debts which may write off your business.

5. *Onerous debt* is a big problem for many businesses. Too high levels of borrowing at crippling interest rates can sink a business. Likewise, building up a large debt which cannot easily be repaid will have the same effect.

Watch out for the following:

- *The cost of venture capital.* Venture capitalists seek a venture capital return from lending or providing capital to your business. This ranges from 15 to 40% per annum in interest rates, management charges, preference shares and other money-making mechanisms.

- *The true cost of MBOs (management buy outs) or MBIs (management buy ins).* An MBO or MBI which is too highly geared can strangle the business in excessive debt and interest charges. Some never recover – and I'm including very large businesses here. Directors may be persuaded to secure personal borrowings against private assets, such as their homes. Losing your home as well as your livelihood and still having debts can be catastrophic. I know of at least one case where the parent company sold off a loss-making subsidiary to its management. Part of the deal was that the subsidiary reverts back to the parent company if certain targets are not met. One of these conditions is impossible to meet because a certain property within the company needs to be sold by a certain date and this won't happen. The parent company has used this tactic to avoid paying out massive redundancy payments to existing management.

- *The cost of onerous leases.* This has been problematic for many businesses, especially where leases have been assigned to third parties by lessees, and the third party has reneged on the lease. The reversion of the lease to the original lessee has put many profitable businesses out of business. One client sub-let to a new business on a sub-lease, whilst it was the lessee. Rentals payable were £120,000 a year. Our client then moved to larger premises. The sub-lessee's business failed and the lessor turned to the original lessee for over £200,000, being rental arrears plus interest. Only strong negotiated evasive action saved our client from bankruptcy. These things happen in business, and business resilience 'what if?'s could have pre-plotted the correct course of action in time.

- *Not paying the Inland Revenue, Customs and Excise (VAT) or the DSS (NIC) on time (or at all).* This can precipitate court action leading to bankruptcy. Apart from harsh penalties, these agencies expect to be paid first, otherwise they can (and will) bankrupt the business. You will have very little leverage in dealing with these government agencies, particularly as in most cases you have collected money on their behalf, such as NICs and VAT as well as PAYE, and not paid it over.

- *Not paying the bank or other lender when your business debts fall due.* This is probably one of the biggest causes of business failure, usually linked to undercapitalisation. At the slightest hint of financial trouble, the lender will seek to limit its liabilities and cut its losses. More often than not, it is the bank which calls in the receivers. Unfortunately, when the business gets into financial trouble, the first port of call is its bank, usually to increase its liability to the bank through further borrowing. The bank or lender has two choices – to extend credit or say 'no'. Most find it easier to say no.

6. *Litigation, fraud against the business and the failure of other businesses* can adversely affect the success of your business. These are mainly *outside factors* over which the business has little control.

The knock-on effect of other businesses closing down is fairly common. For example, your business is a major supplier of radiators and tubing to a car manufacturer. The car manufacturer goes out of business – so do you. Or your suppliers go out of business, so you cannot supply the main client and both businesses are affected.

It is a much more serious business if your company is sued, or enters into expensive litigation and loses. The costs and damages could cripple the business. Likewise, business fraud and theft often left undetected for years, can seriously impact upon business profits or put your company out of business. One only has to look at the recent Barings Bank case where a trader in Singapore 'lost the bank'.

7. *Many factors are the results of economics.* Increased competition, recessionary factors, being in the wrong business at the wrong time, losing a market (e.g. the corner shop being closed down due to the opening of a hypermarket in the area), are some of the aspects of supply and demand related to business failure. After all, if something has to be blamed, it may as well be poor trading conditions, or the price-cutting activities of similar businesses in the area. Certainly many of these are contributory factors to business failure.

There again, were you in the right business at the right time? What marketing sensitivity analysis did you do, and are you still doing? Were you correct in starting your business at the depth of the second greatest recession this century? Did you consider all factors of business resilience? Could the business make it in these conditions?

8. *Not making a realistic business plan* causes business failure. Many businesses fail not because the idea wasn't great, but because the cost of getting the idea into a saleable commodity was too high. Keen business owners and management believe the business around the idea will succeed. Being optimistic (who isn't with a great idea!) their business

plan reflects their optimism – in fact with those fantastic projected cash flows, who needs capital? The business will be self-generating before long. Wrong!

Unrealistic business plans or those incapable of fulfilment, or those not given *enough time* to succeed are really errors of judgment by the business owners. It is almost impossible (especially if undercapitalised) to have a three-year business plan succeed in one or two years. Yet, 60% of business plans give over-optimistic cash flows and profits projections. It is no wonder that less than 2% of business plans put up to venture capitalists for funding are ever funded. The venture capitalists know that of the 2% of companies funded by them, only 30% of those will ever be truly successful.

9. *Loss of business confidence* causes failure. This aspect can be shown by the following actions:

- directors and partners withdrawing their loan accounts
- lenders withdrawing their capital
- suppliers and buyers going to competitors
- investors and banks withdrawing their support
- directors asking to be removed from public office
- withdrawal of personal guarantees (if possible).

The causes of these actions are many – from overspending the business's money (usually by directors living beyond the means of the business), to a major calamity such as the death, disability or retirement of a key director or employee. Even the personal bankruptcy of a director or partner or sole trader can cause this effect.

Whatever the reason, those initiating the action are signalling a loss of confidence in the business and, by implication, its management. It could be downhill fast for the business unless remedial action is taken.

10. *Legal and regulatory aspects* can cause a business to fail. While the actions of lobbying groups such as trade unions may cause substantial losses to a business today, it is more the legal and judicial actions of the courts and EU which may force a business to close its doors to a new business and sales opportunity.

Health and Safety regulations, new environmental laws, sweeping regulatory powers ranging from fishing to manufacturing to financial services have caused businesses large and very small to close down. The cost of compliance is just too great. In the financial services sector alone, 1993–95 saw massive fines imposed by regulatory bodies on life offices, fund managers and individual firms for not complying with the training and competence regulations. The knock-on effect has been the sale of some companies and the closing down of sales forces of others.

Manpower (and jobs) in these direct sales operations has fallen from a high in 1990 of 240,000 people to less than 80,000 people today.

The above reasons for business failure are complex and one or more of them can be applied analytically in any given situation. However, my reason for mentioning them in the first place is not to put off the budding entrepreneur or those in business already - but solely with the intention of prevention being better than cure. If you know what is out there; if you know what the consequences of certain actions are; then you are better prepared for dealing with any eventuality which may arise. Success today is no guarantee of success tomorrow. The following strategies should go a long way towards ensuring that you stay in business, and that you know how to deal with some of the aspects which arise if your business gets into financial trouble. There is no point in developing wealth-building objectives only to lose everything at the final hurdle through lack of planning.

---

### STRATEGY #218
### Immediately, if the business is in trouble – buy 90 days of time

---

You cannot be expected to make snap decisions when under tremendous financial pressures. Your first action must be to relieve the pressure, so that you can plan effectively. This is the case even when you think that a business disaster is imminent.

How do you buy time? Although you can do this yourself, you probably need to appoint a trained negotiator with banking and credit control skills. Most creditors, lenders, government agencies and the like will allow you sufficient time to come up with a satisfactory solution. You can't be expected to run your business whilst fighting fires on all fronts. Apart from the personal stresses involved, you need to take a step back to appraise the situation coolly. So you need a 'holding action'.

This is accomplished by having your negotiator write to all creditors, banks and other interested parties. They will be told to contact only the negotiator, not you. They will be promised satisfactory responses in due course, once the negotiator has assessed the situation.

The success of this approach is akin to third party endorsement. For example, if *you* say you're a great businessman, it does not have the same effect as if *someone else* has said it. If your creditors know they are dealing with a professionally-appointed negotiator, they will be more inclined to work more *effectively* with that person than with you.

# STRATEGY #219
## Consider your business options for survival

You and your business will have the following broad range of options available for consideration:

- given time, to sort out the business's financial problems; or
- to make an *informal* agreement with creditors (and others) to pay them in good time; or
- to make a *formal* arrangement with creditors (and others) to make payment as agreed with the majority of them and made an order of court. This is called a CVA or Corporate Voluntary Arrangement; or
- to call in the receivers and apply for a bankruptcy or liquidation order; or
- to wait for a creditor to apply to have your business wound up.

Each of these actions has a different set of consequences. If the business is a 'no-hoper' then the options from a CVA to liquidation will have more appeal. If the business is worth salvaging or the setback is merely temporary, then a 'soft landing' can be negotiated.

If creditors think that there is hope for business continuance and therefore payment, they will probably agree to an informal arrangement with the eventuality of payment – even if a lesser amount.

Your biggest hurdle is agreement from the Inland Revenue, Customs and Excise and DSS, but this has been successfully negotiated in the past and can be done in the future.

Some creditors may wish to take pre-emptive action by applying for CCJs (county court judgments) but this is to be resisted in order to protect your business credit lines.

If a CVA is agreed with the majority of your creditors (75% of value at the creditors' meeting), then your business can continue, subject to the making of your agreed payments each month. These usually range from about 20p to 25p in the pound. If the business defaults, it can be wound up. Although CVAs are relatively new, they are a viable alternative to bankruptcy and your credit ratings are not adversely affected. In fact, only the creditors on 'the list' will know of the business's problem, and no adverse credit referencing is usually compiled.

---

**STRATEGY #220**
**Do not be forced into liquidation or**
**bankruptcy without first considering a CVA**

---

Insolvency practitioners are only too keen to liquidate your business. That's how they make their money. You do have alternatives available to you – so don't be rushed into anything. Always take professional advice before you act. If you trade in *insolvent circumstances* (with no hope of profitability and without sufficient assets to back up your liabilities) then *it is a criminal offence* for all directors involved in the business. However, don't be over hasty. Many businesses make losses year after year, but are not insolvent in terms of the definition.

If you feel that the business can be salvaged (or sold) then consider a corporate voluntary arrangement – a CVA – first.

---

**STRATEGY #221**
**Critically review and assess the business**

---

Whatever course of action you eventually decide upon, you need a *plan of action* almost like a business plan with cash flows, but one which is designed to turn the business around and set it on its new course, following certain actions. Certainly banks, lenders and some creditors will want to see some of this planning.

---

**STRATEGY #222**
**Protect the business assets from loss or**
**attachment by creditors**

---

As a director, you have a duty to do this anyway. Some assets may be attached by creditors, others not, by law.

If you know that the business is going to fail and you dispose of assets or hide them from creditors – in 'fraud of creditors' – then your creditors can still attach those assets, whether moved to offshore trusts or to a pension fund.

However, assets generally built up within a pension fund are usually safe from creditors of the business. I say usually, but this has not always been the case. It has been known for creditors, where the director or individual has given personal guarantees, to wait for the pension fund to mature and then to attach the tax-free cash lump sum payment accruing to the individual.

Specialist advice should be taken in respect of shares and fixed assets held in trust individually and beyond the reach of the creditors.

---

## STRATEGY #223
## Try to separate one company's business from another

---

Even though you may operate more than one business, if it can be shown that one business controlled the other, then your creditors may apply for a 'joinder application' and recover their debts from one or the other.

Usually, though, one company in a group can go insolvent, with creditors only able to recover what they can from that company.

---

## STRATEGY #224
## If a partnership, the same rules apply: however you may need an IVA

---

Partners usually have unlimited personal liability known as 'jointly and severally liable' for partnership debts.

Responsibilities and liabilities are dictated by the partnership agreement and, failing that, the 1890 Partnership Act, which was recently amended.

Unless liabilities and debts are expressly limited and this fact is made known to creditors at the time of the transaction, then all partners are liable for each other's business debts.

In this case, partners will contemplate an IVA (individual voluntary arrangement) on a group basis, rather than a CVA.

A sole trader (not in a company) will also contemplate an IVA as opposed to going bankrupt.

---

## STRATEGY #225
## Make sure you have enough working capital in the business

---

This is where the tricky negotiating bit comes in. If your regular bank is also one of your creditors being negotiated with, then sources of additional working capital are going to be out of the question for this bank to consider – unless it really believes that your actions will turn the business around.

You will, in all likelihood, require additional sources of finance to keep the business going during the negotiating period. One good thing – you won't have to pay creditors for 90 days, so massaging your cash flow is already working for you.

Some of the finance avenues open to your business are:

- ask your bank
- ask other banks to rebank you at a higher level of borrowings
- try the government guaranteed loan scheme for small businesses
- massage cash flow
- everyone takes a reduction in pay
- remortgage your home – but *only as an absolute last resort*. Even then, think twice before you do this. Your home is at risk if you do.
- new investors, especially for tax reliefs under the EIS (Enterprise Investment Scheme)
- your business may appeal to a 'business angel' wishing to invest in a turnaround business
- shareholders asked for more capital
- directors can increase their loan accounts
- factoring and invoice discounting
- commercial loans on business-owned properties
- loans from directors' only pension funds
- sale and lease-backs of property
- employee share owner trust schemes (ESOTS)

Debt consolidation loans are also available personally to individuals in the business. These are usually secured against property though.

The message for all business owners and management teams is that when the business is getting into trouble, they should seek professional help as soon as possible.

The following strategies will help those businesses with *specific* problems which may lead to business failure if not attended to appropriately.

Undercapitalisation is one of the major reasons of business failure. The business does not have enough money to sustain itself. Often businesses start off being badly capitalised and then desperately try to keep afloat. The worse the financial position gets, the less inclined the banks are to bail you out.

## STRATEGY #226
## Make sure you have enough capital in the first place

If your business plan has a capital requirement of £500,000 and you can only raise £250,000, then don't go ahead with your plan.

It is a commonly-held view that by asking banks and investors for smaller amounts of capital these are more likely to be granted than larger ones. Bank managers and investors will critically examine the position. If they feel that the business is unlikely to make it, you won't get their support. One banker told me that some business plans seen by him are up to 50% under-funded in their need requirements. Business owners request too little in the first place; the cash flows are not there and the business collapses.

## STRATEGY #227
## If the business suffers from a lack of business oxygen, then recapitalise it or get out while you're ahead

If you could have pumped more cash into the business, you probably would have (whether your own money or someone else's). Sometimes it's only a matter of managing cash flow effectively, staving off cash out-flows as long as possible, whilst waiting for the new contract to begin, or a debtor to pay. However, in other cases, the business cash flows are just not there (nor will be there) and drastic action must be taken.

If a small business, the loss of the business usually has a knock-on effect with the business owners' personal guarantees being called in. This could result in the loss of the family home and other assets as well.

Your gut reaction is probably to hang in there as long as possible hoping for a positive result. The problem is that if others (such as creditors) hear that the business is in trouble before you tell them, they begin taking their own evasive actions. Banks are very quick to react, recovering overdrafts and loans from your bank accounts when you least expect it – and least want it. In fact, that is one action you can definitely count on, unless you are well prepared for it.

Take the case of a West Midlands motor component manufacturer. A quality BS 5750 company employing 113 people, they started paying their own bills late because their debtors were paying them late. One month a major blue chip company did not pay at all as expected, causing the managing director to ask the bank for an extension to the overdraft from £100,000 to £150,000, mainly to meet salary commitments. The bank refused to grant the extra facility. The company then managed to get their prime debtor to pay up (£70,000) and paid the blue chip debtors' cheque into their bank account, breathing a sigh of relief. All's well that ends well?

Not so. The bank immediately claimed the £70,000 in reduction of the existing overdraft facility, thereby plunging the company into an even greater crisis. Eventually the bank called in the receivers and the company went out of business – yet it had millions of pounds of contracts to be fulfilled, if it had had time to see them through.

Banks don't take prisoners. They have short memories and if the slightest hint of financial trouble is there – unless they have more to lose than you have to gain – they get nervous and pull the plug on the business.

If you are a very very small business, such as a one-man band, always quit while you're ahead. It's easier to start up again, doing something else, then getting deeper and deeper into debt. You're actually not doing anyone any favours by staying in business.

---

## STRATEGY #228
## Correct timing of your actions is essential. So, always act at the appropriate time

---

This holds for all strategies or factors in this chapter. Time is certainly of the essence, as is timing. But acting too late, or not at all (because you didn't see the warning signals) can spell disaster. For example, take the case of the company in the previous section brought to its knees by its own bank.

- The company should have known the bank was hostile – it would not extend the business's overdraft facilities, and had asked for it to be reduced in the past.
- The business had developed a history of erratic banking practice, being reliant on buyers paying when they could – often six months late.
- The business had major contracts with blue chip companies worth millions of pounds, but instead of jumping for joy and having a new belief in the business when the £70,000 was paid into the business's bank account, the bank acted precipitously calling in all loans and overdrafts and taking what was already there to satisfy its own debt first. This is not an uncommon occurrence – it happens all the time.
- The business, thinking ahead, should have paid the £70,000 into

an account with *another* bank (where it had only savings, no loans).

- It should have had extended dialogue with its usual bankers and obtained the bank's position in writing. Even then, it should only have 'drip fed' the usual bankers, satisfying interest payments until such time as new facilities or new bankers were sought.
- By acting early, the company could have been saved. If it had changed bankers earlier, its position would have been stronger. Because the business did not communicate with its existing bankers enough, the bank acted on its own information (usually creditors asking if the business is OK) and initiative and pulled the plug.

*Remember – always have more than one bank account for your business.*

---

### STRATEGY #229
### Check your 'business resilience' areas

---

Continually apply 'what if?'s to all aspects of your business. If a problem is even a remote possibility, learn how to uncover it and then plan to deal with it and the effects of the problem on the business.

Dealing *now* from a position of strength is far preferable to a weakened position later.

---

### STRATEGY #230
### Build strong management teams and train them adequately

---

Business owners work *on* the business; management teams work *in* the business.

Poor and bad management practices can be overcome with proper management training and the instilling of financial disciplines and systems. Do a management audit of management tasks and standards to be judged against key result areas. The answer lies in team building which is an effective training technique. Success-oriented achievement training linked to performance reward programmes should focus management on managing the business for wealth-creation and profit.

## STRATEGY #231
## Build systems to manage cash flows on a daily basis

Businesses stay alive through proper cash flow management. The business systems should include computerised management accounts with cash flows in and out and the dates when these occur. An additional column can be added for when the latest dates of payment can be made.

Some businesses have one system, with a parallel system operated by their accountants for double-checking. This is useful for VAT, PAYE and other payments.

Check how much credit can be given and for how long. Check how long it takes to get debtors to pay. Are discounts offered for speedier payments?

Many businesses assign a person (or team) to account receivables to get the money in as quickly as possible. This can be part of a customer service programme.

## STRATEGY #232
## Rebroke your borrowings for a better deal

It may pay you to shop around. If your business is paying higher interest rates on loans taken out when interest rates were very high, then some lenders are prepared to offer a better deal to secure your business account. Packaged deals involving overdrafts, loans, factoring and invoice discounting could be better propositions all around. You may wish to keep all debt and business liabilities with one bank and have a second bank account, which is always kept positive, with a different bank. Savings can be made if you shop around.

## STRATEGY #233
## If borrowing venture capital, check the cost structures – they may cripple your business

Venture capital costs come in many guises. They range from a capital raising fee (up to 15%) to annual management fees (up to 5% or more); interest payable on loans (up to 20% or more p.a.) and preference share dividends. Some companies are paying up to 40% per year in interest and other charges. Work out the internal rate of return in your business

(IRR) and compare that with the cost of new capital. See also Chapters 3 and 6.

---

### STRATEGY #234
### If contemplating an MBO or MBI, check out the leveraged debt burden – can the business sustain it?

---

Although directors may put in some cash, the bulk of the deal will be leveraged through the company taking on an enlarged debt burden. Some companies never recover from this (in addition to their other liabilities) and management spends all its time refinancing or rearranging debt packages with banks instead of building the business. Again, check out the cost structures of venture capitalists and debt providers and try to limit your own risk on your personal assets.

---

### STRATEGY #235
### Renegotiate onerous leases

---

If you are left holding an onerous lease (where, say, you sub-let a fixed property and the sub-leasee has reneged, thereby causing the property rentals to revert to you, or where your business has failed, but you signed personal guarantees), then the position can be renegotiated to affordable levels. I know of a number of cases where the landlord lessor has been negotiated down to a reasonable and affordable level. This practice requires considerable skill and negotiation and you are best advised to have a professional third party negotiator to do it for you. In one case, termination of the lease was set by the lessor at £130,000. The eventual deal negotiated was for £40,000 – a saving of £90,000 and a win/win situation for both parties.

---

### STRATEGY #236
### Learn to communicate and then negotiate with the Inland Revenue, Customs and Excise and other government agencies

---

The natural reaction when bad news comes from the Inland Revenue or other agencies is to batten down the hatches, shut off all communication and hope that the problem goes away. If only things were that simple! The key here is effective communication skills. My father was very good at this. He would agree with everything said and then go his own way. It was most frustrating. When the Inland Revenue believe there is nothing further to say, that's when they launch into the attack – so keep them talking. Your professional negotiator should buy you at least 90 days' time. Letters can be sent to all creditors explaining that you are reassessing the business's financial position at present, will soon be making contact with them to appraise them of the position and your refinancing, and all correspondence should go to your professional advisers.

---

## STRATEGY #237
## Negotiate the best bank deals – always have at least two bank accounts

---

Banks exert financial power. They can cause the collapse of your business and they know it. The answer is simple – don't get into unilateral defensive positions with your bank. Give yourself some options. Open other bank accounts with different banks. Whilst your business is strong, negotiate facilities, even if you have no use for them right now. Get your professional adviser to 'tout' your business to a number of banks, saying you are reviewing your present arrangements. This will stand you in good stead later should things go wrong. The second bank, where you have built up a positive savings relationship, will be better disposed towards requests for financing than a newcomer.

---

## STRATEGY #238
## Take out insurance cover against litigation, fraud and other calamities which may strike the business

---

If your business does not have existing insurance coverages, then do something about it. As a minimum your business will have employer's liability. A number of policies are available to cover Inland Revenue, DSS and Customs and Excise investigations (for a premium of about £300 a year); others cover litigation and damages as well as fraud on the business. This form of 'business umbrella' coverage should also include 'Directors and Officers and Trustees liability' cover, which is now tax deductible (for premiums) to the business. Cover is not expensive when viewed against possible losses which may occur if you don't do anything.

## STRATEGY #239
## Continuously reappraise business sensitivity analysis and business resilience factors

It is always easier to cope with factors which are known to the business. It is more difficult when the unknown and unexpected happens. For example, actions of competitors taking your clients, normal market forces operating such as scarcity of essential raw materials; the sudden loss of a major contract. How will the business react to these changes? Some of them are so subtle that you don't known what has hit the business before it is too late to do anything about it. How resilient is the business to withstanding these changes? What alternatives are planned to counter them? Business sensitivity analysis should be an ongoing part of any business. A business prepared could be a business protected. If you expect a downturn in six months' time which will affect cash flow, then organise alternatives now.

## STRATEGY #240
## Incorporate those factors into your ongoing business plan which must be believable for success

Few business plans hit their targets exactly. Many are optimistic about future cash flows and events occurring. The key is to ensure that sufficient time is allocated to realise the objectives and targets of the business plan. As a rule of thumb, add another one third to your present time line for success. If you make it in the original time, you're ahead. Pressure to perform unrealistic time targets may affect the business decision-making adversely. You may be tempted to opt for short-term 'quick fix' solutions instead of sticking with your long-term plan. To ensure success, it is better to have a gradual build-up of business over a longer period, so be prepared to fund the business for that longer time. It is in the business development phase that most companies run out of capital and require additional funding.

Businesses rarely run 100% according to plan. Income takes longer to come in to businesses than expected and the once-optimistic cash flows could be seriously reduced. Again, the key lies in cash flow management. This includes efficient management of capital from investors.

Remember – even with adequate initial capitalisation, the business still only has a limited chance of success. It is how effectively management responds to the business-building issues and how it deals with business resilience which either makes or breaks the business.

---

## STRATEGY #241
## Overcome the loss of business confidence by creating business optimism

---

Even if things are going badly – be positive, confident and optimistic. Be prepared to nip negative issues in the bud and deal strongly with management and employees as well as customers, showing a positive attitude. If things are depressing you, take comfort from Brian Tracy in *The Psychology of Achievement*, who advises you to 'fake it until you make it'. At least show a positive attitude, even if all around you is doom and gloom.

Respond quickly to the underlying causes of dissatisfaction. Consider alternative courses of action and always have pre-planned alternatives available – don't wait until the last minute to do something. Having the will to succeed is vital. Remember, Thomas Edison failed 11,000 times before perfecting the filament for the light bulb. Colonel Sanders of Kentucky Fried Chicken was turned down by 1,000 restaurants before one offered him a royalty on his chicken recipe. They didn't give up; they just tried different ways of becoming successful.

---

## STRATEGY #242
## Get to know the law and regulations surrounding your business. Understand what business you are in

---

Business compliance knowledge will keep you in business where others will fail. Understand your business environment and what regulates it. Learn what you can and cannot do to grow your business legally.

The best method of updating yourself is to read about it. Attending seminars relevant to your business and its environment will also help. Compliance may also bring with it new opportunities. For example, in the financial services sector, with the advent of full disclosure of commissions, the salesmen in the industry dropped by over a third within six months. Some firms saw the opportunity for an open declaration of fee-based financial planning, rebating all commissions to clients. Their businesses are booming.

Not complying with the legislators (at home and in the EU) and regulators can drive you out of the business. There may be nothing wrong with your business as a vehicle for wealth-creation, but if you don't follow the rules, or if you break them, you will soon be out of business.

The consequences of a business in trouble could lead to a total loss situation. You and fellow business owners could lose their value in the business itself, but in addition the following may result:

- loss of business assets
- loss of the family home and other assets
- disintegration of marriage and dispersal of family
- being barred from future directorships
- being unable to obtain credit
- ill-health caused through stress
- general lowering of the will to succeed
- employees losing jobs; redundancies cause ill-health and family break-ups

Sometimes the above consequences cannot be avoided. They will happen. However, if you know about the consequences, then it will enable you to be a better planner. You can engineer a 'soft landing' for both you and the business – not everything need be a hard knock. If you can do it on your own, no doubt you will. However, most people are too close to the action to know what to do and when to do it. A part of wealth-creation is *wealth-retention* – and by following the courses of action outlined above, you may be able to retain more of what you have or enough to start again.

## Key points summary

- The objectives were to develop strategies on how to deal with businesses in financial trouble.

- *Reasons* for business failure give early warning signals on what to look out for. There are ten comprehensive reasons for businesses failing, followed by over 20 strategies on how to deal with them.

- Communication, negotiations and continuous reappraisal of the business are the most important features. Use a professional negotiator for best results.

- Saving the business and protecting its assets as well as the business owners' assets is vital, but not always possible. However, *retaining wealth* is as important as creating it and these strategies will be essential reading for all business owners.

# PART 2

# Business Tax – Reducing Strategies

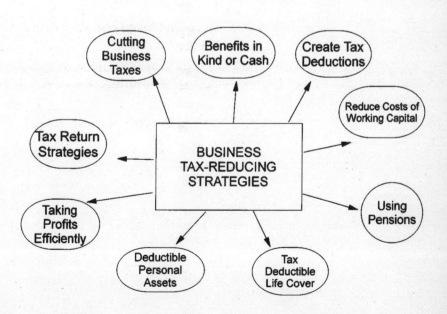

INCREASING CASH FLOWS AND PROFITS

# CHAPTER 15

# Tax Return Filing Strategies

*You are entitled to expect the Inland
Revenue to be fair by settling your tax affairs
impartially, by expecting you to pay only
what is due under the law, by treating
everyone with equal fairness.*
**The Taxpayer's Charter 1994**

**Objective: Save on tax penalties and interest whilst reducing
business and personal taxes, and the chances of an
audit**

There are many people who feel that they have to absorb anything
which the tax system throws at them. Over their lifetimes they will
probably pay more in taxes than any other payment and, indeed, many
people feel obligated to do so. For much of their tax lives there is the
overriding fear of the consequences of rocking the tax boat, or inviting
unnecessary attention to their affairs and of accepting everything without question.

   This fear is not from any real threat, it is only a fear which results
from lack of knowledge of the procedures which govern the basis of our
tax laws. However, over the years, the Inland Revenue has developed a
code of practice or charter which outlines the rights of individuals to
fair treatment and assistance from the Inland Revenue with their tax
affairs. The Inland Revenue has to provide an efficient service to taxpayers and to be accountable to taxpayers for what it does.

   The Inland Revenue has come under pressure to perform efficiently but, like everyone else, has cost constraints. The chances of an audit from either the Inland Revenue, the DSS (for National Insurance contributions) and Customs and Excise (for VAT) has not been as great in the past, but as these tax collection agencies become more efficient, will surely increase. The best thing the business taxpayer can do is to be fully prepared for the eventuality of an audit. The second best thing is to take out insurance cover for investigations costs. Policies start at about £250 per annum for smaller businesses. Cover is up to £60,000 in costs incurred by the taxpayer in meeting the demands of any investigation.

---

## STRATEGY #243
## Keep your tax bills as low as possible

---

There are a number of rules which every individual and corporate taxpayer should follow to avoid allowing their tax affairs to get out of hand. Apart from the fact that most people cannot remember events and transactions which occurred, say, six years ago, if ill-prepared over a number of years, the taxpayer will be greatly disadvantaged in his dealings with the tax authorities.

The system of assessment of individuals and smaller businesses (not companies) is in the throes of enormous upheaval with self-assessment currently being phased in. The Inland Revenue will be particularly vigilant as there are big opportunities for reducing profits – quite legitimately – but the taxpayer must watch out for anti-avoidance legislation.

The three basic rules to follow which will keep your tax bills as low as possible, and reduce the chances of audit, are:

*Rule 1: Keep in control* and don't let your tax affairs get out of hand. If you do, you are only storing up trouble for the future. This strategy means that you must keep clear and accurate records of all income received and of any expenses made and allowances available to offset against your income. Your records should be kept up-to-date, at least on a monthly basis.

- *Communicate* with the Inland Revenue and other agencies to keep them informed of any changes in circumstances. For example, on an individual basis, new personal circumstances such as marriage, separation, divorce, unemployment, retirement are events to be notified to the Inland Revenue. So are new sources of income or losing a source of income. Where the taxpayer is a business entity, then changes in tax codings, PAYE, redundancies, fringe benefits

begun or ceased, sale of business assets and so on must all be notified to the Inland Revenue – not at once, but in time with the tax
returns of the business.

- **Check your tax bill** payable. If the figures are not correct, then
  write to the tax office and tell them. If you disagree, you can appeal
  to the commissioners.

**Rule 2: Make the right choices.** The choices made by you can drastically affect your tax bill. These are choices concerning the family and
claiming allowances; job choices with regard to perks and fringe benefits as well as retirement planning and paying for education. If in
business, the spread of taxpayers through employing the spouse or
other family members can save tax; claiming capital allowances and
rolling them up for future years; effectively dealing with business
losses and creating new tax deductions; claiming maximum expenses;
registering for VAT; retiring and selling the business; getting tax relief
on investments; offsetting share losses against capital gains; using the
home in the business, are all examples of choices to be made which
affect your tax bill. These are only a few of the many areas which
require consideration and which will certainly save taxes.

However, if the right choices are *not* made, then these savings will be
lost.

**Rule 3: Act within the time limit.** If the taxpayer does not act within
the time limits, then penalties, interest and other sanctions may apply.
All tax law is concerned with time limits, which can be as short as 30
days or as long as six years or more.

By keeping to these three basic rules, you will limit the chances of a tax
audit (or at least an in-depth one) and can claim valuable deductions
and allowances, thus reducing your tax bill.

The Inland Revenue is committed to keeping down taxpayer's costs
– it is in their Charter for taxpayers. Quite poignantly, the Charter ends
with the words:

In return, we need you
- to be honest
- to give us accurate information
- to pay your tax on time
All we ask is that you keep us up-to-date with your tax affairs."

## STRATEGY #244
## Keep in control but use an aggressive tax return preparer to help you

The key is to find an aggressive tax return preparer who will work within the tax laws so that you pay the least amount of taxes. If you don't have one already (or even if you do), ask him what level of tax he paid last year. If not satisfied, don't use him – if he can't do it for himself, he will be unlikely to do it for you.

What you or your business do not want to do is to pay tax unnecessarily. If tax deductions and allowances are due to you, you have a right to claim them. The Inland Revenue estimate that over seven million taxpayers have money owing to them. Don't be one of them.

## STRATEGY #245
## Make the right choices – prepare your own return at least once

The best way to become familiar with your own tax affairs is by preparing your own returns. Whilst you will probably not become a tax expert, you will get to know generally what you can and cannot do. By becoming your own tax expert, you will be better placed to advise and instruct your accountant or tax preparer in what to claim or not.

## STRATEGY #246
## Always act in time in relation to your tax affairs

If you personally, and the business corporately, do not act in time in relation to your tax affairs, then the following may happen:

- Interest and other penalties may be chargeable on late or overdue taxes.
- You may not be able to claim valuable reliefs and deductions. This is particularly the case when having to make certain elections within given time periods.
- Your situation could tie up valuable management and administration time, which the small business can ill-afford.
- You may invite an investigation of your tax affairs, or an audit.

It is therefore most important to keep to all deadlines in dealing with the tax authorities. It is especially important to have your tax affairs in order if self-employed, with the new regime of self-assessment beginning. Whilst the following dates are deadlines, always act at least a week beforehand to ensure that you meet them. The following are the main deadlines only. If a company, then corporate year ends will dictate many deadlines.

## A. The self-employed

Self-assessment will apply from 1996/97 [FA 1994, ss 178–199 and Schedule 19; FA 1995, ss 103–116 and Schedules 20 and 21].

You have the choice to work out your own tax (or not) under the self-assessment rules. Self-assessment will apply to tax returns sent out in April 1997. The filing date is 31 January 1998 to file a return relating to 5 April 1997 tax year end.

If you wish the Revenue to work out your tax, the return must be in by 30 September 1997. If late, then penalties will apply.

There is no change in the PAYE system. However, other tax payment dates will be standardised. Tax on all sources of income will be due every six months on 31 January and 31 July.

*The tax dates for self-assessment are as follows:*

| | |
|---|---|
| 1 January 1996 | 1st instalment preceding year basis. |
| 1 July 1996 | 2nd instalment preceding year basis. |
| 31 January 1997 | 1996/97 1st instalment due 'on account'. |
| April 1997 | 1996/97 return issued. |
| 31 July 1997 | 1996/97 2nd instalment due 'on account'. |
| 30 September 1997 | 1996/97 return filed if Inland Revenue to calculate tax. |
| 31 January 1998 | 1996/97 balance due. |
| 31 January 1998 | 1996/97 return filed if self-assessed. |
| 31 January 1998 | 1997/98 1st interim payment due 'on account' (based on 50% of 1996/97 tax paid directly on all income). |
| April 1998 | 1997/98 return issued. |
| 31 July 1998 | 1997/98 2nd instalment due 'on account'. |
| 30 September 1998 | 1997/98 return filed if Revenue to calculate tax. |
| 31 January 1999 | 1997/98 balance due. |
| 31 January 1999 | 1998/99 1st instalment due 'on account'. |
| 31 January 1999 | 1997/98 return filed if tax self-assessed. |

If figures are not available, under the new rules for 1996/97 onwards, best estimates will have to be used. It will no longer be appropriate to put 'As agreed' or 'To be agreed' on your tax return after those dates.

## B. Corporation tax returns

Companies and unincorporated bodies such as clubs, are charged to corporation tax [FA 1990, s 91; FA 1994, s 182] [TMA 1970, ss 11AA; F(no. 2) A 1987, s 82]. The new 'pay and file' system where companies have to estimate and pay their tax not later than nine months after the end of the accounting period, was introduced by the Inland Revenue a few years ago. A statutory return (Form CT200) with supporting accounts, must be filed within 12 months after the end of the accounting period.

Between 1 April 1996 and 31 March 1998 (on a date to be given), companies will have to 'self-assess' their corporation tax, and be responsible for it. The company cannot ask the Inland Revenue to work out its tax bill in the same way that the self-employed can. The Revenue will have 12 months to select a company return for audit. If it has not done so by then, the return which was self-assessed will stand, unless fraud, negligence or inadequate information comes to light.

## C. Other important deadlines

*The following deadlines were given for important dates.* The exact day is given for the 1995 tax year in brackets. Whilst the month will usually be the same, the latest date schedule for the year should be obtained from the Inland Revenue.

| | |
|---|---|
| May (19): | Employers to file end-of-year returns (Forms P14, P35, P38/P38A). |
| June (6): | PIID forms due (returns of benefits for employees). |
| June (16): | Class 1A (company cars and fuel) National Insurance contributions due. |
| June (30): | Second instalment Schedule D tax 1995-96 due. |
| July (5): | Last day to elect for a personal pension or retirement annuity contribution paid in 1995/96 be given in 1994/95. |
| July (19): | PAYE quarterly payment date for small employers. |
| October (5): | Last day to make an Enterprise Investment Scheme investment related back to the previous tax year. |
| October (19): | PAYE quarterly payment date for small firms. |
| October (31): | Filing of personal tax returns due. |
| December (1): | Payment date for higher-rate tax and capital gains due from previous tax year. |
| December (29): | The date for payment of current tax year's Schedule D income tax is 1 January. To avoid penalties, pay |

early.
Closing date for reclaiming Class 2 National
Insurance contributions paid in the previous tax year,
on the grounds of low income.

## D. Deadlines for claims or elections

By the end of the tax year in question (e.g. 5 April 1996) claims or elections for assessment or reassessment must be made. If not made, then these valuable reliefs or deductions could be lost forever. The main ones for *businesses* are as follows:

- In relation to trading losses, for example, by 5 April 1996, a loss which was incurred in 1992–93 should be set against other income of 1993–1994. A loss incurred in 1993–1994 should be set against a capital gain realised in 1993–94, or carried back where permitted.
- Claiming capital gains tax retirement relief on ill-health grounds for a disposal made in 1993–94.
- Electing to treat plant or machinery purchased in 1993–94 as a short-life asset for capital allowance purposes.

There are many personal reliefs and assessments to be claimed or made, some going back for six years. For example, claims for personal allowances for 1989–90 must be made by 6 April 1996.

---

## STRATEGY #247
## Get all returns in on time to avoid penalties

---

It's bad enough having to pay the tax, but even worse if penalties or interest are payable. For some, however, it may be more convenient (for reasons of cash flow) to pay the interest rather than the amount owing, until such times as payment can be made.

## 1. The self-employed

The self-employed will be subject to the following penalties: for 1996/97 late returns, there will be automatic penalties, plus interest and surcharges where tax is underpaid. If tax is overpaid, then repayment supplements are allowed (interest on overpaid tax).

a) *The surcharge on late payments is:*
5% of any tax not paid by 28 February.
A further 5% of any tax still not paid by 31 July.

b) *Automatic penalties for late returns are:*
£100 if the return is not made by 31 January; plus
£60 a day if failure to pay is declared by the tax commissioners;
£100 if failure is not declared by the commissioners and a return is not made by 31 July;
Further penalties of 100% of the tax adjudged owing if a year late (if a return has not been made by next 31 January). This does not apply to partnerships.
Other penalties apply where fraud or negligence is applied to reduce provisional payments.

c) A penalty of up to £3,000 for failure to keep records relevant to your returns for five years and ten months from the end of the tax year if in business, and for 22 months from the end of the tax year if not in business.

d) Interest on overdue tax or on overpayments of tax generally fluctuates in line with commercial interest rates and between October 1988 and March 1995 has seen a high of 13% and a low of 5.5%. At the time of writing it was 7% (September 1995).

Interest is payable from a 'reckonable date' which is usually the date when tax is actually due for payment. By agreement or otherwise (if appeals are made or postponement given), the date interest runs from may be varied – or even backdated if fraud or negligence in reducing tax payable is alleged.
Interest paid is not tax deductible.

## 2. Companies

If returns are not sent in by the due date, then automatic fixed penalties are payable and other tax-related penalties if the return is more than six months late.

- Failure to notify a liability 12 months after the end of the accounting period incurs a maximum penalty of 100% of the tax payable.
- Failure to submit a corporation tax return under pay and file (accounts after 30 September 1993) incurs an automatic penalty of:
  ·£100 if up to three months late
  ·£200 if more than three months late
  ·10%–20% of tax payable if unpaid after 18 months.
  ·If considerably late, then penalties increase substantially, e.g. £1,000 if the third consecutive late return over three months.
- Negligence or fraud in returns or accounts has 100% penalty of the amount equal to the tax lost.

Interest on overdue tax for corporations at 6 March 1995 was 7% p.a. Interest on overpaid tax was 4% per annum. Note that there are also company law penalties for filing late returns.

---

## STRATEGY #248
## If subject to penalties and interest, negotiate an offer with the Inland Revenue

---

The Inland Revenue can either institute proceedings against the business (or personally) or accept an offer not to do so. The amount can be negotiated and the penalty reduced if disclosures are voluntary and the taxpayer co-operates and the offences are not too grave.

This strategy can save you thousands in not undertaking proceedings and further aggravation from the Inland Revenue. The Revenue has the power to reduce interest as well as penalties.

If reasons for non-payment of tax are genuine, such as cash flow problems, the Inland Revenue is usually reasonable in giving you time to pay in instalments.

If the Inland Revenue suspects fraud, negligent conduct or evasion, it can open up past assessments for up to 21 years. If not, it can only go back for six years without alleging fault.

---

## STRATEGY #249
## If self-employed, make full use of the transitional rules for filing purposes

---

For 1996/97, transitional rules will apply which allow an averaging so that, in most cases, the amount assessable will be half that of the two year period ending in the tax year 1996/97.

The effect of these rules is that *only 50% of the profits* of a business are taxed in each of the accounting years ending in the tax years 1995/96 and 1996/97. This presents a wonderful planning opportunity for the self-employed.

It will, therefore, be beneficial for there to be higher profits in these accounts years than in the accounts for the years ending in the tax years 1994/95 and 1997/98.

The new rules can greatly affect your cash flow. If business profits are increasing, you are likely to pay more tax sooner. If profits are reducing, then you will pay less tax sooner.

The new transitional rules are designed to phase in the changeover from a preceding year basis (profits from last year taxed in this year) to a current year basis (profits taxed in the year in which they arise).

Very careful planning is required, especially if sole traders and partners are considering incorporating.

---

### STRATEGY #250
### Make full use of personal pension contributions during the transitional tax filing periods

---

Personal pension contributions made by the self-employed are not taken into account when calculating profits. They are made by reference to net relevant earnings for a tax year and effectively reduce taxable income.

This is most significant for the two accounting years in the transitional period as profit is effectively halved. Thus, any expenditure which is relievable and takes place in these years will also, in effect, be halved. Such expenditure will only attract half of the tax relief it would normally enjoy.

However, personal pension contributions made in this tax year will attract full tax relief as they will reduce taxable income on a £ for £ basis.

It may pay the sole trader or partners to postpone capital expenditure during the transitional period and maximise personal pension contributions instead.

Watch out, though, for profit manipulation as it may trigger anti-avoidance provisions.

---

### STRATEGY #251
### Claim all refunds due immediately

---

Remember that a refund is a return of your own money, usually without interest or a thank you letter, that you never owed in the first place. (Interest is only payable to you from the end of the year of assessment following that in which you paid tax. This interest is, however, tax-free. Sometimes the Inland Revenue is at fault, or errors have been made in calculations, or new deductions are possible, sometimes creating losses. For example, pension contributions may trigger a tax deduction, giving rise to a refund, even for previous years.)

Unless the Inland Revenue is paying interest at a higher rate than you can achieve elsewhere, get your money out of their pockets as quickly as possible. Follow-up if necessary to do so. It is estimated that over seven million individual taxpayers are owed unclaimed refunds from personal and other deductions not being claimed.

If owed a refund or you can claim back taxes, get your return in to the Inland Revenue as quickly as possible. Individuals can use a repayment claim form R40. Always document your claim in writing.

---

### STRATEGY #252
### Use the same principles to claim for overpaid VAT and NIC contributions

---

Income tax and corporation taxes are not the only taxes which carry interest and penalties for non-payment or under-payment, or pay interest to you for over-payment. The same situation applies particularly to value added tax (VAT) and also to National Insurance contributions (NICs).

VAT is administered by the Customs and Excise. Any business with an annual turnover of £46,000 must register for VAT. Below that level, you register voluntarily.

VAT is not a tax on profits as such. It is a tax on the consumer that is collected in stages for businesses throughout the business chain, and eventually by the business supplying the customer. In this way the business becomes a tax collector. If the business fails to charge for VAT and account for it, it will be liable for VAT and penalties. This situation could obviously affect profits.

The basic rule is that VAT is chargeable on the supply of any goods or services where money is payable (or money's worth) and where supplied in the course or furtherance of any business.

Some supplies are taxable for VAT, with a standard maximum rate of 17.5%. Goods or services may also be taxable but zero rated. Zero rating gives entitlement to recover VAT on underlying costs, whereas exemption does not.

An expanding business may wish to register for VAT voluntarily if below the VAT turnover threshold, at present £46,000, as VAT on costs would be recoverable. VAT must obviously also then be charged on supplies.

VAT returns must be submitted with full payment by the end of the month following the end of the VAT accounting period. Some businesses do not issue tax invoices (retailers, possibly) and where this occurs, VAT is due on the gross taxable income received during the VAT period. Your strategy must always be to issue VAT invoices, unless on the retail scheme.

VAT legislation and rules are complex and Customs and Excise have a large enforcement division with very wide powers of inspection. If there are errors, then assessments will be raised for under-declared VAT and penalties and interest charges imposed. Penalties are as follows:

- Late registration                5% to 15% of the net tax due.
- Late returns                     surcharges ranging from 2% to 15%.
- Misdeclaration penalty           15% of additional VAT assessed when specific limits are exceeded.
- Interest charges                 at a prescribed rate enacted by Treasury order. Usually only imposed if there has been a loss of revenue.
- Penalties                        over 60 regulatory offences give rise to penalties.
- Fraud                            100% of tax involved or less for civil cases. Three × amount if criminal cases or imprisonment.

Customs and Excise do make mistakes as do businesses. Usually they are reasonable in accommodating the business. There have been a number of recent cases where VAT has successfully been argued against, and the taxpayers have won. VAT paid on sports subscriptions has had to be returned to members of sports clubs recently, as well as partial VAT for the supply of spectacles by opticians, VAT reclaims on surrendered road fund licences, and a pending European court decision input on VAT on the company car could be very costly for the Exchequer.

Strategies should cover all taxes, not only taxes on profits or income. If reclaims may be made for VAT and National Insurance contributions overpaid, or claimed back, then ensure that the proper tax filing procedures are made and adequate records kept.

## STRATEGY #253
## Reduce the chances of an audit

You will send a clear signal to the tax authorities that you or your business are 'audit material' if you don't keep proper records, if you file returns consistently late and are sloppy about your business affairs. On the other hand, if you always file returns on time, send in written explanations, and pay your dues promptly, the chances of an audit are much diminished. The audit is nothing more than proving what a good record keeper you are.

You must become familiar with audit procedure and knowledgeable on your own affairs. The more you learn on how to report income, deductions and other relevant facts, the less the chances of an audit.

Don't allow an audit to drag on. The longer the investigation takes, the more chances there are of deficiencies turning up. Always behave impeccably in an audit. Here are some rules from Charles J Givens' book, *Wealth Without Risk,* on how to behave in an audit.

- Say little; smile a lot. Never volunteer information.
- If you feel strongly about your position, let the auditor know. Often the auditor will let the point go in your favour.
- Provide as much documentation in your favour as possible for each point in an audit.
- Don't give up, even if you don't have all the documentation.
- Don't make too many concessions.
- Don't be rushed unless you feel hurrying will work in your favour.
- Don't complain about the tax system; the auditor pays taxes, too.
- Don't try to tape-record the conversation.
- Act with confidence that you're right. You probably are.
- Tax auditors are not well paid. If a tax auditor sees you driving a Mercedes or wearing a Rolex, he or she will not be sympathetic. Take off fancy jewellery and wear conservative clothes.
- Give the auditors adequate space and other facilities to carry out the audit.
- Be courteous to the auditor and avoid being abrasive or argumentative.
- Don't present your receipts in a brown paper bag. The auditor will assume that, if you're disorganised, there must be errors on your tax return somewhere.

If you feel strongly about your case, don't be afraid to object or appeal against decisions.

## Key points summary

- Changes in the ways in which tax is collected for companies and to be collected for the self-employed will have the effect of bringing taxpayers up-to-date instead of lagging years behind with returns. There is no escaping the current year basis of assessment.

- Good and accurate record keeping is essential to claim deductions, file returns on time and to avoid an audit investigation.

- Timing is most important to avoid penalties and interest. There are a myriad dates by which returns of one kind or another must be filed.

- Pay attention to VAT and other taxes, such as National Insurance contributions, where penalties may also apply.

- By adopting proper tax filing methods, the business can save thousands of pounds otherwise spent in management time and taxpenalties. Big savings can be achieved by knowing your way around the tax system and claiming all that is due to you.

# CHAPTER 16

# Cutting Your Business Taxes

*There is no art which one government sooner learns of another than that of draining money from the pockets of the people.*
**Adam Smith (1723–1790)** *Wealth Of Nations*

### Objective: Reduce business taxes by up to 50%

Companies pay corporation tax and advance corporation tax (ACT) on profits; unincorporated businesses pay income tax assessed on the business owners. Other taxes include capital gains taxes (CGT) on asset disposals, valued added tax (VAT) on purchases, stamp duties, inheritance taxes, National Insurance and so on – in fact, quite a taxing business.

The main partner in any business is the taxman. Like it or not, the taxman can help himself to between 20 and 40% of the business's profits. His partners include the VATman and the NIC collector, who will take another 10 or 20% of value from the business. The extent to which you want these largely unwanted partners in *your* business is entirely up to you.

If you fail to claim your legal entitlement to deductions and deferrals, as well as capital allowances for which the business qualifies, then you are giving away business value which should otherwise accrue to the business owner. In short, you should have a clearly-defined tax reduction strategy for your business. How is it that for identical businesses with the same turnover and expenditures one will pay at maximum levels of taxation, whilst the other will pay nothing at all? It all comes down to preparing specific tax reducing strategies.

---

### STRATEGY #254
### Aggressively prepare the business tax reducing strategies

---

It is the right of every business and individual to arrange their affairs in such a way as to avoid paying taxes.

Lord Clyde (in Ayrshire Pullman Motor Services and Ritchie *v* IRC) said that the Inland Revenue will put the 'largest possible shovel' into your stores and will take every advantage to deplete the taxpayer's pocket under the taxing statues. He goes on to say that the taxpayer *in like manner* is entitled to prevent the depletion of his means by the Revenue.

There is no doubt about it – the Inland Revenue can take an unreasonably large share of your income and savings. By astute planning, much can be done to avoid this situation. However, passive resistance by doing nothing will accomplish nothing. The business needs to know how far it can go without bringing into play the anti-avoidance legislation. To do this, it needs advice from aggressive tax advisers.

---

### STRATEGY #255
### Take out tax investigations insurance to limit your risk

---

It is a fact that most people and businesses fear the Inland Revenue. It has, over the years, nurtured this fear to ensure compliance and payment of maximum taxes. As a result, the business fearing an investigation prefers to 'sit tight' and not claim everything which is its due.

Businesses, however, have an obligation to their owners and shareholders to maximise profits. They also stand a much increased chance of an audit or investigation, in any event, because the Inland Revenue and other agencies (Customs and Excise for VAT and the DSS for NIC) are becoming better geared for this. The Inland Revenue recently announced a close working relationship with the DSS to collect NIC (National Insurance contributions) on employee benefits. Whether the business taxpayer likes it or not, there is a 3:1 chance of an investigation of some kind over the next three years.

Investigations are costly for the business in fees and tying up time.

Insurance cover is available to pay for fees incurred in investigations, and every business should have it.

---

## STRATEGY #256
## Claim all deductions, even when in doubt

---

The worst that could happen if a deduction is claimed which is later unsubstantiated is that it is disallowed. This increases your tax-paying situation. However, you are no worse off than you were before claiming the deduction which you believed was claimable. If in doubt, claim it.

If your tax preparer is timid (for fear of drawing attention to the business's practice of claiming deductions) then change him.

---

## STRATEGY #257
## Define the business's policy in relation to making profits

---

Any business can substantially reduce its taxes by reducing the amount of profits available for taxation. Some businesses show no profits year after year and therefore pay no taxes.

Yet against this scenario must be weighed other important considerations. In the main, most businesses do not wish to be known as 'loss making businesses'. This may affect the corporate image of the business in the marketplace, as well as its perceived strength in the eyes of creditors and suppliers.

Be prepared, then, to pay some taxes. The reason for this is that in order to show that the business is profitable, it must produce profits. Profits will be taxable. The balance, after tax, is then available to shareholders as dividends, or to the company as retained reserves. If a sole trader, net profits accrue directly to the business owner. If in a partnership, they are allocated and taxed individually, the partners themselves increasing their capital accounts.

If there are no profits, then there are also no dividends for shareholders (unless there is a distribution from previously-taxed profits). The business may, therefore, be caught on the horns of a dilemma. To avoid taxes may make the business 'unprofitable', but to reward business owners who are shareholders requiring dividends, can only be done from after-tax profits. A balancing act is therefore required, and proper planning is essential.

## STRATEGY #258
## Reduce business taxes by claiming all deductions

Any business may claim expenditure incurred in the production of its income. Items of expenditure 'wholly and exclusively' for the purposes of trade are allowable [TA 1988, section 74 (a)], whereas those not 'wholly and exclusively' for the purposes of trade will be disallowed.

There are a myriad Inland Revenue statements of practice, press releases and extra-statutory concessions which need to be considered, not to mention the case law and detailed tax rules which have to be taken into account when assessing taxable profits. Whilst the tax legislation may say one thing, often interpretation of the law and specific rules may vary. To give the Inland Revenue its due, most clients have found its staff are helpful in formulating the correct approach. If in doubt, ask them whether your approach is permissible or not. They are, after all, only interpreters of the law and its rules. If you feel you have a case to make, then appeal against adverse decisions.

The Revenue has bound itself by its own code of practice – the Taxpayers' Charter. One of the codes is that you 'pay only what is due under the law'. The Inland Revenue must operate a uniform interpretation of the tax legislation, and thus treat all taxpayers alike. If in doubt as to interpretation, the Revenue will issue a statement of practice. If you believe that the Inland Revenue interpretation is wrong, you may appeal to the Commissioners. Where the law is believed to be onerous, the Inland Revenue will issue an extra-statutory concession to enable the taxpayer to get fair treatment.

As taxpayers can order their personal and business affairs in the most suitable way to reduce their tax liabilities, it just does not make commercial sense not to claim for every deduction, allowance and reduction of taxes possible.

## STRATEGY #259
## Maximise business tax deductions

The computation of profits for the self-employed and partners is different from that for companies. The way in which deductions are handled can also be different. The position of the self-employed is reviewed first, and then companies. Remember, the greater the level of tax deductions claimed the less tax is payable. Critically examine all items of expenditure and those capital payments which qualify for capital allowances. The lists of deductions following each category are not exhaustive but do give a good idea of what can be claimed.

## 1. Self-employed

Accounts should be prepared to reflect a trader's earnings for a year, rather than purely on cash received. Accounts must be prepared on the 'earnings basis' for the first three years of a business before a switch may be made to a cash basis.

Prior to the Finance Act 1994, profits were ascertained before capital allowances. For businesses which started after the 1993/94 tax year, capital allowances are treated like any other business expense. Businesses in operation before 5 April 1994 will be phased into the new treatment basis from 1997/98. With the changes to self-assessment, the 'preceding year' basis of assessment will be abolished from 5 April 1996. There will be a transitional period of assessment to get all self-employed and partnerships on to a 'current year' basis of assessment by 1997/98.

In 1996/97, only 50% of profits will be taxed, and although there are anti-avoidance rules to prevent the shifting of profits, tax planning is possible and can be brought to bear to maximise this position. This tax planning would include changing the dates of accounting periods, obtaining a tax advantage which was not the main benefit expected by the arrangement; the arrangement to be entered into solely for bona fide commercial purposes; and profits 'shifted' are below a minimum threshold. Existing firms will have certain options on how their profits are taxed and when, and there is substantial scope for tax planning.

The self-employed do not pay PAYE, they are assessed on a 'Schedule D' tax assessment basis. As such, the self-employed have more scope to reduce their tax bills than employed people. There are more expenses to be claimed and they are easier to claim. They also have loss relief, which can be set against other taxable income, or carried back against total income for the previous three years (in the earlier years of the business).

Smaller businesses with a turnover of less than £15,000 need not complete detailed accounts. All that is required is turnover, expenses total and net profit figures. Above that turnover figure, more detailed accounts are required.

The self-employed may deduct the following from income to arrive at taxable income and profits:

- Normal business expenses, such as purchase of goods, wages of employees, rent of business premises and business rates.
- Expenses incurred from using the home in the business. This is

usually a proportion of lights, water, electricity, cleaning, telephones, rent, mortgage interest etc, which is based on a calculation of business usage and private usage as a proportion of total usage.

- If the business is renting out properties (either furnished or unfurnished) then expenses may be claimed against rentals. These include rents you pay, water rates, general maintenance and repairs, fittings and furniture, insurance, cost of using agents to collect rentals, interest payable on loans to purchase or improve investment properties, management fees, legal fees on leases, accountancy fees, costs of collecting rents, such as travel costs, service and security costs, wear and tear costs (usually at 10% p.a.), the council tax.
- If not registered for VAT, then any VAT suffered will form part of your expenditure (except for business entertainment VAT) and is deductible. Similarly, if you are registered for VAT then, if unable to recover all input tax from Customs and Excise, the non-deductible amount will count as expenditure.
- Costs of insurance in the business.
- Hotel and travelling expenses on business trips.
- Car and vehicle running expenses including fuel, road tax and insurance. Capital allowances are allowed against the car value each year (usually 25%) which also reduces taxable income.
- Cost of raising loan finance.
- Legal expenses on debt recovery and employees' service agreements.
- Contributions to local enterprise agencies and TECs.
- Bank interest charges. Other bank charges.
- Business subscriptions and magazines.
- Tools.
- Special clothing necessary in the business.
- Bad and doubtful debts.
- Gifts advertising the business, with a value of up to £10 per person.
- Repairs to business property.
- National Insurance contributions for staff.
- Pension contributions, sickness contributions and other allowable employee benefits for staff.
- 50% of self-employed Class 4 National Insurance contributions is allowable against taxable income. This is the NIC payable by the self-employed on profits. (In 1995/96 Class 4 contributions of 7.3% are calculated on profits between £6,640 and £22,880.)
- Advertising.
- Capital allowances are given for the tax year in which the profits of an accounting period are taxed. In the year of purchase, a first year allowance is claimable and then a writing-down allowance on the reducing balance.

- Post-cessation expenses are now allowable [FA 1995, section 90]. Expenditures and allowances are not given automatically. They must be claimed. It is important that you know what is claimable and what is not. It is also important to know what is taxable and what is not. Many tax-free items may inadvertently be taxed.

*The following are not generally claimable or allowable:*

- Expenditure for private usage. When expended for both business and private usage, the private usage portion must be added back. If not 'wholly and exclusively' for the purposes of trade [TA 1988, section 74(a)], then expenses are disallowed.
- This includes rent, light, heat etc, when you live in the business premises – all private usage is a disallowed expenditure.
- Motor expenditures when used privately.
- Private telephone bills.
- 50% of your own Class 4 National Insurance contributions.
- Depreciation on assets is not allowable. However, capital allowances are.
- Expenditure on capital items, such as cars, machinery, computers is not allowable expenditure. Again, capital allowances may be claimed. [TA 1988, section 74.]
- Your own earnings and Class 2 NICs are not allowable deductions. Drawings must be added back for tax purposes.
- Entertainment expenditures are not allowable deductions. [TA 1988, section 577.]
- Gifts to customers above £10 in worth, which are neither food, drink, tobacco nor a voucher for such goods. [TA 1988, section 577.]
- Illegal payments. [Finance Acts 1993 and 1994.]
- Lease rentals on expensive cars costing above £12,000 for the sole trader or an employer. A proportion of the lease rental is added back as a disallowable expense. [CAA 1990, section 35.]
- Provisions for bad debts if general. Specific reasonable provisions may be made. [TA 1988, section 74 (j).]
- Remuneration not paid within nine months of the year end, such as bonus payments to employees, are then disallowed. [FA 1989, section 43.]
- Pension contributions made by the sole trader himself cannot be used to compute taxable profits but may be an allowable deduction from taxable profits. [FA 1993, section 112.] Other payments may not be a deduction in arriving at profits, but may be a deduction from personal taxable income, such as certain annual payments or royalties. [TA 1988, section 74 (p) and (q).]
- Legal costs in connection with the acquisition of capital assets are

disallowable, as well as legal costs in connection with renewing a lease of more than 50 years.
- Professional costs incurred in connection with tax appeals are not allowable as they relate to tax on profits as opposed to an expense incurred in earning profits.

If in doubt, deduct it.

## 2. Companies

A limited company pays corporation tax and not income tax on its profits (as a sole trader or partner does). If a company pays dividends, then advance corporation tax (ACT) is payable on them. This is offset against a company's mainstream tax liability.

From a tax deduction and allowances point of view, the position is similar to that of a sole trader or partner. In general, expenditure incurred 'wholly and exclusively' in the production of trade income would be deductible. Certain expenditure is specifically excluded as a deduction (such as business entertainment) and some expenditures (on capital assets) are not allowable, but rather qualify for capital allowances.

However, the following additional situations apply for companies over that allowable to the self-employed:

- Directors' remuneration is an allowable expense in computing taxable profits.
- National Insurance contributions paid on employees' wages (including directors') and on the provision of private fuel and cars to staff are allowable against profits. (No part of a sole trader's or partner's own Class 2 and Class 4 contributions is directly allowable against profits, but 50% of the Class 4 contributions is allowable as a general deduction but this changes in 1996/97.)
- Companies have a wider scope with bigger deduction capacity than the self-employed. For example, pension contributions are continuous, even if the company is making a loss, which cannot be the case for the self-employed.

---

## STRATEGY #260
### Make the best use of capital allowances to reduce taxes

---

Capital allowances are normally given for the tax year in which the profits of an accounting period are taxed. In the year of purchase, a first year allowance is claimable and then in subsequent years, there is a writing down allowance on the reducing balance.

Allowances must be proportioned for private use of a business asset. Capital allowances reduce taxable profits.

## CAPITAL ALLOWANCES (1995/96)

|  | Initial allowance on cost | Writing-down allowance on reducing balance |
| --- | --- | --- |
| Plant, machinery, equipment |  | 25% |
| Computer software |  | 25% |
| Motor cars (maximum £3,000 p.a.) |  | 25% |
| Vans, lorries |  | 25% |
| Office furniture and equipment |  | 25% |
| Insulation of factories and warehouses |  | 25% |
| Patent expenditure on patent rights |  | 25% |
| 'Know how' expenditure |  | 25% |
| Mineral extraction |  | 10%–25% |
| Factories and warehouses | 20% | 4% (on cost) |
| Agricultural buildings | 20% | 4% (on cost) |
| Public highways and roads | 20% | 4% (on cost) |
| Hotel buildings | 20% | 4% (on cost) |
| Houses under assured tenancies |  | 4% (on cost) |
| Enterprise zone buildings | 100% or | 25% |

Capital allowances mean big tax deductions. The implications are as follows:

- Allowances for sole traders and partners are available against trading profits for the relevant tax years.
- Loss relief may be claimed if they increase a loss or turn a profit into a loss.
- For sole traders and partnerships, special rules apply for the phasing-in of self-assessment [FA 1994, ss 211–214 and Schedule 20, para 9]. Allowances should not be lost because of the averaging

rules for 1996/97 where existing businesses are phased in. Capital allowances will be treated as trading expenses.

- Allowances for a trading company are deducted in arriving at trading profit. Profits could be turned into losses and corporate loss relief claimed.
- For both individuals and companies, allowances may be carried forward, if not set against other income or profits.
- Specific claims must be made for allowances – they are not automatic. Companies use form CT200 or an amended return. Allowances must usually be claimed within two years from the end of the accounting period – and up to six years if profits and losses for that period are not settled.
- Not all allowances need to be taken in full, which will enable better use of other reliefs and allowances first.
- Capital allowances are not deducted from the cost of an asset in computing a capital gain, but will be if computing a capital loss.

## STRATEGY #261
## If profits are too low, make a partial allowances claim only

If allowances are more than profits, or if a trading loss is suffered and no tax is payable, then don't claim the whole of the capital allowances. This would keep the written down value for tax purposes higher to give larger writing down allowances later. These may then be set against future trading profits.

This is especially the case if you have other reliefs and allowances which must be used – such as personal allowances which would otherwise be wasted – then reduce your claim for allowances. Keep the computations available for future years though.

## STRATEGY #262
## Avoid losing relief for allowances by claiming in time

For plant and machinery allowances (these include capital equipment such as computers and fax machines) there is an additional requirement for expenditure to be notified to the Inland Revenue within two years from the end of the period (and an even shorter period under self-assessment).

So, notify the Revenue by letter, even if a claim has not yet been made. Show what the amounts are which have been expended and the categories – office equipment, furniture, computers, lorries.

---

## STRATEGY #263
## If self-employed, use capital allowances to turn trading profits into trading losses

---

Any losses can be relieved against other income. The self-employed will no longer have the flexibility of including or excluding capital allowances when making loss claims because capital allowances will be treated as trading expenses for existing businesses from 1997/98.

The only way then to use allowances to vary the amount of the loss will be by disclaiming plant and machinery allowances. However, there is still time to plan for the reduction of trading profits through capital allowances. Trading losses may be carried back against the income of earlier years.

---

## STRATEGY #264
## If a company, don't take allowances to use other current year reliefs

---

Companies may wish to leave profits high enough to use reliefs which are only available in the current accounting period. These may include group reliefs for losses, and current year expenditures.

---

## STRATEGY #265
## It may pay you to lease a car, rather than buy it

---

The writing down allowance is 25% a year when you buy a car. However, if a car is leased, the whole of the leasing charge is deductible from taxable profits (less any charge for private use and the restriction of the car to £12,000 cost to the leasing company). It may pay you to plan to lease the car and have 100% deducted now, rather than buy it and write down its value; 25% on a reducing balance may take eight years to write off.

---

### STRATEGY #266
### Always buy plant and machinery on the last day of the financial year

---

Buy on the last day of the financial year, rather than the first day of the next year, so that you get the full year's capital allowance; even though legally yours, you have not yet paid for the asset – or if it's on hire purchase, the same applies.

---

### STRATEGY #267
### Go for maximum loss reliefs to reduce taxes

---

If self-employed, trading losses may be deducted from:

- Other income of the same tax year
- All income of the next tax year
- Trading profits of future years
- If the loss arises in the first four tax years of a business, all income of the preceding three tax years, but set off against the earliest years first.

The self-employed must set off losses against other earned income first, then against investment income. If personal allowances and reliefs may be wasted, then perhaps it is better to carry forward the whole loss to offset it against future profits. This is because you can't claim all tax reliefs and only part of a loss. The whole of the loss must be set off first.

For a company, the trading losses may be claimed as follows [TA 1988, section 393 (A91); (2); 393(1); 242 and section 402]:

- Set off against current profits
- Carry back against earlier profits
- Carry forward against future trading profits
- Set off against franked investment income (dividends received from other companies)
- Group reliefs.

A company's losses will already include capital allowances which have been claimed. In addition, the set off against trading profits will include capital gains.

## STRATEGY #268
## Generate losses to get back tax paid and benefit the business owner

A large tax-reducing payment may cause a loss for the current year to be set off against trading profits. It may also give the opportunity to go back for up to three years [TA 1988, ss 393(1)] or to carry forward against future profits [TA 1988, ss 393(1) (2)]. For example, a substantial pension contribution payment may have this effect. By reducing profits in previous years, tax would be repaid – good news if it was paid then at higher rates.

After a trading loss has been set against all profits of the current period, any balance may be carried back and set against the profits of the last three years, starting with the last year. The business must have been trading in the earlier period. This set off can be made against any profits, not only trading profits, so may include capital gains taxed in that year.

Tax already paid is repaid. Tax due but not paid need not be paid. The loss claim may cause surplus ACT (advance corporation tax) to arise, which can also be carried back for six years, or forward and also used against mainstream tax liabilities. The net effect of creating a loss by making a substantial pension contribution is a repayment of tax as well as a large tax-free growth vehicle, the pension fund. It may also save taxes due to be paid.

It's always better to pay yourself first, rather than the Inland Revenue.

## STRATEGY #269
## Reduce taxes by making large pension contributions

The last strategy showed how pension contributions can be used to create losses and get back tax. Pension contributions are 100% deductible to an employer. They are also 100% deductible (within the funding limits) to the self-employed.

Pension contributions reduce taxable income and therefore taxes payable. If the business is looking for deductible expenditure to reduce taxes, then by far the best investment for 100% deductibility is pension contributions.

If made individually, they also reduce the individual's taxable income – at his or her highest rates of tax.

---

### STRATEGY #270
### Set up an ESOT to reduce taxes

---

An employee share owner trust (ESOT) is one of the most powerful tax planning tools available – in some ways even more powerful than pension funding. Why? Because it has the ability to funnel tax deductible cash back to the company and can significantly reduce the cost of working capital.

This is because the setting up costs of the ESOT are tax deductible – as is capital borrowed to fund the ESOT. Interest on the loan is also tax deductible. Even if the company set up the ESOT (it must must hold 10% of the shares in the company to qualify) to defer tax or to claim tax reliefs, it will be in a time suspension for at least seven years before the Inland Revenue claws back any tax owing by disallowing previous reliefs. This will occur if employees do not buy shares from the share trust.

If the shares are not taken up by employees from the ESOT within seven years, then tax reliefs can be clawed back. However, the company will have experienced significant tax relief for a long period if there was no take up. See Chapter 19 for further comments, especially the double reliefs from gearing an ESOT with a pension fund.

---

### STRATEGY #271
### Decide on whether commercial property should be held by the company or the pension fund

---

The pension fund is a useful vehicle for other things apart from paying pensions. For example, a business owner's pension fund, such as a SSAS, may hold commercial property which it purchases. It then rents the property back to the business. Rents payable as well as loan interest paid to the pension fund by the business are tax deductible to the business and are not taxed in the pension fund.

The business should set high levels of commercial interest rate for its payments to the pension fund. The higher the better. This is because the business can more or less set the rate of interest return for the pension fund. And it's all tax deductible to the business – so long as it's commercial.

However, if the business purchased the commercial property and not the pension fund, then capital allowances would apply. After the initial 20%, however, 4% a year is hardly likely to excite anyone. Rather make the tax deductible contributions to the fund, which purchases the property.

## STRATEGY #272
## Make tax deductible investments

The self-employed and companies may get 100% tax relief for investing in enterprise zone properties (EZTs).

Pension contributions are tax deductible investments for both the
self-employed and companies.

The self-employed may also invest in venture capital trusts and
enterprise investment schemes for income tax relief (as may any individual over the age of 18) as well as capital gains tax deferrals.

There are no other investments which attract tax relief, apart from a
company investing in an ESOT to fund it for its employees.

Tax deductible investments can reduce profitability whilst creating
large tax deductions, thus saving tax individually or corporately.
Whilst less is available for dividends, the cash diverted into investments will continue to build wealth for the business or the individuals
in it.

## STRATEGY #273
## Reduce the incidence of all taxes, not only business taxes

Careful planning using the existing legislation and tax rules can generate substantial tax savings in capital gains taxes (annual exemptions,
holdover and rollover reliefs, retirement reliefs); inheritance taxes
(annual exemptions on transfers, estate exemptions, business property
and agricultural reliefs, the use of the nil rate band); income taxes
(deductible expenditures, capital allowances and reliefs); corporation
taxes (the same) and others such as VAT, stamp duties and the saving
of National Insurance contributions (NICs).

Take NICs for example. Certain employee benefits can be given
which save NIC of 10.2% for a business. Bonus payments attract Class
1 NIC at the full rate. If the company buys a car and transfers the asset
to the employee, then NIC is saved. If a bonus of, say, £30,000 was
awarded to an employee or director, then the company pays £3,060 in
NIC Class 1 contributions and the employee or director incurs tax of
£12,000. If the company buys a car instead and gives it to him, then the
£3,060 in NIC is saved. The tax charge is not immediate either as it is
not PAYE, but a PIID benefit.

Compare an unincorporated business with a company. Both have
four business owners, each earning £80,000. The National Insurance

bill (1995/96) is as follows:

| Partnership | | Company | |
|---|---|---|---|
| | £ | | £ |
| Class 2 | 1,196.00 | Employees' Class 1 | 8,170.24 |
| Class 4 | 4,742.08 | Employer's Class 1 | 33,640.00 |
| | 5,938.08 | | 41,810.24 |

The incidence of tax in this case is the very high level of NICs payable in companies compared to the self-employed. Self-employed businesses or partnerships should carefully examine their circumstances before becoming incorporated. It is no wonder that companies are constantly searching for NIC avoidance schemes to save on this open-ended tax for companies.

The strategies in this chapter have shown how the business can create significant tax deductions, allowances and reliefs enabling it to cut taxes by up to 50% or more – whether self-employed or a company.

## Key points summary

- Businesses must claim what is legally their right. The Inland Revenue and other taxing agencies are the biggest profit-sharing partners of any business.

- Businesses fearing investigations can take out insurance cover to provide fees to cover these.

- Business taxes can be reduced generally by over 50% (and sometimes 100%) through claiming all deductions and creating new ones, as well as losses.

- Businesses should aim to reduce *all* taxes, not only taxes on income or profits.

# CHAPTER 17

# Benefits in Kind or Cash?

*You can't make someone else's choices. You shouldn't let someone else make yours.*
**General Colin Powell, '13 rules to live by', *The Book of Lists***

**Objective: To use fringe benefits and tax avoidance schemes to increase wealth**

Whether the employer pays the employee in cash, or in a mixture of salary and 'perks', the usual financial position for the employer is fairly neutral. The cost of providing benefits in kind is more often than not worked out in the remuneration package so that if salaries or wages alone are paid, they will be higher than a package of salary and other benefits. Yet, there are certain benefits which may be given to an employee which have tax saving advantages to the employer. These are usually in the form of savings of National Insurance contributions (NIC).

To the employee, the situation is not as clear-cut. He or she will pay income tax on salary or wages under PAYE, deducted at source, and may also pay additional income tax on the value of the benefit given by the employer, unless it is specifically exempt, such as pension fund contributions.

The scope for the employer to rationalise and optimise employee benefits is obviously vast. Apart from the obvious savings to be made by buying employee benefits in bulk, the company or business can secure employee loyalty and give incentives through the provision of 'perks' and other benefits in kind. This is also an opportunity to reward employees for exceptional performance.

From the viewpoint of employees, however, there is a mixed reaction. Some cannot effectively use the 'perk' or benefit provided by the employer. They would prefer to have the additional cash, or salary as wages, and then make their own benefit arrangements. In these cases, the employer has either not communicated the 'benefit' value sufficiently, or the employee is not sufficiently impressed to want it. This then has a spiral effect with the employer offering nothing further to 'ungrateful' employees, who themselves have nothing further to consider.

Often the 'perk' is the result of a salary sacrifice or the foregoing of a salary increase to provide for it. Sometimes the employer expects a 'like for like' contribution from the employee (for example, with pension funding) and the take-up from employees will vary according to their perception of the value of the benefit. The only way around this inertia in the acceptance of 'perks' and additional benefits is proper communication of the values and costs of the benefits. This can be accomplished through regular benefit statements.

---

### STRATEGY #274
### Provide a benefit and 'perk' review and reporting process

---

Employers should, in any event, have a regular annual review, incorporating a value and cost analysis of the benefits and perks. This will not only indicate what value they are getting for their money, but also enables an accurate assessment of costs and liabilities. These costs are usually given as a percentage of payroll and are used for financial analysis and control purposes. Regular monitoring and feedback also indicate trends and usage. Obsolete benefits and perks (due to changing legislation, cost and value changes) must be discontinued or upgraded and changed.

A full corporate benefit audit will indicate the extent of the employer's commitments and liabilities, as well as indicate benefit values to the parties.

### BENEFIT REVIEW PROCESS

1. *Corporate benefit audit*    Critically examines values and costs of providing benefits and perks.

↓

2. *Cost survey and review*    Critically examines costs of providing

individual perks and benefits with
individual cost breakdowns for
employees and a total cost summary
for the business.

↓

3. *Benefit and 'perks' review*     Critically examines the benefit values
for employees individually and gives
total benefits purchased by the
employer as well as employees.

↓

4. *Review of current market*     Gives the total market spectrum of
*availability*                    what perks and benefits are available,
their maximum allowable amounts and
the costs of providing benefits and
perks at a maximum level.

↓

5. *Benefit and cost statements*  Provides for each employee a written
statement of what benefits and perks
they have, what the costs of providing
the above are for each employee, and a
consolidation of the total amounts for
the employer.

↓

6. *Management of this process*  Provides continual communication of
the benefits to the employee in relation
to the costs of provision, to establish
added value and benefits worth.
Provides a basis for monitoring, as well
as feedback of the process in the best
interests of the employer and the
employee.
Provides a basis for the introduction of
new perks and the deletion of obsolete
and unused ones.

↓

7. *Interaction planning*        Provides a basis for optimising wealth
for employees through individual
financial planning for best provision
according to individual needs and
preferences.
Provides a basis to link the employer's
benefits and perks to the individual's
existing personal benefits and to
optimise these.
Provides a basis of feedback on needs

requirements and attitudes within the
business environment, essential for
future planning.

↓

8. *Evaluation and*          Based on monitoring, feedback,
   *re-evaluation*           research and scenario planning, the
                             employer may assess the impact of its
                             policies.

↓

9. *Further corporate benefit*   The cycle begins again, this time
   *audits*                      implementing changes in policy as a
                                 result of previous actions.

The business will wish to keep under review the impact of its policies
on motivation, reward, incentivisation in terms of value and cost. It
will also wish to examine the tax and legislative consequences of its
actions in a changing environment. In doing so, it will take into account
the business's preference for, or aversion to, risk. The risks are:

- Risk of failure of management policies.
- Risk of investigations from the Inland Revenue, DSS and Customs
  and Excise.
- Risk of providing benefits and perks – the financial risk of increasing cost liabilities.
- Risk of not providing benefits and perks – the reward or incentive
  motive which remains unfulfilled.

Having established the position of the employer and the employee in
relation to providing benefits in cash or kind (perks), the next step is to
examine what benefits are available, and what their taxation consequences are.

---

### STRATEGY #275
### Ascertain the taxation position of benefits in
### kind for employer and employee

---

Fringe benefits are a part of life. Employees may receive a company car,
have luncheon vouchers, have their medical bills paid, have their
accommodation and overseas trips paid for, and have the use of mobile
telephones, to mention just a few. To most, the perk or fringe benefit
could be better than getting a salary increase.

Some employee benefits or perks received from the employer are taxable in the hands of the employee, some are tax-free and some are

allowable expenses. Some are taxable in the hands of certain classes of employee (PIID employees) and exactly the same benefit is tax-free or not taxed in the hands of others (such as non-PIID employees).

Each employee and the benefit received must therefore be separately considered. In addition, some benefits and expenses may receive a negotiated dispensation from the Inland Revenue, where no tax is payable. Allowable expenses are not taxable either because the employer is reimbursing the employee for his or her expenditure in the course of the job. These are usually mileage allowances, removal expenses, subsistence allowances, cost of professional subscriptions and flat rate expenses in certain industries. [TA 1988, section 201.]

In general, benefits in kind are taxable for directors and 'higher paid employees' under TA 1988, sections 153–168. Those earning below £8,500 p.a. (except for certain directors) will not be taxed on their benefits from the employer. These are non-PIID employees. Those employees earning at the rate of £8,500 p.a. or more, and directors, must have form PIID completed to be assessed on the cost to the employer of benefits in kind received by them.

Where the employee is not a PIID employee, but receives a benefit which is convertible into cash, then the benefit will be taxed. There are also the criteria for assessing National Insurance contributions.

The government intention is that all employees must pay tax on the whole of their earnings whether received in cash or in kind. To not affect lower-paid employees too harshly, the limit of £8,500 was established in 1979 and has not changed to date.

Where remuneration, together with benefits and reimbursed expenses, is £8,500 per annum or more, the employee is subject to PIID benefit assessment. Be careful here – it is the *rate* of pay at £8,500 p.a. which is the deciding factor, not the *actual* pay received. If monthly pay is £2,000 then the annual amount at that rate is £24,000 – over the PIID benefit. The fact that the employer may only intend to pay the employee for three months of a year (a total of £6,000) is not considered.

Any remuneration plus the value of benefits and reimbursed expenses below £8,500 p.a. are not taxable.

However, a PIID or P9D return may still have to be made to record reimbursed expenses and other benefits, or if a director – even earning below £8,500 p.a. or if excluded under section 168 of the Taxes Act 1988. To be an excluded director, he or she must earn less than £8,500 in remuneration and benefits, be employed on a full-time basis (or work for a charity or non-profit making company) and hold less than the company's ordinary share capital (together with close family and certain other associates).

## STRATEGY #276
## If both spouses are employed, then shift otherwise taxable benefits to the lower-paid employee

This is a perfectly legitimate way of providing tax-efficient benefits. However, watch out for TA 1988, section 154 (1) where, if the benefits are substantial, the Inland Revenue may still seek to tax the higher-paid employee or director under rules where the benefit was made to that employee's household by reason of his or her employment. This may even be the case where the recipient (the lower-paid employee) was also a company employee, i.e. the spouse.

The way around this is to make the benefit available to anyone in the employment category, not only specifically to one or more employees – for example, subsidised mortgage arrangements. Remember, it is the quantum of the benefit in kind which is important, i.e. the cost to the employer of providing the benefit.

The employee is free to negotiate his or her remuneration or benefits as they see fit. Perhaps Mr A receives mostly salary, his spouse mostly benefits. The level of £8,500 is so low in any event, that it is unlikely that 'substantial' benefits will result.

## STRATEGY #277
## Establish totally tax-free benefits – for any category of employee

There are certain benefits which are not taxable, even for otherwise assessable PIID employees. These tax-free benefits are as follows:

- Awards under suggestion schemes.
- Long service awards.
- Luncheon vouchers up to 15 pence a day.
- Provision of representative accommodation.
- Rail strike costs, public transport costs and allowances.
- Removal expenses, up to £8,000.
- Retraining.
- Retirement benefits, such as pension contributions.
- Sports facilities.
- Staff canteen and dining facilities.
- Use of a pool car.
- Workplace nurseries and crèches.

- Clothes specially needed for work.
- Discounts on goods and services, so long as employer is not out of pocket.
- Employees' outings up to £50 per person per year.
- Allowable fees and subscriptions to professional societies.
- Food and drink, if provided for all employees.
- Gifts, but not money on retirement.
- Gifts not from employer if cost under £100.
- Life insurance – cost of provision if approved scheme.
- Loans which qualify for tax relief.
- Scholarships and apprentice schemes awarded by employer.
- Season ticket loans if total of cheap loans is under £5,000.
- Sick pay insurance costs if approved scheme.
- Staff suggestion schemes – up to £5,000.
- Books and tuition fees for training.
- Transport between home and work for the severely disabled.
- Travel costs for late night journeys, if conditions are met.
- Profit-related pay – the tax-free portion, if approved scheme.
- Parking paid for by employer.

There is wide scope for planning employee benefits around tax-free benefits for all employees, including directors.

---

## STRATEGY #278
## Establish taxable benefits in kind for PIID employees and directors qualifying for them

---

Taxable benefits in kind can be a tremendous 'perk' for employees. The reason is that the true cost of provision is absorbed by the employer. The cost to the employee is the tax cost of having the value of the benefit included in taxable remuneration as opposed to having to pay for the benefit itself. It is even more efficient for using some benefits, where the add-back cost is only the difference between the Inland Revenue's official rate of interest and what the employee pays. This scenario is best illustrated as follows:

| Benefits | Gross cost to employer (example) | Tax cost to employee |
|---|---|---|
| Asset used by employee | £10,000 | $20\% \times £10,000 = £2,000 \times 40\% = £800$ |

(The cost to the employee is only the £800 tax charge on the asset costing £10,000, the assessable value being 20% of market value i.e. 20% ×

£10,000.)

For the employee to purchase this asset using his or her own net disposable income would have meant gross income of £16,666 before tax, i.e. if the employee is taxed at 40%, then £10,000 to buy the asset is obtained from £16,666-(40% × £16,666). To have the full use of the asset for £800 (the tax charge) would therefore be considered by most to be a good deal.

If the employer paid the school fees of the employee's children, then it is more likely that the full benefit will be taxable.

| Benefit | Gross cost to employer | Tax cost to employee |
|---|---|---|
| School fees | £10,000 | 40% × £10,000 = £4,000 |

It is still preferable for the employee to pay only £4,000, instead of the full £10,000 school fees costs.

To the employer in both cases, the benefit would be tax deductible, giving a net cost of £7,500 for the £10,000 benefit provided if the corporate tax payer pays tax at 25%.

Note that fringe benefits and taxation apply to any employer/ employee relationship, not only to companies.

## TABLE OF TAXABLE BENEFITS IN KIND SUMMARY

| Benefit | Tax | | NIC |
|---|---|---|---|
| | Directors and employees earning £8,500 a year or more | Other employees | All employees and employer |
| Assets given to employees, or if sold or lent | Costs to employer if new, or market value | Second-hand value, if any | Chargeable if asset can be exchanged for cash |
| Assets used by employees | Usually 20% of market value | No charge | No charge |
| Company car includes private use | 35% of list price | No charge | 10.2% of benefit figure |
| Company car fuel | Scale charge | No charge | 10.2% of benefit figure |
| Company van includes private use | Scale charge £350–£500 | Scale charge £350–£500 | 10.2% of benefit figure |
| Commodities, gold, fine wines, diamonds, etc. | Market value | Market value | 10.2% of market value |
| Credit cards, charge cards | Net cost to employer | Net cost to employer | Chargeable if asset can be exchanged for cash |
| Interest on card | No charge | No charge | No charge |

| | | | |
|---|---|---|---|
| Fees and subscriptions (not approved) | Cost to employer | Cost to employer | No charge |
| Non-cash gifts from 3rd parties (not employer) costing £100 or more | Cost or market value if cost unknown | Cost or market value if cost unknown | No charge as not provided by employer |
| Hairdressing at work | Cost to employer | No charge | No charge |
| Living accommodation provided without strings attached | Usually annual rateable value with special rules for property costing over £75,000 | Annual rateable value with special rules for property costing over £75,000 | No charge |
| Living accommodation as a condition of employment or security risk | No charge unless apportioned | No charge unless apportioned | No charge |
| Loans of money interest free or below the official rate, and above £5,000 in value | Difference between interest paid and the official rate | No charge | No charge unless written off |
| Loans of assets | Taxable value | No charge | Chargeable if asset can be exchanged for cash |
| Luncheon vouchers over 15 pence a day | Balance between 15 pence and actual cost is a taxable benefit | Same as for directors | No charge |
| Cash for coffee machine | Taxable value | Taxable value | 10.2% charge |
| Non-cash voucher | Cost to employer | Cost to employer | No charge if cannot be surrendered for cash, usually |
| Cash vouchers | Cost to employer | Cost to employer | 10.2% charge only if turned to cash by surrender |
| Transport vouchers, season tickets | Cost to employer | Cost to employer | No charge if cannot be surrendered for cash, usually. Some are, though, if PAYE on this amount |
| Payment of employees' personal liabilities | Cost to employer | Cost to employer | Liable to NIC at 10.2% |
| Mileage allowances | Taxable if in excess of business expenditure or tax-free rates | Same as for director | Chargeable if in excess of AA/FPCS rates |
| Medical insurance | Cost to employer | No charge | No charge |
| Mobile phones and fixed car phones, unless refund personal use | Fixed taxable value of £200 | No charge | 10.2% |
| Mortgage – low interest or interest free | Taxable values less tax reliefs if loan qualifies | Same as for directors; same possibility of no charge depending on circumstances | No charge to NIC |

| Loans written off | Tax liability at value | Tax liability at value | 10.2% chargeable |
|---|---|---|---|
| Petrol for private use in company car | Taxable value of scale charge | Tax payable on scale charge unless directly provided by employer | 10.2% chargeable |
| Relocation allowances | Taxable value | Taxable value | 10.2% chargeable |
| Removal expenses over £8,000 | Cost to employer of £8,000 | Cost to employer over £8,000 | 10.2% chargeable |
| Scholarships for children where no trust fund | Cost to employer | No charge | 10.2% chargeable |
| Scholarship and apprenticeship schemes for above £7,000 and other conditions | Taxable benefit above that current at cost to employer | Same as director | 10.2% chargeable |
| Season ticket loans above £5,000 | Taxable on the full amount of all loans | No charge | No charge |
| Unapproved benefit schemes such as FURBS | Value of benefit | No charge unless the benefit takes the employee over £8,500 | No charge |
| Executive sports and health clubs memberships (limited) | Taxable value or cost to employer | No charge | No charge |
| Staff suggestion scheme payments of over £5,000 | Taxable value on difference | Taxable value on difference | 10.2% chargeable |
| Excessive training costs | Individually assessed | Individually assessed | 10.2% chargeable if allowances |
| Legal, financial services and other benefits advice paid for | Taxable benefit | No charge | 10.2% chargeable benefit in kind |
| Council tax payment | Cost to employer | No charge | 10.2% chargeable |

Some things are benefits in kind and chargeable as such to income tax and/or NIC. However, other 'benefits' such as the grant or exercise of non-approved share options will give rise to a tax charge payable on any profit or gain arising. These types of 'benefits' have not been included as 'perks' or 'fringe benefits' as the charge to tax does not usually arise unless a specific event happens.

## STRATEGY #279
## Make good benefits in kind for previous years

If the employee has been taxed on the benefit in kind in previous years and now wishes to personally pay for the private use of that benefit, there is no time limit for doing so.

Further remuneration could be taken before the year's assessment is determined and used to make good benefits provided in earlier years. This is something which could be done if outstanding penalties and interest from prior years' incorrect returns are outstanding (because of incorrect past reporting of benefits).

---

### STRATEGY #280
### Make assets available for employees to use, then write them off

---

The tax charge to employees where assets are made available for use by the business is only 20% per year. Once the asset has depreciated in value sufficiently, the market value of the depreciated asset will become the tax charge if given to the employee and written off. The employee ends up with an asset (which has cost the employee a negligible amount) for which he had full use and enjoyment and then he or she gets to keep it. Alternatively, replace the old asset and continue to write it off at 20% of its market value. Remember, the only cash outflow for the employee is the tax on the 20% valuation each year.

---

### STRATEGY #281
### Employees may gain significantly by making their own contributions towards the cost for private usage of company assets

---

It may pay the employee to make a contribution for private use to avoid all tax charges, for example with company cars. This would reduce the assessable benefit on a pound for pound basis.

In respect of the list price of company cars, the employee can contribute towards the cost of the car subject to a maximum deduction of £5,000.

---

### STRATEGY #282
### If the employee wishes to have a more expensive car, pay the maximum allowable contribution then reduce the annual payments

---

It would not pay the employee to reduce the list price beyond £5,000, the maximum deduction allowable. Because of this (cars are taxed on the list price of the car when first registered, not on its cost) if the car is under four years old, it would pay the employee to make annual payments instead in return for being allowed to use the car for private purposes.

---

### STRATEGY #283
### Make sure that company car mileages are maximised for lower scale charges

---

If the company car completes 2,500 business miles per annum or more, then the assessable benefit is reduced by one third. Where it is 18,000 miles or more per annum, then it is reduced by another one third, thus making it a two thirds reduction. These levels of reduction apply from the 1994/95 tax years onwards. Prior to that (1993/94) there was an increase by 50% in scale charges for less than 2,500 business miles a year.

In addition, if the car is four years or older at the end of the tax year, then a further one third is reduced.

---

### STRATEGY #284
### Keep a logbook for all employees to ensure exact business and personal mileages are made

---

Apart from good bookkeeping practice, these logbooks are useful to save the company extra NIC1A – National Insurance contributions collections on company car and fuel benefits at 10.2% for private usage, as well as additional VAT in respect of the fuel used for private mileage.

If the DSS does not have actual figures, it will assume private usage. The increased costs to any business with a large fleet of cars used by employees can be enormous.

It may be better for private usage to be covered by the employee in full, thus avoiding further NICs payable by the employer.

---

### STRATEGY #285
### Operate company cars without taxes payable

---

This may seem like a tall order. However, by using vehicles aged four years and older and ensuring business mileage of 18,000 miles and more, the total paid could reduce substantially.

Take the example of a car costing £12,000:

If it was four years old or more, doing a business mileage of over 18,000 miles a year:

| | |
|---|---|
| Price of car | £12,000 |
| 35% × £12,000 | £4,200 |
| Reduce by ⅔ for 18,000 miles | (£2,800) |
| | £1,400 |
| Reduce by ⅓ age allowance (4 years) | (£467) |
| | £933 |
| Less employee contribution for private use | (£600) |
| Taxable benefit | £333 |
| Tax payable at 40% | £133.20 |
| Tax payable at 25% | £83.25 |
| Total employee outlay: 40% | £733.20 |
| Total employee outlay: 25% | £683.25 |

If the car was new, doing a business mileage of 8,000 miles a year:

| | |
|---|---|
| Price of car | £12,000 |
| 35% × £12,000 | £4,200 |
| Less employee contribution | (£600) |
| Taxable benefit | £3,600 |
| Tax payable at 40% | £1,440 |
| Tax payable at 25% | £900 |
| Total employee outlay: 40% | £2,040 |
| Total employee outlay: 25% | £1,500 |

---

## STRATEGY #286
## Use expert advice for massive savings on company car benefits

---

Savings can be made for both employers and employees if the correct planning and costing mechanisms are put into place early enough. For example, NIC1A is a tax paid by the employer on the scale charges on the value of company cars and fuel provided to staff at 10.2% (in 1995/96). Much of this can be avoided by using logbooks and employee contributions.

The cost, list price and type of vehicles used are important and how they are used in the business is vital to reduce tax charges.

Many firms of accountants have software programmes indicating the best usage of company cars and whether additional cash should be given to the employee to purchase his own car and run it, or whether the business should do so. Whilst more freedom may be given to the employee, there are also other factors to take into account, such as image of the company; effect on other benefits, such as pensions from increased salary; reimbursement of expenses for business mileage; fleet discounts not being available to employees individually, and so on.

The area is a complicated one and calculations need to be considered from both the employee and the employer to get to a net benefit position. The employer can help with increased salaries, provision of cheap or interest-free loans, reimbursement of expenses for business mileage, help with contacts for better deals, and so on.

It may mean a careful balance of company car (or lower grade cars provided by the employer), with mileage allowances and personal contributions for private usage. Financial modelling is required to consider all the possible variables.

---

### STRATEGY #287
### Keep records to substantiate claims for entertainment and other allowances

---

A travelling and subsistence allowance will count as the taxable income of the director or employee. A tax deduction may be claimed for any part of the allowance shown to have been expended for business purposes.

To substantiate claims for tax deductions, a record-keeping system is vital. It may be better not to have the allowance, but to reimburse the director or employee directly for business expenditure to avoid benefit-in-kind taxation.

Reimbursements or round-sum allowances for entitlement are disallowed as a tax deduction to the employer. However, the employee may claim a P11D deduction for expenditure for genuine business purposes. Yet, if the allowance was not specifically for entertaining, the employer would get the corporate tax deduction. However, the employee would not get a deduction for entertaining, only any other business expenditure.

---

### STRATEGY #288
### Make maximum use of beneficial loans

---

In the 1995/96 tax year loans may be made interest-free to individual employees of up to £5,000. This is in addition to loans which qualify for tax relief such as loans of up to £30,000 for house purchase.

In other words, the employee can be given company money as a benefit, free of any taxes. Usually there is a charge for directors and PIID employees on the annual value of beneficial loan arrangements. The taxable portion of the loan would be the official Inland Revenue rate of interest (say 7.5%) less what the employee pays, say 2%, making 5.5% the interest rate chargeable to tax.

For example:

Amount borrowed: £10,000 at 2% annual interest (£200).
The official rate is, say, 7.5%. The loan will be taxed on interest of (7.5%-2% = 5.5%).

$$5.5\% \times £10,000 = £550 \text{ (taxable benefit)}$$
$$\text{Tax on } £550 \text{ at } 40\%: £220$$
$$\text{at } 25\%: £137.50$$

Even though the loan is a benefit to the employee, for £420 cash outlay (interest of 2% plus tax payable) he or she has the benefit of £10,000. The amount payable each year until the loan is repaid is the actual interest plus the difference between the Inland Revenue official interest rate and the amount of interest paid. The total payable of £420 represents interest of 4.2% for a higher rate taxpayer and 3.37% for a basic rate taxpayer on an outlay of £337.

Non-PIID directors or employees would have no tax charge arising; nor would PIID directors where the loans totalled less than £5,000 (although watch out for Companies Act contraventions). There are further exemptions which apply – for example, where the loan is for the payment of inheritance tax or capital gains tax, or to buy a life annuity for someone aged over 65.

There is a tax charge if the loan is written off, as well as NIC payable, since the loan then becomes 'earnings'. However, if the employee dies and the loan is forgiven, no tax charge arises.

---

## STRATEGY #289
**Make maximum use of foreign travel – benefits in respect of foreign travel may be tax-free, even for your spouse – so long as properly minuted and documented**

---

Overseas travel expenses are usually deemed to have been 'necessarily' incurred in performing business duties and no benefit in kind should arise. However, where there is a dual purpose, such as a holiday at the end of a business trip, then the element would be a taxable benefit in kind.

If a spouse accompanies a director or employee and the employer pays all of the expenses, then a benefit in kind may be assessed on some or all of the expense if not seen to be necessary for business purposes.

However, where the board of directors minute their decision that the director or employee be accompanied by a spouse or family member, it may satisfy the Inland Revenue that no benefit in kind arises. It will also be necessary to show that the spouse or other relative was able to perform certain tasks which could not be performed by the employee or director.

This may be the ability to speak a foreign language, or if the director or employee was in poor health and required assistance.

All receipts should be kept and records substantiated. Where the employee may be able to get entertainment expenses which are not added to his or her tax liability, these will not be allowable to the company as a business expense.

---

### STRATEGY #290
### Examine tax avoidance schemes for legal minimisation of taxes

---

Tax avoidance is legitimate practice, tax evasion is not. If a benefit can be obtained tax-free, then the employer should carefully consider this aspect. Some benefits are not subject to tax in any event, being specifically excluded by the legislation, such as pension contributions, profit-related pay, parking, sick pay insurance costs and so on.

There are, generally speaking, two immediate kinds of taxes to pay on earnings. The first is income tax, the second is National Insurance contributions (NIC). Some employee benefits and benefits in kind do not incur NIC, either because the benefit is exempt, or it does not fit into any general category for NIC.

Class 1 National Insurance contributions are payable on earnings, which generally means on money paid to an employee. Contributions are also due on benefits in kind which can be turned into cash by surrender (but not by sale) such as premium bonds. So if the employer pays the employee his wages in premium bonds or vouchers changeable for cash, then income tax is payable on the benefit, as well as NIC. If the item has to be sold first, then it is usually not liable to NIC contributions. If the employer purchases the asset (such as a car) and gives it to the employee, then no NIC is payable, although the value of the car will suffer income tax.

Both employees and employers pay Class 1 National Insurance contributions. Whilst that paid by employees is limited in respect of earnings to £2,042.56 in 1995/96, the NIC for employers has no upper limit. Employers will pay NIC at 10.2% on all assessable benefits. For example, if a director is paid a bonus of £100,000, then the company has to pay NIC of £10,200.

The saving of NIC is therefore a big issue and has spawned a large industry of tax advisers. Basically, if the benefit is subject to PAYE, it will be subject to NIC. The real challenge over the years has been to reward employees with bonuses and benefits-in-kind which do not attract NIC. Better still is if there is no NIC and no P11D benefit to pay either.

Whilst it all comes down to a definition of what is and what is not 'pay', there are traps and pitfalls to be wary of. Some benefits are chargeable, depending on how they are provided. Take, for instance, the case where the company contracts directly with the supplier, for example by paying the employee's home telephone bill or by buying a season ticket. In both of those cases, no NIC is payable. However, there will be a benefit-in-kind income tax charge for a P11D director.

The government has become increasingly frustrated with methods of paying or rewarding employees. As a consequence they have done two things:

1. Brought the benefit into the PAYE net as opposed to merely a P11D benefit.

2. Extended the definition of pay specifically to include benefits in the form of gilt-edged securities, shares, debentures, units in unit trusts, national savings certificates, options, futures, gold bars and bullion, fine wines, premium bonds, assets exchangeable for cash, commodities, assets traded on a recognised investment exchange and vouchers to obtain any of the above assets (but not vouchers which cannot be exchanged for cash or a mixture of goods and cash).

Whilst this is the present position, there are a number of NIC avoidance schemes, which enable lump sums to be paid to or for employees, which avoid NIC. Some of these also happen to avoid P11D benefits.

---

## STRATEGY #291
## Investigate the use of NIC avoidance schemes for wealth-creation

---

The objective is usually to provide a tax deductible benefit to the business, whilst incurring no other tax liabilities. The benefit is usually subject to income tax in the hands of the employee, but NIC is saved at

10.2%. The employee now has an asset which may be kept or sold. If sold, it is usually to repay debt or for further investment purposes, including geared pension arrangements.

## STRATEGY #292
## Choose the level of risk which the employer is willing to accept

The level of risk is the risk of being investigated by the Inland Revenue, the DSS and Customs and Excise (for VAT). The 'better' the avoidance scheme, the greater the chances of investigation.

An acceptable level of risk may be paying bonuses in a different 'non-pay' form with NIC savings only, but the risk levels will increase if the scheme includes saving corporate NIC as well as PIID benefit-in-kind taxation. Saving NIC would excite the DSS, saving PIID would ignite the Inland Revenue.

Yet this is a corporate decision and the majority of businesses have practised one form or another of it for years. It is a principle of UK law that one can do anything legal to save tax. Unable to rule on the legality of the schemes in question, the government merely takes the benefit into the tax net in the future.

The one area, however, which it would find most difficult to do anything about is where the company makes a payment into trust for future employee benefits or retirement benefits. The payment is tax deductible to the company. There is no NIC payable because no employees are mentioned; there is no PIID benefit either as no taxable benefit has vested. The employee has access to the benefits on offer as well as investments.

NIC avoidance schemes are alternative vehicles to pension arrangements for the creation of wealth outside the business. Even the payment of dividends by a company could be a conscious attempt to avoid the payment of NIC through additional remuneration – a perfectly legal way, though, of redistributing money from the business. Other methods of using investments instead of pay as a bonus will avoid NIC, so long as they have not been specifically legislated against.

---

**STRATEGY #293**
**Take out an investigations insurance policy to be on the safe side**

---

This type of policy will cover the costs to a business of DSS, Inland Revenue, Customs and Excise and other investigations (which any business stands a one in three chance of having, in any event). It usually costs from about £250 a year and covers fees in legal and accounting work to rebut investigations of up to £60,000 worth of fees.

This type of insurance cover is a sensible precaution if engaged in tax saving activities.

---

**STRATEGY #294**
**If not happy with any NIC or tax saving scheme, obtain professional advice first**

---

Professional advice may mean taking counsel's opinion, or clearing things with the DSS or Inland Revenue first. In any event, the business's accountants should be involved in this part of your strategy planning.

The offering of benefits in cash or kind has profound financial and corporate implications for the business. It does involve including employees in the decision-making process, but will be more applicable to directors and employees with higher earnings wishing to limit their tax liability. At the same time the employer will strive to make the employee benefit programme tax-efficient as well as cost-efficient.

## Key points summary

- A thorough overview is given of the tax-free and taxable benefits in kind available.

- The process is described of how the employer interacts with the employee in establishing need requirements and controlling costs.

- Strategies are given to reduce taxes and National Insurance contributions, which increases money available for wealth-creation.

CHAPTER 18

# Use the Business to Create Big Tax Deductions

*My rule always was to do the business of the day in the day.*
**Duke of Wellington (1769–1852)**

**Objective: To create tax deductible benefits for business owners and employees**

Given the choice of enriching the Inland Revenue's coffers or your own, the natural instinctive reaction is to do whatever you can to keep more of what you have whilst capitalising on what is available to you. The practice of wealth-creation applies equally to business owners as it does to employees in the business. Everyone will try to get the best deal for themselves. In the final analysis, people work to retire – to make enough so that they do not have to work again.

The key to personal enrichment is the business itself. It is the power-house which will make all things possible, provided it recognises the aspirations of the business owners *and* the employees in the business. Some do and some don't – after all, employee expenditure saved means greater profits for the business owners. Having said that, most businesses recognise the need to have reward and recognition structures in place, as well as adequate remuneration policies for their employees.

After all, the management wants a happy and contented workforce, striving to increase performance, so that profits continually increase.

The biggest expenditure for people during their lifetime is not paying off the home, or educating the children, but paying taxes. In fact, up to 70% or more of your income goes out in taxes of some kind or another – income taxes, VAT, road taxes, council taxes, capital gains taxes, inheritance taxes, stamp duty and the like. Tax planning is big business. It supports an army of accountants, tax preparers, financial advisers and tax planners, all with one aim in mind – the reduction or elimination of taxes within the law. What you end up with eventually will be the direct result of your effective tax-reducing strategies not your income or investments.

Your tax plan will turn usual expenditures into tax-deductible items. It can also be incorporated with what the business gives you or allows you to have. To increase the individual's net disposable income or take-home pay need not cost the business any more. All that is required of the business management is an open mind and the ability to co-operate with the people in the business. It is your duty to yourself to pay as little tax as possible. It is also your right to construct your own tax-reducing plan and to implement it.

---

## STRATEGY #295
## Develop your personal tax-reducing plan

---

The tax system works on the basis of taxing not your total income, but the amount of income left after all deductions and allowances have been taken off. It is supposed to operate without conscience and to be applied fairly. How is it, then, that half a dozen individuals, each earning exactly the same, will pay different amounts of tax? Some may pay thousands of pounds; others will pay nothing at all. The key lies in re-arranging your affairs in such a way that all legal deductions are utilised so that you pay less in taxes. This is your right.

What you cannot do is to claim deductions to which you are not entitled or not declare all of your income. This is tax evasion and is most severely dealt with by the tax authorities. However, tax avoidance is perfectly permissible. Your tax avoidance plan will enable you to reduce your taxes by 50% or more, year after year.

## STRATEGY #296
## Determine if the business can take over some of your expenditures

There are certain employee benefits which can be purchased more cheaply through the business, than if you, as an individual, were to pay for them yourself.

These are mainly:

- life assurance
- income protection or permanent health insurance (PHI)
- critical illness benefits
- private medical insurance
- disability insurance coverages
- car insurance
- pension benefits
- health and protection benefits generally

The reason for this is that exactly the same benefits can be purchased in bulk by the business for a group of employees, creating cost savings. As a result, the risk is spread, but also the cost reduces because of lower charges and costings of the benefit. If the employee paid for the benefit provided by the company, the company would only have the cost of administering the benefit. Yet the savings to the employee could be substantial.

Take, for example, Jill Harris, a 45-year-old business executive, who has been paying for the following benefits personally. Compare her individual costs with the costs of purchasing *exactly the same* benefits through the business:

|  | Individual costs (p.m.) £ | Using the business (p.m.) £ |
|---|---|---|
| Life cover | 47 | 3.5 |
| PHI | 120 | 4 |
| Critical illness | 40 | 3.75 |
| Private medical insurance | 52 | 20 |
| Disability cover | 15 | 2 |
| Car insurance | 35 | 19 |
| TOTALS PER MONTH | £309 | £52.25 |

When the personal expenditures were 'transferred' to the business, then savings of £256.75 resulted in Jill's case. In addition, if the business was paying for these costs, most of them would be tax deductible to it. The net cost (after tax relief) would be below £40 for the business to supply these benefits. Yet Jill would have to earn (if a higher rate taxpayer) £772 before tax just to meet these expenditures individually!

In this case, the business has been used to increase Jill's net disposable income by over £3,000 a year. This saving could be used for additional pension contributions. Pension contributions create tax deductions individually, creating further savings of £400 for every £1,000 spent in Jill's case on pension funding.

Note that, of the above items, it is likely that only the car insurance will be added back as a benefit-in-kind for individual tax purposes.

---

### STRATEGY #297
### Use the business to create tax-free income of at least £4,000

---

Under the profit-related pay rules, a business with an Inland Revenue approved profit-related pay scheme can give tax-free pay to employees. This is based on a formula of the lower of 20% of pay, £4,000 or actual profit-related pay. In financial terms, this is worth an extra £1,600 to a higher-rate taxpayer and £1,000 a year to a basic rate taxpayer.

As all businesses must have the intention to create profits (or they would be out of business), they have nothing to lose (except the set-up costs) by implementing a profit-related pay scheme.

---

### STRATEGY #298
### Use profit-related pay for further tax deductions

---

The employee, better off as a result of profit-related pay tax-free income, can now create a further deduction from taxable income by investing in plans which are, in turn, tax deductible.

The most obvious choice is to maximise pension contributions, relievable from taxable earnings at your highest rate of tax. Alternatively, you may prefer an investment in a qualifying enterprise investment scheme company (EIS) for relief from your actual tax liability at the lowest rate (20% in 1995/96).

The double gearing effect of profit-related pay and pension contribution deductions means that the Inland Revenue will have totally funded your pension contribution and further rewarded you for allowing them to do so.

The position gets even better if, as a taxpayer, your income is usually at the higher rate, but profit-related pay and pension contributions reduce it to the basic rate of tax. This would generate a further tax saving of 15% on the income which was reduced to the basic rate.

| | |
|---|---|
| Salary | £28,000 (40%) |
| Profit-related pay | (£4,000) |
| Personal allowance | (£3,525) |
| Pension contribution | (£1,600) |
| Taxable income | £18,875 (25%) |

The difference in tax rates as a result of the combined effects of profit-related pay and the pension contribution (which at £1,600 is the tax saving on £4,000) is 15% (40%-25%). Without profit-related pay and the pension contribution, the tax rate would have been at its highest level (40%). With it, total taxable income in this case drops by about 20%, disregarding the personal allowance. What is more, the pension contribution has not cost you a penny!

---

## STRATEGY #299
## Use the business for perks and fringe benefits, many of them tax-free

---

Remuneration packages can be designed in such a way that they not only include salary, but other benefits as well (see Chapter 17). The cost to the business is the same, but the benefits to the employees are greater than if salary alone was given. This is particularly the case if the benefit or perk is tax-free or if the tax value added back to income is less than if salary only was received. This is shown as follows:

| | Individual package | | Cost to company |
|---|---|---|---|
| 1. Salary | £50,000 | | £50,000 |
| (net after-tax income) | £35,215 | Tax £14,785 | |
| 2. Salary | £30,000 | | £50,000 |
| Tax-free perks | £10,000 | | |
| Taxable perks/benefits | £10,000 | | |
| (net after-tax income) | £19,215 cash | Tax £10,785 | |
| | + perks of £20,000 | | |

Both packages carry equal pension benefits. The employee will decide if it is better value to take only salary and to buy individual benefits, including a company car, or whether it is a better deal to have the package of benefits from the company, which include a company car. Taxable perks or fringe benefits may not be added back at the full value. For example, 35% of the list price of the company car (if under four years old) is added back each year. The value of the total benefit package would have to be greater than that of salary alone. As shown earlier, the cost of purchasing individual health, protection and other benefits can be at least five times greater than if 'purchased' through the business.

---

## STRATEGY #300
## Get your personal assets tax deductible

---

Using the strategies in Chapter 22, by starting your own business from home, or as an employee working from home, you can achieve large tax deductions and allowances on your personal assets used in the new business.

Allowances for the purchase of computers, cars, fax machines, audio visual equipment and recreational assets, such as boats and aeroplanes will all be deductible from your income. Expenses, such as a proportion of rent, mortgage, heating costs, lights, water and other utilities, employing the spouse, and other business expenses are all deductible to you, if properly structured for personal business and tax reasons.

---

## STRATEGY #301
## Don't only make tax-motivated decisions – be commercial and benefit-oriented

---

Not all benefits are tax deductible. If you only plan around tax decisions you may never realise your overall goal of maximum wealth-creation. Some investments are not tax deductible, but they do grow free of taxes or capital gains – such as personal equity plans. Your personal risk preferences may be more cautious and in certain instances you may be weighted towards taxable, more secure investments, such as building society fixed deposits. Every individual will have a different plan of action and a different route to realising his or her goals.

Set your investment and retirement goals and plan your funding levels to get there. If you only invest in tax deductible investments, such as pensions, remember that there are also tax restrictions when you come to take your benefits. For example, the maximum pension which you can fund for is two-thirds of final salary (which is capped at £78,600 in 1995/96), after 40 years of service. Most people who rely on pensions alone will retire on less than 50% of their final salaries. Yet, what they actually want and need is 100% of final salary.

There is a danger of only planning around tax-based decisions and investments. For maximum wealth-creation, what is required is a bene-fit goal, not a tax goal. Reducing taxes will give you the extra income to make other investments to reach your benefit goal.

---

## STRATEGY #302
## Make loans to employees to enable them to increase their wealth

---

An employer may now make loans of up to £5,000 to employees, interest-free and with no benefit-in-kind taxation payable by the employee on the loan. If the loan is written off, then this becomes a tax-able event, even if the employee has ceased to be employed by the business [Taxes Act 1988, section 160].

The employee could use the loan to pay off debts, for investment pur-poses or to redeem part of the capital on a mortgage, thus saving thousands of pounds of future interest payments. He or she could also make tax deductible pension payments or investments, thus generating the ability (in taxes saved) to repay 25 to 40% of the loan within 12 months.

---

## STRATEGY #303
## Pay interest on director's loan accounts

---

A director's loan account is sterile money. It does not grow, and more often than not, interest is not paid to the director for leaving his money in the business. It is also at risk of total loss, should the business cease to exist.

Directors are rewarded in many ways – salary, perks, fringe benefits, dividends. Dividends are paid from after-tax income, which includes Advance Corporation Tax (ACT) and Corporation Tax. Dividend pay-ments are not tax deductible to the company. However, interest payments are, and it would pay the business to make deductible loan interest payments and the director to receive them. If the director's loan account could be replaced with other financing, the director could

invest this for capital growth. A £50,000 directors' loan account, if
invested at 10% growth over ten years would amount to £129,687!

---

### STRATEGY #304
## Decide on whether to take salary or dividends

---

Taking salary or extra salary by way of bonus payments must be viewed
against taking dividends. Salary is a tax deductible item in the business; dividends are not. Salary is a before-tax payment; dividends are
an after-tax payment. However, no National Insurance contributions
are payable on dividends, as they are on salary. Taking extra salary may
mean a stronger base to take into account when making pension contributions: the higher the salary, the more the contributions to pension
funding made by the business.

From the company's point of view, savings can be made by paying
dividends. These savings are National Insurance and increased pension
costs. However, as pension costs are tax deductible (as are some
National Insurances – Class 4 at 50%), these costs are marginalised to
some extent. Dividends may be irregular, but salary becomes expected,
which could cause cash flow problems in the future.

The one advantage with dividends is that they can be streamed and
paid to the shareholder. This is a way to get income paid to a spouse or
other family relative who may hold shares, with a lower tax rate (even
though there is a tax credit on dividends at 20%, higher-rate taxpayers
will pay more).

For some companies, the debate is academic only – not all directors
or employees hold shares, so dividends may be out of the question.
There is a combination of salary and pension contributions, covered in
Chapter 17, which far outweigh the payment of dividends.

---

### STRATEGY #305
## Buy more shares to increase your wealth

---

Emerging UK companies, mostly unquoted, which have come through
one of the biggest recessions in history, show a form of business
resilience which is to be admired. These are the companies which will
give dynamic growth in the future, with venture capital returns. A venture capitalist investing in a company like this would seek a return of
at least 30 to 40% a year in growth of share values.

Growth companies which eventually list on the Stock Exchange can
bring large returns to investors.

If you're working in the business and can see its potential, try to buy shares from the business owners. This is often best set up by having an employee share owner trust (ESOT) to purchase shares from the company for the benefit of employees.

Linking profit-related pay to the ESOT can produce the means of payment for the shares. Any dividends earned will then be for the benefit of the shareholders.

Employees will also feature in the plans of the business owners wishing to sell up and retire. By selling to management (and employees) – a management buyout – the business owners have created a market for their own shares. It makes sense to begin the share purchase route relatively early, to get employees used to the concept of share ownership and earning dividends.

The business can also give share options to enable employees to become stakeholders as well as future owners of the business. The better they perform, the better the share option deal.

---

### STRATEGY #306
### Partnerships should create artificial share option schemes to motivate employees

---

Partnerships don't have shares, so their employees cannot share in the growth and performance of the business. Well, they can – but only through bonuses, not shares.

To give employees a stake in the business, set up a phantom share scheme. Call it the Business Partnership Share Scheme. Each year the partners decide how much of the profits will go to employees. By using profit-related pay and personal investments such as PEPS within the share scheme, the employee will have a scheme linked to the stock market but reflecting the growth of the Business Partnership. This is a powerful motivating tool with no tax consequences for the employee. He gets tax-free pay and investments which grow tax-free.

---

### STRATEGY #307
### Use the business to reduce personal outgoings

---

The marginal cost to the business of providing tax-deductible benefits is lower than the marginal cost of the employee or director paying for benefits from non-deductible after-tax income.

If the business can subsidise mortgage and school fee payments, pay for fringe benefits such as accommodation, attendance at conferences and holidays, cars and other leisure assets, then this is a cash flow saving to the employee or director. There may well be an add-back for tax purposes, but it will always be cheaper to pay the tax than pay for the benefit individually out of after-tax earnings.

In this way, businesses can assist in wealth-creation by employees by freeing assets which would otherwise have been spent. Those can now be invested by or for the employee.

---

### STRATEGY #308
### Use the business for big tax deductions

---

You get the benefits, the business gets the deductions. If the employee provided his own benefits, the only deductions available to most are pension contributions. Every other payment made (unless in the course of business) is not deductible. Naturally there are exceptions such as those allowances conceded by the Inland Revenue over the years – but again linked to being 'necessarily' incurred for employment purposes.

The situation is different for the business. There are very few disallowable expenditures (such as business entertaining), most expenditures for the employee or for the business being tax allowable or deductible. Where the employee can derive some personal use from business assets there can be a tax charge if you are an employee earning over £8,500 a year or if a director, or connected through shareholdings. Many employees can use the company's assets free of any taxes. Others will be taxed on the benefit as a benefit in kind.

Business and work should also be about enjoyment and fun. Try it some time – you may get to like it!

### Key points summary

- Tax deductible benefits can be created for business owners and employees.

- However, don't lose sight of the commercial and economic aspects as opposed to a total preoccupation with tax reliefs. Don't be totally tax driven.

- Business and personal tax reduction strategies can save thousands of pounds and these savings are shown in this chapter. You can increase your take-home pay by a *minimum* of 20%.

# CHAPTER 19

# Reduce the Cost of Working Capital

*Economy is going without something you do
want in case you should, some day, want
something you probably won't want.*
**Anthony Hope (1863–1933)** *The Dolly
Dialogues* (1894)

**Objective: To reduce the cost of working capital and to improve
cash flow whilst accomplishing business objectives**

Companies are best judged by their liquidity. If they don't have available funds, in the form of cash or facilities (such as overdrafts)
available, then they may have difficulty in meeting their debts as they
come due. In fact, a business with a positive net value could be techni-
cally insolvent. By July of 1995, borrowings by small to medium-sized
business had dropped from 51.5% of funds employed to 35%.
Businesses on the whole are either getting stronger or making greater
use of equity, reducing their reliance on borrowings from banks.

The continuous flow of cash to any business is its lifeblood. Without
it, it's as a car without petrol – nothing wrong with the car – it just can't
go anywhere.

---

### STRATEGY #309
## Determine where the business cash comes from

---

Business cash can come from many sources

- retained profits from trading
- shareholders' capital
- sale of assets
- sales of new shares
- trading income, sale of stock
- directors' loans
- loans from directors' pension funds
- bank loans
- overdrafts
- investment income
- lines of credit (but not counted as cash)

The most important source is trading profit. If the business cannot generate cash flow from its internal activities, it will fail. There is only a limited supply of cash from other sources, and this is usually depleted quickly unless regularly topped-up. If the business coffers run dry, then illiquidity of the business, coupled with the inability to pay debts, is all that is required to face bankruptcy. These aspects are largely covered in Chapters 3 and 6.

This chapter is largely concerned with reducing the costs of working capital to the business, whilst fulfilling the business's overall objectives.

*Working capital* is usually defined as the surplus of current assets over current liabilities. Current assets (usually trading stock and debtors) are constantly converted into cash to pay current liabilities.

Example of current assets are:

- Stocks of raw materials
- Debtors
- Investments (short-term)
- Cash at bank and in hand
- Pre-paid expenses
- Work in progress and finished goods in stock

Current liabilities include the amounts falling due to the creditors within one year.

By reducing cash expenditures and the cost of using cash, more is available for the business, thus reducing pressure for funds from other sources. The fact of the matter is that either the business directly supplies the cash from current assets, or it engages in external debt funding. The most common source for the latter is by way of bank overdrafts and loans, both of which have interest costs and must be repaid.

Essentially then, solutions are sought to improve the flow of cash in and out and around the business, by making use of legitimate processes and schemes. Many of these use acceptable Inland Revenue tax reducing methods resulting in less being paid out in taxes and more cash thus being available for other things. Our overall objective is to free the cash flow.

---

## STRATEGY #310
## Outline the business objectives which need to be implemented with a cash or cost requirement

---

The corporate objectives may comprise the following:

- increase in pension funding
- implement employee benefit programme
- implement directors' benefit programme
- bonus payments as initiative and performance awards to executives
- purchase of premises
- investments of surplus funds
- marketability of company shares
- employee and director share schemes
- employee incentivisation schemes
- building of corporate image and profile
- happy and contented workforce
- protection of the business – Keyperson provision
- arranging of new capital or loans for new production processes and other areas
- new marketing initiatives
- reduction of corporate tax liabilities

The above objectives may fail to be implemented for lack of planning as well as insufficient funding. However, most objectives can be achieved with proper structuring.

---

### STRATEGY #311
## Establish the extent of creditworthiness of the business and its sources of funds

---

Once the business has established the costs of implementation of its objectives, it will then seek to establish its financial position (now and in the future) to service the implementation of its objectives.

All of this will come down to cash flow and whether it is in surplus or requires funding. Eliminating or reducing costs will also positively affect this outcome (see Chapters 3–6).

---

### STRATEGY #312
## Use the ESOT (ESOPS) model to reduce the cost of working capital and achieve other business objectives

---

Employee share owner participation schemes (ESOPS) or trusts (ESOTs) mean different things to different people.

**To the business they mean:**

- a lock-in and retention of employees/managers
- happy and contented workforce owning a stake in the business
- a way of introducing new, cheaper and tax-efficient capital into the business
- a means to obtain present and future marketability of shares
- a means to guarantee the sale or transfer of new or existing shares in the business
- an investment of surplus funds (if available)
- arrangement of new capital, or replacing older, expensive capital with newer, cheaper capital
- a reduction of corporate tax liabilities
- provision of share schemes for workers

**To the employee they mean:**

- a stake in the business
- a method of obtaining shares without having to pay hard cash for them now
- a later funding method without personal outlay to pay for shares
- a future income stream from dividends
- recognition as a valued employee

- a share in the production of the result of his or her labour
- a means to build wealth

The ESOT is an employee share owner trust, set up by the company for the benefit of its employees.

To date, businesses have only seen it as such. However, it is also one of the most dynamic working capital funding devices.

There are two types of ESOTs, a statutory one (where the rules governing the scheme are legislated for, governed by the Finance Act 1989) and a case law ESOT, where tax reliefs apply as a result of legal precedents and legal principles enshrined in our law.

The words 'ESOT' and 'ESOPS' are largely interchangeable and 'ESOT' will be used here.

---

**STRATEGY #313**
## Understand the cash flow inherent in the ESOT arrangement

---

STEP 1

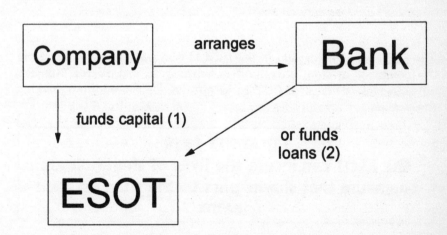

The company arranges funding of capital from a bank or uses its own funds to fund the ESOT at a minimum of 10% of its shares by value. This process may be repeated as often as required.

Capital funded is *tax deductible* to the company. Interest payable is *tax deductible* to the company. Either the company or the ESOT may service the loan.

STEP 2

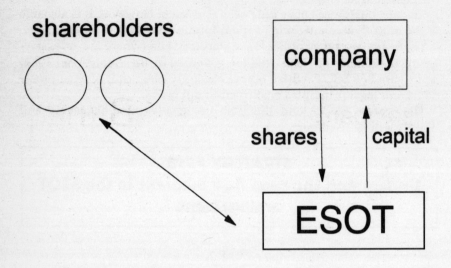

The ESOT uses the capital in the trust to purchase shares either from the company or from shareholders wishing to sell shares. Special, advantageous deferral of CGT rules applies for shareholders making these sales.

---

### STRATEGY #314
### The ESOT can insure the lives of shareholders to ensure that shares pass to the trust on their deaths

---

The trustees of the ESOT can effect a life policy and pay the premiums. On the death of the shareholder, the ESOT receives the proceeds from the policy which it then pays to the estate of the deceased, in exchange for shares.

 The arrangement can be formalised in a unilateral sale of share agreement or in conjunction with existing double option or Buy and Sell arrangements. As the trust cannot sell the shares, the agreement will be one-sided.

## STRATEGY #315
## The company uses the new working capital to repay the bank or as additional cash in the business

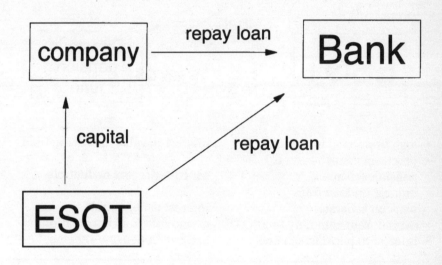

Either the ESOT or the company can repay the loan and service the loan debt. Most of the main clearing banks have a specialised ESOTs' lending department to assist businesses with their funding requirements.

## STRATEGY #316
## Achieve double gearing on tax deductibility by using a loan from a director's pension fund

So long as the loan is used for genuine commercial purposes, there should be no problem in its usage. The company borrows from the bank and uses the funds borrowed within the business. It may make pension contributions to a director-only pension scheme. If the pension scheme is a new one then there is a two-year waiting period for a borrowing requirement of 50% (25% if less than two years). The company then borrows cash from the pension fund to fund the ESOT.

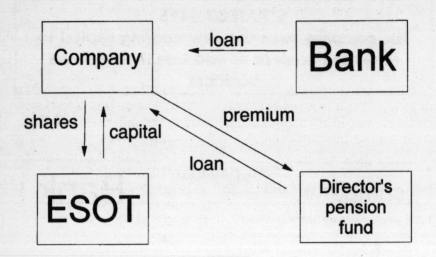

- loan from bank to company:     interest payable and deductible
- premium contribution to
  pension scheme:     contribution tax deductible
- interest on loan from
  pension scheme:     interest is deductible
- capital from company to ESOT:     deductible from corporation tax
- interest to pension scheme:     tax-free in pension scheme

---

## STRATEGY #317
## Achieve big tax and interest rate deductions for the company through using the ESOT cash flow cycle

---

Consider the following example:

Express Tyres and Rims Ltd wishes to acquire further capital to implement its business objectives. It has over 100 employees with at least five years' service and directors with varying levels of shareholdings. The company is prepared to give up 10% of its equity for an ESOT that it has established to incentivise its employees. There is a directors-only pension scheme that can accept additional funding. The company has an existing overdraft, which is considered expensive.

The capital requirement is £500,000 (£400,000 working capital and £100,000 pension contributions).

The company sets up the ESOT, the costs being £10,000. It borrows £500,000 from the bank at 10%, which it uses to fund the ESOT. The

ESOT purchases shares from the company (the Finance Act 1989 expanded section 153(4)(b) of the Companies Act 1985 to permit financial assistance to a company's employee share scheme). The cost of setting up the ESOT is an allowable deduction for tax purposes (from 1 April 1991).

The company now has £500,000 cash. It pays a pension contribution of £100,000 that is corporate tax deductible. The pension scheme has an immediate loan value of 25% now and 50% after two years. The company requires further borrowings for commercial purposes (service bank interest, working capital, further funding of the ESOT) and borrows from the pension fund, paying a market interest rate to the pension fund. This interest is a deductible expense in the company. In addition, the interest received by the pension fund is not taxable in the fund and increases the fund value accordingly.

This plan will:

- create additional tax deductions, including that of the capital used to fund the ESOT
- provide for the sale and marketability of the company's shares
- increase the value of the director's pension fund
- decrease the cost of working capital substantially, by the following deductions:

> 27.25% (average corporate tax rate) on capital amount
>
> 27.25% (average corporate tax rate) on interest payments

| | |
|---|---|
| Example: working capital | £400,000 |
| interest at 10% to bank | (£40,000) |
| tax saving generated on capital deduction: | £109,120 |
| less interest paid on loan | (£40,000) |
| add tax saving on interest being deductible | £10,912 |
| net savings | £80,032 |
| new net working capital: | £480,032 |
| after paying interest on loan | |
| | |
| Cost of working capital in first year | -16.67% |

- Generate surpluses which can be used to fund the company's objectives

Assuming the company profits (net of other expenditure) are £1 million in this tax year, then the tax position is shown as follows:

## No gearing

| | |
|---|---:|
| Company profits | £1,000,000 |
| Overdraft interest on £500,000 at 10% | £50,000 |
| **Taxable** | **£950,000** |
| *Tax payable* | |
| First £300,000 at 25%: £75,000 | |
| Next £650,000 at 35%: £227,500 | |
| Total £950,000 at 31.84% | £302,500 |

## With gearing

| | | |
|---|---:|---:|
| Company profits | | £1,000,000 |
| ESOT borrowing | £500,000 | |
| Interest on borrowing at 10% | £50,000 | |
| Pension contribution: | £100,000 | |
| Pension fund interest loan at 10% on £25,000: | £2,500 | |
| Cost of setting up ESOT: £10,000 | £10,000 | |
| Allowable deductions | | (£662,500) |
| Taxable | | £337,500 |
| *Tax payable* | | |
| First £300,000 at 25%: | £75,000 | |
| Next £37,500 at 35%: | £13,125 | |
| Total £337,500 at 26.11% | | £88,125 |

The *tax saving* (£302,500-£88,125) is therefore £214,375.

What then is the overall effect of this process? This is shown in the following strategy, which not only has the effect of reducing the cost of working capital to the company, but has substantial other benefits.

---

### STRATEGY #318
### Generate large benefits from a geared ESOT

---

A geared ESOT will create benefits for the company, directors and employees, which is shown below. It also shows the liabilities generated and the net benefit value.

## BENEFITS AND LIABILITIES

| Benefits to company and employees | | Liabilities generated | |
|---|---|---|---|
| Tax savings of | £214,375 | Overdraft/loan of | £500,000 |
| ESOT value | £500,000 | Interest payable | £52,500 p.a. |
| Pension scheme | £102,500 | Loan from pension fund | £25,000 |
| Cash – working capital | £400,000 | Set up costs paid | £10,000 |
| Cash – working capital | £25,000 | | |
| Totals | £1,241,875 | | £587,500 |
| Net benefits value | £654,375 | | |

*The annual cost* of providing a total benefit of £1,241,875 is £52,500, or 4.23% gross. (Note that the set up charge for the ESOT would only be included in the first year. As it is paid by the company, it will not be an outstanding liability to be satisfied in future years.)

## CASH FLOW POSITION OF COMPANY: 1 YEAR

### With gearing

| Cash in | £ | Cash out | £ |
|---|---|---|---|
| Net profits | 1,000,000 | Set up costs ESOT | 10,000 |
| Loan from bank | 500,000 | Pension contribution | 100,000 |
| Capital for ESOT | 500,000 | Loan to ESOT | 500,000 |
| Loan from pension fund | 25,000 | Interest on loans | 52,500 |
| | | Tax payable | 88,125 |
| Totals | 2,025,000 | | 750,625 |
| Net effect: £1,274,375 | | | |

### No gearing

| Cash in | £ | Cash out | £ |
|---|---|---|---|
| Net profits | 1,000,000 | Overdraft interest | 50,000 |
| Loan/overdraft | 500,000 | Tax | 302,500 |
| Totals | 1,500,000 | | 352,500 |
| Net effect: £1,147,500 | | | |

Apart from the increase in working capital, the company has established a formidable range of benefits and increased its net cash position. It has also significantly reduced its corporation taxes payable

– with a tax saving of nearly a quarter of a million pounds and a percentage saving of over 70%!

---

### STRATEGY #319
### Make the process even more effective through using a put and call structure with the bank

---

Because the ESOT has to pay interest (if the company does not do so) out of a dividend stream that has been taxed, the financing can be improved by using a put and call structure. Here, a UK tax paying bank buys the shares over which it enters into put and call options with the ESOT. The ESOT's obligations are guaranteed by the company.

The bank can now use the ACT credit that accompanies the dividend income on the shares. It can also claim tax deductions on the funding cost at 33%. This should reduce the cost to the company of running the ESOT.

The costs of providing the ESOT as an employee benefit are reduced using this route as opposed to issuing new shares and the dilution this brings for shareholders.

---

### STRATEGY #320
### Use the savings generated to satisfy business objectives

---

These may be to repay the overdraft or other loans. More funding of the ESOT in later periods is also possible which will mean that more shares can be purchased and new working capital introduced. The pension fund can be further boosted or its loan repaid. Cash is available for corporate investments to pay dividends or to increase employee benefits.

---

### STRATEGY #321
### Assist the employee to purchase shares in the ESOT through profit-related pay

---

The employees must take up shares within seven years. However, they have to pay for them. The company can establish a PRP scheme to provide the additional cash to pay for the shares. This in turn enables the ESOT to finance the interest debt on the loan, which is otherwise financed through dividends or by the company. In this way, employees can get their shares without having to affect their disposable income.

---

**STRATEGY #322**
## Set up a profit-related pay scheme (PRP) to reduce the outflow of working capital and improve cash flows

---

In 1987 a mere 26,411 employees were on PRP. By March 1991, this had grown to 350,100 employees, and today it is over one million employees. It is a growth area for businesses to give extra cash to their employees without paying for it.

Some surveys (by IDS) have found that PRP is not really a motivator for employee performances. They found it to be a 'tax-free bonus' which did not affect the retention or recruitment of workers. The unions fear job losses as a result of it, and also a squeeze on pay packets if profits fall (*Independent on Sunday* 28 July 1991). The same report also mentioned that a typical factory worker on a 36-hour week could increase his basic wage of £11,682 by £1,862 to earn a total of £13,544 as a result of PRP.

In any event, if profits in the business fall, job losses may result, with or without PRP, as well as decreases in pay.

If PRP does not motivate or incentivise employees, then surely the answer is to link this exciting concept to benefits that do. Share purchase is one of these.

Profit-related pay is governed by TA 1988, sections 169–184 and Schedule 29, FA 1989, section 61, and FA 1991, section 37, as well as later regulations and statements of practice from the Inland Revenue.

A scheme must be registered with the Inland Revenue and any profitable group, company or firm may participate. Some employers, such as local government, are excluded, as are controlling directors with 25% or more interest.

Essentially, parts of the employee's earnings come to him or her tax-free if the employer registers a PRP scheme and profits are made. All this means is that the employee pays less tax and as a result has more money to spend.

The PRP formula is: the lower of 20% of PAYE or £4,000 or the actual PRP paid.

For example:

Mary Miller earns £18,600 on PAYE. 20% of £18,600 is £3,720, which is less than £4,000. Mary can have £3,720-worth of her pay completely tax-free. This is worth an extra £930 to Mary to spend how she wishes.

It is also equivalent to a 5% pay rise.

Consider another example:

Tom Miller earns £40,000 on PAYE. 20% of £40,000 is £8,000, so Tom can only have £4,000 (as the lower of 20% or £4,000) on PRP. This gives him an extra £1,600 in take-home pay – in Tom's case an increase in pay of 4%.

Businesses have been taken to task for misusing the PRP scheme for their own ends and not benefiting employees. For example, businesses will calculate PRP and reduce salaries accordingly, thus saving vital cash flow. The Inland Revenue may become interested if flagrant abuses occur. However there is a case for phased PRP that increases employee' incomes and saves the business cash flow. This is generally at salary increase time. The business uses PRP to provide the salary increase, which saves on cash flow.

A 5% salary increase on a payroll of £1,000,000 is £50,000, which could be diverted through PRP and saved as cash flow. (Note that National Insurance contributions are still payable on PRP.)

---

## STRATEGY #323
## Use directors' (or partners') loan accounts in the business to improve working capital

---

If paying interest for expensive working capital on loans from banks or raising working capital through issuing new shares, which may also be expensive, it may be cheaper for directors' loans to be introduced into the business to replace expensive working capital. Naturally, there is a risk to the director of losing his money, and the lost opportunity cost of his money growing in value elsewhere, as the business may pay lower interest or none at all.

Individuals borrowing money to inject into the business by way of loan accounts may have the interest on the borrowings tax deductible to them.

Although directors' loans to the business are fairly standard practice, the strategy for the director is usually to increase personal wealth. If this is not possible through the business, then the director should consider withdrawing his investment so that it may increase in value elsewhere. After all, a director's loan made to the business in 1980 for £50,000 will still only be worth a much devalued £50,000 in 15 years' time (1995). There is no capital growth on a director's loan account.

It may be better for both the director and the business to use a loan account redemption scheme. The director withdraws his loan account and invests it in a growth investment, which is in turn assigned to the bank as security against a lower-costed overdraft or loan, which the business services. At least the director (or partner) is now in a growth medium for investment purposes. Tax deductible interest is paid by the business to the bank.

The business is assured of continuing working capital and may have reduced the cost of it due to the security offered by the director.

---

### STRATEGY #324
### Use all available tax deductions and capital allowances to reduce tax. This restricts cash flow leaving the business

---

Businesses don't always claim all the tax deductions that they are entitled to, or capital allowances (see Chapters 16 and 18), nor do they put into effect cash outflow reducing schemes, involving National Insurance contributions avoidance (see Chapter 17).

By finding additional tax breaks, or tax reducing methods, as well as savings on interest and other payments, the business can significantly cut the cost of its working capital, retaining more cash for itself.

There are also credit management strategies (see Chapter 5) which will assist the business in obtaining credit as well as getting money in faster.

---

### STRATEGY #325
### Consider borrowing from your pension scheme, rather than from the bank

---

The business can only borrow from a directors' or partners' pension scheme, such as a SSAS. It cannot borrow from an employees' pension scheme, although it has, in the past, had access to surpluses that it used for business purposes – and can still save pension contributions cash flow by taking 'holidays' in employee schemes and not paying premiums.

Borrowings from a directors' pension fund do have restrictions, but there is no reason why a pension fund cannot be substituted for your bank. At least the money is there when you need it. For a pension fund which is more than two years old, 50% of assets can be borrowed; if less than two years old, 25%. The Occupational Pension Schemes (Investment of Scheme's Resources) Regulations 1992 state that a loan may only be made if:

- necessary for the employer's business
- for a fixed term
- at a commercial rate of interest
- it contains a written agreement to the effect that it will be repaid if the borrower is in breach of the conditions of the loan, ceases to carry on business or becomes insolvent

The beauty of the pension scheme loan is that the business is paying interest to its own pension fund and not the bank. The interest is tax deductible to the business and not taxed in the pension scheme. The business can set its own rate of return, so long as it is commercial. In this case the higher the better. The beneficiaries are the prime wealth-builders of the business. It stands to reason that maximum pension funding should be done to build up your business's private bank.

It is not only reducing the cost of working capital, but also ensuring its adequate provision, that is vital to the business.

## Key points summary

- The business should review its cash flow needs and the cost of servicing working capital. This cost can be substantially reduced, and the levels of working capital increased through appropriate strategies.

- Strategies involving employee share owner trusts, profit-related pay, loans from pension schemes and directors' loan accounts are described.

- Without positive cash flow, the business will fail.

# CHAPTER 20

# Tax Planning with Pensions

*There is only one success – to be able to spend your life in your own way.*
**Christopher Morley**

**Objective: To structure tax planning to increase pension funding significantly by freeing up money which would have been paid to the Inland Revenue**

Is it really possible for 'ordinary people' to create multi-million pound retirement plans? I believe it is, so long as you start early enough and allow the wonder of compound interest to do its work for you. Every day in the UK, people are beginning to realise that this dream is possible and putting their action plans together.

---

**STRATEGY #326**
**Determine what you have to do to build up a million pound pension fund**

---

Naturally you need a lot of time. You also need the resources. If not self-employed or a business owner, you need your employer's help to restructure your employee benefits so that (at no extra cost to your employer) more money is available for your savings programme.

The government will do its best to stop you. On the one hand it wants its citizens to be self-sufficient in retirement and to build up their own retirement savings. On the other hand, it makes it difficult by restricting you legally from attaining your objectives from pension funding. How is this possible? It sets limitations:

- Limitations on the levels of *contributions* to approved pension schemes. If employed, you are limited to 15% of your taxable earnings. If self-employed, you are limited to a percentage of net relevant earnings – from 17.5% to 40%, which rises with age. In fact, if you pay too much, it must be repaid to you *and* you suffer tax penalties (at least 35%). Even employers are limited in their pension contributions made for you.
- Limitations on what you can *fund for*. Funding for occupational and personal pension schemes is capped at a pension no greater than ⅔ of final salary with a maximum salary of £78,600 (1995/96) – the earnings cap. No matter what the *potential* might be, your efforts will be limited by State intervention.
- Limitations on what you can *take from your fund*. The amount of tax-free cash is limited for both occupational pension schemes (tax-free cash is based on the formula 2.25 × annual pension, so the maximum is 2.25 × £52,400 = £117,900 cash lump sum payable, where £52,400 represents the maximum pension at ⅔ of the earnings cap) and personal pension plans (25% of the accumulated fund).
- Limitations on what *type of money* may be used to fund pensions. If you have no 'net relevant earnings' but plenty of interest income or dividend income – too bad. You can't use it to qualify for increased pension contributions.

The problem with pension scheme funding is that it is tax-based (maximum ⅔ pension) and not *benefit*-based, where you need to fund for 100% or more of final remuneration.

This means that you are forced to build your funds partly from pension contributions and partly from other sources.

Whatever the fund accumulation process, the principle remains the same – investments are made to generate funds for use in retirement.

## CONTRIBUTION AMOUNTS REQUIRED AT VARIOUS AGES TO HAVE £1 MILLION AT AGE 65

| Age | Term years | Contribution p.a. | Interest 10% compound | Value |
|-----|-----------|-------------------|-----------------------|-------|
| 20  | 45 | £1,265    | 10% | £1m |
| 25  | 40 | £2,055    | 10% | £1m |
| 30  | 35 | £3,355    | 10% | £1m |
| 35  | 30 | £5,530    | 10% | £1m |
| 40  | 25 | £9,250    | 10% | £1m |
| 45  | 20 | £15,900   | 10% | £1m |
| 50  | 15 | £28,600   | 10% | £1m |
| 55  | 10 | £57,100   | 10% | £1m |
| 60  | 5  | £150,000  | 10% | £1m |

Broken down into monthly figures, a 20-year-old needs to save £105.42 per month; a 40-year-old needs to save £770.83 per month; a 50-year-old needs to save £2,383.33 per month to accumulate a retirement fund of £1 million.

---

## STRATEGY 27
## Get your pension contributions tax deductible

---

Within the limits laid down by the Inland Revenue and various legislation and regulations, your contributions will be tax deductible.

For example:

Assume Mark Eardley is age 40, self-employed, with net relevant earnings of £50,000 p.a. He may contribute 20% (£10,000) to his personal pension plan. He wishes to retire at age 65. To accumulate his £1 million fund at age 65, assuming a 10% compound interest growth rate, he need only contribute £9,250 p.a. but assume he contributes the full £10,000.

| | |
|---|---|
| Taxable earnings | £50,000 |
| less personal allowances £3,625 | |
| less pension contribution £10,000 | -£13,625 |
| Tax to pay on | **£36,375** |
| is | **£10,745** |
| *without* pension contributions: tax | £14,745 |
| Net cost of contribution (£10,000 - £4,000 tax saving = £6,000) | |

Put another way, Mark spends net £6,000 a year (£500 a month) to accumulate his fund of £1 million. Total net cost will be £500 × 25 × 12 = £150,000 over the 25-year period. In fact, Mark is ahead, because he only required £9,250 a year to build his fund at 10% compound interest per year. That extra £750 per year will increase his savings by over £80,000 (at 10% compound growth p.a.)

---

### STRATEGY #328
### If employed, make the calculation using your maximum 15% deductible contribution

---

15% of remuneration of £50,000 = £7,500 p.a. contributions to an AVC or FSAVC. This should build a fund of over £800,000 for a 40-year-old retiring at age 65, at a net cost of £4,500 per annum after tax relief.

---

### STRATEGY #329
### Use your unused tax reliefs to maximise your contributions

---

You may qualify for the 'carry-back' or 'carry-forward' provisions for unused tax reliefs as described in Chapter 8. The following example shows the position for Sam Robinson, who has an existing retirement annuity:

She was born on 2 April 1952. He must make his contribution for the current year and can then go back to the 1988/89 tax year (if currently in the 1994/95 tax year). He would have to pay £15,360 into his plan by 1 July 1995. He then goes back to 1988/89 and begins to use up reliefs from that date onwards. The relief available in that year is £254. The example will give the tax deductible amounts for each year:

| Year of assessment | Net relevant earnings | Percentage relief | Maximum relief available |
|---|---|---|---|
| 1994/95 | £76,800 | 20% | £15,360 |
| 1993/94 | £62,086 | 20% | £12,417 |
| 1992/93 | £29,897 | 20% | £5,979 |
| 1991/92 | £29,998 | 20% | £5,999 |
| 1990/91 | £25,593 | 20% | £5,118 |
| 1989/90 | £9,012 | 20% | £1,802 |
| 1988/89 | £1,452 | 17.5% | £254 |
| Total | | | £46,929 |

Using 'carry-back' and 'carry-forward' will significantly assist you with increased funding for retirement purposes. In this example, a total of £46,929 can be contributed for tax reliefs. Note that greater reliefs are possible with a personal pension plan, if an older person, as 40 per cent is the relief allowed from age 61 and over, whereas 20 per cent is the largest allowable amount for retirement annuities.

---

## STRATEGY #330
## First use maximum pension funding, then the best tax-efficient investments to achieve your funding goals

---

The most tax-efficient medium for building funds tax-free (without any capital gains tax or income taxes) is to use an approved pension fund. Not only is compounding occurring off a larger capital base, but tax deductible contributions reduce the net cost of the investment to you.

Go for the maximum amount possible within your disposable income means. This is the best investment you will ever make.

Then, if above the funding limitations, consider alternative investments for your fund to build up. These must be growth oriented.

- *Personal equity plans* (PEPS) also have no capital gains taxes, nor income taxes on their funds. However, the contributions are not tax deductible. There are also funding limits that, in 1995/96, are £9,000 per person per annum.

- *Venture capital trusts* (VCTs) are more risky, being investments into unquoted companies, but the risk is spread on a pooled investment basis. Tax relief for contributions is 20% on investments up to £100,000 per person and relief is up to the level of your tax liability. Dividends and capital gains are tax-free. The investment is for at least five years.

   There is a wide range of growth investments, including unit trusts, investment trusts, insurance bonds, and the like to choose from. You may wish to have a managed portfolio if your investments are large enough for one.

---

**STRATEGY #331**
## Always take your tax-free lump sum in retirement

---

At retirement (see Chapter 31) you have a choice of taking the whole of your pension fund as an annuity or pension or part of it in tax-free cash and the balance as an annuity or pension.

Greater flexibility for future growth is possible (as well as control of your investments) if the tax-free cash lump sum is taken. You may even purchase an annuity with this cash (a PLA – Purchased Life Annuity) which is more tax-efficient than the annuity from your fund.

Reinvestment will help you to accumulate further funds. The best investment medium for personal pensions is to leave your money in the pension fund for as long as possible (age 75 maximum). It will continue to grow in the fund, compounding tax-free.

---

**STRATEGY #332**
## Get your employer to help you – or if you are the business owner, help yourself – to accumulate retirement wealth

---

Many strategies for personal wealth accumulation are given in Chapter 9 and elsewhere. Employers can help to free up cash (which will still be tax deductible) through:

- restructuring employee benefits
- saving on NIC at 10.2%, which can be applied for the employee's benefit (see Chapter 17)
- setting up pension schemes and AVC facilities
- setting up a profit-related pay scheme (PRP)

The PRP provides non-taxable employee income of up to £4,000, creating additional net disposable income of £1,600 (for a 40% taxpayer) and £1,000 for the 25% taxpayer. It's money they never had in the first place and a 20-year-old can build his or her £1 million retirement fund from that alone!

After all, an organisation must be profitable to stay in business and PRP is the most efficient way of distribution avoiding income taxes.

Business owners will find pension planning can be used to export built-up wealth from the business to the individual most tax efficiently. Higher funding levels of SSAS and EPP arrangements give impetus to this approach. Contributions made by the business are tax deductible to the business and thus reduce the incidence of corporate taxation.

---

### STRATEGY #333
## Plan an interaction between personal financial planning and business benefits

---

If the business doesn't provide the benefit, then the employee has to make it up personally. Employees willing to sacifice their own income for cheaper-costed group benefits should arrange for interactive financial planning. Potential savings are great and can be applied to retirement funding schemes.

It is possible to provide for a comfortable retirement and to do so tax-efficiently and effectively. Get to it!

### Key points summary

- A structured approach to tax-efficient retirement funding is described.

- The key is to start as early as possible and to know what is available in the form of tax planning mechanisms.

- There need not even be additional outlay by the employer, who could use profit-related pay and benefit restructuring to assist the employee financially, thus enabling the individual to create personal wealth.

- Instead of paying higher taxes to the Inland Revenue, these can be substantially reduced through deductible pension contributions.

# CHAPTER 21

# Getting Your Life Cover Tax Deductible

*The idea is to die young as late as possible.*
**Ashley Montague, 'Pieces of Good Advice',**
***The Book of Lists***

**Objective: To get the least expensive life cover for the business and individuals**

Life insurance is a commodity. This means that it should be sold, in the main, on price. Why pay £1,000 a year for £200,000 worth of coverages, if you can get exactly the same amount of cover elsewhere – but for £750 a year?

Individuals and businesses stay with the same insurers for a number of reasons:

- loyalty
- laziness – been a customer for many years, so why change?
- reputation of life office is good
- products are reasonably costed
- advised to use a particular life office by a broker
- medical reasons mean they cannot qualify for further coverages
- older people may pay more if they change

- ignorance – they *think* they've got the best deal

However, life assurance is, in fact, the *same product* wherever it is brought. Some companies are better than others, some do have better charging structures, but, in the main, the product is the same.

Changing underwriting practices have generally brought about cheaper premiums over the years, with discounts for non-smokers and healthier lives assured. Many now view life assurance in the same way as car insurance – there could be cost savings through rebroking and consolidation of prices.

---

## STRATEGY #334
## Obtain a review of all life coverages – you may get a better deal

---

A client recently wanted to increase her life cover by 50% so that a tax-free lump sum would be provided for her child. As a single parent, she was concerned that no provision would be made for him. She had effected a life policy in 1990 for £73,000, a maximum cover, whole of life policy. Now she wanted to increase coverages by £100,000.

| Year | Company | Cover | Premium |
|------|---------|-------|---------|
| 1990 | Company A | £73,000 | £15 p.m. |
| 1995 | Company A | £173,000 | £46.50 p.m. |
| 1995 | Company B | £173,000 | £35.80 p.m. |

It was better value for the client to take out a new policy for the full amount, than to have company A increase the existing coverage. The client was five years *older* at the time of the increase, and the premiums proportionately had reduced for *exactly* the same type of policy. Exactly the same principles will apply where the business owns the policy and wishes to increase coverages.

---

## STRATEGY #335
## Don't only review life cover – include all protection benefits in your review

---

The same review principle applies for permanent health insurance (PHI), critical illness cover (CIC) and disability and health coverages. There may either be premium savings to be made, or benefit enhancements for the same amount of money. See also Chapter 9 on group scheme protection benefits.

---

### STRATEGY #336
### Never buy life assurance policies for making investments

---

There are many elements which make up a life policy premium. These include the following:

- cost of life cover
- cost of underwriting
- cost of medical examination and health premium costs
- reinsurance costs
- policy issue costs
- policy administration costs
- commissions
- cost of bonuses guarantees (reversionary bonus policies)
- investment management costs
- investment element, if there is one
- profit element for the life office

Life funds are taxed. Surplus premium, after deduction of the above costs, is applied for investment purposes. If the cost of cover (or other costs) increases beyond expected costs, then the investment element is reduced to pay for the cost of cover.

All too often one hears, 'I like the term policy, but don't want it because I won't get anything back.' Your estate or heirs will, if you die within the term, or the business and surviving partners or shareholders will, if the policy proceeds are for their benefit. The only reason why you get nothing back on a term policy is because it has no value. Investment into a life policy, taken out for protection purposes, is not a good deal. The only ways to get money out are:

- by surrendering it
- by taking loans against it or from it
- by selling it (endowments mostly qualify but not life policies)

Most of these actions are associated with penalty charges, although surrender values from some companies have recently improved following consumer pressures on charges and poor values.

There are far better investments around, such as pensions, PEPs, investment trusts – to name only a few. Investing in a life policy – as an investment – is usually poor value. The exception is a single premium whole of life, better known as an insurance investment bond. This is set up specifically for investment purposes.

---

### STRATEGY #337
### You never get what you think you are paying for – learn how the life office keeps your investment if you die

---

Take the following example:

| | Cover | Investment Value |
|---|---|---|
| Whole of life standard cover policy after ten years of paying the premium | £100,000 | £36,000 |

What do you get if you die – £100,000 or £136,000? In fact, all you get is the face value of the policy – the sum assured. The investment element is retained by the life office. Your *loss* is the additional £36,000 which, if invested elsewhere, could have gone to your heirs, or business beneficiaries.

---

### STRATEGY #338
### Never buy joint life policies – they only pay out once

---

A joint life whole of life policy is much favoured by mortgage lenders and, of course, life offices. Two lives are insured, with a premium for two lives, to pay out on the first or the last dying person.

For example, Trevor and Mary have taken out a joint life, first death, whole of life policy with cover of £200,000. This will pay out on the death of the *first* person, a sum of £200,000. The second life assured has *no* life cover.

They have *paid double* for only one payout. The premium costs are roughly the same for two *separate* policies. With separate policies, the total payout will be £200,000 each, i.e. £400,000. In any event, you have far greater flexibility with separate policies. You may also think a joint life policy is providing the coverages required, but it is not. Review your coverages position immediately in case the latter is the situation.

## STRATEGY #339
## Choose the best coverages at the lowest price

The following table shows how the costs of policies increase for the same coverages:

| Type of policy | Cost of cover | Premiums |
|---|---|---|
| Term cover | cheapest | 100 |
| Renewable term | 5% | 105 |
| Convertible term | } add up to 10% | 105 |
| Renewable and convertible term | | 110 |
| Whole of life (maximum cover) | not much difference in cost from term cover at, say, 20 years | 105 |
| Whole of life minimum cover | more expensive | 500 |
| Whole of life standard cover | even more expensive | 750 |

If the requirement is for life cover only, usually choose term or maximum cover whole of life. *Term* pays out only within a certain term if you die. *Whole of life* pays out on death, whenever that occurs.

Note that while whole of life maximum cover is the cheapest form of whole of life cover, premiums could increase or cover reduce at (usually) the 10-year review of the policy carried out by the life office. Premiums payable at that stage may not support the cost of life cover from the very small investment element in this type of policy. You may have to increase premiums or suffer a reduction of life cover.

## STRATEGY #340
## Always include waiver of premium benefit on a life policy

Waiver of premium (WP) is a disability benefit. If you become disabled permanently and cannot work, the life office will continue to pay your premium for you. The cost is usually 1%–2% of the premium. As you stand a six times greater chance of becoming disabled than of dying before age 65, it makes sense to include this coverage. In fact, financial advisers have been sued in the past for not suggesting it to their clients.

---

**STRATEGY #341**
**Get your life cover tax deductible if an individual**

---

Whilst Life Assurance Premium Relief (LAPR) was discontinued in 1984, it is still possible to get tax deductible premiums, if an individual (or partner), by taking out a *pension term policy*.

You must qualify for 'net relevant earnings' in the normal way. An amount up to 5% of net relevant earnings can be used to provide a lump sum payable from a personal pension plan, if death occurs before age 75.

For a pension term policy, you don't need to effect a separate pension plan. The term life cover can stand alone if required. However, there are premium restrictions. Premiums used to provide life cover must be included as part of the maximum contributions permitted.

For example:

Mary Miller earns £20,000 'net relevant earnings' a year and is aged 35. She is married and requires £200,000 worth of life cover to age 65, for family protection purposes. The premium for a term policy for £200,000 cover for 30 years is £40 per month (£480 p.a.). She pays £2,000 a year into her personal pension plan at the present time.

Net relevant earnings test: 17.5% × £20,000 = £3,500
Premium test:   5% × £20,000 = £1,000

Mary *could* (although here she is only spending £480 a year) spend up to £1,000 in tax deductible term premiums. If not, she has 'contribution space' for a further £1,020 p.a. in pension contributions.

The net cost to Mary as a 25% taxpayer for her tax deductible life cover is £360 (£480-£120) per annum – a saving of £120 through tax reliefs by using this route.

---

**STRATEGY #342**

**If in a partnership, use tax deductible pension term policies for partnership protection; if a company, take out qualifying term cover for tax deductible premiums**

---

Partners can get tax relief in this way for paying premiums on pension term policies which are the subject of partnership Buy and Sell or double option agreements. See Chapter 11.

Some company owned life policy premiums are tax deductible, whilst others are not. It all depends on the structure of the policy and other factors.

A company may wish to insure a Keyman or to cover a loan with life cover. To obtain the tax deduction of the premium, the following conditions must be met:

- term policy
- term of five years or less
- not renewable, nor convertible term
- no surrender value
- solely to provide protection for loss of profits
- the life assured must not be a significant shareholder (usually less than 5%)

The proceeds will be taxable in the hands of the company. However, the premiums will have been tax deductible, thus reducing, by 25% or more, the cost of providing the life cover.

---

**STRATEGY #343**

**Companies requiring better coverages, or where the deductibility provisions are not satisfied, should opt for longer terms or whole of life**

---

It may be in the company's interest to provide life coverages for longer periods than five years. In these cases, term policies or whole of life policies are used, according to the circumstances of the company. The following are the tax implications for companies:

*Term policies* not qualifying because of terms longer than five years, or if renewable and/or convertible, or where the life assured has a material interest in the company, will have the premiums not deductible and the proceeds still taxable.

*Whole of life policies* effected after 13 March 1989 will not have their premiums tax deductible. The proceeds will be tax-free. However, there could be a charge to tax if there is a gain (calculated on the difference between the surrender value and the premiums paid) arising when the policy pays out.

Gains are treated as the company's income and chargeable under Schedule D Case VI.

---

## STRATEGY #344
### Always get clearance from the Inland Revenue for the deductibility of qualifying term assurance premiums

---

The clearance should be in writing and is usually given by the local tax office. It must be applied for and is not automatic. The Inland Revenue will check to see if the policy qualifies for its premiums to be tax deductible under the rules.

---

## STRATEGY #345
### Ensure that policy proceeds remain tax-free (qualifying policies)

---

If a qualifying policy becomes non-qualifying then a tax charge may arise, i.e.

- death of a life assured or maturity of the policy which has previously been made paid-up within the first ten years, or 75% of the term of an endowment policy if shorter.
- surrender, assignment for money or money's worth (or an excess) will be a chargeable event only if it occurs before the expiry of ten years, or 75% of the term of an endowment policy if shorter; or if the policy was made paid-up within that period.

Generally, gifts of policies are not chargeable events, nor is death or maturity if premiums were paid in full, or where the policy has existed for ten years or more.

> # STRATEGY #346
> # To avoid inheritance taxes, write your policy in trust

If the proceeds of your policy fall into your estate, then IHT could be payable. Ignoring the effect of the 'nil rate band', the following is the position, allowing for inheritance taxes payable:

|  | £ |
|---|---|
| Net estate | 500,000 |
| Policy proceeds not in trust | 100,000 |
| **Taxable** | **600,000** |
| Tax at 40% | 240,000 |
| Balance for distribution | 360,000 |

In the example above, 40% of the proceeds were lost to IHT charges. By writing the policy in trust for a spouse, child, dependant or any other party, proceeds pay out to the trustees on death, thus by-passing the estate. There is a further advantage in that these proceeds are available immediately and not held up by probate or disputes. It would save tax in this case of £240,000 – a substantial extra amount for heirs.

Trusts enable policy proceeds to devolve tax-free and may be used by individuals and business owners alike.

Note that company-owned term policies held in trust will still be income taxable in the company's hands when they pay out. Shareholders and partners paying premiums may hold their shareholder or partnership agreements in trust with IHT saving consequences.

Personal pension plans should also be written into trust to avoid IHT consequences. Trusts are provided free by life offices and product providers on standard forms. Alternatively, pay a visit to your solicitor.

## Key points summary

• Shop around for the best-costed coverages. Review life and other protection policies for better deals.

• Don't use life policies as investments; never buy joint life policies and watch out for other rip-off practices from life offices.

• Get your life cover tax deductible and keep the proceeds tax-free.

• Use trusts if possible to avoid inheritance taxes.

# CHAPTER 22

# Making Your Home, Recreational Assets and Foreign Travel Tax Deductible

*Don't be no Ant-man. An Ant-man has very low horizons.*
**Winston Groom The Wit and Wisdom of Forrest Gump**

**Objective: To use the home and other assets in the business for legitimate tax deductions**

Whether you are employed or self-employed, you may use the home and other assets quite legitimately for the conduct of your business and obtain valuable tax deductions for their use. Employees are more restricted in what they can claim, but the self-employed (or partners) and even those operating small businesses from home have a much wider scope for using 'personal assets' in the business. The intrepid business owner may even make money from the use of recreational assets, such as boats, caravans, aeroplanes and snowmobiles and claim deductions for using them. You can also structure your business affairs in such a way that foreign travel becomes tax deductible to your business. It all depends on what sort of business you have.

The income tax rules usually tell you what is specifically not allowed. By implication then, the taxpayer can plan around what is not disallowed. In fact, the worse that can happen is that you make what you consider to be a legitimate claim and find that the Inland Revenue does not allow the deduction.

By planning your tax affairs properly, however, many thousands of pounds can be quite legitimately saved by using personal assets such as the home, vehicles, computer equipment, storage space, telephones, fax machines and recreational assets. The secret to successful claiming of deductions (and allowances) lies in a number of factors, which are covered below.

---

## STRATEGY #347
## Set up a business from home to enable deductions to be claimed

---

There are literally thousands of different kinds of businesses which can be operated from home. In fact, the general trend in the UK economy, following many years of recession and redundancies, has been for people to set themselves up in business. Rather than incur the expense of renting business properties, they operate from home. Over a million new businesses have been set up in the last 15 years in this way.

There is no law which says you can have only one business. Even if you are employed elsewhere (as a Schedule E taxpayer), there is nothing (apart from your employer) legally to stop you from having a second business, or for your spouse or partner to have one. There is also no income tax law or other law which says that the business owner must always make profits either. So long as your *intention* is to make a profit and to run a business on commercial lines, you can make business losses on your business (or second business) and set those losses off against other taxable income – at least for three or four years, if not longer.

Another common myth is that people won't do business with you if you work from home, that your business won't do as well as if it operated from business premises in, say, a town centre, and that you must be as close to your customers as possible. Whilst some of these aspects will, no doubt, appeal to larger businesses, people can do business wherever there is a good communications network. If you have a telephone, fax machine and computer modem (for the Internet or workstations), it is no different from the purpose-built office in the town centre. Unless the business is dependent on a through-flow of people (walk-in custom) then working from home can save you thousands.

---

### STRATEGY #348
### Make sure that a 'business' is set up – at least have the outward trappings of one

---

You should have proper letterheads, business cards and other stationery. Many print shops will make up a pack for you with the necessary paperwork, including invoices and other documentation.

The cost for a 'starter-pack' is usually about £20. Decide on whether the business will operate as a sole trader (you or your spouse or partner), or as a partnership (you *and* your spouse, partner or a third party) or as a small company. The costs of setting up a company (and running it) can be as low as £500 a year. All structures of business require separate planning, depending on your circumstances.

Some people may decide to turn their hobbies into a business. Make sure that, if this is done, it would not be seen by an outsider as just your continuation of the hobby, i.e. with no profit motive. The intention to operate a business must be visibly established. One way of expressing this intention is to open a separate bank account for the business.

Next, make a list of all the assets which will be used in the business.

---

### STRATEGY #349
### Compile an asset and usage list for the business

---

If some of the assets are used for personal use, then allocate a time period for personal and business use.

The reason for the asset and usage list is to enable you not to forget to claim your deductions and capital allowances.

A typical list would be:

- mortgage or rents payable
- use of one or more rooms in the house
- share of electricity/gas/water/oil
- cleaning and cleaning materials
- Council Tax
- telephone(s)
- fax machine
- computer hardware
- computer software
- filing cabinets
- storage space
- audio visual/television and video equipment/projectors and film equipment
- motor vehicles
- other assets
- cost of using family members as employees or help in the business
- other charges, fees, domestic expenditures attributable to the business
- books for reference work, library, subscriptions
- insurance

Also, make a list of the costs incurred in actually setting up the business from home – items purchased, stationery and so on, as follows:

- extra lighting requirements
- filing cabinets
- stationery and letterheads, cards, invoices
- heavy duty carpet protector (essential)
- desks, chairs, office furniture
- office equipment
- telecommunications costs and cable
- answer machine
- computer equipment
- computer software
- artwork, advertising
- office supplies etc
- insurances

Next to each item on the list, note its cost, date of purchase and business usage. The generally-accepted rule for using the home in the business (or the business in the home) is that the domestic costs are proportioned according to their usage between private and business use.

For example, if the square footage of house space is 1,500 sq ft and the office or business usage space is 200 sq ft, then the proportion is 200/1,500 = 13%. This means that 13% of domestic costs – lighting, heating, water and so on – may be deductible for business purposes.

Items such as cleaning, where the business portion requires greater input, can be proportioned on a different level to reflect the true position.

---

## STRATEGY #350
### Don't use the business area of the house exclusively for business purposes, but 'almost' exclusively

---

This may seem a strange thing to say but there is a strong reason for doing so. If any area of the main residential property can be shown to have been used exclusively for business purposes, then there is a danger that when you come to sell the home, the part of the capital gains tax exemption for selling your own home will be lost.

Usually a balanced position is struck, whereby the home is used 'almost' exclusively, so that you get the income tax deductions for running the business, but don't incur the CGT charge on selling the home.

---

## STRATEGY #351
### If self-employed, claim the use of the home and other assets as tax deductions

---

If running a business from home on your own account (not for the employer's account, which is covered later), then to claim relevant expenditure as a tax deduction under the Taxes Act 1988, section 74(a), the expenditure must have been incurred 'wholly and exclusively' for the purposes of trade.

Some expenditures are deductible in this way; others are deductible as 'capital allowances'.

For example, if you use your car for business purposes and business travelling, you can claim for the business proportion of car expenses, and also the business proportion of capital allowances on the car value when you first started using it for the business.

If the home telephone is used for business calls, then a deduction may be claimed. Expenses from using part of the home can be allowed against taxable profits if they are 'wholly and exclusively' for trade, in the fixed proportions shown earlier.

Apart from the 'wholly and exclusively' stipulation, to be deductible expenses must be of a revenue, not a capital nature.

The expense must be for business purposes. If private and business use has occurred, then the private expenditure portion is removed and the business portion is usually allowable. However, should the expenditure be for the sole purpose of the business, any incidental private benefit would usually be ignored.

The self-employed or business owners who are not employees of other businesses may claim any reasonable expense in connection with the business.

Assume a small business is started this year from home:

|  | £ |
|---|---|
| Other taxable income (e.g. salary from employers) | 10,000 |
| Trading income this year from own business | 3,500 |
| Allowable expenses (10% proportion): | |
| 10% rent/mortgage interest | 1,200 |
| 10% of utilities | 150 |
| 10% of services | 200 |
| 20% of car expenses | 240 |
| Telephone (business portion) | 840 |
| Other allowable business expenses | 490 |
| TOTAL EXPENSES | 3,120 |
| Capital allowances % cost | |
| 1. Car: 25% × £5,500 | 1,375 |
| 2. Computers: 25% × £3,500 | 875 |
| 3. Other short life goods: 25% × £1,200 | 300 |
| TOTAL ALLOWANCES | 2,550 |

In this scenario, the individual has trading income of £3,500 and expenses and capital allowances of £5,670, making for a business loss of (£2,170) in its first year of trading.

This loss can be utilised to reduce other taxable income of £10,000, down to £7,830 and for a 25% taxpayer is worth £542 in tax saved.

Whether used as an expense or a capital allowance, the net effect is that personally-owned assets can be geared to reduced business profits and personal taxes.

## STRATEGY #352
## Get part of the mortgage or rent tax deductible at marginal not restricted rates of tax

If part of the business premises is used for the purposes of a trade or profession, then up to a maximum of ⅔ of the rent paid for the premises will be allowed as a deduction. This may be increased if the circumstances warrant it. [ICTA 1988, section 74(c).]

Mortgage interest attributable to the business premises portion is deductible. The balance of mortgage interest is not, save for the part allowed under MIRAS, which is in itself restricted (to 15% of £1,720 = £258). As with rents above, it may be possible to agree a higher amount, of up to ⅔, with the Inland Revenue if the business premises are exclusively apportioned within the home. Beware the capital gains tax implications, though.

---

### STRATEGY #353
### Buy a second property and use that for business premises or letting out

---

Either way, the *full interest* on any loan used to purchase a second property for business purposes (which includes letting out the property or a part of it) is deductible from business profits. You will not be restricted as you are with MIRAS relief only on your principal residence. A second property will give you scope for additional deductions, such as full interest relief.

---

### STRATEGY #354
### Deduct business property rates or the business proportion of council taxes

---

Whilst council tax paid on your main home is not allowed as a business expense, the proportion rules usually apply and these 'rates' may be proportionately allowed if operating a business from home.

However, if the residence has been assessed for both council tax and business property rates, then the latter is claimable in full as a deduction.

---

### STRATEGY #355
### If no business is proposed, but spare rooms can be let, reduce your taxes substantially

---

Running a business from home may be too much for some people. However, many have extra income needs and may have spare rooms in the house to be let out. Whilst rental income is taxable, 'rent a room relief' allows an exemption of £3,250 on gross annual rentals. This is equivalent to a 40% taxpayer earning an additional £8,125 tax-free!

There are many deductions which may be claimed in connection with letting rooms and furnished lettings, if run as a business – again, another way of reducing taxable income or profits from other sources.

---

### STRATEGY #356
### Claim deductions for using recreational assets

---

Whilst the number of owners of private aircraft, boats, pleasure craft, snowmobiles and other recreational assets (including caravans and houseboats) are not as numerous as homeowners, the budding entrepreneur can make money from his pleasurable assets.

For example, if you own a boat, organise fishing or cruising charters; similarly with an aeroplane, making private charter flights for profit.

All expenditures in your stated endeavours will be allowable against your taxable profits. Who knows – you may even make a loss, but it won't stop you from enjoying yourself!

If assets are purchased specifically for business use, then capital allowances will apply. This is particularly useful for expensive personal assets purchased to use in your new business. Over a four-year period, your pleasurable assets could have been tax allowable against your business profits or rolled forward to be offset as losses in future years.

---

### STRATEGY #357
### If employed, still use the house and other assets to reduce your taxes

---

Employees working from home for an employer (not themselves), who incur expenditure in connection with their business activities for their employer (such as sales reps working from home) may deduct certain of those expenditures.

Schedule E employees would only have a claim for Schedule E expenses, which can include home expenses [TCGA 1992, section 158(1)(c): SP5/86]. Where it can be shown that the claim was not based on any specific proportion of the house being used, then usually a capital gains tax charge will not arise when you sell the house. However, if it does, then consider using annual exemptions for capital gains tax or future roll-over reliefs where applicable.

Employees, to claim expenses, must prove that they have been expended 'wholly, exclusively *and necessarily*' in connection with their employment. In fact, very few expenses satisfy this onerous condition and some expenses are specifically allowable by statute or by concession.

If it is necessary for the employee to work at home, he will be able to claim a proportion of the cost of heat, light, water, telephone and fax calls as well as other expenses which can be connected with the work from home. If a room is used exclusively for work, a proportion of the council tax is allowable as well as a proportion of rent or mortgage interest.

The employee will also be able to claim capital allowances for providing (buying) equipment which is necessarily provided for use in the job, less a proportion for private usage [CAA 1990, ss 27,79]. An allowance for business use for a car may be claimed anyway (there is no 'necessary' test).

If the employee has to borrow money to finance the purchase of the equipment, then interest on the money borrowed may be deducted from his or her earnings over four tax years [TA 1988, section 359(3)].

If the employer pays the expenses or some of their value to the employee, then this is taxable in the employee's hands, leaving the employee to claim relief for the allowable part.

Employees working from home can then achieve much of what the self-employed can achieve by way of deductible expenses and capital allowances, thus reducing taxable earnings. However, special rules do apply in certain instances and employees should discuss their circumstances with their employers.

The house is the most valuable asset for the vast majority of the population. On its own it will fluctuate up and down in value, depending upon market conditions. If the home can be 'leveraged' to create new opportunities and tax deductions, then its value as an income generator (of more disposable income) is not to be underestimated.

---

## STRATEGY #358
## Get your foreign travel tax deductible

---

When considering the type of business being set up from home (or otherwise), if you have a love of foreign travel, then make provision for it as part of your business plans.

For example, visits to foreign suppliers, attendance at conferences overseas and visits to international trade fairs and international customers are some of the ways of combining business with pleasure. Whilst the taxman doesn't like you to claim private holiday expenditure at his expense, he cannot complain if you enjoy yourself whilst doing business. After all, if it's not fun, it's probably not worth doing.

The government will also help you to get to your exotic destination by providing export incentives and cash to attend overseas trade fairs and exhibitions.

You may deduct the cost of travel, hotel accommodation and business marketing and promotional expenditure. However, entertainment expenditure for foreign clients, even whilst abroad, will usually not be allowed. A spouse or partner in the business may accompany you on the business trip in a business partner, employee or hostess (host) capacity; or if you are in ill health or in need of assistance.

It would be correct and proper for the business to compile an itinerary showing business contacts and meetings to be held. This should be filed with tickets and other expenditures to support any claim.

If children accompany you, do not claim any expenditure on tickets and costs for them. They are not a deductible business expense for these purposes and could draw unnecessary attention from the Inland Revenue.

Setting up a business from home will enable you to have fun and enjoy doing business. Whether you travel to the Middle East to purchase carpets, or to South Africa for semi-precious stones, you should find a useful market amongst friends and businesses when you get back home.

## Key points summary

- The home is a useful asset which can be leveraged for tax deductions and used to build wealth.

- Whether you are self-employed or employed, the home and other personal assets, as well as recreational assets, are most useful for capital allowances, expense deductions and for setting up a business.

- Foreign travel for business reasons can also be a deductible item.

CHAPTER 23

___

# Getting Rid of Your Business Profits

*Corporations have neither bodies to be punished, nor souls to be condemned; they therefore do as they like.*
**Edward, First Baron Thurlow (1731–1806) in Poynder, *Literary Extracts* (1844), Vol. 1**

**Objective: To reduce the incidence of taxation on profits, whilst building wealth for the business owners**

There are a number of different points of view on the treatment of 'profits', mainly dependent upon the structure and size of the business.

Even the word 'profits' is not all it seems. Most people associate it purely with a cash surplus in the business that can be distributed to the business owners. However, 'profit' is not cash. Its measurement is determined by accounting conventions, some of which have nothing to do with cash flow. An example is depreciation, which is charged on property and plant, and reduces profit.

In this chapter, though, 'profit' is treated as the amount the business has, *after paying tax*, for distribution to the business owners or to be retained by the business. However, this has a cost – a tax cost. To pay a dividend, the company must *first* pay tax on its profits. To take excess cash out of a partnership, tax must first be paid, and a sole trader will pay tax on money accruing in excess of deductible expenditure. The strategies which follow will concentrate on two distinct aspects.

*Firstly*, how to reduce the incidence of taxation, which inevitably involves expenditure of some kind, and thereby reduces profits.

*Secondly*, how to distribute profits in the most efficient manner, or how best to use profits to build wealth.

As profits are taxable, it actually costs the business money to be profitable. Therefore, one must seek the most efficient way to get money out of the business or use it within the business.

---

## STRATEGY #359
## Understand the business cycle to profits

---

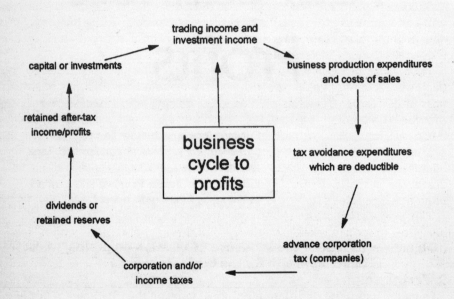

At any point on this cycle, financial and corporate decisions can be made by managers or business owners to increase or decrease the incidence of profits and its distribution or retention.

Some of these can be pressure points where specific actions are initiated. For example, making pension contributions is a tax avoidance measure which reduces profits and therefore reduces taxation. It thus reduces the amount available for dividends or retained after-tax income, which may leave less capital for investment in sales generation. Each action will have some form of alternative counter-action or effect.

---

### STRATEGY #360
## Determine the business's and individual's perspectives in respect of building wealth through the business

---

Different perspectives can be translated into business goals. These will differ, depending upon the structure and size of the business.

## 1. Sole Trader

He or she *is* the business. If the business fails, losses are borne by the sole trader business owner, personally. It may even mean the loss of further personal assets, secured against loans for the business.

Success in business, however, brings its own rewards. The sole trader will endeavour to build wealth as far as possible *outside* the business, and in the most tax-efficient format possible. He or she will seek to reduce taxation and to maximise income.

There is no question of retaining high levels of after-tax income in the business – it cannot be done, because of the personal nature of the business undertaking. If the business needs more cash, the business owner provides it. Although separate bank accounts are kept for personal and business needs, their ownership rests in the business owner personally.

The sale of the business would be difficult – the business owner *is* the business, especially if he or she has not replicated themselves. On death, the best which could be hoped for is a sale of business assets – often at a 'fire sale value'.

The *perspective* of the sole trader therefore focuses on tax-efficient measures to reduce taxes payable and build personal wealth, which is itself protected.

## 2. Partnerships

Partners share in profits and liabilities equally, or in proportion to their partnership shares, or by agreement. Essentially, though, a partnership is by far the most *vulnerable* business structure because each partner is jointly and severally liable for the business debts of the partners and the partnership. This liability can be restricted if the partnership incorporates.

Partners are even *more vulnerable* because very few firms structure their partnership agreements properly. A partner may work for 40 years, building up his or her capital account in the business, only to find that the partnership cannot afford to pay out its value, on retirement in full (usually by instalments) or even on death, because it requires the cash for working capital. (See Chapter 11.)

Profits in a partnership are apportioned as income to each partner and then taxed in that partner's hands. Pre-1994/95 partnerships have assessments made on the firm rather than on individual partners. Profits are assessed in one amount where the tax is paid by the firm, with each partner jointly and severally liable. This assessment to tax takes into account how the income is divided and their personal allowances and other deductions. This form of assessment ends in 1997/98, after which time partners are separately assessed.

Partners who began a partnership after 6 April 1994 are taxed separately, with individual assessments raised, rather than on the firm. Individual partners will not be jointly and severally liable for the total amount of tax payable by the partners. Partners will be taxed under Schedule D, except for a *salaried* partner, taxed under Schedule E.

The traditional perspective has been for partners to build up their capital accounts in the business (capitalised income not taken as drawings) which then accrue for their wealth-building. Capital accounts will only accrue *after tax*. This means that partners will give attention to tax-efficiency planning *within* the partnership itself. In addition, *personal* tax avoidance planning will be used to reduce the incidence of taxation and the building of personal wealth.

Partners manage the partnership assets for their own benefit and those of the other partners ultimately. Their overall perspective on profits will be the greatest accumulation of their capital accounts possible. However, problems could occur with *transferring* wealth on retirement or death.

At normal retirement date, the partners should consider either retiring or staying on in the partnership.

Partners are jointly liable for VAT owed by the firm up to the date of notification of retirement, not the actual date of retirement, and this liability needs to be addressed when considering retirement.

On retirement, the retiring partner's tax liability is based on a full year's assessment which could raise a residual liability in retirement. Under the current year basis of assessment, liability beyond retirement will be subject to 'overlap relief'. If profits are down, then ensure that overlap relief is not lost, but captured at the full rate of 40%.

At retirement, part of the partner's capital account is a realised capital gain which is triggered. The partner should ask if there is a revaluation of any previous surpluses as liabilities may arise on past revaluations of partnership assets.

The partner may be better off by deferring retirement and dying 'in harness'. If not, then there is a possibility that business property relief at 100% is in danger. If the partner is in ill-health, then consider staying on as a partner and don't retire.

If the partnership has old 'Buy and Sell' clauses in its partnership agreement, then these must be taken out. Buy and Sell clauses give a binding contract for pre-sale of the partnership share which would disqualify the partner from business property relief. Rather use a double option agreement which enables the full business property relief exemption of 100% from inheritance taxes on death.

If the partner is forced to take early retirement or is expelled from the partnership, then the following considerations are important, as they impact on future wealth planning of the partners.

For example, an exit from the partnership may be coupled with a restraint of trade or the payment of a lump sum, or an annuity. There may be a high price to pay if not properly planned.

Also, there is no tax relief for the payers of a lump sum. If there is a pay-off, what will be the best route to take? Naturally, one would wish to maximise the net after-tax benefit. If a lump sum is paid to the retiring or expelled partner, then one must look to capital gains tax reliefs and retirement reliefs.

The first step is to look for a rebasing election to create a loss as a result of goodwill. In addition, one must also look to indexation, which will eliminate a gain, but not a loss, following the new rules in 1993. The partner may inherit a 1982 value (the year of rebasing) even if he or she only became a partner say last year. The big problem is in trying to locate accounts prior to 1982 in order to establish these values.

For retirement relief to apply, the partner must be at least 55 years old (50 in 1996/97) and either have enjoyed a share of the business or an asset used in it. For maximum retirement relief, the partner should have owned the asset or share for at least ten years. It is the length of time that you were a partner, not the length of time since the asset was bought which is the important factor here.

The partnership and early retiring partner should consider the different implications of paying and receiving a lump sum, or an annuity, or being retained through a consultancy agreement. If an annuity, then entitlement to it should be in the partnership agreement. One should not mix the payment or consideration of an annuity and lump sums together. If so, the annuity could be capitalised and treated in the same way as the non-deductible lump sum.

A consultancy arrangement would have to satisfy the 'wholly and exclusively' test for deductibility of the payments under the agreement. This is not the case with an annuity. However, consultancy payments are 'net relevant earnings' for pension contribution purposes, whereas annuity payments are not. One must give equal consideration to the tax position of payers in order to maximise the compensation package.

Bear in mind that the exiting partner will require releases from loans, finance arrangements and professional indemnity on retirement, as well as full indemnity against partnership debts. The retiring partner could still be liable for partnership debts and actions and should retain

PI cover for 'run-off' once retired.

This is a complicated area and professional advice should be sought to maximise retirement and early leaving benefits from a partnership.

If the partnership contemplates a husband and wife situation, this could be useful to obtain greater retirement reliefs. Whilst it is generally inadvisable for both spouses to have unlimited liability (perhaps one should be an employee), both have retirement reliefs. The spouse should be brought in as a partner before disposing of the business, to maximise this relief.

Under the legislation at present you do not have to be an active partner to get the relief. As long as you were a 'sleeping' partner for ten years, then each will get at least £250,000-worth of relief at 100% and 50% of the balance up to £1 million.

## 3. The Company

The business owners of a company are its shareholders. However, they may not (if they have smaller shareholdings or are passive investors) be able to influence company policy on how it operates, having to take advice from management on what is best for the company. However, the assumption is made here of a smaller business with shareholders active or reasonably close to the business.

Companies are not as vulnerable as sole traders or partnerships. Shareholders are not responsible for the business's debts – only the business is. However, their capital and therefore their wealth is at risk. The return to shareholders is in the form of increasing capital values of their shares, as well as the expectation of dividends as an income flow. Therefore, the *perspective of the shareholders* is mostly *retained profits* to increase share values and dividends (from after-tax income) and dividends to increase income.

This may be at odds with management who do not own shares, who would wish to build wealth through pre-tax avoidance schemes and increasing income. However, assuming that shareholders are also management, this allows a *perspective* of getting profits out of the business in the most tax-efficient manner, whilst enabling the business to continue as a powerhouse of ongoing wealth-creation. Taking out too much could affect cash flows and working capital, as well as capital creation through retained reserves, which in turn affects the stability of the business.

*Perspectives* will therefore *focus* on tax reduction strategies, optimising profits and a dividend policy if tax-efficient.

## 1. Profit strategies for sole traders

---

**STRATEGY #361**

**Make maximum use of business deductions, allowable expenses and capital allowances**

---

Using the strategies in Chapters 16, 18 and 22, claim the maximum deductions for business expenditure, allowable by law. Make sure that full expenditures incurred in using the home and personal or recreational assets in the business are claimed for. This will have the effect of reducing taxable income and therefore tax payable. Use the strategies to build personal asset wealth through the business.

---

**STRATEGY #362**

**Introduce your spouse, or other family members, into the business to spread income, reduce taxes and use up personal allowances**

---

You may pay family members who are employees a commercially justifiable salary, provide them with a car and make payments into a pension scheme for them. See Chapter 13.

Taking family members into partnership may be a logical extension of your business objectives and can give more flexibility in the allocation of profits.

It is also a useful succession planning tool. Bringing in family members (or others) will allow the business to continue if you die or retire.

Spreading the load and 'keeping it in the family' is a justifiable way to create new taxpayers and get more income tax-free. One of the best ways to increase family disposable income is by spreading taxable income to make use of personal allowances which every taxpayer has.

For example:

Net profits earned by Sam Noble this tax year will be £30,000. He employs his spouse in the business at £10,000 and he takes out £20,000.

1.   *The position for Sam only:*
     Profits                                      30,000
     Less personal allowances                      3,525
                                                  26,475

     Tax payable:    20% of 3,200:          640
                     25% of 21,100:       5,275
                     40% of 2,175:          870
                                         (6,785)

     Balance: net disposable income £23,215 (30,000-6,785)

2.   *The joint position for Sam and Mary:*

| Sam | | Mary |
|---|---|---|
| 20,000 | Profits/salary | 10,000 |
| 3,525 | Allowances | 3,525 |
| 16,475 | Taxable | 6,475 |
| (3,958) | Tax | (1,458) |
| £16,042 | Disposable balance | £8,542 |

Combined tax: £5,416 (a saving of £1,369) or 20% saving.
Increase in disposable income: £1,369 for both of them together.

---

## STRATEGY #363
## Increase pension funding to further reduce taxation and build wealth

---

Pension contributions will further reduce taxable income and enable the sole trader to invest in one of the most tax-efficient investments available – a pension fund. The fund itself is not taxed and grows tax-free.

If you use the spread of taxpayers in the last strategy, the taxman can fund your pension contribution – at no cost to you! In fact, cash generated can now be used for further tax deductions.

For example:

Sam is now a 25% taxpayer as is Mary. Both contribute a total of £1,369 to personal pension schemes.
*Tax saved:* 25% × £1,369 = £342.
This saving can, in turn, be used for further pension funding!

In fact, both Sam and Mary should *maximise* their pension provision if possible, not only using other tax savings, but also other available 'net relevant earnings'. If Mary was an employee, as opposed to a partner, then she could have an executive's pension with a higher funding rate and savings on National Insurance contributions for the business. (See Chapter 13.)

---

### STRATEGY #364
### Make full use of personal investment and other tax deductions

---

Apart from pension funding, the sole trader can invest in EIS (Enterprise Investment Scheme) or VCT (Venture Capital Trust) schemes – up to £100,000 investment gives £20,000 tax relief off an actual tax liability. This is a particularly relevant option if wishing to roll-over a capital gain and defer capital gains tax. Another tax deductible investment is the EZT (Enterprise Zone Trust) where 100% deduction is available. Both of these investments should be considered high risk. There are no other investments which are tax deductible or give relief from tax, apart from pensions and a small relief on interest from investing in your home. (MIRAS or interest relief is limited to 15% of the interest on a £30,000 loan e.g. loan interest 10% × £30,000 = £3,000 × 15% = £450.)

Don't neglect other tax reliefs such as the married couple's allowance, which is transferable between spouses – use the higher-rated taxpayer to receive this tax benefit, not the lower-rated taxpayer.

---

### STRATEGY #365
### Invest (profits) after-tax income wisely to build up personal wealth

---

Once the sole trader has readjusted his or her tax-planning for maximum efficiency and made whatever pre-tax deduction and investment arrangements are appropriate, investments are made from after-tax income.

In other words, profits, having been taxed, are then allocated according to the risk profile of the sole trader investor. (See Chapters 28 and 30.)

Some capital is held back or allocated for further business development, invested in property and premises, and used in the business. This is translated into a base for further wealth, or to sell the business eventually for a significant gain.

Strategies for tax assessment are covered in Chapter 15. See also the following strategy for the new assessment rules for the self-employed.

## 2. Profit Strategies for Partners

Some of the profit-taking strategies for sole traders apply equally to partners and will not be repeated here. These are in respect of:

- making full use of business deductions, allowable expenses and capital allowances.
- if possible using the spouse in the business.
- increasing pension funding to reduce taxation and build wealth.
- making full use of personal investment and other tax deductions.
- investing after-tax income wisely to build up personal wealth.

The following strategies apply more specifically to partnerships and partners in maximising their profits.

---

### STRATEGY #366
### Improve the profit position of the partnership through understanding the new assessment rules

---

These rules apply to all self-employed people, but have specific application for partners. The preceding year basis for taxation will be replaced by a current year basis for taxation.

Businesses commencing after 5 April 1994 will be assessed on the new current year basis immediately. *Existing businesses* will have a transitional year for the tax year 1996/97 and move fully on to the new basis for the year 1997/98.

Get ready *now* for the new *current* year basis. What this means is that taxable profits in one year (say this year) are earned in the accounts year ending in the tax year *before* the year of assessment (say last year). Payments are due on 1 January and 1 July of each year. What will happen is that under the new rules (the current year basis applies from 1997/98), the profits earned in that year will be taxed in that year. Tax payment dates will change to 31 January and 31 July each year. You will get an extra month to pay!

However, in order to make the changeover from the preceding year basis to the current year basis, there will be a phasing-in or transitional period. This will begin in the 1996/97 tax year for *existing* businesses. New ones will already be on it (the current year basis) from 5 April 1994.

It is these transitional rules which open up a new opportunity for tax planning with profits.

The transitional rules allow an averaging so that the amount assessable will be half that of the two-year period ending in the tax year 1996/97.

This means that only half the profits of a business are taxed in each of the accounts' years ending in 1995/96 and 1996/97.

It will, therefore, be beneficial to have higher profits in those accounts years than in the accounts years ending in the tax years 1994/95 and 1997/98.

*Example: Transitional accounts years planning*

| | | | |
|---|---|---|---|
| Have lower profits | 1994/95 | | |
| Have higher profits | 1995/96⎫ | profits £50,000 ⎫ | 50% is |
| Have higher profits | 1996/97⎭ | profits £100,000⎭ | £75,000 |
| | For this tax year, profits are assessed on 50% of 95/96 and 96/97 | | |
| Have lower profits | 1997/98 | | |

If business profits are *increasing, more tax* will be paid sooner. If business profits are *reducing* you will pay *less* tax later. Your strategy is to plan your cash flows and profits over the next few years to take advantage of the opportunity for lower taxes on profits. This may mean bringing forward planned expenditures or postponing them as the case may be. This applies to all self-employed (Schedule D) taxpayers only.

---

### STRATEGY #367
### Reorganise partnership borrowings to get maximum relief on interest payments

---

The changes to the tax assessment rules may have an adverse effect on the amount of loan interest able to be deducted.

The interest on an overdraft or bank loan is an allowable expense (usually) in arriving at the firm's profits.

As the previous strategy indicated in the accounts year 1996/97, profits are averaged over the previous two years and assessed at 50%. This means that only 50% of interest payments made by the firm will qualify for tax relief.

Financial reorganisation of the firm's borrowings may be required to overcome this problem:

- Either the partners *themselves* arrange for substitute loans, claiming 100% of the interest as a deduction for providing finance to the

firm or to increase partnership capital; *and/or*
- Restructuring of financing takes place, possibly with a 'balloon' of interest arrangement over the critical period; *and/or*
- Cash flow planning is undertaken, especially for firms with large loans or overdrafts.

---

### STRATEGY #368
### Organise tax planning around partnership capital accounts to maximise and preserve wealth

---

Partnerships in England and Wales are not legal persona as they are in Scotland. In England and Wales, it is the individual members of a partnership who are trading and not the partnership itself.

However, for taxation purposes, income tax for the partners throughout the UK is assessed in the name of the partnership. Under self-assessment (1997/98) and new partnerships from 6 April 1994, joint assessment is abolished. Partners will be directly assessed.

Once partnership expenditures and allowances are deducted from trading income, then the whole of business profits are treated as the partners' income and taxed under Schedule D.

If there is a partnership agreement which stipulates how much the partner may draw down for personal use, this is strictly adhered to, with the balance of after-tax profits being loaned to the business by the partner. This is called the capital account and is largely used to fund working capital and capital expenditure.

The interaction between the partner and the business is therefore far greater than that between the shareholder and the company, for example. The partnership is largely then valued on the basis of the combined value of these capital accounts and goodwill. The word 'goodwill' arises from the future value of expected income from probate and executors' fees on wills held by solicitors' practices. They were valued on the worth of their value – in that case 'goodwills'. It has therefore come into common parlance as the invisible future value of the business.

Some partnerships specifically exclude goodwill from their partnership agreements – others have a formula for determining what it is. In the main, though, the *value* of each partner's share will be determined by the value of his or her loan account in the business – the capital account. The only problem is that partners bind themselves by agreement on how and when to take out their capital accounts. Often agreements will state that on retirement or death or leaving the firm, the capital account will be paid in instalments, with or without interest.

This is because the partnership:

- has not sufficient other capital to suffer a large reduction in capital at once – working capital will suffer
- has not provided for the fact that at some time capital will be withdrawn
- has not provided partnership protection policies to ensure immediate payouts in the event of death or disability.

This practice can have a disastrous effect on the wealth-building of the individual partner. His death could occasion the termination of the partnership or even result in bankruptcy – as could his retirement. There is an additional burden on the remaining partners, who now have one less fee earner, to increase earnings to pay out the leaving partner. Some just give up.

Quite frankly, the capital of the leaving partner is at great risk and his or her strategy must be to ensure payment of it as soon as possible.

The *strategy* of the partnership should be:

- Replace capital accounts for leavers with bank financing; *and/or*
- Create a savings fund where a percentage of profits is invested each year, to contribute a leaver's capital; *and/or*
- Create forms of alternative payments, and retain the capital account.

In connection with the above, some partnerships have a policy of maximum pension contributions. The retiring partner leaves his capital account behind, substituting the tax-free cash lump from his personal pension plan or SSAS arrangement for it. In addition, he receives a pension. As partnership profits are generated by the whole firm, of which the partner is a member, it is akin to the profits of a company in some ways. Value is reflected in compound growth pension funding instead of shares in this case.

A little known fact is that, in the absence of any agreement to the contrary, the heirs of a deceased partner have *an immediate call for cash* from the partnership on the death of the partner. This cash call is for partnership value. Partners must, therefore, have partnership protection insurance to protect the partnership and its assets.

To maximise personal wealth, the partner should make use of other personal investment and tax-reducing strategies.

Partners remaining in the firm can also pay out an unfunded pension and lump sum, which is deductible to them individually. This strategy may offset the continued retention of the capital account, the repayment of which has no tax reliefs attaching to it.

## STRATEGY #369
## Tax planning around partnership losses to preserve partners' wealth

In general, losses may be carried back and set off against other income, or the partner will have the choice of setting losses off against income in the year of the loss, or against income of the following year, or to carry losses forward to offset against trading income in future years.

Your strategy is to take loss relief in a year when subject to *higher* rates of tax, rather than in low income years.

Note that on the death or retirement of a partner, losses which have not been relieved cannot be carried forward. However, the carry-back of terminal losses may apply. Proper tax planning is most important to make full use of what is available to reduce taxes and build wealth.

## STRATEGY #370
## If you contributed too much partnership capital, get paid interest

Interest paid to a partner on his own capital by the partnership is not an allowable expense, but an allocation of profit. However, payments made *beyond* the agreed amount of contributed capital is entitled to interest at 5% p.a. [Partnership Act 1890, s 24(3)]. This is an allowable expense to the partnership but taxable in the receiving partner's hands under Schedule D, Case III.

## STRATEGY #371
## Make sure that excess allowances over tax due on partnership share is set off against other income

Any excess allowances over tax due on a partner's share of taxable profits can be set off against any other income that the partner might have.

---

### STRATEGY #372
## Maximise pension contributions as repayment of capital accounts may be slow

---

As mentioned in previously, if the circumstances (and previous history of the firm) are such that slow repayments of capital accounts occur, then each partner either changes the system or makes maximum provision himself for tax deductible pension funding.

Pension funding is the major method of building personal wealth outside the business, and of taking our pre-tax profits, so to speak, in the form of pension contributions.

---

### STRATEGY #373
## Pay unfunded pensions and cash lump sums to retiring partners

---

Partners who usually postpone pension decisions due to a lack of structure or urgency should consider the following.

Payment of a pension may be made from the profits of the continuing partners. Partners will therefore only face the expense of pension provision at actual retirement. This enables them to:

- maximise capital in the business
- find new partners to shoulder the burden
- cope with retirement partners' needs

The partnership can pay a pension to retiring partners. This will be deductible to the other partners in their partnership proportions. To qualify as earned income for allowances, the pension must:

- be paid in accordance with the partnership agreement or supplementary agreement
- not exceed 50% of the average profit of the retiring partner for the best three of the last seven years before retirement
- allow a tax-free cash sum of 25% of the notional accumulated sum to be taken
- be allowed to increase and/or be paid to a spouse or dependant
- allow 5% of net relevant earnings to provide term life insurance cover
- be paid direct or by the purchase of an annuity

Such a 'fund' may be used for the benefit of a partnership. No loans are allowed if a fund is established, but the scheme can purchase commercial property from the partnership and lease it back on commercial terms.

Partners may therefore provide for pensions in a tax-efficient manner without having to set aside capital. The unfunded scheme has its limitations, especially where profits fluctuate, and pensions will probably be lower than if conventionally funded. It should not be relied upon as capital may not be available at the exact time when it is required.

## 3. Profit strategies for companies

Depending on the business objectives and management policies of the company, taking the needs of the shareholders as well as the strength, well-being and status of the company, into account, it will:

- endeavour to make best use of tax reducing strategies pre-profit taking; *and*
- decide on the best wealth-creation terms for shareholders.

Usually there is a conflict between these two objectives. Most tax-reducing strategies involve expenditure of one kind or another. Expenditure which is allowable against taxable income will ultimately *reduce* the amount available for shareholders by way of dividends. For most closely-connected companies, this does not pose a problem, as the shareholders are usually its directors. For large companies with more shareholders, some of them unconnected, the company will formulate a dividend policy commensurate with the stage of the business growth.

In the final analysis, it comes down to a sensible balance or mix. The directors would want to retain sufficient capital for capitalisation and working capital needs, now and in the future. At the same time, they would wish to maximise their personal wealth either through:

- increasing value of their shares or share options (if they have them)
- dividends
- bonuses
- other wealth-creation plans funded by the business, such as pensions and NIC avoidance schemes.

The main challenge, having decided on business planning policy, will be the allocation of *pre-tax profits* to funding internal schemes and cash flows, and the allocation of *post-tax profits* to dividends and retained reserves.

# STRATEGY #374
## Paying dividends or bonuses – decide which is the best route

The Taxes Act 1988, s 834(3) has dividends taxable in the year in which they fall due for payment. A dividend from a UK company carries a tax credit [TA 1988, section 231; FA 1993, section 78].

When a company declares and pays a dividend, it must pay ACT (Advance Corporation Tax). The current rate of ACT is 20/80ths of the dividend, or 20% of the grossed-up amount.

The tax credit available to those receiving dividends is restricted to 20%. Thus a dividend of £80 is treated as gross income of £100.

Individuals receiving dividends, who are liable for tax at 40%, will have to pay an additional 20% on dividend income. If an individual is not subject to higher rate tax, the 20% tax credit is deemed sufficient. At present, this represents a saving of 5% on the basic rate of 25%.

Other taxable income is always taxed *first* in the hierarchy and then dividend income.

For example:

Assume Roger received dividend income of £80,000 in 1995/96. The tax credits total £20,000 and the 'gross income' is therefore £100,000. Roger has other income (which is taxable), after allowances and reliefs, of £21,000. His tax liability is as follows:

- at 20% on the first £3,200
- at 25% on the next £17,800
- at 20% on the balance of the basic rate band: £3,300
- at 40% on £95,700

There are various levels of tax efficiency in deciding whether executives should take bonuses or receive dividends. Likewise, for the company, it may be more economical to pay bonuses rather than dividends as a form of wealth extraction. For example, for profits up to £300,000, it is more economic to pay dividends than bonuses. Over £300,000, the marginal rate of corporation tax at 35% comes into play and as profits rise, a point is reached where the additional corporation tax exceeds the saving of National Insurance and bonuses become more economical.

One should consider the effect of regular dividend payments on share values. Probably it would be better to have different classes of shares which have different dividend entitlements.

## Dividends versus bonuses: Net effect (1995/96)

Assume the trading profit in the company was £100,000. This could be paid by either a bonus or by way of dividends, or both. The executive is already a 40% taxpayer on other earnings. At different levels of corporation tax it may be better to take a dividend rather than a bonus, and vice versa. The following calculations will indicate the best routes for various corporation tax rates.

1. *At 25% corporation tax, it is better to take dividends*

| **Bonus route** | | |
|---|---|---|
| Bonus | £90,744 | Employer's NIC |
| Tax | £36,298 | £9,256 |
| **To director** | **£54,446** | |

| **Dividend route – 25% corporation tax company** | |
|---|---|
| £75,000 × 100/80ths (grossed up) | £93,750 |
| Tax credit at 20% | £18,750 |
| **To director (£75,000-£18,750)** | **£56,250** |

The dividend of £75,000 arises as follows for a 25% tax rate company. Mainstream tax payable is £25,000.

| | |
|---|---|
| Dividend | £75,000 |
| ACT £75,000 × 100/80ths - £75,000 | £18,750 |
| Balance mainstream Corporation Tax (£25,000 - £18,750) | £6,250 |
| | **£100,000** |

2. *At 33% corporation tax, it is better to take the bonus (£54,446)*

| **Dividend route – 33% corporation tax company** | |
|---|---|
| £67,000 × 100/80ths (grossed up) | £83,750 |
| Tax credit at 20% | £16,750 |
| **To director (£67,000-£16,750)** | **£50,250** |

The dividend of £67,000 arises as follows for a 33% tax rate company. Mainstream tax payable is £33,000.

| | |
|---|---|
| Dividend | £67,000 |
| ACT £67,000 × 100/80ths - £67,000 | £16,750 |
| Balance mainstream corporation tax (£33,000 - £16,750) | £16,250 |
| | **£100,000** |

3. *At 35% corporation tax, it is better to take the bonus (£54,446)*

| Dividend route – 35% corporation tax company | |
| --- | --- |
| £65,000 × 100/80ths (grossed up) | £81,250 |
| Tax credit at 20% | £16,250 |
| **To director (£65,000-£16,250)** | **£48,750** |

The dividend of £65,000 arises as follows for a 35% tax rate company. Mainstream tax payable is £35,000.

| | |
| --- | --- |
| Dividend | £65,000 |
| ACT £65,000 × 100/80ths - £65,000 | £16,250 |
| Balance mainstream corporation tax (£35,000 - £16,250) | £18,750 |
| | **£100,000** |

4. *Summary of the dividend vs bonus routes*

| | |
| --- | --- |
| Bonus to director | £54,446 |
| Dividend '25%' company | £56,250 |
| | (+£1,804 |
| | or 3%) |
| Dividend '33%' company | £50,250 |
| | (-£4,196 |
| | or -8%) |
| Dividend '35%' company | £48,750 |
| | (-£5,696 |
| | or -10%) |

The director, in this case, is better off with a bonus payment for a company paying corporation tax at 33% or 35%, but better off with dividends where the company pays 25% in corporation taxes.

> ## STRATEGY #375
> ## Improve the position of the director by making a pre-tax pension contribution for him

It will be considerably better value for the director to have a bonus and pension contribution compared to either a bonus or dividend, as shown by the following example. Assume the company will spend £100,000:

| | |
|---|---|
| Bonus (after employer's NIC £5,153) | £45,372 |
| less 40% tax | £18,148 |
| Available cash | £27,224 |
| Pension contribution | £50,000 |
| | **£77,224** |

The company will still spend a total of £100,000, made up of bonus, employer's NIC on the bonus and the pension contribution.

The net position for the executive is £77,224, made up of bonus plus pension. (The company also saves further NIC through the reduced bonus.)

The bonus/pension split in value or wealth-creation terms is considerably better than the bonus alone or any of the dividend positions. It also largely overcomes the problem of reinvestment of the bonus or dividends, as the pension route (for part of package) provides a tax-efficient investment medium.

---

## STRATEGY #376
## Make use of other NIC avoidance schemes to reduce taxation

---

(See also Chapter 17.) The business may wish to benefit executives by diverting bonuses or salary increases into schemes which avoid National Insurance contributions payable by the company. Whilst the Inland Revenue do their utmost to outlaw these schemes through new legislation (the latest attack being to close the loophole offered by commodities received as payment or bonuses by directors – such as gold, wines etc), there are still a number around which are widely used.

In essence, they may provide the following:

• Payment to a director falling outside the 'benefit in kind' NIC rules. Result: no company NIC. Usual corporate reliefs and deductions apply.
• As above, but the scheme is structured so that no charge gives rise to a PIID benefit either, so no tax results in the employee's hands.

This is a legitimate means to transfer wealth to individuals, avoiding various taxes. *You can do anything legal to AVOID tax, but don't do anything to EVADE it.* See Chapters 16, 17, 18 for further details.

## STRATEGY #377
## Take out investigation insurance policies if utilising avoidance schemes

The chances are the company may at some stage (in any event, whether avoiding tax or not) come under intensive investigation from the DSS (for NIC), from Customs and Excise (for VAT) and from the Inland Revenue (for taxes), and this can be a *very* costly event.

Cheap investigations insurance cover is available from about £300 a year and covers the costs of investigations up to, say, £60,000 worth of fees.

## STRATEGY #378
## Utilise all personal allowances and reliefs to reduce taxes

You build personal wealth from what you retain, not what you have to give away in taxes. This is covered in Chapters 16 and 18.

## STRATEGY #379
## Make sure the business is deducting all it can in capital allowances and business expenditures

Bigger deductions give rise to bigger profits, so the company should regularly carry out internal checks and audits as well as credit management controls.

## STRATEGY #380
## Borrow from a director's pension fund rather than a bank

Interest payable to the pension fund is tax deductible to the company. Interest paid to the pension fund accumulates free of all taxes. This is an important strategy to increase wealth and to keep the cycle of financing 'within the business' alive.

## STRATEGY #381
## Invest retained profits wisely

Retained profits are after-tax profits held as reserves in the company and capitalised. They are also a measure of wealth in the company, available for distribution on liquidation (to creditors, then shareholders). The value of the balance sheet and subsequent shareholders' value is increased if profits are retained in this way.

Many companies have idle cash balances not earning any interest (or negligible amounts), some millions of pounds being on call, but never called upon. The answer is to have a proper investment policy for growth or income or property purchases for excess cash. This aspect is covered more fully in Chapter 30.

## STRATEGY #382
## Sell shares and retain wealth by using capital gains tax exemptions

Ultimately the shareholder will wish to sell shares in the company or pass them on to future generations for dividend flow or subsequent sale.

There are capital gains tax reliefs and business property reliefs available on retirement, sale of shares or on death. This allows you to maximise your wealth position without paying additional taxes.

In some circumstances, the company may have to set up specific exit routes for shareholders – in other words, make their shares more marketable. This is accomplished internally through ESOT arrangements and other share purchase and share option schemes, and externally via the Alternative Investment Market (AIM), the Stock Exchange or sales to private investors.

## Key points summary

- Profits may be taken out of a business on a pre-tax basis or after-tax.

- Pre-tax involves the use of wealth-builders, such as pension schemes and NIC avoidance investments.

- The different choices for when to take dividends or bonuses are given.

- After-tax means using dividends, if a company, or intensive personal financial planning if a sole trader or partner for investment purposes.

- The question of whether to leave profits in the business to add value can only occur *after* tax.

# PART 3

# Business Wealth-Creation Strategies

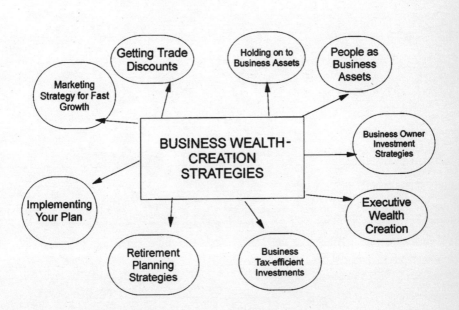

# CHAPTER 24

# Marketing Strategy for Fast Growth

*Marketing is like a little wheelbarrow – it just stands there unless you push it.*
**Making Your Business Really Fly seminar, 1995**
*The enigma of marketing is that it is one of man's oldest activities and yet it is regarded as the most recent of the business disciplines*
**Michael J Baker, *Marketing: Theory and Practice*, 1st Edition, Macmillan 1976**

**Objective: To develop the best marketing strategies to grow the business sales faster**

The business owner needs to make an in-depth analysis to determine how the business may achieve its true potential. The important factor here is how to increase revenue without spending thousands of pounds on high-risk marketing activities – in other words, working *smarter*, not harder.

Marketing is activities undertaken by the business which lead to increased sales and revenues which, in turn, lead to greater profitability. Marketing activities also lead to customer awareness and customer servicing which follow on from customer satisfaction.

Why is marketing such an important function? Well, some goods and services may sell themselves, but generally they don't and they have to be promoted in order to get the sale. It doesn't matter how good the service is, or how excellent the quality of the product, the bottom line is that if no one knows about it, it isn't going to sell.

The ultimate aim of marketing strategy is to help the decision-makers to focus the strengths of the organisation so that they can achieve the maximum advantage in a competitive marketplace. Strategic planning must direct this concentration of power to be effective.

---

### STRATEGY #383
### Define the marketing policy of the business

---

The business decision-makers will formulate marketing strategy and decide the policy of the business in respect of how it will achieve its aims. These aims and objectives will be the result of the 'why?' behind the decisions of the business, and are usually:

- To increase return on equity invested. What must be done in the business to increase the bottom line profitability?
- To capitalise on strengths and opportunities by taking advantage of changes in the marketplace.
- To reposition the business, taking into account what competitors are doing. This may mean changing customer perceptions of the products and services offered by the business.
- To take *action* decisions based on the formulation of business policies.

In order to accomplish these objectives, the business must know exactly what the *current situation* is, how it got there (and what decisions were made to get there) and where it wishes to go from its present position. It must then determine what steps have to be taken to get to where it wants to be (future position). Finally, it must determine what additional knowledge, skill or resources it requires to achieve its strategic objectives. The marketing policy of the business is then translated into various strategies and actions for implementation.

The *strategic variables* to determine the range of products or services for the business must then be determined, with appropriate strategies for each.

## STRATEGY #384
## Formulate the strategic variables necessary to ensure maximum returns for the business

What must the business have or do in terms of capabilities and resources in order to attain its corporate objectives? The following will determine the scope of products and markets for the business. The *strategic variables* are in brackets.

1. *Products or services offered (Products/services)*
What decisions must be made to get *more* of the business's products and services to the marketplace?

2. *Distribution of products and services (Distribution channels)*
The methods of distribution of products and services to the market determine what the markets are and, indeed, what markets will be served. For example, multi-level marketing, chain of stores, whole-saling.

3. *The needs of the market (Markets)*
The business may have a commitment to serve a particular market with particular products or services – such as office supplies, computer paper, car parts, cleaning materials.

4. *Available technological capability (People, finance)*
Does the business have the technological capability? This will determine the products, services and markets served. Examples are computer software, electronics, scientific support.

5. *Available production capability (People)*
The production facilities of the business will determine the products and services offered, as well as the markets to be served. Examples of the latter are office equipment, kitchen appliances, furniture. Can the business cope with and supply products and services on time?

6. *Sales methods (People)*
The ways in which products and services are sold determines what they are and the markets to be served. Examples are direct sales, retail sales, direct mail, mail order.

7. *Availability of natural resources (Products, services, finance)*
Has the business access to adequate raw materials and natural resources such as water, fuel, gas? The availability or otherwise will

determine its future strategies.

**8.** *Future growth possibilities (People, finance)*
The size and future growth rate in market share will determine the products or services offered and the markets served.

**9.** *Sales volumes and profitability (Finance, people)*
The profitability of operations determines the products or services offered and the markets to be served.

The key strategic variables of products are determined by the above 'driving forces' of the business. These determine markets, products, services, capabilities and resources which are *focused* in the strategic objectives of the business.

Often, the product or service itself is the key driving force of the business. Without it, there is no business organisation. A major life office features this aspect in its communication to sales people – everything begins with the sale of a policy. Without sales, the business will fail.

---

### STRATEGY #385
### Develop a marketing strategy for the business

---

Every aspect of strategic planning for the business ultimately results in market planning so that the way the business performs in the marketplace may be improved.

The businesses which succeed are those which have the *clearer vision* of their current position, where they are going, who they are, their future prospects and what they stand for. These are not necessarily the businesses with the greatest resources or capabilities at their disposal, but those with the capability to exploit their strengths whilst compensating for their weaknesses. These businesses bring the best minds in the business organisation to focus on the best market opportunities available.

They will achieve excellence in profitable niche areas, determine how they are different from competitors (and superior to them), know which market areas are the most valuable to exploit and will be able to get the whole organisation behind achieving market dominance.

Concentration of business power is the essential requirement for all strategic success – being able to think, plan, live and implement strategy in each area of activity.

More specifically, the marketing strategy will be segmented into individualised marketing activities to accomplish financial and profitability strategic objectives.

The specific marketing strategy of the business will essentially be contained in a 'marketing business plan' and will detail the following areas to plan the marketing campaign:

- Reasons for the particular strategy.
- Which markets, what products or services?
- The how, what and who – implementation and action plans, with time lines.
- *Competition*, sensitivity analysis and any adjustments, for increasing sales, in product or service price, quality, quantity and types of customer, which need to be made. This may include discounting or price-cutting or a different approach to a previously non-marketed market segment.
- The known *successes* and *failures* in this marketplace and the reasons why.
- The method of *distribution* of the marketing message – the media, advertising, PR (public relations).
- The *resources* required, from production capability and resources to finance required.
- The *targets* for increasing sales and therefore *profitability* which are forecasted (after evaluation of the additional financial expenditure and provision of manpower and other resources).
- Results of a 'test' marketing campaign would be a vital ingredient for future strategic decision-making.

In short, the planning of the specific marketing activity will require an assessment of strategic variables relevant to it. These must be co-ordinated into the whole and then implemented. If not, the business ends up with a wheelbarrow full of good ideas and plans, but no one to push it.

---

## STRATEGY #386
## Ask specific questions relative to the business's marketing activities

---

What are you doing to push the marketing wheelbarrow?

- When was the last time that you or the business undertook a specific marketing activity?
- How many hours each week are allocated to marketing by the business?
- How much money is allocated to marketing each month?
- How effective are you in pushing the marketing wheelbarrow?

## STRATEGY #387
## The big secret is to implement one thing and to run with it

The problem is that there are so many good ideas associated with marketing goods and services, that the natural inclination is to try them all. However, this scattergun approach is not very effective and actually dilutes your concentration and distorts your strategic focus.

The secret is to decide on one marketing strategy and to run with it. If that one succeeds, stay with it. If it fails, then try a different marketing plan.

Marketing is not an exact science. What works perfectly well in one area for one firm may be a disaster for another firm trying the same strategies. People are different, timing is different, products and services are different. The marketing function or activity may only require fine-tuning for the best effect. Ever tried to tune into a radio station or television channel? It may only require the minutest of adjustments for the perfect reception or picture, or you could be miles away from target. You will never know unless you try.

So, if thinking about a marketing plan, the most inexpensive method of research is to 'test market' the product or service first. Do not overload yourself – trust your own people to get on with the job – but if they are only 80% as efficient as you are, you can always 'fine tune' for the extra percentage.

## STRATEGY #388
## Determine exactly what the marketing activity will be

The marketing business plan will give the component parts of the marketing strategy. Some of these will relate to the *specific* marketing activity which is required.

There are a number of ways to grow the business fast. Most of them relate to customer service, and are to:

- increase the number of customers which you want.
- increase the number of times they come back (repeat sales).
- increase the profitability by increasing the average pound value of the sale.
- increase the effectiveness of the business. This is best achieved by systematising what you do.

Customers must be encouraged to spend. Determine *how effective* the business is in each of the above areas. In many profitability evaluations, the successful companies were those that never stopped improving in the areas of quality, innovation and service. The following variables made companies more profitable:

- excellent customer service
- high quality products and services
- market leadership

Each component will have an underlying activity or number of activities which must be done. For example, Nemesis Ltd wants to increase sales and will undertake the marketing activities in the following table, leading to increased customers, repeat sales, increasing profitability and increased effectiveness of the business. The product is a high quality computer software programme, the company is a market leader and has an excellent and well established after-sales service. However, it is not well known because the business has a relatively short track record.

The company has put together a marketing strategy to win more market share. The various activities to be undertaken are described as follows:

| Activity | Action | Expected result |
|---|---|---|
| Marketing to new customers | 1. Advertising in local press, computer magazines and journals, with coupons requesting information. | Heightened awareness leading to increased sales |
| | 2. Telesales to small business users. | Leads and responses for 2,000 new customers in 6 months. |
| | 3. Public relations exercise, articles and editorials through PR company. | Ongoing exercise to increase awareness and reinforce the sale. |
| | 4. Offer a money-back guarantee, if not completely satisfied. | Reinforces sales and buying decisions. |
| | 5. Full *internal* marketing programme for employees in the business. | Information and awareness of what the business is doing. |
| Marketing to existing customers | 1. Mailshot to customers offering upgrades of programmes, with guarantees, and training if required. | Repeat sales, client bonding, competition lock-out. |
| | 2. Include copies of advertising and editorials on the company which have appeared in the press. | Reinforcement of previous sales. |
| | 3. Telecommunications for customer service. | Reinforcement of company as a top quality company. |

Each of the *actions* can be broken down into further activities. For example, 'Telesales to small business users' is also an *activity*. Who, what, when, how, what cost, what expected results, training, monitoring of results, lists, directors, inside staff or external organisations do the work?

With each activity is a *task*. Who is going to do it, or arrange it and then implement it? Don't let the wheelbarrow stand idle for want of someone to give it a push.

The activity could be as simple as the one in the following example from my own case files. A practice of veterinary surgeons had been conducting their business in one area for many years. Within the last two years, three new competitors had set up in the same area and were slowly and competitively drawing existing customers (patients), and the possibility of new ones, away from the practice.

A number of aspects were quite apparent after an investigation of the practice's present position. Sales income was indeed falling. The practice had had 15,000 dog, cat, bird and horse patients over the years, none of them databased, but on a card index system. It had recently built new kennels, a private animal hospital and recovery rooms with underfloor heating. All were under-utilised.

A decision was made to computerise the client list and then to send out a mailshot to all previous and existing customers/patients' owners. It emphasised the new facilities and underfloor heating in the kennels for owners going away or with sick pets in recovery. It also mentioned that certain animals required regular inoculations against disease and possibly now was the time for that job!

The result was a 30% increase in existing customers making repeat sales within 90 days!

This mailshot was followed up six months later with another, offering cheap pet insurance and a discount on a pet health-check. The result was a 27% increase in repeat sales.

The cost of the activity (the first mailshot) was:

| | |
|---|---|
| Databasing costs: | £350 (teenager on vacation) |
| Mail-out costs: | £5,000 |
| New income (repeat sales): | £150,000 |

Add to this customer satisfaction (and bonding) with heightened awareness of what is on offer, and people will buy.

*Too often the fault lies in the fact that customers are unaware of what you do, sell, offer and have available. Once they are aware, they respond.*

```
┌─────────────────────────────────────────────────────┐
│                   STRATEGY #389                       │
│               Have a marketing budget                 │
└─────────────────────────────────────────────────────┘
```

Ever heard the saying, 'You must speculate to accumulate'? Corporate goodwill only goes so far, with free press editorial for example. Beyond that, your marketing activity is going to cost the business money. Some businesses spend 20% or more of turnover on marketing activities. Direct mail organisations may spend up to 60% or 70% of turnover solely on marketing activities. Yet, other businesses will spend next to nothing. Examples of the latter include professional practices such as solicitors and accountants, and other businesses existing solely on referrals.

Pay close attention to the financial side of marketing and ensure that a proper marketing budget is established with defined costings for marketing activities such as advertising, public relations, mail-outs, postage, stationery, telesales, the internet and so on. In fact, whatever the cost is going to be, to get the goods or services to the marketplace and sold in increasing volumes must be budgeted for.

Plan the marketing budget within given cost constraints. Use different approaches to reduce costs. For example, if your promotion to the buying public is to send out an expensive glossy prospectus costing £10 each, then it is better to send out a 'mailer' telling the target audience about the product and the brochure first, including an invitation to buy with a reply-paid card. Only then send out the expensive glossy brochure to your targeted audience. We call this the 'Two-Step' marketing approach.

Successful businesses will usually spend at least 10% of turnover on marketing and related activities to increase sales, and therefore profitability. The only problem is that the business does not suffer marketing fools gladly. This gives very little scope for target market experimentation because of the cost of failure associated with it. This in turn stifles marketing innovation. The business should therefore be prepared for marketing development costs.

Not all marketing activities need affect cash flow. Chapter 25 on barter and trade discounts will show you how to advertise, get PR, and increase sales without spending hard cash.

## STRATEGY #390
## Only take small steps, one at a time

It is important to build on success. Try your selected marketing activity. If it works, build on it, gradually going for larger groups of customers and sales. If it fails, try a different approach.

Don't try a scattergun approach. Focus attention on one marketing strategy or activity and dynamise that. Rather move from one to another than trying all at once. For one, you may give your own marketplace a confusing message. For another, it may be difficult to monitor progress.

This advice or strategy can be used with *each* product or service offered by the business.

Another important factor is that if all the marketing force and energy was spent on a number of different fronts at once, you would run out of marketing finance and energy a lot sooner. Money lasts longer if carefully focused on the desired marketing activity.

## STRATEGY #391
## Get the message across – you can have the best product or service but if no one knows about it, you won't sell it

How true. This is a message brought home to many businesses in every field of endeavour. If no one knows about it, how can it possibly sell? Sales mean marketing. Marketing means activity, awareness and sales. This is a perpetual cycle.

From personal experience in running a large training organisation, the most important thing was getting bottoms on seats. In other words, you could have the best training organisation in the world, with the most qualified trainers, but if you have no one to train, you don't have a business. The success of the business usually comes down to how good the marketing is.

## STRATEGY #392
## To increase sales, always give a guarantee

Those businesses surveyed by us over the years were more successful if the product or service was accompanied by a guarantee.

The guarantee must be marketing oriented – in other words, an offer

of money back if not completely satisfied. It should also be uncondi-
tional. If the client or customer is not happy with your product, take it
back, exchange it for another – do whatever must be done to retain the
client. The word soon gets out and it spreads fast, especially if related
back to bad service.

One company even replaces goods *whenever* the fault occurs or dissatisfaction arises. This can be turned into repeat sales. For example, if
after a number of years the customer wishes to bring the product back,
the company will replace it at half the cost. The returning customer
often makes other purchases at the same time.

If guarantees are offered, they are a very strong tool for reinforcing the
sale. It must be good if backed up by a meaningful guarantee. If doing
mail order promotion and advertising, you must, by law, have a money-
back guarantee or at least a cooling-off period with a return of goods and
services within a certain period. The business can use this to its advantage by promoting the 'if not completely satisfied' guarantee. How does
*your* business guarantee its goods and services?

---

## STRATEGY #393
## Go for repeat sales and customer bonding

---

It is easier to sell to someone who has satisfactorily bought from your
business in the past. In fact, it is cheaper to market new products and
services to existing customers – they expect it. If customer trust is there,
repeat sales and new sales should be easier.

Some products are very difficult to achieve repeat sales on. By their
nature they may last forever or satisfy one-off needs requirements. This
is why innovation on existing products is so important. Take a look at
the computer hardware and software industries. The salesman selling
the hardware will tell you it will satisfy your needs for the next ten
years. Yet in a year's time he will be back trying to sell you the latest
technological improvements – and you will buy because you don't
know any better. Yet your existing equipment will still do the job perfectly well.

Repeat sales are usually well supported with product branding and
awareness campaigns. Often the original sale is made and the repeat
sale is something completely different, such as an accessory. Take the
pet shop industry. Once you have bought your parrot, the bird should
usually live for some time. Where the pet shop makes its real money is
through selling you bird food, a cage, mirrors, swings, water bowls,
toys, lice powder and a host of accessories: cost of one parrot £25, cost
of accessories £125! Even a £1.50 white mouse can cost you £75 for all
the little extras, and as for a £350 pedigree dog . . .

The art of selling, therefore, lies in getting the customer to spend more. It will come as no surprise that petrol stations with shops selling sweets, cards, books, maps, gadgets, drinks, flowers and so on sometimes make more profits from the sale of accessories than from fuel.

What are your accessories? How do you package your goods or services? How do you make it easy for the customer to come back to you?

---

## STRATEGY #394
## Strive for customer satisfaction at all times

---

It is a fact that companies with a market perception of excellent customer service (along with high quality products and services, as well as market leadership) are more profitable. Many studies have been made in this area and all have found that a satisfied customer will come back and spend more with the business. A dissatisfied one will not (unless there is a monopoly). Moreover, a dissatisfied customer will increase the sales of the competition and drive away some of your other customers.

The objective of fast growth for the business will be stimulated significantly through a satisfied customer base which will lead to repeat sales, heightened market awareness, retention of customers and higher levels of profitability.

---

## STRATEGY #395
## Ensure that the business has a customer care programme

---

The message is simple. If you value your customer, then care about him. What many businesses fail to appreciate is that it is not only the marketing department or PR individuals who are responsible for satisfaction of the customer. It is *everyone* in the business. Make the entire business team *aware* of the company's marketing strategy and customer care programme.

Plenty of sales have been lost when the telephone is first answered. A brusque receptionist, not trained in customer care, can lose valuable clients. The problem is that you will never know. Many customers, fed up with the unanswered telephone, will just go elsewhere with their business. One company shows that it cares by offering a free product if the telephone is not answered in two rings – this is their guarantee of service.

Take the case of the production manager with no inter-personal skills. A customer wishes to have further product details and the production manager supplies them. The client is not entirely satisfied and occasions an argument. The production manager, incensed, tells the client 'where to get off'. Result: a glowing victory for the production manager (in *his* opinion); a lost client to the business.

A customer care programme requires training – more often than not supplied by external consultants and trainers. In fact, this route is probably the best way to get the message across to those whom you know couldn't care less about the customer. The impact will be greater if someone outside the organisation is used. Everyone, from the chief executive to the receptionist, should be involved.

If customers are valued – then tell them. Ask the customer for feedback on the business and its service. The strategy of quality leadership asks the question, 'How does the *customer* define quality?' What quality differences does your customer perceive in buying from the opposition or from you?

Exactly what does your customer buy from you? What must you do to be perceived by your customers as being the quality leader in the marketplace?

---

### STRATEGY #396
### Always get testimonials from satisfied clients or customers

---

Third party endorsement is always the best method of referral. It enables the product or service to sell itself. 'If it was good enough for him, it will be good enough for me.'

Do not be afraid to ask satisfied customers for a letter telling you how pleased they are. Then use these, or portions of them (with the customer's or client's permission), as part of your business promotion campaign.

---

### STRATEGY #397
### Target the market and market to the target

---

Define exactly who the customers of the business are, or who you want them to be. Then design your marketing programme to target this group as exactly as possible.

For example, a legal practice wishes to move away from conveyancing and mortgage work towards small business employment law, wills for executives and insolvency work.

| Existing clients | Shift to | New clients required |
|---|---|---|
| • low to medium income groups for house buying<br><br>• mortgage arrangements<br><br>• client referrals from estate agents (drying up)<br>• retain mortgage service | → | • small business with at least 3 directors or partners<br>• insolvency work with small businesses |

| Marketing to clients for existing services | Shift to marketing for new clients | Marketing to new clients for new services |
|---|---|---|
| • referrals from estate agents<br>• existing clients who wanted services<br><br>• literature only, no marketing activity | → | • define what is being offered<br>• seminars, telesales for appointments, referrals from business management consultants<br>• contact existing clients to ascertain those in companies' employ for new services to be offered<br>• marketing activity to target market |

The more *specific* the target marketing, the better the result.

---

### STRATEGY #398
## Use the best promotional tools to market the business's products

---

No one can argue with the fact that the best promotion is free promotion. Whilst it is important to obtain newspaper editorial or advertorial (you take out an advertisement and then you get free editorial coverage and promotion), it cannot be relied upon as the only promotional tool for the business.

There are many different types of promotion vehicles to be considered, depending on available budget finances and the particular circumstances of the product and the target audience to be reached.

The list is not exhaustive, but the following promotional tools are well used by businesses:

- media – TV, radio, press
- advertising – newspapers, magazines, billboards, flyers
- seminars
- personal contacts
- testimonials
- sponsored events
- incentives and discounts
- direct mail and coupon or reply-paid returns
- packaged advertisements on other products
- telesales, telefaxes, internet information
- directories, the Yellow Pages, the Thomson Directories
- Chambers of Commerce
- special events and hospitality promotions
- giveaways

Make sure that all presentations are quality ones. There is nothing worse than a 'tacky' presentation, such as a blurred, many-photocopied sheet, or one devoid of colour or interest. The quality of your presentation will reflect the quality thinking behind the business.

---

### STRATEGY #399
## Develop your own marketing skills

---

Small businesses with limited budgets should at least be aware of what marketing can do for them to increase sales and profits.

Even the most simple newsletter or letter for a mail-out can be constructed in-house. Send it to a PR firm to be polished for maximum effect if you have to, but do not be afraid to design your own. Once you have done so, show it to a few clients or customers for their critical opinions on what you have done. For example, the mail-out to the customers of the veterinary practice mentioned earlier was compiled by one of the vets with no outside help. The main message is one of communication.

Perception also plays its part. Some campaigns even do better if they appear more 'homespun' as opposed to professionally-produced glossy newsletters. There are many courses available on marketing skills and presentations, and of course a wide range of software to choose from for desktop publishing.

Press contacts are also most useful. Consider that you may spend £5,000 on an advertising campaign. It may be better value to feed a journalist for, say, £100 and have an article written on you and the business. In fact, for £5,000 you could have lunch with at least 500 journalists, editors and people of influence – or what about selected clients?

Advertising, to be successful, must be continuous, over a number of insertions (say half a dozen) or over a period (every week in the same place). One-offs seldom bring home the bacon.

---

## STRATEGY #400
## Keep the profile of the business as high as possible, at all times

---

The marketing and PR profile is an important aspect of the business. For many years businesses believed that it was only their customers who were supposed to be affected by marketing activities, such as advertising. Not so. In fact, the employees and sales team feel good at seeing the business being promoted on a continuous basis. They refer to the promotion when talking to customers and it strengthens their beliefs.

It also comes down to what I call third party endorsement. Why is it that your typed message to clients does not have half the impact of a photocopy of an advertisement placed by you in a prestigious newspaper or magazine? It may have exactly the same words. It will even look like an advertisement, but the fact that it was in *The Times* (even though you paid for it) was a form of third party endorsement.

To keep the profile of the business high at all times means that positive press and public relations are most important. Why do people buy from your business and not from the competition (or vice versa – why do people buy from the competition?) Even if your business is smaller than those of your major competitors, properly targeted PR and press can certainly psyche out the marketplace, leading to increased sales. If you have testimonials or a good, positive message to use an endorsement, so much the better. People who are buyers are automatically drawn to the market leaders as first choice. If not a market leader, then some other significant buying advantage must be displayed, such as quality or price.

Employees must be properly briefed that only one or two executives will make comments to the press and no one else. All press and PR should be circulated to all employees.

---

### STRATEGY #401
### If you fail at marketing, keep on fine-tuning: don't give up

---

Not every marketing effort is a resounding success. Many attempts will fail to get the desired results from sales; however, you will have achieved greater marketing awareness.

Learn to be persistent. If the product is right for the market (if the price is affordable) people will buy it. It is a numbers game at the end of the day – the more people aware of it, the greater the level of sales.

One firm of tax publishers sends out the *same* mailshot up to five times a year to the *same* customer base. Their experience is that the first three 'warm up' the target market. Most customers buy on mail-outs three and four and number five is there for reinforcement. This now happens year after year, yet when when they sent out their first mail-out, there were no takers. Having plenty of mail-out literature they sent it out again. Still no sales. And again – this time a few sales resulted, so out it went a fourth time, when the majority of customers bought. Often it's purely a case of the client seeing that the business still exists.

---

### STRATEGY #402
### Do regular surveys amongst existing customers and prospective ones

---

Surveys conducted on a regular basis are part of the market research of the business. They will give a 'feel' for the market and enable the business owner to 'read' the market. This information is valuable in that it enables the business to target its marketing more effectively.

## STRATEGY #403
## If using direct marketing letters to clients or prospects, have your letter professionally prepared for maximum effect

Practice has shown that the placing of certain messages, how the letter is constructed, what information it contains, how long it is and whether it has a 'PS' or not, can critically affect its effective usage as a sales tool.

Constructing the perfect marketing letter will increase sales substantially. My own business has experimented with various formats and styles and some certainly are much more effective than others. Where the key elements of your message are placed is most important. The reader's attention must be grabbed immediately. Most people read the headline then flip to the end to see who the letter is from (taking in the most important message in the 'PS') before making a decision to read the letter at all.

It is not good sending out a mailshot if it is not followed up. After three days, the customer is beginning to forget the letter, after a week he's unlikely to remember it at all. The most effective method is to telephone within a day or two of the target receiving the letter. Alternatively, telephone the customer/client and state that the letter is in the post and that once he's read it, you will call back.

## STRATEGY #404
## Make it easy for the customer to say 'Yes'

The best methods are reply-paid cards (which are already addressed and require no stamps) or self-addressed envelopes. Customers who have to put your important letter to one side whilst searching for an envelope, writing out your business address and then finding a stamp, may lose interest.

On the bottom of the reply-paid card you can advise the customer to use an envelope if he wishes it to remain confidential.

---

### STRATEGY #405
### Always respect the privacy of the customer or client

---

Only make contact at times convenient to the client and then only if appropriate – not during meal times, for instance, if telephoning or making appointments.

It is important to use only customer-oriented people for these tasks, who can act naturally and don't oversell the product or service. Always be courteous, never rude or 'pushy'.

Never argue with the client – if it is inconvenient for him, establish a more convenient time for the conversation.

---

### STRATEGY #406
### Sell the 'sizzle' not the steak

---

In the main, buyers buy the *benefits* of the product or service, not the product itself. It is what the product or service can *do* for them or *add value* which is important. Draw up a list of the *benefits* of the service or product and familiarise your sales staff with them thoroughly before contacting customers.

For example:

*Product:* Mobile telephone, made by Redicon; plastic encased 24-digit electronic circuit amplifier with multiple reception boosters. Cost £99 + VAT. ('Steak')

*Benefits:* Clear reception wherever you are in the country; no connection charge; lowest tariff of all mobile telephones; small enough to fit into your pocket and light enough not to be a burden when carried; essential as a communications tool when late for appointments or if your car has broken down. More expensive than others but better quality and easy payments available. Free calls for the first month. Money back guarantee if not completely satisfied. ('Sizzle')

---

### STRATEGY #407
### If price is a problem, don't talk price, talk benefits and quality

---

In competitive circumstances, when faced with identical products, the customer will make a decision based on price. However, most products are not identical, or if they are, they may be differentiated through packaging. The customer wants to know what the product or service can do for him or her. The sales process is to add value by giving the benefits and qualities of the product or service and then to ask the customer if price is a problem. People mostly buy what the product or service can do for them and price is often secondary. Higher prices can be reinforced with guarantees and higher levels of service.

---

### STRATEGY #408
### If telesales, sell the appointment, not the product

---

One of the biggest marketing mistakes in telesales is to have (untrained) canvassers attempt to sell the product or the service over the telephone. For one, the client cannot see it, or see it demonstrated. For another, it is unlikely that the telesales canvasser knows the product and its benefits well enough to be totally effective. For sales to occur, the client usually has to be seen. This is especially the case when presentations have to be made, or what is being offered is a long list of alternatives, depending upon the needs requirements of the client or customer.

All the telesales canvasser is selling is the *appointment* for a member of the sales team to visit the client. It is then up to the salesman to make the sale. This is usually the position when selling services or products. However, when selling *advertising* space or soliciting charitable donations or direct selling (e.g. car insurance) *where appointments are not necessary*, the customer will make a buying decision over the telephone and telesales are a superb medium for this.

## STRATEGY #409
## Only buy qualified lists and leads for marketing purposes

The business may decide to mail-out to 40,000 unknown customers and will purchase a list for this purpose. A response of 0% up to 15% can be expected, depending upon what it is. Anything above 3% as a response is considered good. The list price is usually about 30p a name, or say £60 per 1,000 names. Sometimes lists are qualified. The customer exists and knows he or she will be contacted. These leads could cost in the region of £5 to £10 each.

Alternatively, a telesales team could charge, say, £350 + VAT for ten corporate appointments – £35 each. The telesales team may have contacted 200 businesses to get the ten appointments though and has done all the hard work for you already. To get a corporate appointment made for you at this price is well worth it.

## STRATEGY #410
## Contact sufficient prospects to ensure success

Marketing is a 'numbers' game. The greater the population exposed to the marketing information, the greater the numbers interested who will make contact.

A general rule of thumb is that newspaper advertising, properly placed, continuous for a period, will attract a response of 0.5% of 1% of the readership of the newspaper. That is, if the circulation is 1 million, then expect a response of 50. That's if you're not giving anything away or having a special promotion with a product or service which has a high demand.

You may wish to 'test' the advertising marketing strategy, and then compare it to say specifically-targeted telesales.

## STRATEGY #411
## Use marketing incentives to gain attention

This may sound astounding to the average reader, but the free pen, the free clock and other similar incentives actually do increase sales enormously. One advertiser, specialising in off the page direct advertising, has a 15%-20% better response by giving away a pen costing less than

£1. People about to spend £100 a month or more on, say, insurances will make their choice solely on the basis of that £1 pen.

The best one yet has to be the 'hospital plan' where everyone wins a cash prize in advance, without actually entering the draw. This is only valid if you complete the direct debit (which, of course, you are told you can cancel if not entirely satisfied). What is amazing is that the cost of the policy is never mentioned. With people desperate to win anything, thousands have signed up (in fact 'winning' the commission which would have been payable to a broker) and, with general inertia, few will cancel the plan.

Marketing incentives will certainly gain the attention of the customer. Discounts on competitive products are one thing, but incentives allow you to hold your price levels.

Create a sense of urgency in your marketing activities – apply within seven days or you lose the offer – to speed up the response and to get sales from potential buyers.

---

### STRATEGY #412
### Avoid the junk mail approach

---

The average household, according to a recent survey, receives over 300 items of so-called junk mail a year in the UK. In the USA it is up to five times that amount.

Try not to give the impression of junk mail – like the *Readers' Digest* mailers which are too much to read, too full, too many. In fact, your mailer need not be expensive either. Often the one-pager which is simple to read, gets a good response. It is also easier to keep.

---

### STRATEGY #413
### Set reasonable time frames to ensure success
### of the marketing strategy

---

Often results are expected too soon. Sometimes it takes months for the full results of a marketing campaign to be assessed. People receive information, and often store it away until they need it. Product requests have been known to come in years later from the same advertising campaign.

However, plan properly and be prepared always to follow-up. Sometimes campaigns are a resounding success and the business cannot cope, thus losing customers. If you suspect that this may be the case, then plan the marketing campaign in 'bite-sized' chunks.

## STRATEGY #414
## Give feedback to the business regularly and monitor results of the marketing initiatives

This aspect is most important and often neglected. It gives valuable information to the business so that alternatives may be tried or financing restructured if an initiative has failed. The business may be depending on the marketing campaign for its cash flow from sales, and early warnings would be in order if the response was slow.

In addition, feedback and monitoring give an opportunity for assessment. If things went wrong, then *why* did they do so? It may be the wrong product for the wrong target market at the wrong price, marketed at the wrong time. One needs to monitor results for success, in any event, if only to justify the continuing existence of the marketing department.

## STRATEGY #415
## Employ professionals to assist your marketing team

People who do marketing all the time are not only better practised at it, but have had the opportunity to hone their skills within countless similar businesses. They have done and seen it all, and presumably they have the experience to be more successful than those who have not really been involved in the marketing process before, nor been successful at it.

Professional marketers added to the team will increase the costs of marketing. However, they will save time and costly mistakes – or at least minimise the risks of failure.

## STRATEGY #416
## Learn the benefit about promoting value and the value about promoting benefits

People want to buy quality products and services at affordable prices. They want to be valued customers receiving added-value and benefits.

If the business learns how to promote the value of its products or services, and the value to the business is in increased sales from promoting the benefits of the product or service, then the business is in a win/win situation with the customer.

In the final analysis, it is 'service which sells' and keeps the customer coming back for more.

---

**STRATEGY #417**
**The business should continually review its market share and market growth matrix to stay ahead of competitors**

---

This is also a survival tactic. Products and services are divided into different groupings which indicate their potential or decline:

1. *Cash Cows*. These products or services have a high market share, but limited possibilities for market growth. Their sales mean cash continues to come into the business at a high level which supports the development of new products or services.

What are the cash cows in your business?

2. *Stars*. These are products or services with high market share and high market growth potential. There is room for further development and exploitation.

What are the stars in your business?

3. *Question Marks*. Sometimes called goats. These are products and services growing at the same rate as the market, but not very profitable. They could become stars.

What are the question marks in your business?

4. *Dogs*. These products or services have low market share and low market growth, as well as low potential. They should not be proceeded with.

What are the dogs in your business?

The concept that marketing as an activity leads to increased sales and greater business profitability is supported by the many marketing strategies given above to enable the business to grow faster.

## Key points summary

- Marketing is an inexact science, dependent for its results on sales and increased profitability.

- The business could fill its marketing wheelbarrow, but still needs to give it a push, otherwise nothing will happen.

- Strategies for marketing do's and don'ts are given for the business, which include regular monitoring and reviews of what the business has to offer to customers and the ways in which this is satisfactorily concluded.

- By adopting many of these simple strategies, the business can gear up significantly for faster growth.

# CHAPTER 25

# Using the Business for Big Trade Discounts

*Cash is king, but barter is smarter.*
**Ivor Tucker 1995**

## Objective: To buy and sell goods and services without affecting cash flow

The following strategies are more appropriate to the modern business which has these objectives:

- Increasing incremental business at no cost.
- Preserving up to 10% or more of cash flow.
- Gaining new business benefits and services previously considered to be too expensive.
- New marketing initiatives at little cost.
- Benefits, goods and services to reward and incentivise employees and customers at little or no cost.

The above applies to any business, from a small sole trader to a large multi-national plc – and it is actually working in practice.

The system of *barter* has been known to man from the earliest of times. Essentially, goods or services are traded for other goods or services, without the necessity of cash changing hands. A unit of exchange is devised which records a value for transactions. To keep the Customs and Excise happy, VAT is payable on all transactions if applicable.

In the UK today, there are literally thousands of smaller barter groups, which are more self-help than business-generators. They have units of exchange ranging from acorns, tokens or buttons to 'trade pounds'. These smaller groups usually supply baby-sitting or dress-making or other services in exchange for the unit of exchange, which can be used to purchase other services or goods. One council in the North West of England encourages its local group by accepting council tax payments in tokens.

These smaller groups work well within communities, obviating the need for cash payments. What this chapter is about is not those smaller community groups but the larger, national barter groups, such as the Capital Barter Corporation, based in London. These larger organisations only have corporate or professional members and are themselves run as businesses. Belonging to one can save your business thousands, as it has mine.

---

### STRATEGY #418
### Understand how the business barter system works

---

Barter is about trade. It is also about saving cash flow and generating new business. It is therefore also about turning non-cash barter transactions into cash transactions for the business – for example, trading something on barter and then selling it on for cash.

This is how the system works. Your business becomes a member of the barter company, paying an annual fee. The barter company makes its money from membership fees and a percentage levied on transactions.

Assume that your business is a hotel. The needs of the hotel will range from the printing of menus and brochures, to purchasing computer equipment and fax machines, to legal and accounting services, holidays for staff, purchasing goods and other services. What the hotel has to offer are 36,000 bed-nights a year, conference facilities and day rooms for seminars, as well as restaurants.

Taking one of its requirements mentioned above: the hotel faces a print bill of £30,000 for menus, brochures and mail-outs. However, a printer has no need for thousands of bed-nights in a hotel (or even that particular hotel) or to gorge his employees on good hotel food night after night. What the printer requires is good legal advice on his

employee contracts, help with his accounts, financing of a new printing press and flights regularly overseas to visit a subsidiary company in
Hong Kong.

The beauty of the barter system at a business level is that each business notifies what it has to offer and what it wants to the centralised
'barter pool'. Usage of the 'pool' clocks up debit or credit balances in
trade pounds, which the parties can spend on their requirements. By
using the barter pool as often as possible, these balances obviously rise
and fall. Each time a transaction occurs, this is notified to the barter
company which, in turn, invoices for its percentage – about 7% of the
transaction's worth.

The trade position of the two participants would then look like this:

| Hotel buys from printer | | £30,000 | worth of printed goods |
|---|---|---|---|
| Printer buys from | airline | £15,000 | worth of fare |
| | solicitor | £5,000 | worth of legal advice |
| | accountant | £3,000 | worth of accounting |
| | hotel | £1,000 | worth of rooms |
| | restaurants | £500 | worth of meals |
| | computer sale | £10,000 | worth of hardware |
| Total | | £34,500 | |

The overall effect is that the hotel has £28,500 worth of debits, the
printer has a net £4,500 worth of debits and various other suppliers
have debits (they owe) or credits (they can spend) in the pool. No single
member is tied to the goods and services of any other and each can trade
with all other members of the pool. Apart from VAT on the transactions, they are subject to normal taxation and accounting laws and
procedures. The settlement of payment is handled by a third party – the
barter company.

---

### STRATEGY #419
### Increase cash flows, as well as balance sheet values, by using barter to grow the company

---

The following examples are of the financial statements of a small
quality hotel with 100 rooms, before and after barter transactions have
taken place. They illustrate how a company can use barter for a small
portion of its expenses and yet significantly improve its net profit percentage and return on capital invested.

The hotel has an average surplus room capacity of 25 rooms per day out of 100, at a room rate of £100 per room. This represents income not earned of £900,000 per year.

The hotel decides to buy the following items:

|  | £ |
| --- | --- |
| Printing | 10,000 |
| Advertising | 10,000 |
| Taxi hire | 3,000 |
| Employment agency | 2,000 |
| Computer system | 5,000 |
| **Total barter purchases** | **30,000** |

The fee to the barter company (7%) is £2,100 in cash, which is its immediate cash cost of purchases.

Over a period, it makes sales of 300 room-nights, earning £30,000 in trade pounds, for which it pays a further 7% or £2,100 in service fees (less than it pays a travel agent to find clients for beds!).

If the marginal cash cost to the hotel for making these sales is 20%, the additional cash cost for making £30,000 worth of purchases and £30,000 worth of sales on barter equals £10,200 or a cash saving of 66%.

This is shown as follows:

## SUMMARISED PROFIT AND LOSS STATEMENT FOR THE YEARS TO DECEMBER 1995 AND 1996 (COUNTRYFUN HOTELS LTD)

|  | 1995 (before barter transactions) | | 1996 (after barter transactions) | |
| --- | --- | --- | --- | --- |
| Sales | £1,000,000 | 100% | £1,030,000 | 100% |
| Cost of sales | £200,000 | 20% | £206,000 | 20% |
| Gross profit | £800,000 | 80% | £824, 000 | 80% |
| Less: expenses | £750,000 | 75% | £754,200 | 73.2% |
| **Net profit before tax** | **£50,000** | **5%** | **£69,800** | **6.8%** |

## BALANCE SHEET AT 31ST DECEMBER 1995 AND 31ST DECEMBER 1996

| 1995 (before barter transactions) | | | 1996 (after barter transactions) | | |
|---|---|---|---|---|---|
| **Assets** | | | | | |
| **Fixed assets** | | | | | |
| Buildings | 3,000,000 | | 3,000,000 | | |
| Furniture and fittings | 500,000 | 3,500,000 | 500,000 | | 3,500,000 |
| **Current assets** | | | | | |
| Cash in bank | 25,000 | | 44,800 | | |
| Stock | 50,000 | | 50,000 | Barter account balance | |
| Debtors | 75,000 | 150,000 | 75,000 | 169,800 | |
| **Less: current liabilities** | | | | | |
| Trade creditors | 100,000 | | 100,000 | | |
| Bad debt provision | 25,000 | 125,000 | 25,000 | 125,000 | |
| **Net current assets** | | 25,000 | | | 44,800 |
| Total employment of capital | | 3,525,000 | | | 3,544,800 |
| **Represented by long-term liabilities** | | | | | |
| Long-term loan (mortgage) | | 2,500,000 | 2,500,000 | | |
| Shareholders' capital | | 750,000 | 750,000 | | |
| Retained earnings (profits) | | 275,000 | 294,800 | | |
| **Total capital employed** | | 3,525,000 | | | 3,544,800 |
| Return on equity (capital and earnings) | | 4.88% | | | 6.68% |

# Summary of the changes to the financial results

*Profit and loss account*

1. Sales increased by £30,000 (new custom through barter).
2. Turnover rises from £1 million to £1,030,000.
3. Cost of sales rises by £6,000 (20% of £30,000).
4. Gross profit rises to £824,000.
5. Expenses increase by £4,200.

*Balance sheet*

1. Bank balance increases, as it saved £19,800 in cash by bartering.
2. Net profit increases by a similar amount to £69,800.
3. Net profit percentage is 6.8% compared to 5% when no barter was used.
4. Return on equity increases from 4.88% to 6.68% before tax.

The results are obvious – the business has increased its *wealth* through using barter.

---

## STRATEGY #420
### Ease cash flow and liquidity by using trade pounds to make normal purchases in lieu of cash

---

Take, for example, a computer manufacturer which buys direct marketing services as part of a new sales strategy. By paying for the mailing lists in trade pounds, cash is saved for other uses.

---

## STRATEGY #421
### Bridge the equity gap when undertaking capital expenditure

---

If the business has invested the bulk of its equity and working capital, it can use barter trade pounds to buy other assets without disturbing its existing banking and financial arrangements. If the business does not wish to take on additional bank borrowings, it can use barter to buy new equipment or services by making additional sales to earn the trade pounds needed to pay for its own purchases.

For example, a marketing services company needing a new photocopier establishes a credit line to buy the copier from another barter pool member.

---

**STRATEGY #422**
**Transact business which would not take place in the cash market because of budget and/or cash flow constraints**

---

This additional business adds to the overall profitability by improving asset utilisation and enabling the business to increase the tools which it uses to generate new business.

For example, a company has exhausted its print allocation budget but needs £20,000 of new printed material for a special promotion for which it has no budget. This would normally have to be deferred until the following financial year. By using the barter pool, it can trade its goods or services for the printed brochures immediately.

---

**STRATEGY #423**
**Save on not having to give credit or waiting for it when making sales**

---

Because of the structure of the barter pool and its payment structure, the company can immediately spend the trade pounds it earns. It does not have to give credit, nor wait for it, from other members.

---

**STRATEGY #424**
**Only pay for what you use and lessen the cash risk of having to sell before you buy**

---

The cash risk of selling before buying is limited to the seller's marginal cost of the product. Members of the barter pool do not bear any of the costs involved in buying or selling goods until transactions have taken place. Thus they only pay for what they use, and this, in turn, provides an incentive for the barter company to provide services which the members need.

## STRATEGY #425
## Use barter to gain new sales

Priority is usually given by members of a barter pool to spend on barter (if possible), rather than using hard cash first. This means that other pool members supplying goods and services will gain new sales. The choice of being able to pay in trade pounds means that this will usually be preferred to cash.

## STRATEGY #426
## Gain access to new markets

Barter offers member businesses great opportunities to gain access to new markets which they may wish to enter. Because the pool reduces competition from the cash market by balancing member buyers and sellers, members gain customers in new market segments.

For example, a recruiting company tendered for an outplacement contract with a major brewery. It was up against half a dozen other better-known competitors. Usually, it would have to reduce its price to have a chance of winning the contract. Using barter, it priced its contract at the full price, but charged 50% in cash and 50% in goods. The real cash cost to the brewery was significantly reduced. The recruiting company sold the goods through the barter pool and generated trade pounds which were used to buy goods and services.

## STRATEGY #427
## Use various pricing proposals for a competitive edge where price is a major factor in winning or losing sales

If the product or service being sold is highly price sensitive, then bring the clients of the business into the barter pool. Barter is then used as a pricing tool, selling goods at a slightly higher total price than competitors, but pricing them in a blend of cash and barter pounds. Because customers pay for their trade pounds at their marginal cost of product, the real cash cost of the product is lower than the competitors'. The manufacturer would then gain additional sales, which would otherwise have been lost.

## STRATEGY #428
## Sell redundant goods and services more profitably through the barter pool

The barter pool can provide a low-risk, low-cost marketplace without management time and involvement for non-core goods or redundant goods and services. These are usually surpluses which are difficult to shift, or the usual markets are saturated. The barter pool can be used to market these goods or services to members who may have a requirement for them.

For example, a company with an empty warehouse may decide to rent this unused property through the barter pool and may even achieve better rental levels this way.

## STRATEGY #429
## Sell surplus or unwanted assets to generate trade pounds

Sometimes a company is paid in assets which it does not itself need. The barter pool provides an ideal medium to dispose of these assets. Lists are regularly sent to members who then make purchases, creating trade pounds which the 'seller' can use to buy the goods or services which it really needs.

## STRATEGY #430
## Use barter to maintain margins whilst reducing the need to discount prices

Most companies trade in the barter pool at their marginal cost of production, which is much lower than their normal selling price. As a result, their trade pounds cost them less in real terms than their face value. Trading can therefore take place at close to list price, which is attractive to businesses whose trading margins are under pressure.

---

### STRATEGY #431
### Use barter to make purchases affordable

---

Frequently a business will delay or decline making purchases of goods and services because of conditions dictated by their current trading circumstances. By selling some of their surplus capacity to other members, such purchases become affordable. Barter also extends budgets by converting unused or surplus assets into tradable value.

---

### STRATEGY #432
### Pay or buy partly in cash, partly on barter

---

Negotiations between pool members may result in transactions which are partly in cash and partly in barter trade pounds. Barter can be the stimulus for the sales which the business did not have or would not get.

For example, a direct marketing company could provide a list, print letters, stuff envelopes and so on, but you would be expected to pay for the postage.

---

### STRATEGY #433
### Join a business discount service for large savings

---

For those not interested in the barter concept, there are alternative ways of increasing net profits and these involve bulk-buying discount services.

There are a number of discount organisations the business can join which, because of their bulk-buying practices, are able to offer significant discounts to the business and its employees making purchases from hard capital goods to holidays.

These discount organisations regularly send out lists of what is on offer, inviting purchases and indicating the discounts offered.

The business can be used as a powerful buying tool for its own wealth-creation, and also for the benefits of its employees. By using barter and trade discount organisations, a business can:

- improve its cash flow and liquidity
- increase profitability by generating business which would not take place for cash

- incur immediate payment in barter pounds which allows for immediate expenditure
- bridge the equity gap
- have performance-based fees
- have access to new markets and semi-captive markets for new sales
- increase market share, especially in new areas
- capitalise on surplus assets and goods which would otherwise remain unsold
- improve margins on sales which would otherwise be discounted
- obtain a competitive edge
- have new opportunities to buy goods with no outlay of cash or stretching of budgets

## Key points summary

- The business is a powerful tool that can create new markets and opportunities for incremental sales without affecting cash flow.

- The system of barter can provide new sales, help liquidity and increase profitability.

- Redundant and surplus goods and services find a ready market through barter.

- Trade discount organisations exist for small businesses to achieve bulk-buying discounts.

CHAPTER 26

# How Best to Hold on to Your Business Assets

*Sooner or later everyone sits down to a banquet of consequences.*
**Robert Louis Stevenson**

**Objective: To keep what you have accumulated; not to lose it or waste it but to grow it**

This chapter is for the benefit of the business owner who, having accumulated wealth through the business, or set up the mechanism to keep the business creating personal wealth, now needs to preserve assets and income streams.

The opposite of preserving and retaining assets is to lose them or their value. Ever heard the expression, 'My business is my pension'? What happens if the business fails, or if the business owner dies? How does the business owner ensure growing prosperity in retirement years, or leave assets intact for future generations? Having built up and accumulated a fortune through judicious management of the business and personal assets, it would be a financial disaster if no thought was given to the protection and preservation of these assets. Unfortunately the biggest losses of business wealth occur, not necessarily through poor management of wealth resources, but through government action, as manifested through the tax system.

Most will agree that it is iniquitous that income, en route to being capitalised, is taxed in both the hands of the business and the individual, and is then open to taxes on death in the form of inheritance taxes or whilst living in the form of growth taxes such as capital gains tax.

This could be the route of £1,000 worth of profits earned by the business:

| | |
|---|---|
| Profits | £1,000 |
| Tax at 25% | £250 (Corporation tax, or ACT at 20%, then corporation tax for the balance 5%) |
| Balance as dividend | £750 |
| Tax in individual's hands | £300 (say 40% higher rate) |
| Balance | £450 |
| Add tax credit on dividends 20% | £150 |
| Balance | £600 |
| IHT at 40% | £240 (40% IHT on death) |
| Balance | £360 |
| Estate charges | £7 (2% of gross estate on average) |
| Balance for heirs | £353 |

In this simplistic example, over two-thirds of the original value (or more) could disappear in taxation alone. However, much of this negative effect could be avoided through proper tax planning and management of investment and assets. There is no point in spending a lifetime of accumulation only to have personal wealth eroded on a massive scale once retirement or death occurs. The following strategies will assist the business owner in the various decision-making processes designed for the preservation of capital resources. Some strategies are common to all business owners, whilst some are more specific, depending on what type of business it is. This is also an area of continuous planning, which changes as personal circumstances change or as factors in the environment (such as increased taxation) change. The overall strategy is how to protect business assets as well as personal assets under different circumstances.

## PLANNING TO PROTECT BUSINESS ASSETS

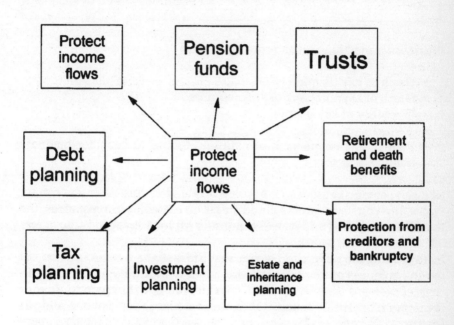

The chapter is broken down into various sections, each relevant to a particular business structure. These are as follows:

1. Strategies common to all business owners.
2. Additional strategies for sole traders.
3. Additional strategies for partners.
4. Additional strategies for shareholders.

Business assets and the values flowing from them during the working life of the business owner through to retirement and then death need to be protected. They also need to be utilised as effectively and efficiently as possible to build maximum wealth. This is accomplished by the business providing an income flow, then a basis for investment and finally a means of enrichment.

## 1. Strategies common to all business owners

---

### STRATEGY #434
### Protect your assets by protecting the business

---

Business protection means protection from:

- Death of key people
- Death of shareholders or stakeholders.
- Disability of key people.
- Avenging creditors.
- Poor management, lack of controls, failure to consider business resilience factors.

If a Keyperson should die or become disabled so that he or she cannot work, then business profits could suffer. In extreme circumstances, the business itself fails and its assets are sold off for a fire-sale value of less than 50% of their worth.

Protecting the Keyperson means that life assurance cover is taken out by the business on the life of the Keyperson. Disability and critical illness coverages should also be considered. If a Keyperson dies or becomes disabled, it usually takes about a year to replace him and his contacts. The effect is far greater on the smaller business totally dependent upon the Keyperson business owner for its survival, and less for larger businesses better able to absorb the financial and human loss. Keyperson cover replaces the individual with cash (see Chapter 10) which makes it easier for the business to continue. Cash introduced into the business in this way has the effect of increasing the value of the business – good news for the survivors!

The death of a shareholder or stakeholder may also affect the business – the more so if the shareholder is involved in the business. Moreover, the heirs of the shareholder may want their newly-inherited shares redeemed and this affects the cash holdings of other shareholders or the company, if they wish to purchase the shares. It is fundamental that buyers want the cheapest price for the shares, sellers want the best possible price. Succession planning using shareholders or partner life insurances provides cash at the right time and price (see Chapter 11).

Finally, businesses in trouble or unable to meet their current liabilities may be pursued by creditors (often relentlessly) and fall victim to bankruptcy proceedings. This a major threat to the assets of the business and business owners should ensure adequate capitalisation, financial controls and management to meet it. Often life savings are at stake and their total loss could have a knock-on effect with the loss of the home and other assets. Strategies for dealing with creditors and businesses in trouble are covered in Chapters 5, 6 and 14.

---

### STRATEGY #435
### Protect your capital, assets and income flows if you become disabled so that you cannot work

---

If the business doesn't provide permanent health insurance (PHI) and critical illness cover, then get your own.

If you become seriously ill, injured or disabled so that you cannot work, find out for just how long the business will be able to support you and your family financially. One thing is for sure – don't rely on the State, as not many people can survive on £52.50 (1995) a week incapacity benefit.

If you are a major contributor to the business's earnings, with you out of the picture, the business will suffer. To support you as well may become unsustainable. It does not matter that you have hundreds of thousands of pounds tied up in the business – it is unlikely that you will have access to it, especially if it's working capital.

Prudent businesses and the people in them take commercial and personal financial survival decisions to protect their earnings, as well as their assets. If there are no earnings, the temptation is to use up scarce capital resources, compounding the problem. Chapter 12 gives the best strategies for protecting income and business assets from disability.

Some PHI policies have long-term care policy benefits, which continue after retirement, but paid for in premiums at today's prices. The best investment you will ever make is by opting for this kind of policy. The reason is that post-retirement nursing home and frail care costs are presently running at over £400 per week. Protecting capital and income after retirement is arguably even more important as the chances of future earnings are nil.

---

### STRATEGY #436
### Protect your assets from creditors and bankruptcy

---

Literally hundreds of thousands of people are directly affected each year through business failures and going bankrupt. Often this is through no fault of their own. They work long hours trying to save the business and themselves, only to lose everything and have to start again.

Roger Levitt, the disgraced financier, when declared bankrupt, was seen driving a Rolls-Royce shortly afterwards. When asked (it was widely reported in the press) how he could afford to do so when bankrupt, he answered that whilst *he* was, his wife wasn't. The lesson is obvious – even when things are going well, plan for every contingency.

To protect your assets from creditors (unless done in fraud of these creditors) make use of trusts, make gifts to your spouse and children, and build valuable pension schemes. In other words, if possible, put your assets beyond the reach of your creditors.

Possibly the best form of trust planning is with pension schemes. Not only are these the most flexible kinds of trusts about, they can hold almost any asset, from investments to commercial property. What is more, the pension fund trustees can buy and sell assets, raise mortgages and loans and, with certain pension funds, provide the business with finance. Pension funds can protect your assets from creditors.

The pension fund is a separate legal entity from the business and is therefore largely protected from the creditors of the business. However, there have been reported cases where creditors have waited for a member of the pension fund to reach pension age to attach his lump sum benefits, which are paid in cash. With the new flexible retirement planning, you can now preserve your fund benefits to at least age 75. If still pursued by creditors, take an annuity, not cash.

Try not to give personal guarantees or security over your home. It is always better to separate personal assets from your business assets. If a bank demands personal securities, you are no worse off remortgaging your home and using the cash in the business instead. At least then, if the business fails, you don't lose your home to the bank. Interest raised to purchase shares or to fund the business is tax deductible to individuals.

Assets gifted to spouses do not incur capital gains tax charges, nor inheritance tax in advance. If your marriage is stable, then the spouse makes an ideal planning tool to spread assets. Gifts, made to children, could crystallise a capital gain; however, if the donor survives for at least seven years then no inheritance tax is payable.

The most common perception is that trusts are widely used to protect assets from creditors. The donor would gift shares, property, investments and other assets into trust for the benefit of named or unnamed beneficiaries and divest himself of ownership of the asset. The more control and discretion held by the donor, the greater the taxation effects in the trust. If the donor reserves any benefits, then there is a possibility that the gifts with reservation rules will apply. In other words, it could be said that the assets were still the donor's and had not legally passed to the trust. Properly constructed trusts can be most effective in sheltering assets, from creditors as well as inheritance taxes. The earlier the assets are transferred, the lower the costs of doing so, if growth assets.

In reality, the inflexibility of trusts, and the cost of setting them up and running them, have meant that only the wealthier sectors of the population use them to any large extent. The use of business property reliefs (up to 100%) has also meant that using trusts as a vehicle for avoiding inheritance taxes has lessened. However, as a weapon in the armoury against attacks by creditors, they can be useful.

---

## STRATEGY #437
## Check that all life assurance and pension policies are written in trust

---

The reason here is to ensure that valuable policy proceeds and death benefits from pension funds do not fall into the deceased's estate for inheritance taxes. Inheritance tax is payable at 40% on the value of net assets in your estate. Policies not written in trust will have the proceeds payable to the estate.

Whilst the first £154,000 (1995/96) of anyone's estate is free of inheritance taxes (the nil rate band), the effect of policy proceeds (which can be substantial) falling into the estate can increase estate values dramatically. By writing policies in trust, the proceeds are paid into the trust outside the estate. There is another valuable benefit from arranging trusts. Probate may take some time to be granted and cash from the estate could be tied up for years. Whilst some income could be advanced to heirs, it is usually insufficient. Policy proceeds in trust are available immediately.

Life policy trusts are different from trusts set up to hold assets, such as shares or property. Life policy trusts really only come into effect on death, and life offices set them up at no cost to you.

Problems arise when policies which should have been written in trust have not been set up in this way. Sometimes the policy has to be cancelled and rewritten in trust. Also, policies in trust cannot be assigned to banks for loans. The trust would first have to be discontinued and then the policy assigned. However, then you run the risk of the policy paying out to the estate, especially if the debt has been settled, where the policy was secured.

Pension policies not written in trust will have the death benefits paid to the estate and subject to inheritance taxes.

Review all policies and decide whether they should be written in trust or not.

---

### STRATEGY #438
### Effect life assurance in trust to provide estate liquidity tax-free

---

Many estates (on death) are asset rich and cash poor. Whilst the testator may have been a millionaire on paper through share values and fixed property, there may be no liquidity in the estate to settle estate debts and pay bequests. Remember that inheritance taxes must be paid first and in cash. If no cash is available to the estate, then assets will have to be sold, if they can be. Sometimes privately-held unquoted shares cannot be sold, nor the family home which is required for the widow and children to live in.

The lack of cash in any estate is a major problem. It may mean selling assets at the wrong time. Assets which have been built up through the business will now be sold, often at a 'fire-sale' value.

The solution is to have life assurance proceeds payable directly to the estate to satisfy estate liabilities, but then they are possibly subject to inheritance taxes. If so, then gear up the sum assured by 40%, i.e. if the amount required is £200,000 before tax, then after tax it is £200,000 grossed up by 40% = £333,333. Tax at 40% is £133,333 leaving the estate liquidity requirement of £200,000.

A cheaper alternative is to write the policy in trust for £200,000 with the spouse and heirs as beneficiaries. They or the trustees would then make a loan of cash to the estate to settle its liquidity requirements. The loan could be settled with assets passing or future asset sales.

---

### STRATEGY #439
### Use business life assurance to protect personal investments

---

Assume that a shareholder, director, partner or even a sole trader has money in the business, either in a director's loan account, partner's capital account or a working capital account. The individual dies, usually at the most inopportune time for the business and family. The business needs his cash more than ever, as does the family. To repay the loan account could affect the liquidity in the business severely. Yet it is also morally unjustifiable to keep it knowing that the family requires the cash.

Whether paid back or not, the value of the loan account still forms a part of the deceased's estate and is liable to inheritance taxes. So, even though the estate doesn't have the cash, it pays tax on it. There are some exceptions which qualify for business property relief on death, but business loans are unlikely to qualify (whereas capital accounts if rated as 'share value' may).

Loan accounts owing cannot therefore be treated as cash in the estate, unless actually paid into it. However, shareholders and partnership protection policies can provide the cash to the surviving business owners to make good the amount owing. The survivors increase their own loan accounts to do this. Alternatively, adequate Keyman cover enables the business to repay business loans, and this is usually the better method.

---

### STRATEGY #440
### Use excess estate liquidity for investments

---

Any policy proceeds in excess of estate requirements can be invested for heirs to provide income or capital growth.

---

### STRATEGY #441
### Capture the growth of investments through an offshore bond investment, in trust

---

One of the best investments is made from money generated by the business and invested in an offshore investment bond. Written in trust, these bonds are useful for post-death planning because of the 'dead sett-lor rules' under section 547 of the Taxes Act 1988. As the taxpayer is dead, no income tax liability attaches to him. Consequently any income for beneficiaries may be received tax-free as a result of this provision.

The offshore bond can be constructed to hold any asset, including property and existing investments. It has an income drawdown facility whilst the business owner is still alive (of 5% p.a. which may be accumulated on a tax deferred basis). If the bond matures, then tax is payable if a higher rate taxpayer at that time. If not, then the proceeds are tax-free.

A useful advantage is to use such an investment vehicle to receive death-in-service benefits from the business's group scheme, which may then be invested for tax-free income for beneficiaries. A letter of wishes is left with the trustees of the group scheme or death-in-service benefits nominating the offshore bond in trust to receive the benefits.

---

### STRATEGY #442
### Make use of trusts to protect assets and capture taxable growth

---

Only set up a trust if assets are worth at least £100,000 or have very high growth potential. For example, when a company is formed, the value of its share is at par (cost price). If the business does well, the growth in value of the shares could be phenomenal. What the trust does is to capture this growth in value outside the estate of the business owner. Similarly with share portfolios and other assets.

For maximum effect, however, the former owner of the shares should give up control and not reserve any benefits to himself. If he does not do this, then the full value could fall into his estate and be taxed at 40%.

The general rule with trusts is, the greater the flexibility and discretion allowed, the more penal the taxation consequences. The less the level of control, the less penal the taxation consequences. For example, trustees are usually taxed at 25% on income received by the trust, but if it is a full discretionary trust, the tax charge is increased by 10% to 35%.

With business property reliefs now at up to 100% on death, the value of trusts to shelter shares and business ownership assets has largely diminished. However, these reliefs will still apply through the trusts, which are also useful to capture capital gains on shares.

---

### STRATEGY #443
### Use a trust to hold business and agricultural assets with 100% reliefs indefinitely

---

There are three main types of trust in use by trust planners today. These are:

- Interest in possession trusts.
- Accumulation and maintenance trusts.
- Discretionary trusts.

*Interest in possession trusts*
If an estate owner has business or agricultural assets eligible for the 100% relief, and such assets are transferred into a flexible interest in possession trust with wide powers of appointment, then the position is as follows:

- *Inheritance Tax* is nil because of the business property or agricultural property reliefs at 100% [FA number 2 1992, Schedule 14]. Note that full relief is now available for land which is let.

- *Capital Gains Tax* can be held over [TCGA section 165]. Possibly one should consider not making the election (the time period to elect is six years – you can get the tax back with tax-free interest) because the gain will crystallise when the life tenant dies. On death, the life interest will terminate and be free of inheritance taxes. The capital gains tax exemption and market uplift will apply [TCGA section 73], but if holdover relief has been claimed, then capital gains tax is payable on the lower of any held-over gain and the actual gain [TCGA section 74].

Interest in possession trusts can be used by business owners for the company to purchase its own shares.

---

## STRATEGY #444
## Get surplus assets out of the company free of all taxes

---

If a family trading company, for example, has surplus assets which it wishes to take out of the company with the least potential tax charge, and the shares are either already owned by or transferred to a family trust in which the family beneficiaries have an interest in possession, then:

- CGT holdover relief is claimed.
- 100% inheritance tax business property relief is claimed.
- Articles of Association are changed to enable the company to buy its own shares. A resolution is passed to buy shares held by the trustees.
- This is a non-approved transfer and therefore is treated as a distribution. The company is liable for ACT (Advance Corporation Tax) which may be offset against the company's mainstream liability. Surplus ACT can be claimed back for the preceding six years.
- The trustees may end up with a capital gains tax loss or no chargeable gain due to the distribution process.
- The 'distribution' under trust law is not part of the income of the life tenants (because it is not distributable to them). It is not accumulated income either and there is no further tax to be paid in the trust.

This way the surplus assets are extracted from the company for the benefit of the trust with no charge to inheritance tax, capital gains tax, income tax or corporation tax in the hands of any of the parties. Always get a clearance certificate under section 707 of the Taxes Act 1988 first. Avoid including the settlor or spouse as beneficiaries as they could be taxed.

### Accumulation and maintenance trusts

These trusts are useful because once assets have been placed in the trust, no further inheritance taxes are payable. Assets transferred are a PET (a Potential Exempt Transfer, which means that the settlor or donor must survive for seven years for total exemption from inheritance taxes).

Payments to a beneficiary or distributions made to one on termination of the trust will not incur an inheritance tax charge. There is no ten-year or interim inheritance tax charge on the trust assets either (as there is with a discretionary trust).

The accumulation and maintenance trust can be used for a variety of purposes, which are as follows:

- A gift of any asset as a PET (Potentially Exempt Transfer).
- A gift of business or agricultural property eligible for the 100% or 50% relief under F(2)A 1992 Schedule 14.
- As a capital tax-free fund for private company shares or land.
- To hold life policies.
- To receive death-in-service benefits from occupational pension schemes where children are nominated. The trustees could use this cash to buy non-cash assets from the deceased's widow.
- To transfer assets (at the nil rate band) from a discretionary trust.
- As a will trust for grandchildren.

### Discretionary trusts

These are the most flexible, but also the most heavily tax-charged types of trust. Assets passing into trust are charged at 50% of the inheritance tax rate (50% of 40% = 20%); there are charges on the value of assets after ten years (at about 6%) and on termination of the trust.

Yet, the transfer of business assets into such flexible trusts by will or during the lifetime of the settlor, with proper planning, can save inheritance tax and capital gains taxes. These provisions are broadly as follows:

- Certain business and agricultural assets can be held in such trusts indefinitely with 100% relief.
- These assets will not be chargeable at the ten-year anniversary dates, nor the interim charges after the first ten-year anniversary

charge date. If the relief applies at the first ten-year anniversary charge date, the charge rate will be nil. This rate will apply until immediately prior to the next ten-year anniversary. This is the case even when the assets have been sold. Beware, however, assets with 50% relief as there is no allowance at this rate and the charge will apply.

- Capital gains tax reliefs and exemptions are more complicated – however, there is no CGT holdover relief restriction for non-business assets [TCGA 1992, section 260].

---

### STRATEGY #445
### Use a discretionary trust for double IHT relief

---

This type of trust can be used to obtain 100% relief in the estate of spouse A and the same in spouse B's estate. Assume spouse A in his will leaves business or agricultural property, plus the value of the nil rate band (£154,000 in 1995/96) to a discretionary trust in favour of his family and including his spouse B.

- Spouse A dies. Business property or agricultural property relief is obtained for the first time at 100%.
- The capital gains tax death exemption and market value uplift is also obtained for the first time.
- A leaves B his investment assets.
- B purchases at arm's length the business or agricultural assets from the trustees.
- B dies. On death after two years from purchase, her estate should also be eligible for the same reliefs and exemptions.
- B suffers no loss of income because she is a beneficiary of the discretionary trust.
- Life assurance could cover the two-year period for eligibility.

Trusts require careful planning and the appropriate legal advice should always be taken but they do provide a useful tax planning tool to preserve business assets for present and future generations.

---

### STRATEGY #446
### Transfer assets tax-free to your spouse

---

In order to make full use of all exemptions from an income tax, capital gains tax and inheritance tax point of view, the spouse is essential for business planning.

- There is no tax charge on assets passing between spouses during their lifetime or death.
- If the assets are income producing, then using the spouse as a tax-payer not only soaks up tax-free exemptions, but also provides an income stream for the spouse. The 1995/96 personal allowance is £3,525. This equates with £5,875 worth of tax-free income for a 40% taxpayer and £4,700 for a basic rate taxpayer.
- Each spouse has a capital gains tax exemption of £6,000 p.a. in 1995/96.
- Each spouse enjoys retirement relief on £250,000 which is exempt and 50% of the next £750,000 worth of business assets.
- Each spouse can use £154,000 of their estates free of inheritance taxes for bequests to third parties, such as children. (The nil rate band.)

Consider transferring shares and other business assets or investment assets to the spouse for maximum reliefs and tax savings.

---

### STRATEGY #447
### Use the spouse allowances and reliefs for investments

---

Considerable savings can be made by spreading investments or cash for investments between spouses. These include:

- Maximum investments into personal equity plans (PEPs) of £9,000 each (1995/96) p.a.
- Each may have a TESSA for tax-free income.
- Each may invest up to £100,000 p.a. into venture capital trusts and qualifying EIS companies.
- Employing the spouse to obtain additional pension contributions reliefs.
- Using the spouse personal allowances for taxable income.
- Using the spouse capital gains tax exemptions when assets owned by the spouse are sold.

This is also a useful strategy to protect assets from creditors.

---

**STRATEGY #448**
# Get double reliefs on retirement when you sell the business.

---

If there were no reliefs on the sale of the business or qualifying assets, capital gains tax would be payable in full on retirement.

However, retirement relief means that substantial savings may be made. To qualify for full reliefs, the business (assets) must have been held for ten years and the parties must be aged 55 or over (50 from 1996/97). Relief is reduced for lesser periods, although continuous but different businesses will count towards the relief.

For example (1995/96):

Assume A sells his business for £1 million on retirement. Full relief applies.

| | |
|---|---|
| Sale of business | £1,000,000 |
| Relief: 1st £250,000 – exempt | £250,000 |
| | £750,000 |
| | |
| Next £750,000 at 50% | £375,000 |
| less annual exemption | £6,000 |
| Taxable | £369,000 |
| | |
| CGT payable at 40% | £147,600 |

Now assume A and B are equal partners and sell the business for £1 million on retirement. Full relief applies.

| | |
|---|---|
| Each sale of business | £500,000 |
| Relief: 1st £250,000 – exempt | £250,000 |
| | £250,000 |
| | |
| Next £250,000 at 50% | £125,000 |
| less annual exemption | £6,000 |
| Taxable | £119,000 |
| | |
| CGT payable at 40% | £47,600 |
| | |
| Total tax, both partners: | £95,200 |

This represents a CGT saving of £52,400.

---

## STRATEGY #449
## Plan your retirement effectively to avoid all taxes

---

If your business and investment assets are substantial, then you can avoid capital gains taxes, inheritance taxes and income taxes by choosing the correct procedures on retirement. However, your planning should begin at least ten years before you retire.

It may mean emigrating to a tax haven and then selling assets to avoid capital gains taxes and inheritance taxes, or offshore investing, or using trusts. Specific planning is also required with pension funds and annuities, where timing is important. Thousand of pounds can be saved for future generations, or to enhance your lifestyle, by taking suitable advice. Remember, it is not what you have, it's what you keep and nurture which reduces the risk of capital erosion and falling incomes in later years.

---

## STRATEGY #450
## Invest wisely and safely according to your circumstances and risk preferences

---

It will come as no surprise that the most speculative investors in the world before retirement become the most cautious investors – almost overnight – on retirement. Previous high level earnings capacity has gone and full-time attention is devoted to what you have accumulated.

For most people, there is no second chance on retirement and value assets must not only be protected but geared for income and capital growth. Proper portfolio planning will be required and independent financial advice sought. Make these crucial planning decisions at least two years before retirement.

---

## STRATEGY #451
## Aim to pay off all debts before retirement

---

For a happy and contented retirement, without financial stress, your aim will be to pay off all debts and liabilities *before* retirement. Failure to do this may burden your capital assets and reduce your income-generation and growth base.

At least five years before retirement, make maximum use of the business to achieve your aims. Instead of an expensive company car, downgrade purposely to make savings to be applied to additional pension funding or bonus diversion schemes to provide cash to pay off your mortgage and other liabilities earlier. Don't wait until the last minute – by then it will be too late and you may have to use lump sums from your pension fund to pay off liabilities – money which should be invested for capital growth and further income.

If retirement means selling your business – begin the planning process (finding a buyer, getting management involved, etc) at least two years earlier. The one thing you have in retirement is time – time to consider what you should have done earlier.

---

## STRATEGY #452
## Make sure that your will is in order

---

Whatever you do, don't die intestate. Dying intestate is a signal to everyone that you didn't intend to plan things properly. Apart from losing the ability to bequeath the nil rate band of £154,000, thus saving thousands in inheritance taxes, you also lose the ability to utilise fully the spouse exemption on death. No inheritance tax is payable on assets bequeathed to a spouse. Lastly, you lose the opportunity to say where your worldly wealth is going. This means that the State gets to divide it up, often delaying probate. It also means that you have lost the opportunity to create will trusts, important to protect minors and immature beneficiaries, and to make double use of the business and agricultural property reliefs, thus creating problems for those coming after you. For example, your failure to nominate guardians for children or to appoint executors and administrators could create problems for your heirs.

If you haven't done so already, do it now – make a will. Incidentally, over 60% of solicitors do not have wills themselves. Ask your solicitor if he or she has one – if he hasn't, change solicitors.

The will is the mechanism which guides estate planning. It activates your carefully-prepared asset disposals and is the vehicle which generates necessary tax reliefs. Make sure your spouse or partner also has a will.

## 2. Additional strategies for sole traders

---

### STRATEGY #453
### If a sole trader, use a self-invested personal pension plan (SIPP) to shelter your assets

---

This type of personal pension plan can be set up for as little as £300 and can be your vehicle to hold investments from cash to property. Contributions made to an approved SIPP can be tax deductible, following the personal pension rules.

You can retire from your SIPP between the ages of 55 and 75 and it provides generous flexibility to plan future income streams. All capital gains on investments compound tax-free and at retirement you can expect a tax-free lump sum of 25% of your fund, the balance of the fund buying you a pension for life – and one for your spouse, after you've died.

The main advantage of the SIPP is the total investment control which you have over your assets and investments within the fund. You may invest in other product providers' pension funds, building society fixed deposits and any manner of approved investments. If you want flexibility and control, choose a SIPP for your business protection retirement planning.

---

### STRATEGY #454
### If a sole trader, take out a life policy to protect your estate from business debts

---

Most business owners don't know it, but if you die, your business debts fall into your estate for settlement.

This means that creditors will benefit *before* your family. The situation is compounded because employees in your business have at least a statutory claim for redundancy from your estate. In other words, the business, instead of preserving wealth, will destroy your wealth if the proper protection measures are not taken.

The sole proprietor or trader is a Keyman. However, as there is no separate business entity (he or she *is* the business) the life policy must be taken out personally. Use pension term to get the premiums tax deductible, and write the policy in trust for family beneficiaries. The trustees can loan the necessary liquidity to the estate to settle estate and business debts.

## 3. Additional strategies for partners

---

### STRATEGY #455
### Make sure that all partnership agreements are water-tight

---

Imagine the following scenario. Patrick is a partner in the firm of Welltodo and Partners and introduced £50,000 into the partnership as working capital, which is reflected in the partnership capital account. He had to take out a loan secured against his home, but receives full interest relief on the loan for the investment into the partnership. Patrick gets on reasonably well with the other five partners in the firm. He has signed the standard partnership agreement which lays out his entitlement to share in profits (and losses), spells out his holidays each year and explains how the partnership bank account works.

As no one from the firm has retired or died, these issues are not really uppermost in anyone's mind. Over the years, Patrick generates substantial profits for the firm, takes some out as drawings and allows the rest to accumulate. The firm expands, taking on new employees and partners. Patrick also separately owns a share of the office building, valued at £250,000 (for his share). His capital account in the partnership is now £300,000 and he contemplates retirement knowing that he has substantial business value.

Patrick retires and it's champagne all round. He would like the firm to pay out his capital account so that he can emigrate to warmer climes and enjoy his old age. The partners have a meeting and conclude that the withdrawal of such a large sum would be disastrous for the partnership. In terms of the partnership agreement, they can pay out the capital account over the next eight years with no interest – at £37,500 a year. Naturally, Patrick is aggrieved. This is not what he wanted and it will greatly affect his ability to generate further income and capital growth in retirement. The partners have taken this course of action because over the next five years two other partners will also retire with even larger capital accounts. Not only will they have to generate fee income for the firm, there are fewer partners to do it. Potential new partners hear about the problem and refuse to come in on these terms.

What if Patrick had died instead of retired? If there is nothing to the contrary in the partnership agreement, then the heirs have an immediate call for cash, which could be disastrous for the unprepared partnership (1890 Partnership Act). It would be even worse for his estate and heirs if the firm could only repay the capital account in instalments – especially if over long periods.

As part of your planning strategy, make sure that all agreements are water-tight. Get them changed if not, following the strategies in Chapter 11. Many agreements for partnerships follow out-dated precedents relating to the 1950s or before. Aspects such as professional indemnity run-off are not even catered for. (You may still be liable for partnership debts, even after retirement.) If necessary, have separate agreements for the sale of your partnership share and the provision of cash at the time it is needed the most.

## STRATEGY #456
## Protect the partner's value with double option agreements

The partners can provide for cash to purchase a deceased or disabled partner's share of the business through life, disability and critical illness policies underwritten in trust. The surviving partners use the proceeds from the policy to purchase the deceased's share from his estate. The most effective method for inheritance tax purposes is the double option agreement. Each party has the option to buy or sell and when one party triggers the option, the other must then perform. This enables necessary cash to be available in full at exactly the time it is required.

If a person is disabled, or suffers a stroke, cancer, paraplegia, or one of life's dread diseases, then the option can also be triggered to buy and sell shares. Some agreements also have a 'buy-back' clause if the dis-- abled partner recovers.

### 4. Additional strategies for shareholders

## STRATEGY #457
## Get unquoted company shares sold at fair market value on death or retirement

Use a double option agreement with insurance coverages as discussed in Chapter 11 for payouts on death. The agreement should contain a valuation clause, which is usually agreed each year, with an uplift in coverages if the value of the business increases.

Retirement strategies are fully covered in Chapter 31. However, business owners and shareholders should bear in mind that unquoted shares are notoriously difficult to sell. Usually they have to be offered to existing shareholders first, and only if declined are they then available to third parties. Minority unquoted shares have very little value for new investors. EIS investors can only buy newly-issued shares; however CGT reinvestment investors may purchase existing shares.

Business planning would indicate that, if at all possible, an employee share trust should be set up to buy the shares at a fair market value (see Chapter 19). If so, then CGT rollover reliefs will apply. Alternatively, investigate the trust strategies in this chapter where the company buys back shares.

Above all, ensure that succession planning is in place. Small businesses probably don't want outsiders (even heirs of the deceased shareholder) in the business and a proper double option agreement should cater for this need to direct shares back to surviving shareholders at a fair price.

Ultimately, the shareholder will either wish to dispose of shares or retain them. If disposal is sought, then the market for the shares must be created (ESOT, listing on Stock Exchange or AIM); if the shares are retained then a stated dividend policy should be sought.

---

### STRATEGY #458
### Always arrange for your unquoted shares to be sold, if possible, on your death

---

Dividends are nice to have, but they are not guaranteed to occur and cash in the bank is *always* a better option. Make sure that shareholder agreements are in place to sell shares to the survivors or share trust on death. Once you have gone, remember there is no one in the business to look after your interests (unless a very close family business) – so plan ahead now.

---

### STRATEGY #459
### Ensure future dividend flows through preference shares

---

Converting shares from ordinary shares to preference shares is not usually considered to be a settlement. If keeping shares in retirement or death, then try to convert them to preference shares. This will at least ensure some income flow in the absence of a double option or Buy and Sell agreement enabling the purchase of shares for cash.

## STRATEGY #460
## If selling shares, make use of rollover reinvestment reliefs

The sale of unquoted shares will be a disposal for capital gains tax purposes. The tax can be deferred by rolling over and reinvesting the gain into other unquoted qualifying companies. The investor can spread his risk by investing in a number of companies or through a venture capital trust which qualifies for these purposes.

You may even pick up EIS reliefs at 20% of your investment up to £100,000 to reduce your tax liability.

At retirement age, retirement reliefs may apply, so that the deferred gain could be 'washed out' of the system then. Make full use of annual exemptions and gifts to spouses to avoid taxes. Rollover reinvestment qualifying companies usually have well-planned exit routes for investors.

## STRATEGY #461
## Get director loan accounts repaid for further investments

If you have a loan account in the business, it has been lying dormant since you left it there. There is no capital growth on loan account cash, although some interest may be payable.

It may be better for the company to pay the director commercial levels of tax deductible interest on his or her loan account, than to pay dividends, which suffer advance corporation tax (ACT) and are not deductible.

Alternatively, look to *replacing* the directors' loan account with other sources of finance. The director can then invest for capital growth and further income as well as making use of tax reliefs. This process should begin at least a year before retirement. The loan account money should not be left in the business once the director has left it. It leads to problems on death, in any event, when the company should be paying it over to the deceased's estate – where it will lose 40% of its value from inheritance taxes. It is far better to redeem the loan account and then to tax shelter it.

## STRATEGY #462
## Use the cheapest and best trusts such as company pension funds to tax shelter assets

Occupational pension schemes such as SSAS or EPPs may be used to hold assets otherwise owned by the company. Whilst this action does weaken the balance sheet, it should create tax advantages and is useful for protection purposes.

The SSAS, for example, could purchase a commercial property which is rented to the company. Interest paid by the company is deductible, and accrues tax-free in the pension fund. The trustees can buy and sell property within the fund, avoiding capital gains taxes. Assets grow free of all taxes.

Problems may arise on actual retirement, when pensions must be paid, as well as lump sums. The properties held may have to be sold (which could be difficult at that time) or loans taken out against them to enable pensions to be paid. It is in the interests of the members of the fund to ensure that sufficient cash contributions are also made to make the fund viable for its pension commitments.

From a tax and estate planning point of view the pension scheme is indeed a flexible trust with none of the tax charges of a discretionary trust and can be used for future generations also employed in the business. From a business planning point of view, the pension scheme protects assets from creditors and can act as a bank with loan facilities.

Above all, the pension fund investment is an ideal vehicle to provide capital and income for the business owner and spouse or partner in retirement.

### Key points summary

- Protection of the business assets leads to protection of personal capital and the retention of wealth.

- All areas of personal financial planning are involved to lessen the incidence of taxation and to promote growth and future income.

- The various strategies describe how to hold on to your business assets using trusts, business agreements, business reliefs and business protection arrangements.

# CHAPTER 27

# The People in Your Business – Your Most Valuable Assets

*It is individuals working within organisational structures who produce the product, make decisions and conceive strategies. Yet because people are a less measurable organisational asset, less easily appreciated by a study of the balance sheet, than material assets or market share, they are often overlooked or forgotten . . .*
**Sue Cartwright, 'Remember the Workers', Sunday Times 1989**

**Objective: To increase profits as a result of increased employee performance**

The newspaper article from which the above opening quotation was made, was written in the context of merger and acquisition plans and has remained with me for many years. Some businesses care about their employees, others don't. This is not a chapter on the recruitment and management of employees, nor their training, nor what jobs they do, but a chapter on *how to retain* and grow the business's most valuable resource – its people.

How is it that some businesses experience a constant turnover of employees, yet others retain a loyal and performance-oriented work force? It is not only a matter of caring, but also one of proper employee benefit structuring and, of course, job satisfaction.

In a survey carried out by the London Business School and Egon Zehnder (1988) of 40 UK acquisitions, all 40 companies conducted a financial and legal audit of the company they wished to acquire. Some of the companies considered the financial implications of employee pension arrangements, but *not one* made any attempt to carry out an audit of the company's human resources to assess the talent being acquired.

---

### STRATEGY #463
### Carry out your own corporate audit of the people in your business and what they are worth to the business

---

What is an individual worth? How do you value him or her? Well, people obviously have a financial value to the business. Then there is also a value attributable to the skills and talents of the individual in the business. These are often left unharnessed because the business does not know *how* to access these skills or is not aware of them. In some cases, the business is not even interested in the skills and talents of their workers – often bringing in more expensive outside expertise for a job, when they have the capability in-house.

In strict financial terms, the individual must be worth:

- the marginal added value of the individual's performance to increasing profits *and*
- the cost of losing the individual and replacing him or her, *and*
- the costs of training and re-phasing the individual as a productive unit of the business.

To the business the individual has a cost and therefore a value. This will differ from business to business and job to job within the business. To the business, some people are worth more than others, and valued more than others.

Let us say, then, that the cost of the employee to the business is reflected as a value of pay and benefits and then valued on a Keyman basis of up to ten times salary. This would include the replacement cost of the employee.

Unfortunately for some, the older the employee becomes, the more he or she costs and, in relation to the job or performance, may not be adding value. The big mistake is then made of trying to change the employee instead of the (now redundant) job.

Compare the value in financial terms of the employee to the business with the financial value of the employee to his family. In the latter case (purely in financial terms), the value of the employee as a breadwinner is measured as:

- replacement income for life
- replacement income on death

Assume an annual salary of £30,000. This increases at 3% per annum for salary increases and includes the value of benefits. Life expectancy of the employee is 38 years, that of the spouse 45 years and within that period dependants will leave the home.

The financial value to the family is an increased income flow until death – in this case, over £2 million in total expected future income. It is the business which provides salary and benefits and later pension benefits, with top-ups from individual investments. Whichever way one looks at it, in salary and benefit expenditures *alone*, over the working lifetime of the average employee of, say, £20,000 p.a. increasing at 3% a year to age 65, for, say, 25 years (in the same firm) will cost the firm over £750,000.

Businesses are paying a lot of money in pay and payroll costs in the long term – usually their largest expenditure – and should expect performance added-value to the business. However, if the business, having made its employee costs outlay, does not invest *further* in the employee, then there could be dissatisfaction and the loss of the employee.

The employee value audit should contain items such as:

- Worth of employee to the business
- Worth of the business to the employer
- Is the employee in the right job or is the job obsolete?
- How can the value of the employee be improved? What must be done to achieve this? What is the price to pay? These are crucial questions requiring crucial answers.

## STRATEGY #464
## Build a team, so that the business owner can work on the business, not in it

When the business owner realises that the business is being run solely on his (or her) skills, then he will realise that the only way to get out of the business is to impart these skills to the rest of the team. In this way, the business owner can work *on* developing the business and not *in* it. Business decisions should be made, not emotional ones. The business owner should not be going into the business each day to stand at the counter selling to customers, but should be developing and managing the business.

The function of a manager is to enforce adherence to systems. Don't overload yourself, trust your own people. Be happy to have 80% of your day freed up by having your team of employees run the business. The business will require an organisational chart, with the functions of each job in each area given.

People love to excel. Given the opportunity and the responsibility, they will grow exponentially. So will the business. Often business owners are themselves the limiting factors in business growth.

To begin the path to rapid growth, the business owner should:

- develop the *systems* required to run the business (better than the business owner could)
- give the *team* (the employees and managers) their functions
- ensure they are properly trained
- systemise the routine things, and humanise the exceptional things
- look at what you get for it, not what you pay for it
- be prepared to pay for expert advice to help the business get to where it is going. It is a fact that small businesses seldom take the advice of outsiders when they need it, or they go for the 'cheap' solution. This is not the right attitude in developing the business.

## STRATEGY #465
## Link the structure of employee benefits to people's needs as well as performance

Employees may be rewarded in many different ways. A business could give a package of employee benefits to its employees and achieve no added incentivisation; yet another could give exactly *the same* package to its employees and achieve added value, increased performance and loyalty. The first business regularly loses employees, the second one keeps them. What then is the secret of success of the second business?

The answer lies in listening to the needs of employees; then telling them what benefits they have and why. In addition, and most importantly, tell them what these benefits have *cost* the business to deliver and what the *value* is to the employee.

The method leading to this success in added value, increased performance, employee retentions and a happy and contented work force, is to link employee benefits to the *needs* of the employees, as well as to their performance. Previous structures studied in depth in business over many years have indicated that a focus on performance alone is not enough. A focus on employee needs, and satisfaction of those needs, keeps employees from becoming dissatisfied (see Chapter 9). A benefit is not a benefit if it cannot be used. Become an interested, caring employer – it doesn't cost any more. It's similar to using 39 muscles in your face to frown and only 17 to smile – it is actually *easier* to be closer to the action, than away from it. Be interested and develop a caring attitude – you can't lose!

---

## STRATEGY #466
## If the business has an employee benefit and remuneration package, then tell the employees how it benefits them

---

Employees either regard their benefits structure as a *right* (they deserve it whatever happens and are entitled to it) or as a *valued-added*, negotiated package, which they are grateful to receive. Which employees are easier to incentivise – those paid as a 'right' or those paid and incentivised for 'performance' and loyalty?

The problem is that if you get something anyway, it has very little added value to you, and greater dissatisfaction may result. However, if the employee is intimately involved with his or her package, understands it, recognises the costs underlying it, and is regularly communicated with in respect of it, then this flexibility (which costs the business no more), is such a powerful motivator that employees more or less have a business within a business.

Examine the traditional position with the newer, open and more flexible position:

*Traditional position*
Remuneration package of salary (plus benefits if applicable) is paid to the employee. There is no further communication except, possibly, access to pension rule books and the type of company car allowable.

Even share options are included on this basis, with little more than a paragraph in the employee's contract of employment and a note in the post.

*Flexible position*
1. The employee is counselled at first hand to find out what he or she has by way of existing benefits provided privately.

2. The employee is given a *total package figure*, within which is flexibility to meet the actual (not perceived) needs of the employee. The usual is *salary + core benefits + flexible benefits*.

   For example, a mortgage subsidy may be more suitable as an employee benefit than a larger company car.

3. Following the selection of benefits, the employee is given an *annual statement* showing the following:

   - salary + benefit structure
   - cost to the business of providing the benefit
   - cost to the employee by way of his contributions
   - present value of the benefits
   - future value of the benefits

4. The employee has the opportunity (usually in conjunction with an independent financial adviser) to reconsider the package annually, as his or her circumstances change.

5. The addition of *performance-related schemes* is communicated in a similar way:

   - share and share options
   - employee share owner trusts (ESOTS)
   - profit-related pay
   - bonuses and commissions
   - NIC avoidance schemes which build wealth

As before, their cost, values, future values and financial tax implications should be shown.

As a result of these measures the employees feel involved, and an integral part of the business. They have basically set their own individual packages within certain parameters. They get regular 'bonding' information and communication and are *part of the team*. As a result, they wish to stay, not leave the business.

## STRATEGY #467
## Regularly update employees on how the business is doing

If a part of the team, they deserve to know. Instead of you having to tell people to work harder, they will intuitively make the decision to help the business perform. Never underestimate the willingness and drive of people to want to do better than expected of them.

Years ago, annually in our business, the executive team would work out how much sales had to be accomplished by each branch for that year. Each branch was then given a figure as its budget. With 20 salesmen in the branch, it was relatively simple to divide this figure by twenty and the result was each person's target.

A better way was to know the capability of each salesman and have the manager work out the targets for each person and give it to them. This was generally acceptable but gave no real scope for beating target. One year we decided to approach each salesman individually and to give him the branch's target and then ask how much he would be able to contribute towards that.

The result was an increase in target by over 50% and in actual performance, the branch's target was exceeded by 30%! Why? Because, knowing the full picture of what had to be done (and not wanting to do less than the average because of peer pressure), people wanted to succeed in what they *themselves* had chosen to do.

Everyone has heard the old adage of making the other person think it was his idea in the first place – in order to get the job done. This method uses the same principle. Give your most valuable assets more responsibility. Then watch them come through for you.

## STRATEGY #468
## Through the business, help employees to build wealth

Employees in the business have basically the same end objectives as the business owners. They need to survive, wish to live a quality life and then retire with an adequate pension and personal wealth. Their only route to all of this is through the business.

If the business's objectives are the same as those of its workers then the route to profitability, success and security should be definite. However, things do not always happen as planned and people leave, or become redundant if the business fails.

However, business owners should be aware of the employees' needs for profit-sharing and wealth-building as part of the reward for building up the business.

Rewards are usually provided through:

- increased salary
- increased benefits
- bonuses
- share options
- shares and dividends
- NIC avoidance schemes
- career advancement/promotion
- profit-related pay

If *a partnership*, the same can be achieved, but by using a 'phantom share scheme' for the incentivisation of the employees (see Chapter 28).

---

## STRATEGY #469
### Business strategies to retain employees and keep them happy and contented

---

One has to ask the question, 'Why would an employee wish to leave?' There could be any one of a number of reasons – ranging from job dissatisfaction to not being paid what the employee thinks he is worth. There may be perceived management problems or whatever.

Always try to establish *why* employees are leaving. The manager/owners can then build up a picture of where the areas of dissatisfaction are, and seek to overcome them: it could be an impending take-over of the company where jobs may be lost and the employee is leaving in advance of the rush (although most wait for redundancy terms); a change in job specification or function; or any other reason.

The 'retention' programme can also be used to recruit new employees.

The business should develop a number of strategies for employee retention, including the following:

- remuneration and benefit packages adequacy
- performance-related rewards
- career path planning and job satisfaction
- caring employer
- attitude surveys to establish need requirements
- communication and bonding between the business and employee
- wealth-building incentives

- well-being, satisfaction, valued and needed employee, team building and employee care programmes.

---

### STRATEGY #470
### Determine what the benefits are to the employee from a business seeking to add value to the employee

---

If the employee recognises tangible impact from the business, then the employee will make a value judgement to stay and *assist the business in its objectives.*

Benefits to the employee should include:

- maximising corporate benefits in personal financial planning
- flexibility within changing circumstances
- being seen as a valued team member by a caring employer
- more personal disposable income arising from tax-efficient and better-costed corporate benefits
- only 'paying for' benefits which are *of use* in the short or long term
- elimination of certain personal financial problems through better structuring
- providing now for post-retirement benefits which would normally be lost from the date of retirement (protection benefits, life cover, car benefits, BUPA)
- the ability to give meaningful feedback to the employer
- creation of personal wealth
- elimination of stress

---

### STRATEGY #471
### Join the 'Investors in People' programmes

---

The government has initiated an 'Investors in People' programme to recognise the value of a trained and motivated employee. Join this programme (if you have not done so already) to show the corporate image of a caring employer positively.

In the final analysis, the business either values its employees, or it doesn't. Many, in fact, do not. These are mostly family-owned businesses. There would be no question of giving off shares to employees for many of them, for example, and such employers think salaries and benefits should be as low as possible, people should be grateful for the job alone, etc. Perversely, this approach does seem to work for some companies, especially where employees are less mobile and caught in the poverty trap, but the continued ongoing loyalty of the employees to the business owners must be questioned in the future – some do not even have pension benefits. Still, businesses do tend to focus on immediate costs rather than longer-term added value and this approach is not surprising.

For the vast majority of businesses, however, the value of the employee is recognised and everything will be done to ensure that the successful performance of the business is mirrored in its policies towards the people within the business who helped to make it all possible.

Don't focus wholly on the cost issues – focus on the end result.

## Key points summary

- Strategies to retain and reward people in the business.

- How valuable is the employee?

- Using the team approach making working *on* the business more achievable.

- Know what employees' need requirements are, so that they can be addressed.

- Communicate with employees for maximum effect.

- Help employees to build wealth through the business.

# CHAPTER 28

# Business Owner Investment Super-Strategies

*The universal regard for money is the one
hopeful fact in our civilisation, the one
sound spot in our social conscience. Money
is the most important thing in the world. It
represents health, strength, honour,
generosity, and beauty as conspicuously as
the want of it represents illness, weakness,
disgrace, meanness and ugliness.*
**George Bernard Shaw (1856–1950)** *Major
Barbara*

**Objective: To develop strategies for people wishing to invest in
businesses, and to realise their investments when it is
prudent to do so**

Investing in any business can be risky – the more so, if the business is
an unquoted company with only internal management controls, and yet
more so if the business is a sole trader or a partnership.

These types of business investments do not appeal to everyone. For
one, they are difficult to find (unless they are start-ups) and for another,
they are difficult to assess once found. However, there are plenty of

investors around willing to accept this level of business risk – according to NatWest Bank, which has a large data base of private investors, so-called 'business angels' have in excess of £6 billion to invest in UK smaller businesses.

For most businesses investors, though, investment is more likely to be merely a 'punt' with spare cash, or a short-term means to save tax by investing in an Enterprise Investment Scheme company under the EIS tax relief rules, or to defer a capital gain. Those wishing to spread their risk may opt for a Venture Capital Trust (VCT) or for the IFP Portfolio of EIS Companies.

These are the more passive investors. Those seeking a more active role (business angels) will ignore VCTs and find their own businesses to become involved with – often a long and arduous process.

The following strategies are designed to show the investor what to look for and how to find it. They will also indicate to the business requiring private investors what has to be done to attract them. Lastly, they will show the investor when and how to get out if the time has come for that.

---

## STRATEGY #472
## Understand why certain investors will seek businesses in which to invest

---

Every investor has a risk profile which will range from extremely cautious and least risky (building society investments) to highly speculative and most risky (shares).

On our sliding scale, the type of investor interested in investing in businesses which are unquoted will be one with a high preference for risk. He or she will have an adventurous outlook, be prepared to speculate to accumulate and can sustain the loss of the whole investment once made. Compare this high preference for risk investor with a totally risk-averse investor – cautious, cannot afford to lose a 'nest-egg' and invests in 'safe' or 'guaranteed' investments, usually only for income. The only risky event for the latter type will be a weekly trip to the newsagents for a £1 lottery ticket.

The high preference for risk investor is therefore likely to be someone who

• can afford to lose the entire investment
• is not retired or living on modest means
• has time to wait for significant capital growth
• has invested in this type of investment before

- has built up smaller businesses to bigger ones in the past and understands this market
- would like bigger returns in capital growth and income flow than conventional investments
- would like an active (or passive) role in the investee company, i.e. would like to follow his money

There may be others, not necessarily of the correct risk profile, who will be persuaded, against their better judgement, to invest by family and friends or business associates.

---

## STRATEGY #473
## Never invest in sole traders, and to a lesser extent (unless a professional practice) in partnerships

Sole traders and partnerships are highly vulnerable business structures. If the business fails, you could be saddled with business debts and liabilities. You should only be considering company investments. The reason for this is quite obvious. How do you invest in a sole trader? The sole trader *himself* is the business. The only way to help a sole trader financially is by making loans or capital gifts. There is no 'share' to reflect the growth in your investment. All you would have is a loan agreement, presumably payable on demand. The same can be said of a partnership, unless you are coming in as a partner where your liability can be limited. Otherwise, not only your capital is at stake, but also the rest of your wealth, due to being jointly and severally liable for the partnership debts.

If a passive investor, don't consider partnerships. The position is different if you will be an active participant in the partnership (as a partner). By law, some businesses can operate only as partnerships (such as solicitors and accountants – and then you should be professionally qualified to be one).

Investors in companies receive share certificates. These may grow in value, reflecting their higher worth if the business is successful. Shareholders are not liable for the company's debts (unless they sign personal guarantees) and their liability is limited to the extent of their capital in the business – which they may lose if the business fails.

If the small business wanting your investment is not prepared to become a company (unless the type of partnership by law described above) then think twice before investing in it.

---

### STRATEGY #474
### Develop an understanding of risk and return
### analysis and ratios. Learn the numbers

---

Given the business plan of the business, you must be able to determine whether to invest in it or not.

Some basic ratios will act as 'pointers' for your decision-making processes. Compare them with other businesses, usually operating in the same sector.

For example, work out the *profitability ratios*:

*Profit margin*
This shows management's use of the resources under its control. Extraordinary items are excluded from this ratio, because they do not represent normal operating profit.

$$\text{profit margin} = \frac{\text{profit before taxes}}{\text{sales}} \times 100$$

$$\text{e.g.} \quad \frac{200,000}{2,000,000} \times 100 = 10\%$$

*Return on total assets*
Profit is closely related to the assets employed by the company.

$$\text{return on total assets} = \frac{\text{profit before taxes}}{\text{total assets}} \times 100$$

$$\text{e.g.} \quad \frac{200,000}{1,300,000} \times 100 = 15\%$$

*Return on owner's equity*
This is the return on the owner's capital (equity) investment in the business.

$$\text{return on owner's equity} = \frac{\text{profit before taxes}}{\text{owner's equity}} \times 100$$

$$\text{e.g.} \quad \frac{200,000}{750,000} \times 100 = 27\%$$

There are literally hundreds of different ratios which can be applied in investigating the performance, liquidity and profit returns for a company, not to mention others which determine what the equity/debt/

preference shares investment amounts should be. Whole textbooks have been written on the subject. Serious investors should get to grips with ratio analysis as a constant monitoring tool of what is happening in the business.

The following table is an example of an abbreviated ratio analysis.

| Company: Constantia plc | 1995 | 1994 |
|---|---|---|
| **Liquidity/capital structure results** | | |
| Current ratio (liquidity 1) | 1.7 | 2.6 |
| Liquidity ratio 2 | 0.6 | 1 |
| Gearing (total borrowings against shareholders' funds) | 44% | 40% |
| After-tax return on equity | 8.5% | 13.3% |
| Pre-tax return on equity | 15.2% | 18.3% |
| Returns on total funds | 10% | 11.4% |
| Asset turnover | 0.9% | 0.9% |
| Net profit % | 11.2% | 13% |
| **Investigating liquidity** | | |
| Sales increase | 8.3% | |
| Buys stock | 79 days | 81 days |
| Pays debtors | 28 days | 28 days |
| Creditors' turnover | 29 | 28 |
| **Investigating performance** | | |
| Gross profit% | 24% | 25% |
| Distribution: sales | 4.8% | 5% |
| Administration: sales | 8% | 7% |
| Administration increase | 24% | |

A quick interpretation of this analysis would show:

- A fall in liquidity ratio, and the gearing ratio requires a further investigation. Check for new financing and also for working capital increases or decreases.
- Returns on equity falling. If asset turnover has not changed, then investigate the fall in the net profit percentage. In this example, the fall in the gross profit percentage could have resulted from an increase in turnover causing a fall in profit margins. Also the 24% increase in administration expenses could explain the fall in the net profit percentage.
- Tax charges have risen, although profit has fallen. Check accounting policies.
- Decline of operating profitability mainly through gearing and tax factors, increasing administration costs, but not sales performance.
- The company could seek further financing to improve its liquidity position in the near future and would have to explain its existing

borrowings and deferred tax liabilities. Internal tightening up on costs is required in administration. Because of increasing gearing levels, possibly the company should consider new equity finance.

The above is a very limited interpretation and is not intended to be comprehensive, only to supply the necessary indicators on how to analyse the figures.

---

## STRATEGY #475
## Learn the important ratios for investors

---

One of the most important ratios for shareholders is to ensure that their dividends are safe, and to achieve this they need profits compared with the dividends payable (dividend cover):

$$\frac{\text{Profit for the financial year}}{\text{Dividend payable}} = \text{e.g. } \frac{120,000}{59,000} = 2.03$$

The company could pay the dividend another 2.03 times which should give comfort to investors.

In addition, investors would want to know what the earnings per share will be. It indicates total earnings (dividends plus retained reserves for expansion) which each share generates. Companies strive to increase earnings per share each year.

Take, for example, a company with 100,000 × £1 shares:

$$\frac{\text{Profit for the financial year}}{\text{Number of issued shares}} = \text{e.g. } \frac{120,000}{100,000} = £1.20$$

Here, £1.20 is earned for every share held by shareholders.

Learn the 'numbers' and become familiar with ratios (see also Chapter 3).

---

## STRATEGY #476
## Learn when to say no to a 'good deal' and when to go ahead

---

Investors in small businesses must develop their own criteria for investing.

For example, their individual criteria could be to:

- Choose an existing company with a strong management team, requiring development or expansion capital to exploit a niche market or opportunity. The company must have a strong track record without necessarily having been profitable in all trading years. This should ideally be in manufacturing sectors and able to offer EIS tax relief; *or*
- Choose a company which is in the high tech sector with a strong management team, which has no less than 18 months' trading record, able to offer a CGT rollover facility and up to 30% of its equity; *or*
- Select a business in financial trouble where the investor can invest and use his expertise to turn the business around. For example, **your criteria** could be to take a majority stake only in the printing sector in the Midlands.

The investor will want a business plan (see Chapters 1–3) on which to base decisions and will want answers to in-depth questions.

In addition, he will require a 'due diligence' exercise to be completed on the business, usually by an accountant, confirming the business plan and that there are no 'skeletons in the cupboard' in connection with the business.

He may also require an investor's subscription agreement, detailing how the business will spend his money.

So, no matter how good the 'deal' looks, always do your homework first; stick to your criteria and due diligence and undertake appropriate research.

---

### STRATEGY #477
### How to link the business's needs requirements with the appropriate investors

---

What are the financial needs requirements of the business? These will be detailed in the business plan. For example:

'The company requires £200,000 from private equity investors. This will entitle them to new ordinary shares offered at £1 each, and be equal to a 35% stake in the business' *or*

'The company requires £200,000 made up of loan debt finance (50%) and private equity investment (50%). The company is open to negotiation, should the same investor(s) be able to provide both. An investor can expect up to 20% of the company in newly-issued £1 shares, which shall be ordinary shares.'

Alternatively, the company may wish to raise new finance as follows:

'40% loan finance
10% preference shares
50% ordinary shares
to a value of £200,000. This is for the expansion of the company into new markets.
The main directors of the company will effect Keyman policies for the amount of capital raised to protect against loss of profits on death.'

The company or business should be fully prepared in respect of its requirements and what it is able to offer to potential investors. Investors may require:

- An investment in respect of their own investment criteria.
- Equity participation with high expected capital gains and a future dividend stream.
- Knowledge of a possible exit route, such as a flotation or sale of the business.
- Tax reliefs under the EIS (Enterprise Investment Scheme) or CGT rollover reinvestment relief. Does the company qualify under the rules?
- An income stream as a non-executive director.
- Investor subscription agreement.
- Details of 'due diligence' undertaken if an accountant has done so.
- To be happy with the investment and not to have to worry about it. Personalities are important. If the chemistry is not there between the management and the investor, he won't invest.
- To make a specific size of investment. This may be too large or too small for the company.
- To spread his investment risk among a number of companies.

---

## STRATEGY #478
## Attract likely investors to your business

---

To attract investors you should:

- Try to accommodate the action points, or as many of them as possible, mentioned in the strategy above.
- Have a clear business plan with a summary to show to investors. This is essential. Include in it any brochures describing the business and its services and other interesting information.

- Be prepared to make presentations to likely investors to sell the proposition to them.

If the business 'stacks up' and the proposition is interesting to investors, then much will depend on the type of investor. If, for example, the investor is a 'passive' type and you are seeking a passive investor, that's fine; but if the investor wishes for an active role and this cannot be accommodated, then, even though the investor has the funds, he won't invest. You must decide on, and try to attract, the correct profile of investor:

| | | |
|---|---|---|
| *Passive* | no involvement | usually invests for tax reasons |
| *Active* | involvement | wants a job; tax relief may or may not be important |
| *Entrepreneurial* | involvement | prefers start-ups or businesses in trouble |
| | no involvement | collects a portfolio of director-ships |
| *Business angel* | involvement | tough character who knows about businesses |
| | no involvement | passive investor, attends board meetings for fees. Both types are large investors |
| *Tax investor* | no involvement (or very little) | forced to invest in unquoted companies for tax reliefs. Wants to spread risk and get the best income and capital growth deal. Can be quite a large investor for CGT reliefs |
| *Ignorant investor* | no involvement | usually a tax relief investor who does not understand the high level of risk. Smaller investor. More suited to VCTs |
| *Other companies* | stake building | often interested for reasons of diversification |
| *VCTs/EIS Portfolio* | active monitoring | need suitable investee companies for their investors |

To sum up:

- a proper business plan is essential
- presentation is everything
- negotiation will be a strong point
- does your business have the correct structure – is it a company, qualifying investors for tax reliefs?
- what is on offer to the investor?
- are there any safeguards?
- what is the exit route?
- are you talking to the right profile of investors?

---

### STRATEGY #479
### Learn how to look in the right places for suitable investments or investors

---

Much depends on the type of investment money which you wish to raise – equity finance or loan finance – as well as how much.

If a very small business, your first port of call is a LINC or Business LINK or associated Chamber of Commerce groups, or the TECs and other affiliates of the DTI (Department of Trade and Industry).

Venture Capital Report, the Capital Exchange, Business Exchange, IFP Portfolio and other groups can examine your business plan and advertise your requirements. NatWest Bank and Midland Bank have 'business angels' data bases, as do many firms of accountants and private investor groups, as well as other business owners.

If you have a larger requirement – usually £250,000 and above – you may wish to try one of the hundreds of venture capital organisations.

For loans, there are, of course, banks, private lenders and secondary lenders.

Be prepared for some up-front fees from finance arrangers, although most work on a success fee. Investment arrangers will want to see some commitment from those seeking finance because often work is done arranging finance which is then not taken up. However, avoid the excessive up-front fee rip-off merchants. The most common complaint from those seeking finance is the amount of times fees have been paid and then nothing is raised. Ask for a track record and testimonials of where money has been raised and talk to those 'happy' and satisfied customers. You'll soon get the measure of the investment arranger.

The average up-front fees and marketing or advertising costs will be about £2,500. This is not that high if you're raising £1 million! For amounts under £50,000, work on about £500.

The best advice is to appoint someone to raise the money for you. It saves you management time and only interested investors will be introduced.

Professional advice is also required so that you do not infringe company law as well as the act relating to public offers which came into effect on 19 July 1995. There are strict rules on making unquoted company offers to the public without a formal prospectus.

If the business has the cash and is raising large amounts (over £1 million) possibly an early listing on the Alternative Investment Market (AIM) is appropriate: the costs – minimum £80,000. (Although there are packages at £50,000, these don't usually include PR and marketing costs.)

---

## STRATEGY #480
## Get up to 60% in tax reliefs for your investors

---

In certain circumstances, investors can qualify for a combination of EIS and CGT reliefs of up to 60% – a CGT deferral of 40% and EIS tax relief of 20%.

Make sure that your company is a qualifying one to receive these types of investors. Interim EIS approval is available from the Inland Revenue if the company qualifies.

---

## STRATEGY #481
## If a business owner or investor, diversify to spread your risk

---

Investing in unquoted companies is usually considered to be higher risk. Out of every ten unquoted companies, one may experience rapid growth and succeed significantly, one will perform reasonably well, and the other eight will either fail or fade away. It is no wonder that venture capitalists only invest in less than 2% of all propositions considered by them.

Risk can also be spread – on a pooled basis through VCTs or EIS funds – or individually selected for a spread through the IFP Portfolio.

Don't leave all your eggs in one basket – invest in more businesses to spread your risk.

---

### STRATEGY #482
### If a business owner, protect your personal assets

---

If you are a sole trader you are most at risk, as you *are* the business. Your investment commitment is total – 100%. Often your house and other personal assets are left as security for business loans. If this is so, and the business fails, you could lose your home.

To protect your personal assets, consider transferring your business assets to a company. Gradually wean yourself off personal guarantees and security offered over private assets. Consider spreading risk by having new shareholders invest in the business or have the government offer up to 85% security on loans under the government Small Firms Guarantee Loan Scheme, available from most banks.

Transfer assets into your spouse's name or into trusts to protect your potential wealth.

If a partner, try to lessen the effect of lending security on personal assets and the same if a director/shareholder. Try to separate personal assets from the business if at all possible.

---

### STRATEGY #483
### Try to limit your business investment risk

---

The investor (or shareholder in an existing business) should seek to limit the risk of loss of his investment by pursuing various strategies:

- Dividends or income flow (non-executive directors). Dividends are unlikely from businesses which are start-ups, as profits are rein-vested. However, more mature businesses can have a dividend policy. Income flow can come from directors' fees or preference shares.
- If tax reliefs for making the investment are possible, take them. The combination of tax reliefs (like EIS) and income flow could return much of the value of the initial investment over a five-year period.
- Investment losses in qualifying unquoted companies are relievable against other income or capital gains.
- Investor subscription agreements with the company ensure that investor's money is spent on the purpose for which it was raised.
- Spread risk amongst various companies, if possible.

## STRATEGY #484
## Know when to get out of your business investment – the exit routes

Business owners find it difficult to comprehend why anyone, once they have invested, would want to come out of that investment – especially if it is a good one.

However, investors in unquoted companies have different reasons for doing so. One of the main reasons is that they invest when risk is at its highest and significant capital gains can be made. As the company matures, the rate of growth slows and this is evidenced usually by increasing dividends to keep investors in the business (see Chapter 23). The investor looking for higher risk investments will want to move out at that stage and take his capital gain, reinvesting it elsewhere.

Other investors may have invested for tax reasons and must stay in for three (CGT) or five (EIS) years and may wish to come out of the investment to invest again for tax reliefs.

It is important for businesses to think about exit routes for investors. These can be:

- flotation as Stock Exchange listing or AIM
- new investors to take out the old ones
- share buy-back
- sale of the business

In addition, the business should start early on to think about replacement capital to exchange for the departing investors.

The investor will learn when prudence is better than returns and whether to stay on as an investor, or whether to go.

## STRATEGY #485
## Build up an investment portfolio of business directorships

Investors can have capital growth as well as income. Some non-executive directors have no equity, but their expertise at board level earns them directors' fees.

Others invest and become non-executive directors. They can expect to earn between 5% and 10% per year from the company for their expertise and direction – as well as to obtain dividends and experience capital growth. Investors who structure a portfolio of directorships can grow with the business, experiencing rising levels of income and capital growth, as well as other benefits.

---

## STRATEGY #486
### If a partner coming into a partnership, especially a professional practice, review all partnership and other agreements first

---

If you are a partner investing into a partnership, beware the small print, or the lack of it. In particular, note the extent of your liability, and how wealth will be transferred from the partnership to you or your heirs. How is your capital account to be repaid, and what alternatives exist in the partnership for structuring a better deal?

Apart from retirement provisions, check out what happens if you (or another partner) dies, becomes disabled, leaves the business, or if the business ceases to trade.

It's no good building up business wealth, only to have it slip away from you because the paperwork wasn't agreed or attended to properly.

---

## STRATEGY #487
### If a partner or shareholder, increase your investment wealth through insuring the other partners or shareholders

---

If a partner or shareholder dies, the cash from the life assurance policies buys his or her shares for the survivors. The deceased's heirs or dependants get cash as the shares are *instantly* marketable on death with insurance coverages. The survivors get the share of the partnership or company without having to find extra cash to do so, as the life policies provide it. See Chapter 11 for further details.

It is one thing to build wealth – it is quite another to protect it, to consolidate it and to retain it. The above strategies will assist both business owners and business investors in their objectives.

### Key points summary

• Investors have different reasons for investing in higher-risk unquoted investments.

• These range from tax reliefs for passive investors under the EIS to venture capitalists seeking high capital gains.

- Investors must understand how to assess business risk by looking at, and comparing, the figures.

- Strategies are given for increasing investment values, as well as exit routes for investors.

# CHAPTER 29

# Executive Wealth-Creation Planning

*Every man is the maker of his own fortune.*
Sir Richard Steele (1672–1729) *The Tatler,*
No. 52

**Objective: Using the business to fund home buying and school fees whilst enhancing savings and future retirement income**

The business can help to create wealth for employees, directors and business owners. Apart from the perceived and actual values attaching to shares or the value of a partner's share as represented by a capital account and share of other assets, the business can be used as a vehicle to achieve a lot more.

Remember, what you spend from after-tax pounds in paying off your mortgage or paying school fees means that not only do you have a net reduction in your available personal disposable income, but you are paying between 25% and 40% *more* because your income is taxed first at your marginal rates and only then applied for your payments.

It has been said that those paying school fees or university fees stand little chance of adequately funding for retirement or having the house of their dreams. Many people, caught up in the recession years of the late '80s and early '90s may be suffering from negative equity and the servicing of large debts. *In addition*, salary increases in the main have barely kept pace with inflation, and many families are going backwards in real terms.

Many are totally reliant on their employers for income as well as for the provision of employee benefits. Naturally, business owners have a far greater degree of flexibility on how they plan their affairs. Employees are relegated to the benevolence of their employers in structuring their private affairs through the business.

Assuming that business owners and employers can be *flexible* in constructing remuneration and bonus packages, there are then significant areas for strategic individual planning.

## 1. STRATEGIES FOR HOME PURCHASE

A house is an asset increasing (you hope) in value. When the mortgage is paid off, your house belongs to you and you are free to deal with it as you please. By comparison, the company car is an asset with (usually) a decreasing value, and is never yours – unless you buy it outright from the company.

Ask yourself the question – what employee benefit would be most valuable to you right now? Helping you buy your home would probably be in the top three on your list – but is seldom offered as an alternative to you.

However, this is a marvellous opportunity for the business to help you build wealth. Also, redeeming your mortgage years earlier protects your lump sums due from pension schemes and endowment policies. These can now be used to create more income for you in retirement.

---

### STRATEGY #488
### The first step is to ascertain if your employer can help you

---

If you own the business, no problem. If an employee or director, then the business may have to review its pay and remuneration policies to give you more freedom in the allocation of your pay package to include home subsidisation.

## STRATEGY #489
## Review your current payments position

How much are you paying per month? What type of mortgage do you have? Is it interest only, or a repayment mortgage? What is the outstanding term to the end of the mortgage period and how much is outstanding?

Do you qualify for MIRAS (Mortgage Interest Relief at Source)? In the 1995/96 tax year this was interest relief on the interest of the first £30,000 worth of mortgage, restricted to 15% of that relief.

Are there early redemption penalties – are you penalised if you pay your mortgage off early?

## STRATEGY #490
## Ask your mortgage lender for a breakdown of your payments schedule

If you do not have such a breakdown, get one. This should show you how capital and interest payments are determined and how much of each you pay off each month.

## STRATEGY #491
## If your mortgage interest rate is too high, try to get a better deal

Remortgages could achieve a lower rate, often by a considerable margin, with a net gain, even allowing for early redemption penalties and transfer costs. Have a mortgage broker do these sums for you.

## STRATEGY #492
## Ascertain the effect of regular capital payments off your mortgage

Most homeowners pay thousands of pounds in totally unnecessary interest payments.

By speeding up the payments from monthly to fortnightly, you can reduce the mortgage redemption term by about six years.

A mortgage is actually a savings account in reverse. The building society lends you money and you repay it with compound interest. Interest charged is assessed on the outstanding capital balance. By reducing the capital balance, you reduce the amount of interest which you pay. A mortgage reduction programme is based on the process of speeding up your monthly mortgage payments to weekly or fortnightly payments. If paying £1,000 per month, then pay £500 per fortnight.

By making the half-monthly payments during the course of a year, you actually accumulate 13 monthly payments. You then use this extra month's payment to reduce your outstanding capital balance. By doing this, you will then reduce the amount of interest you pay by thousands of pounds over the term of your mortgage.

This can be done without any legal fees, without having to change to another lender or change your mortgage. There are no refinancing costs or bank charges and no additional insurance required. Some building societies (like the Yorkshire Building Society) are even selling fortnightly mortgages now. Others allow you to increase capital payments regularly; others insist that you build up capital first and only pay off mortgage loan capital once a year.

The following example will best illustrate how you can pay your mortgage off early, through no additional outlay. It applies to a capital and interest mortgage for 25 years at 11% interest, £75,000 mortgage loan.

| If monthly payments | | If fortnightly payments |
|---|---|---|
| £222,634 | Total payments to building society | £178,484 |
| £0 | Mortgage balance | £0 |
| £75,000 | Equity in home | £75,000 |
| 25 years | Mortgage term | 18.5 years |
| £0 | Interest saving | £44,000 |
| After 25 years | Owning the home | 6.5 years sooner |

If this was an endowment mortgage, then not only would the home be paid off sooner, but the endowment could mature for a considerable sum (say the original £75,000 loan amount) at the original date and be used for other purposes, as the house was paid off 6.5 years earlier.

Alternatively, look at the value of your endowment policy right now. Consider selling it or surrendering it to pay a capital sum immediately off your mortgage, thus reducing the term even further and saving thousand of pounds' worth of interest. Without having to pay endowment premiums either, you could make further capital payments off your mortgage more regularly, or fund an alternative investment such as a personal equity plan or a pension.

---

## STRATEGY #493
## Ascertain from your mortgage lender when the most appropriate time would be to make capital payments

---

Timing is crucial here. Some mortgage lenders only allow additional capital payments to be made at certain times during the year. You may have to build up your own capital to pay off an annual lump sum. Get permission in advance from your lender to make capital reduction payments. At least one bank operates a speeded-up mortgage repayment scheme, paying your mortgage off weekly or fortnightly (instead of monthly), which has the effect of paying off capital earlier and shortening the length of the term of the mortgage.

A greater effect can also be achieved by making one extra mortgage payment, which is essentially what happens when you change to a weekly payment basis i.e. 52 weekly payments instead of 12 by one month payments. (Four weeks in a month equate to 48 weeks in a 12 month cycle. However, there are 52 weeks in a year, and the weekly payment effect produces the extra four weeks of payment.)

---

## STRATEGY #494
## Determine how the business can help you – what does it actually pay and why?

---

The business can assist you in a number of ways. Each method has different payment and tax consequences. Some methods can be combined.

- Business pays off capital (and/or interest) amounts as an employee benefit or loan.
- Business pays off interest amounts by subsidising your payments.
- Business provides 'tax-free' income through profit-related pay which you use to pay the mortgage or pay off home loan capital
- Business considers other methods, such as a plan to provide additional savings to build up a sum to repay the mortgage loan in full at a later date.

---

**STRATEGY #495**
**Generate additional cash by restructuring benefits to help you buy your home earlier**

---

The business has a number of options open to it.

It can, for example, rearrange your pay package in such a way that additional cash is produced to subsidise your mortgage payments or interest payments. You might, for instance, take a reduced company car benefit. Savings generated in reduced HP or lease payments plus tax savings in reducing from a higher cost car to a lower cost car are then applied to the mortgage subsidy.

You are better off in terms of personal wealth-creation because part of your pay is now building your wealth through helping you purchase your home earlier.

Direct mortgage subsidies will also be a benefit in kind (similar to the car benefit) and its value will be taxed as a benefit in your hands. However, the net effect is better for you in cash flow terms.

This is illustrated as follows:

Jonathan Grant has a 25-year endowment repayment mortgage. Seventeen years remain of the term. Monthly mortgage interest payments are £800, being roughly an interest rate of 10% p.a. on an £80,000 mortgage loan. He also previously had a company car valued at £10,000 attracting benefit taxes of £3,500 p.a. By moving to a cheaper vehicle, savings are produced of £6,188 per annum in lease and tax payments. This saving is to be applied to a mortgage subsidy for Jonathan.

---

**Present position**
**(in simple terms)**

| Company cash flow | | Jonathan cash flow | |
|---|---|---|---|
| Cost of car p.a. | 10,000 | | |
| Benefit tax on car | 0 | Benefit tax on car | 3,500 |
| NIC1A to company | 1,500 | | |
| Insurance/other | 2,000 | | |
| Net effect (company) | 13,500 | Net effect (Jonathan) | 3,500 |

---

| New position in simple terms) | | | |
|---|---|---|---|
| Cost of car p.a. | 6,000 | Cost of car p.a. | 0 |
| Benefit tax on car | 0 | Benefit tax on car | 2,100 |
| NIC1A to company | 612 | | 0 |
| Insurance/other | 700 | | |
| Net effect (company) | 7,312 | Net effect (Jonathan) | 2,100 |

Company savings: £6,188

The company is no worse off by applying £6,188 to subsidise Jonathan's mortgage. In addition, Jonathan saves £1,400 which can be applied to the benefit tax on the mortgage subsidy.

| | |
|---|---|
| Mortgage to pay p.a. | £9,600 |
| Company subsidisation benefit | £6,188 |
| **Balance for Jonathan to pay** | **£3,412** |
| | |
| Benefit tax to pay by Jonathan at 40% × 6,188 | £2,475 |
| Total to pay | **£5,887** |
| less previous tax savings on car benefit | (£1,400) |
| **Net cost to Jonathan for mortgage** | **£4,487** |

The reduction, therefore, is £5,113 per annum. This represents a substantial cash flow saving to Jonathan of 53%, net of all taxes; plus this position includes all taxes paid for his company car. What a winning position to be in!

---

## STRATEGY #496
## Use the special Inland Revenue rules on interest payments to pay mortgage interest

---

Mere subsidisation of your mortgage payments attracts full benefit in kind taxation.

Special rules apply where only the interest is paid for. There, the Inland Revenue taxes you on the *difference* between the Inland Revenue official rate of interest and the interest rate paid by you. The difference in interest rate is the benefit to you.

This can be illustrated by the following example:

David has an interest-only mortgage of 10% per annum on a £100,000 mortgage. Mortgage interest payments: £10,000 p.a.

The company is prepared to pay 5% of this interest on behalf of David. The Inland Revenue 'official rate of interest' is, say, 7%. The difference in interest rates between what the company pays and the official rate is 2%. David is calculated to have received a benefit in kind of 2% worth of interest, which is taxable.

|  | Calculations | Payments |
|---|---|---|
| Mortgage interest to pay (10%) |  | £10,000 |
| David pays 5% |  | (£5,000) |
| Company pays 5% |  | (£5,000) |
| Tax to pay: at 40% | (2% × £10,000) |  |
| 40% | (£200) | £80 |
| at 25% | (2% × £10,000) |  |
| 25% | (£200) | £50 |
| Company pays £5,000 (no NIC is payable on this benefit) | | |
| David pays £5,080 less MIRAS | | |

The net cost to the company after tax relief at 25% is £3,750.

Previously, in real terms, David would have paid (£10,000 + 40% of £10,000) = £14,000 (less MIRAS) as he pays from after-tax income – if a higher rate taxpayer. Now he pays (£5,080 + 40% of £5,080) = £7,112, a saving in net disposable income of nearly 50%.

This saving can be applied against further capital reductions (which will not be taxable – as if the case where the company pays) of the mortgage, or tax deductible pension contributions.

---

### STRATEGY #497
### Decide whether the business pays off capital or interest for you

---

The different methods of calculating benefit in kind taxation for capital payments (direct subsidies) or interest-only payments (paying mortgage interest) should be seriously considered. Subsidising loan interest payments could be more beneficial as it is only the difference between the 'official' rate of interest and the real interest rate on the payment.

The 'official' Inland Revenue interest rate is set by the Treasury from time to time. It is usually quite close to the bank base rate. Over the last five years it has gone from a high (November 1989 to November 1990) of 16.5% to a low in June 1995 of 6.5%, with an average of 7.7% between 1994 and 1995.

There are also special more beneficial rules which apply where loans or subsidies are for your home.

---

**STRATEGY #498**
**Consider whether to subsidise below the MIRAS level of relief**

---

As you get MIRAS (Mortgage Interest Relief at Source), you should use the *value* of this exemption first and then have the business subsidise above this level. However, the level of MIRAS relief has fallen so drastically over the years, that the saving could be marginal, and you may be better off by having the full amount subsidised.

MIRAS relief applies to interest on the first £30,000 worth of mortgage loan, but is capped presently at 15% (1995/96) of that amount. An example would be: 10% interest on £30,000 loan = £3,000 × 15% = £450 relief only.

---

**STRATEGY #499**
**To avoid benefit in kind taxation completely, employ your spouse in the business at under £8,500**

---

Benefit in kind taxation does *not* apply in certain circumstances. An employee earning less than £8,500 p.a. who satisfies the following conditions will pay no benefit in kind taxation [ICTA 1988, sections 153–168]:

- Someone who earns under £8,500 p.a. (including value of the benefit and reimbursed expenses)
- Someone who is not a director in terms of the definition
- Someone who does not hold more than 5% of the company
- Someone who is a full-time employee
- Someone who has a remuneration and benefit package which is less than £8,500 p.a.

Considerable savings can be made by transferring the mortgage to the lower-paid spouse, satisfying the above conditions, and then have the business subsidise the mortgage.

Often mortgages are in joint names and this is often better as you can then split the subsidy on higher mortgages for best tax advantage.

---

### STRATEGY #500
### Get your whole home loan covered for free

---

There are numerous strategies which may apply here and each should be carefully considered. For example:

- The business introduces a profit-related pay (PRP) scheme. This produces an amount of 'free' or non-taxable income. Under the rules, a 40% qualifying taxpayer can get an extra £1,600 a year and a 25% taxpayer gets £1,000 extra income tax-free (1995/96). In some cases, this can be enough to pay your tax bill when the mortgage is subsidised!

- If you have an endowment mortgage, you can change to a pension repayment mortgage, using the 15% deductible pension contribution allowance for an AVC/FSAVC allowed to individuals on company pension schemes (or higher amounts for personal pensions if no company scheme). The company savings in NIC with this scheme and your tax reliefs combine to enhance the plan significantly. At retirement you have a larger 'fund' and therefore a greater tax-free cash amount to redeem your mortgage.

---

### STRATEGY #501
### If using the NIC and pension plan, sell your endowment policy or surrender it to repay further capital off your mortgage

---

As interest compounds on your outstanding mortgage loan, reducing the underlying capital amount owing by as much as possible saves you many thousands of pounds in the long run in saved interest payments. These savings can be applied to further personal wealth-creation.

### Key points summary

- Any business can provide a mortgage subsidy or direct capital redemption as an employee benefit.

- The tax treatment differs depending on the type and amount of the subsidy.

- Using proper tax and financial planning you can get your most valuable asset – your home – completely free or at least paid off many years earlier with substantial interest savings.

## 2. STRATEGIES FOR PAYING SCHOOL FEES

As with home buying, the business can be used as a vehicle to pay for school fees. The strategies of obtaining employer approval for more flexible employee benefit structuring (if an employee or director) are exactly the same for child education planning as are those for home buying. There are also strategies for the self-employed and those in partnership.

Private education in any form is an expensive business. It has been said that those on the school fee paying treadmill seldom have enough extra resources to provide for adequate retirement funding or even adequate home buying. The sacrifices made by parents are monumental and well-recognised.

If you have no private capital resources (or even if you have, but would rather earmark these for wealth-building) then usually school fees are met from after-tax income. To pay school fees of, say, £10,000 a year for a higher rate taxpayer requires earnings of at least £14,000.

The one kind of inflation which will never disappear is that of school fees. On average, school fees increase by about 11% per year. The high cost, on an increasing basis, often requires intensive financial planning.

---

### STRATEGY #502
### Confirm the flexibility of your employer to restructure your pay package

---

School fees subsidisation needs the co-operation of your employer. If this is not forthcoming from the business, don't worry, there are other strategies outside the business which can be employed, such as lump sum advance payments, pension loan arrangements and school fees discounts by negotiation with the school.

---

### STRATEGY #503
### Rearrange your remuneration package or divert your bonus annually

---

The business can pay your school fees (and you pay employee benefit taxation on the amount paid).

You can take a salary reduction or your remuneration package can be restructured, possibly reducing the level of one benefit (e.g. company car) and increasing another (school fee subsidy).

Either way, the business is no worse off, the amount paid is tax deductible to the business, but taxed in your hands.

National Insurance contributions (NIC) are usually payable by the employer on the value of the benefit.

Instead of taking a salary increase, ask for a school fee subsidy payment. Make sure, though, that your benefits paid in this way still 'count' for pension purposes. Likewise, if a bonus is payable to you, think about diverting it into school fees payments.

---

### STRATEGY #504
### Examine bonus diversion schemes to pay school fees

---

Any bonus paid to a company executive or employee attracts income tax at highest rates as well as NIC (at 10.2% currently) on such payments as salary. (10% in 1996/97.)

There are a number of NIC avoidance schemes available which save the company money as well as the executive. As these 'loopholes' arise, so the government acts to close them. However, it is a fundamental principle of our law that you can arrange your affairs in any legal way to avoid tax. (See Chapter 17 for further information.)

---

### STRATEGY #505
### Get the Inland Revenue to pay for your school fees – and retire comfortably

---

If you are paying school fees out of income, have little or no retirement funding in place, and satisfy other criteria, then this powerful savings plan is for you.

Paying school fees out of income is one of the most tax-inefficient ways of doing things. My client, Timothy Renbury, had precisely this problem. Private education for his two sons and a daughter was costing him a fortune – over £15,000 a year – after tax.

Timothy had made very little pension provision because of the annual drain of cash into the private school system. He owns his business which he considers to be successful and is a higher rate taxpayer. Although, at a pinch, he could continue to pay school fees out of income, it meant paying more tax with fewer tax deductible items personally.

What Timothy really wanted was peace of mind. Our strategy for him was to make maximum pension contributions, which at his age gave 20% tax relief (as a sole proprietor). At the same time, a school fees loan was arranged, secured against his property, for repayment in 17 years' time – at retirement. (You can also get unsecured loans.)

He estimated that he would need about £80,000 worth of loan at that stage to pay school fees over the period. Interest is payable on the loan, but only on the amount actually drawn down. With tax relief at 40% on his pension contributions, and interest at only 8% to 10% on the loan, plus the fact that now school fees were paid from *before tax* income (or loan capital), meant that Timothy was financially ahead of the game.

Traditionally school fee loans are linked to endowment policies as repayment vehicles, but these have no tax deductible premiums and are themselves paid from after-tax income. The acceptance by the school fees loan lender of the pension cash *lump sum* as the repayment vehicle meant that Timothy had achieved the same effect as the endowment (i.e. providing a tax-free lump sum to repay the loan) but with pre-tax money.

In addition, he also has an annual pension in retirement, generated by this plan, of up to £30,000 a year (depending on annuity and fund performance rates at that time) which he never had before. Also, his present net disposable income is *greater* because of the tax-reducing effort of the pension contributions.

In effect, the Inland Revenue has paid for the school fees because the pension contributions are tax deductible at his highest rates of tax and the lump sum from the pension fund is tax-free.

There will be those who say that the pension scheme is to be used exclusively for retirement purposes. However, if Timothy had not structured his payments in this way, he would not have met his pension objectives either. Careful planning using the business can create massive personal wealth and security for later lifestyle needs. Less than 5% of people are fully funded on pensions – for the best tax-free growth investment available.

The same strategy can be used for house mortgages – get the Inland Revenue to buy your house!

---

## STRATEGY #506
## Effective use of a lump sum to reduce the cost of school fees

---

Most private schools have a facility to pay an up-front lump sum into a savings plan run by the school. You can 'lock-in' guaranteed non-escalating school fees by using this method. School fees inflation is presently about 11% per year so this is a considerable saving over the period.

The school has your money in advance and is prepared to be generous.

---

### STRATEGY #507
## Be prepared to negotiate fees with the school for substantial savings

---

Parents who cannot afford the full fees (and even those who can) have nothing to lose by asking for school fees deductions. Often annual savings of 25% to 33% can be made in this way. After all, private (public) schools are run as a business and they would rather have a pupil at reduced fees than no pupil at all.

Often the best way is to get your school fees planner to *negotiate* this aspect on your behalf, rather than doing it yourself.

---

### STRATEGY #508
## Have the business set up an educational bursary or scholarship fund for the children of employees

---

Much has been said about the employee restructuring his/her remuneration package by doing without one benefit in order to have another. In this case, the business may decide to have its own bursary or scholarship fund to assist in the provision of educational fees for the children of employees.

The taxation implications are that scholarships awarded will give rise to a taxable benefit in kind, unless the employee is himself the holder of the scholarship. If the scholarship awarded to the child of the employee parent was not awarded by reason of the employment and 75% of the scholarship awarded by the employer's fund is awarded to children whose parents are not employed by the company, then there is no benefit in kind taxation [TA 1988, s 331 and s 165(1)]. Being assessed as a benefit in kind is always preferable to paying school fees from after-tax income.

---

### STRATEGY #509
### Have the business make a contribution to your favourite charity – the school or university

---

Public schools or private educational institutions more often than not have charitable status. A business making charitable contributions would involve the following tax implications:

A UK resident company may make a payment or donation to charity and have it deductible as a charge on income in computing the company's profits, if it is a qualifying donation [TA 1988, s 339]. The following are some of the conditions which apply to being a qualifying donation:

- It is not a covenanted payment to charity
- It is not already deductible in computing profits
- It is paid by the company to the charity after deducting an amount equivalent to the income tax thereon
- The donation must be a sum of money
- The company must certify to the charity that it has deducted tax from the payment
- The donor company must not itself be a charity

The charity reclaims from the Inland Revenue the tax deducted by the company. There are other minimum rules for 'close' companies. Individuals may also give to charities through a payroll giving scheme [TA 1988, s 202], where the employer deducts an amount up to £900 from the employee's wage or salary and pays that over to a charity. This method gives tax relief at the highest rate as PAYE operates on the salary less the amount of the donation.

The employee can specify a particular charity. It is up to the employer, though, to operate the scheme. Gift Aid [FA 1990, s 25 and F (No. 2)A 1992, s26] is another way in which the government seeks to get taxpayers to support charities. This scheme gives income tax relief at the highest rate for substantial cash donations to charity. The charity can claim the tax from the Inland Revenue to top up on the donation received.

Check with the school or university bursar to ensure it has the proper level of charitable status to accept these donations.

As a totally unrelated and separate issue, see what bursaries or scholarships are being offered by the school to needy parents.

## Key points summary

• Using the business to pay for your children's education can be cost-effective for the business as well as the employee.

• Careful planning is required to pay for school fees at the same time as building your personal wealth. Both objectives are entirely possible with the strategies outlined above.

## 3. STRATEGIES FOR FURTHER WEALTH-CREATION

The executive or employee will be looking at every possible way of increasing personal wealth and through this accumulation ensuring a financially happy future and stress-free retirement.

Subsidising mortgage loans and school fees are ways of reducing the outflow of personal disposable income by using the business to funnel tax-efficient cash in the right direction. This method can also be used to pay for elderly parents' frail care and nursing home costs, holidays abroad and other financial commitments. Less is going out, so more is available to spend on other things or for savings.

---

### STRATEGY #510
### Give shares or share options to reward performance and build wealth

---

There are other strategies which are purely designed to create additional wealth. Some executives and employees have shares or share options in the business. Others do not, nor will they ever have. However, those who do will be able to exercise their options or sell their shares when the time is right and make a capital gain which is part of their wealth-building portfolio. Capital gains tax may be deferred by reinvesting the gain into unquoted companies which qualify for these purposes. Eventually they may be taxable unless some other relief, such as retirement relief, applies.

Where shares are held, then the holder will expect capital growth as well as a future dividend stream. However, not all companies are prepared to give up equity (especially smaller family-owned companies) and alternative wealth-creation means must be sought.

## STRATEGY #511
## Alternatively, reward performance with bonuses or bonus diversion strategies

Whether shares are available or not, the executive may receive a performance-related bonus. This is taxable and subject to National Insurance contributions at 10.2% by the company. (10% in 1996/97.)

Bonus diversion schemes exist which save the National Insurance contributions being paid, and possibly also the benefits-in-kind taxation. Bonuses and other payments are made to, or on behalf of, the executive, either in cash or in kind, and then are usually sold and immediately reinvested by the executive.

Naturally the government is keen to limit the extent of how these schemes operate and does restrict certain of them from time to time. However, if it can pay the company to make better use of its money, and even to tax shelter it, whilst rewarding executives (who may be at their pension funding limits), then bonus diversion schemes are a likely means of doing so.

## STRATEGY #512
## If in a partnership, make full use of bonus diversion schemes

The above scheme may be used to divert partners' bonuses into a tax-sheltered environment as well. However, where bonus diversion is most important is for the employees of a partnership who will never have a stake in the partnership unless they become partners.

How do you motivate a partnership employee? By setting up a 'phantom' share scheme and diverting a salary increase or bonus diversion into it – that's how. So long as all the employees agree to its rules, they may have a 'share option' or hold a stake directly in the scheme. The scheme is made even more efficient through profit-related pay. Savings in National Insurance contributions are possible for the partnership, and tax efficiency for the employees. Their 'shares' are invested in the share trust fund into unit trusts, investment trusts, PEPs and other investments giving them an exposure to the stock market. Some view this as being preferable to an investment in the business itself!

The power of motivation for increasing employee performance can be greatly stimulated in this way for partnerships. Yet its application is largely unknown.

Chapter 31 deals with retirement and business exit strategies.

Executive wealth-creation is a focused activity which will maximise pension funding first and then concentrate on other options such as shares and executive wealth-creation plans, all of which are covered elsewhere. Chapter 17 (on benefits in kind or cash) has a full description of NI avoidance schemes for executives, and Chapter 8 deals with pension strategies. Other chapters cover the hundreds of ways of making the most of employee benefits, tax planning, investing properly and taking profits from the business.

All of these strategies are discussed in great depth and will not be repeated here. Every man is indeed the maker of his own fortune and should plan accordingly.

## Key points summary

- Executives could benefit from having the business fund or subsidise home buying or paying for school fees, two of the most costly areas for any employee.

- Even if benefits-in-kind tax is payable, it will always be cheaper for the executive if arranged in this way.

- Wealth-creation does not only mean finding ways to spend less personal cash. It also means wealth-building using shares, options, pensions, bonus diversion and tax shelter schemes.

- Even employees in partnerships can benefit from wealth-creation schemes – something impossible usually unless they become partners.

# CHAPTER 30

# Tax-Efficient Investments for Businesses

> *If a man looks sharply, and attentively, he shall see Fortune: for though she be blind, yet she is not invisible.*
> **Francis Bacon (1561–1626)** *Essays*: 'Of Fortune'

**Objective: To use the best available tax shelters for the business and the people in it**

Once the business has begun creating wealth, it must then develop investment strategies to harness it and preserve it. It is no good at all if the business fails to use what it makes to provide a better financial future for itself and its owners.

Wealth-retention and creation through the business is the *ultimate objective* of the business owners and shareholders personally. Internal investments will add to the strengths of the business itself, whilst external investments via the people in the business will increase their wealth personally. Internal investments are those made by the business; external investments are those made by or for the business owners and employees.

## WEALTH ACCUMULATION

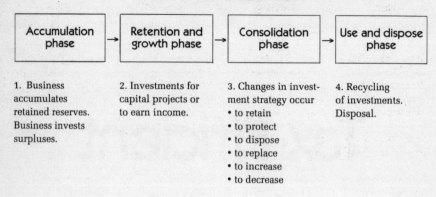

| Accumulation phase | → | Retention and growth phase | → | Consolidation phase | → | Use and dispose phase |
|---|---|---|---|---|---|---|

1. Business accumulates retained reserves. Business invests surpluses.

2. Investments for capital projects or to earn income.

3. Changes in investment strategy occur
 • to retain
 • to protect
 • to dispose
 • to replace
 • to increase
 • to decrease

4. Recycling of investments. Disposal.

---

## STRATEGY #513
## Determine the investment policy of the business and its attitude to risk

---

Usually the investment policy of the business is determined according to which phase of the business growth cycle it finds itself in.

## BUSINESS GROWTH CYCLE AND INVESTMENT POLICY

The business growth cycle shows the business attitude to risk and capital at various stages of the development cycle, the link to surpluses and the investment policy in respect of these surpluses:

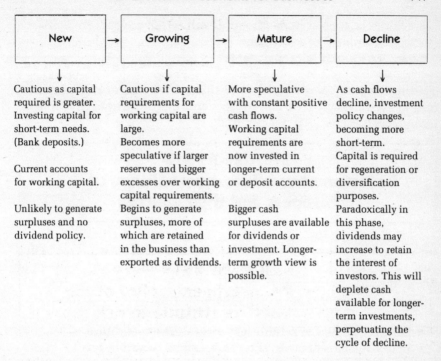

| New | Growing | Mature | Decline |
|---|---|---|---|

Cautious as capital required is greater. Investing capital for short-term needs. (Bank deposits.)

Current accounts for working capital.

Unlikely to generate surpluses and no dividend policy.

Cautious if capital requirements for working capital are large. Becomes more speculative if larger reserves and bigger excesses over working capital requirements. Begins to generate surpluses, more of which are retained in the business than exported as dividends.

More speculative with constant positive cash flows. Working capital requirements are now invested in longer-term current or deposit accounts.

Bigger cash surpluses are available for dividends or investment. Longer-term growth view is possible.

As cash flows decline, investment policy changes, becoming more short-term. Capital is required for regeneration or diversification purposes. Paradoxically in this phase, dividends may increase to retain the interest of investors. This will deplete cash available for longer-term investments, perpetuating the cycle of decline.

Businesses with rapidly increasing cash surpluses will be actively looking for the best investment medium, whether for income generation or growth.

## STRATEGY #514
## Determine the availability of investment resources

Capital and income for investments will usually come from the following sources:

- shareholders' capital
- directors' loan accounts
- retained reserves from after-tax profits
- cash from pre-tax surpluses or profits
- unused portion of loans
- sale of assets
- investment income
- dividend waivers
- operating efficiencies and cost reduction exercises

- windfalls, such as trade discounts and barter, payouts on insurance policies (death of a Keyman)
- tax, VAT and other repayments

Trading income should not be considered for investment purposes, only banked in short-term current accounts for future transfer to longer-term deposit accounts if not required.

---

### STRATEGY #515
### Determine the future expenditures of the business and their sources

---

Business expenditures should be calculated over at least a three to five year period – longer if significant capital expenditures are expected or planned.

These expenditures are usually the following:

- Working capital expenditures – operating expenditure
- Employee benefit costs, such as pensions contributions
- Administration and other fixed costs, computerisation
- Variable costs associated with production and sales processes, purchase of stock and raw materials
- Capital expenditures, such as plant and machinery
- Dividends and dividend policy
- Bonuses and commissions
- Legal, accounting and other fees
- Acquisition and merger costs
- Property acquisition costs

Expenditure items must be 'cash flowed' and their times and rate of expenditure noted. Investment policy and strategies can then be implemented for either short-, medium- or long-term investments.

For example, the business may wish to *save* for future capital expenditure rather than take out loans for it.

---

### STRATEGY #516
### Link the business's investment strategy to tax shelter and tax deductible investments

---

The return on the investment increases significantly depending on its tax-efficiency.

1. For example, a *sole trader* makes the investment and assumes a 10% interest return on a £100,000 investment. The investment is tax deductible as to the capital sum invested. If the business owner pays tax at 40% on the return and receives tax relief at 40% on the investment made, then the following illustration shows a net return on the investment of 46%.

| 40% business owner: 1st year | | | |
| --- | --- | --- | --- |
| Interest return | 10,000 | 10% | (taxable) |
| Tax 'return' 40% relief | (£40,000) | 40% | (relief on capital) |
| Total initial return | gross | | 50% |
| | net | | 46% |

2. If a *company* made the same investment, then a net total return would be 42.5%. For instance, if a '25%' corporation tax company with investment of £100,000, interest at 10%, capital deductible, interest taxable:

| 25% company: 1st year | | | |
| --- | --- | --- | --- |
| Interest return | £10,000 | 10% | (taxable) |
| Tax 'return' 25% relief | £25,000 | 25% | (relief on capital) |
| Total initial return | gross | | 35% |
| | net | | 42.5% |

The above two scenarios can now be compared to investments which offer no tax reliefs on capital, with the interest taxable; which only shows a total net return of 7.5%.

For instance, with investment of £100,000, interest at 10%, interest taxable:

> Interest return: £10,000 (taxable) 10% gross
> Net of tax (25%): £7,500
> Net return: 7.5%

Tax shelters, investments with deductible capital (and interest) will give bigger net returns than those which are merely taxable. In addition, the effect of capital gains taxes (and inheritance taxes etc), could further reduce the total investment returns over any given period, which includes the realisation of the investment, or otherwise. The business's investment strategy should reflect its preference for risk as well as making use of tax-efficient investments.

---

## STRATEGY #517
## Determine the investment range for any business to invest its funds in

---

The following table shows likely investments for the business to consider, depending on its risk profile, capital or income requirements, and need for growth and tax reliefs requirements.

| Investment | Level of risk | Income | Growth | Tax relief |
|---|---|---|---|---|
| Current account | lower | yes | no | no |
| Offshore current account | lower | yes | no | no |
| 90-day call account | lower | yes | no | no |
| Fixed deposits | lower | yes | no | no |
| Guaranteed income bonds | low (but possible capital risk) | yes | no | no |
| Bank instruments (treasury, bank acceptances etc) | low | yes | no | no |
| Corporate bond | medium/high | yes | capital may fall | no |
| Treasury bonds, local government, other bonds | low (but capital risk) | yes | capital may fluctuate | no |
| Offshore bonds | medium/high | yes | yes | no |
| Endowment policy | medium | no | yes | no |
| Unit trust | medium/high | no | yes | no |
| Investment trust | medium/high | no | yes | no |
| Share portfolio | medium/high | some | yes | no |
| Unquoted company | high | dividends | yes | no |
| Enterprise zone trust | medium/high | yes | yes | yes |
| Pension fund | low | no | yes | yes |
| Property | medium | yes (rent) | yes | no |
| ESOT | low | no | yes (in trust) | no |
| Employee benefits | low | no | no | yes |
| NIC avoidance schemes | medium | no | yes (for employee) | yes |
| Retained reserves | low | no | no | no |
| 'Hard' investments (yacht, works of art) | high | no | yes | no |

## STRATEGY #518
## If a sole proprietor, shareholder or partner, determine the investment range for (personal) investments

If you are the sole proprietor (or to a lesser extent, a partner) in the business, the business investment mix will revolve to a large extent around personal risk objectives. A shareholder (or employee with investment money) will usually use the same investment strategy, depending upon risk preference or risk aversion.

| Investment | Level of risk | Income | Growth | Tax relief |
|---|---|---|---|---|
| Current account | lower | yes | no | no |
| Offshore current account | lower | yes | no | no |
| 90-day call account | lower | yes | no | no |
| Fixed deposits | lower | yes | no | no |
| Tessas | lower | yes | loyalty bonus only | tax-free income |
| Other bank instruments | lower | yes | no | no |
| Guaranteed income bonds | low/medium | yes | no | no |
| Corporate bonds | (possible capital risk) high/medium | yes | no (capital may fall) | no |
| Corporate PEPs | high | yes | yes | no |
| Treasury bonds | low | yes | possible | no |
| Government, other bonds | low/medium | yes | possible | no |
| (note that capital may fluctuate up and down with *any* bond) | | | | |
| Offshore bonds | medium/high | yes | yes | no |
| Endowment policy | medium | no | yes | no |
| Personal Equity Plan (PEP) | medium/high | no | yes | grows tax-free |
| Unit trusts | medium/high | yes | yes | no |
| Investment trusts | medium/high | yes | yes | no |
| Share portfolio | high | yes | yes | no |
| Enterprise Investment Scheme | higher | dividends | yes | yes |
| Unquoted non-qualifying companies | very high | dividends | yes | no |
| Venture capital trusts | higher | dividends (tax-free) | yes | yes (20%) |
| EIS fund | higher | dividends | yes | yes (20%) |
| Alternative investment market (AIM) | higher | dividends | yes | no (unless EIS company) |

| | | | | |
|---|---|---|---|---|
| Qualifying unquoted company for CGT reinvestment relief | higher | dividends | yes | yes (40%) |
| Share portfolio | high | dividends | yes | no |
| Enterprise Zone Trust (EZT) | high | yes | yes | yes (100%) |
| Pension fund contribution (self-invested pension plan or other type) | low | no | yes (tax-free) | yes (40%) |
| Fixed property | medium | rents | yes | no |
| 'Employee benefits' and share schemes | low | no | possible | yes on some |
| Hard investments (works of art etc) | high | no | yes | no |

The above are generally representative of the types of investments to be considered. As a general rule, lower risk investments with 'guaranteed capital' will have no growth and are usually income-producing.

Higher-risk investments usually have capital at risk and therefore expect higher returns in respect of growth, with little or no income. The individual may wish to limit capital risk by having *cash* investments within a growth portfolio.

Most people are concerned with the risk of loss of capital as opposed to the risk of what they may earn beating inflation in the long term.

## STRATEGY #519
## Select the most tax-efficient investments for surplus cash and invest in tax shelters

Once the business has decided on its investment strategy, in accordance with its business objectives, and made the necessary allocations for further expenditure (using shorter-term usually fixed interest investments), it can invest its surpluses by choosing a mix of investments. Some investments are more tax-efficient than others. Tax-sheltered investments may even be protected from creditors (such as pensions – but only if there is no fraud).

By investing in tax-sheltered investments, the investment begins tax-efficiently and the shelter ensures its continuance. These types of investments are the best wealth-builders.

---

## STRATEGY #520
## Your best tax shelter is the business's pension fund. Maximise contributions to it

---

Contributions to a pension fund are tax deductible to the business and to the individual making allowable contributions.

Once made, the contributions compound tax-free within the pension fund. The value of the contributions made are not taxed in the hands of the individual members of the fund. Nor are they taxed as a benefit in kind.

The company or employer does not pay NIC on contributions, saving 10.2% on cash flow. (10% in 1996/97.)

If the business gets into trouble, the pension fund stands outside the business and is for the benefit of its members.

Because the pension fund itself is not an asset of the business, it is not reflected on the balance sheet. However, its existence is known and this strengthens the profile of the business.

The employer-owned scheme for directors or partners (SSAS) may be used as a source of funds. Loans are available to the business for commercial purposes. Loans taken by the business must have interest paid at a commercial rate. This interest is deductible to the business, but *not taxed* in the pension fund itself. The business can virtually set its own rate of growth in the fund at higher levels.

Pension funds in surplus could help the business's cash flow by taking contribution holidays – another example of its flexibility.

---

## STRATEGY #521
## Use a pension scheme to protect the assets of the business

---

The business's property (premises) could be purchased from a third party by the owner's pension scheme (SSAS) and rented to the business.

The trustees of the pension fund have wide powers and can take or make loans, arrange mortgages and so on.

The rental income paid by the pension fund accrues free of all taxes in the pension fund, and is tax deductible to the business.

The pension fund is in effect a trust which is most flexible. Purely discretionary, it does not suffer tax charges like other trusts, nor does it have to cease after 80 years.

Property held in this way (see Chapter 26) may be utilised by future family members (so long as they participate in the business) for as long as there are future family generations. They simply become members of the pension fund.

Business assets can therefore be protected within a pension fund. A SSAS can even purchase shares in the sponsoring company – usually up to 5% worth. The pension fund is your most tax-efficient tax shelter. Individuals in business (sole traders or partners) may use a self-invested personal pension to hold property and other investments. On retirement, tax-free cash is payable to members. The pension itself is taxable.

---

### STRATEGY #522
### The company or business may invest in other tax-efficient investments such as EZTs

---

Any individual or business may invest in an Enterprise Zone Trust (EZT) investment, and obtain 100% tax relief – the amount of the investment is unlimited, but long term.

The only problem is that EZT investments are fairly scarce, because EZT zones, where investments are made, have filled up, leading to a shortage of investment opportunities.

Some Enterprise Zone Property Trusts offer a pooled arrangement where investors share in the capital allowances related to the property. Investors would expect an income from the property investment (rental income of, say, 7%) as well as a capital gain.

---

### STRATEGY #523
### A company may invest in an ESOT – an Employee Share Owner Trust, for tax shelter and working capital enhancements

---

Capital, either borrowed from a bank (or other source) or given by the company to the ESOT, is tax deductible to the company. The ESOT uses the cash to purchase shares in the company or from shareholders.

If purchased from the company, the company receives cash which can be used as working capital, or invested elsewhere – for example into tax deductible pension contributions. The full gearing effect is covered in Chapter 19.

The ESOT is a tax shelter for employees, who take up shares (which can be funded through profit-related pay) and receive dividends. However, it can be used as a store of wealth by the company. The ESOT can be used to funnel tax-efficient cash to the company. It can also be used as a tax-deferral vehicle. If the shares are not taken up by employees within seven years, the tax reliefs are 'clawed back'. The company would have had the benefit of the tax reliefs for a number of years, though.

---

### STRATEGY #524
### The business should make investments (usually in property, plant and machinery) for capital allowances

---

Capital allowances (see Chapter 16) are another form of tax relief, but given in a different way. If the investment qualifies for capital allowances, then the capital cost of the investment is 'written off' or 'written down' for tax purposes, over a number of years, depending upon its Inland Revenue-assessed life expectancy.

---

### STRATEGY #525
### Qualify the company to receive Enterprise Investment Scheme (EIS) or capital gains tax (CGT) reinvestment rollover investments

---

The company could become a tax shelter to private equity investors seeking tax reliefs for their investments.

Many investors do not qualify for tax deductible pensions (because they do not have 'net relevant earnings' or are too old) but they do get 20% of their investment – up to £100,000 (1995/96) off their actual tax liability – and no capital gains tax on their capital growth, per person, per year.

Investors may require an unquoted company to rollover their CGT liability and defer their capital gains – often to age 55 (50 in 1996/97) when they can benefit from retirement relief. By combining an EIS with a CGT investment, reliefs of 60% are possible.

Companies receiving these investments for equity will have additional cash for investment purposes, over and above working capital requirements.

Often the new capital is raised for a specific purpose such as corporate expansion, to make an acquisition, invest in property, or whatever is detailed in the business plan.

---

### STRATEGY #526
# Invest in legitimate NIC avoidance schemes to build executive wealth

---

Tax avoidance is OK, tax evasion is not. Businesses or individuals may arrange their tax affairs in any legitimate way to avoid the payment of taxes. It is worth repeating the following words of Lord Clyde (in Ayrshire Pullman Motor Services and Ritchie *v* IRC) in relation to how the taxpayer may protect assets from the taxman:

> No man in this country is under the smallest obligation, moral or other, so to arrange his legal relations to his business or to his property as to enable the Inland Revenue to put the largest possible shovel into his stores. The Inland Revenue is not slow . . . to take every advantage which is open to it under the taxing statutes for the purpose of depleting the taxpayer's pocket. And the taxpayer is, in like manner, entitled to be astute to prevent, so far as he honestly can, the depletion of his means by the Revenue.

Legitimate investments or bonus payments constructed in such a way as to avoid National Insurance contributions (NIC) and other taxes legitimately can be significant tax shelters for the business as well as employees.

The use of trusts, investments and specific modes of payment enable the individual to build wealth outside the business – tax-efficiently. Some schemes avoid NIC, PIID benefits and other taxation – savings which can be utilised elsewhere by the business for investment purposes.

---

### STRATEGY #527
# Get the best interest rates for short-term investments

---

Many businesses invest in current accounts earning little or no interest. Some have millions of pounds of idle money gathering dust, not interest.

A generally unknown fact is that up to 3% more can be obtained through utilising an offshore interest account with a reputable bank or building society, invested for 90 days, but with flexible no-penalty accessibility.

At the time of writing (1995/96):

> Current account (UK bank) average: 2%
> Offshore account (with flexibility): 9%
> Difference: 7%

Seven per cent on revolving capital of £1 million is £70,000 worth of interest lost.

Many businesses keep their money in current accounts for undesignated cash flows – and never use it. Research has shown literally millions of pounds lying unutilised in current accounts, sometimes for years, earning almost nothing.

Business should carefully assess future cash requirements, and invest the excess until required.

---

## STRATEGY #528
## Pay the best interest rates for loan account money

---

Any director or partner leaving his director's or partner's loan account to lie fallow in the business is making a poor investment decision. Granted, it may be spare capital, but directors may also have borrowed the money in the first place to lend it to the business. He or she may even be paying (albeit deductible) interest on the money borrowed, but loan account money will *always* be dead money to the director. It will *never* grow, as it is not invested, only loaned. An amount of £50,000 loaned to a business 30 years ago is still only worth £50,000 (less in value for inflation). The *opportunity cost lost* could be 30 years × 6% compound growth on £50,000 = £287,174; at 10% compound growth it would have been a massive £872,470. This position is made even worse if no interest is payable.

If the director is in for the long term and wants his money in the business, it may be better to put it in as equity, not loan capital. The level of risk is the same if the business goes down. However the upside of capital growth in shares and dividends far outweighs the downside of low or no interest and no capital growth in a loan account.

A director's loan account is the worst possible long-term investment strategy for him – great for the business (to have free money) but bad for the director and his or her wealth- building programme. Replace it with bank finance if possible and allow the director to invest for growth.

---

### STRATEGY #529
### Review investment arrangements regularly – at least once a year

---

Regular reviews are essential to keep pace with changing business circumstances. In Chapter 8, it was seen how easy it was to allow review arrangements to slide with respect to investments within a pension scheme – the loss of end fund value over 18 years is 20% for a 1% investment loss of performance today.

Constantly review individual and business cost savings and investment strategies. By squeezing a bit here and a bit there, vast savings can be made. Once made, these should be judiciously invested for further growth or income for the business.

---

### STRATEGY #530
### If a partnership, build up an investment fund to pay out capital accounts or pensions

---

The problems with partnership agreements and the fact that capital accounts are mainly used for working capital in the business (usually with the payment of no interest), lead to greater problems on death or retirement.

At a critical time, when the business needs the capital account money the most, it has to give it up. In fact, under the 1890 Partnership Act, heirs on death have an immediate call for cash (unless other arrangements are made) and this could cripple the business.

The best solutions are:

- a savings fund to pay out retiring or deceased partners
- a phased payment plan, say beginning five years before retirement of the capital account – possibly to boost pension funding
- maximum pension funding – or the partners pay a lump sum and unfunded pension to the retired partner or his dependants (and the firm keeps the capital account for a longer period)
- staying on as a partner and dying 'in harness' so as to maximise business property reliefs on death

Partners' wealth is often at great risk left in the partnership. If bank finance can be exchanged for personal capital, then do it.

---

## STRATEGY #531
## Help employees to build personal wealth. The 'knock-on' effect makes for wealthier businesses

---

Offering employee benefits, pension benefits, share options and schemes, profit-related pay and wealth-building arrangements to executives and employees – whether reward oriented or performance oriented – will tie the employee and his or her loyalty to the business. Performance-related schemes will improve the business's performance and wealth.

This really is a case of spending now to accumulate later. However, in many instances the business owners are the wealth-builders, and those who look after their people will have their people look after them (see Chapter 27).

It is easy to motivate company employees by giving them shares or share options in the company – but employees of a sole trader or partnership have no such structure. The answer is to build a 'phantom share scheme' using profit-related pay and personal equity plans. A trust is set up for employees and the better the business does, the more it contributes a part of its profitability for its employees. It could give a taxable salary increase, but the motivating effects of that are soon lost. It is far better to build the 'Horace Parminter Partnership Share Scheme' and for employees to be a part of that – better still as they will be invested actually in the investment market, and their investment risk will be spread.

Business owners must invest their business's cash surpluses sensibly, whether in fixed interest or growth investments. In the last fifteen years I have yet to see a seminar specifically organised to advise businesses on where to invest the business's money – a couple of separate or individually direct product presentations, but nothing else. That must tell the reader something.

## Key points summary

- The business wealth-creation cycle is shown as well as different investment policies, depending upon the stage in the business development cycle of the business.

- Cash surpluses are then developed for investment against the risk profile and needs of the business.

- The importance of tax shelters, such as pension schemes is discussed.

- Strategies for companies, sole traders and partnerships are shown for investment wealth-creation.

# CHAPTER 31

# Business Retirement Planning Strategies

*Retirement means having twice as much
husband on half as much money.*
**Institute of Financial Planning Conference,
1994**

**Objective: To get the most from your retirement plans – ensuring
a comfortable lifestyle in retirement**

Retirement plans do not only include pension benefits. A well-rounded retirement plan will include investments in equities and fixed interest for growth and income, a pension fund with options for a tax-free lump sum and other income and capital sources.

In an ideal world, by the time the retirement date has arrived, the individual will have considered various options and be taking expert advice. Earlier chapters of the book will have encouraged maximum pension funding as being the most tax-efficient method of capital creation and will have enlightened him or her on how best the business may be used to achieve the individual's personal objectives. In addition, there will be company shares or business value to be decided upon, such as capital accounts for retiring partners, as well as the ongoing relationship between the business and the retiree.

Retirement planning begins at least ten years before actual retirement date. The individual enters into a 'Retirement Countdown Planning Process'. Every future move is plotted and structured in advance.

When I developed the first UK clearing house for pensions and annuities some years ago, I was guided by the fact that available knowledge for retirees was at worst fragmented and at best one-sided. Decisions on retirement benefits were made in a flash, often causing a loss of fund value and reduction of benefits of 50% or more. Once lost, through selecting the wrong options, these benefits are *never* recovered.

Our research further showed that the greatest dilemmas affecting investors in retirement were:

- not enough income in retirement
- previously speculative investors become extremely cautious investors
- the inability to increase income and capital in retirement
- getting locked into the wrong type of annuity rates
- fear of living too long on income which devalued because of inflation
- not having properly planned maximum wealth-creation when they had the opportunity to do so

Our survey at the time (1990) asked retirees at least two years into retirement: 'What would you do over again if you had the opportunity, having experienced retirement?' The overwhelming majority said they would have put more resources into planning for retirement, double or more if they could have done so. Most were worried about living too long on dwindling income.

The strategies in this book have been largely for creating wealth from the business. The final section (Chapters 24–31) is designed to *maximise* what you have built up and retain it.

It is important to understand the demographics of ageing in a world where everything is accelerating, to understand why ongoing wealth-creation and retention is essential to business retirement planning.

For example, the fastest growing segment of population in the USA is the 85-years and older group. This trend is similar in the UK, with the fastest growing age group projected to 2020 being 75 and above. (Percentage interpolations compiled from the 1992 population projections of the Government Actuary's Department: 1995 to 2000 = 7%; 2000 to 2010 = 4%; 2010 to 2020 = 12% growth in this age group.)

People born in modern times are living much longer. For example, an individual born 30 years ago will retire at age 65 and die, on average, at age 73.

Someone born early in 1900 will have been aged 14 at the start of the First World War in 1914 and aged 32 in 1932 – the time of the Great Depression. That person would only have experienced a life of toil, retiring at age 65 and dying at age 70 on average. However, his grandson will retire earlier at age 60 and will live another 23 years and 8 months to age 84.

So, in two generations, the grandson will have been *retired* for five times *longer* than his grandfather was. His wife will go on to age 88. During that period, the general level of prices will double or triple.

'Risk' in the twentieth century has been connected with the possibility of *losing* your money, whereas 'risk' in the twenty-first century will be to *outlive* your money.

---

## STRATEGY #532
## Begin the retirement countdown process by reviewing and evaluating your retirement assets

---

A through review is essential, showing the present position of your retirement planning portfolio. This will usually comprise the following components:

|  | Spouse 1 | | | Spouse 2 | | |
|---|---|---|---|---|---|---|
|  | Value | Lump sum | Expected income | Value | Lump sum | Expected income |
| Current pension fund |  |  |  |  |  |  |
| Paid up pension funds |  |  |  |  |  |  |
| Unfunded schemes – FURBS |  |  |  |  |  |  |
| **Investment assets** |  |  |  |  |  |  |
| Equities/unit trusts/investment trusts/PEPs |  |  |  |  |  |  |
| Fixed interest deposits/Tessas |  |  |  |  |  |  |
| Bonds |  |  |  |  |  |  |
| Hard assets |  |  |  |  |  |  |
| Other |  |  |  |  |  |  |
| Other |  |  |  |  |  |  |
| **Company shares** |  |  |  |  |  |  |
| Share options |  |  |  |  |  |  |
| **Partnership capital accounts** |  |  |  |  |  |  |
| **Partnership share value** |  |  |  |  |  |  |
| **Director loan accounts** |  |  |  |  |  |  |
| **Money owed to you/loans made by you** |  |  |  |  |  |  |

**Maturing policies**
Endowments
Single premium insurance bonds
Surrender value – life policies
**Assets likely to be sold**
**Assets let/rented out**
**Inheritances (possible)**
**Consultancy or other**
**employment income**
**State pension**
**Other assets**
**Totals (assets plus inflows)**

£    £    £    £    £    £

---

## STRATEGY #533
## Review your liabilities and cash flow outgoings at retirement date

---

This should be more or less the same as at present in respect of house-hold expenditure, provision for holidays, running a motor vehicle and so on. Mortgages will probably have been paid off but, if not, include mortgage payments. You may have to set aside a lump sum to replace the company car and other older items.

| | Joint | Spouse 1 | Spouse 2 |
|---|---|---|---|
| Household expenditures | | | |
| Living expenditure – food, entertainment | | | |
| Utilities – lights, water, gas | | | |
| Motor vehicles and fuel | | | |
| Mortgage/rent/nursing home | | | |
| Council tax | | | |
| Insurances – general | | | |
| Holidays | | | |
| Gifts | | | |
| Servant/char/cleaning | | | |
| Taxes – income tax/CGT | | | |
| Clubs, subscriptions | | | |
| Second properties | | | |
| Life assurance premiums | | | |
| Medical insurance premiums | | | |
| Medical expenses | | | |
| Other | | | |
| **Totals – cash outflows** | £ | £ | £ |

## STRATEGY #534
## Balance or reconcile your inflows with your outflows at retirement

| | |
|---|---|
| Total cash inflows: | £ |
| Total cash outflows: | £ |
| Balance | £ |

## STRATEGY #535
## Get your financial adviser or planner to fine-tune your calculations and present a written report for you to work from

This financial planning report should indicate the following areas, depending on your individual circumstances and objectives:

- Cash flow income and expenditure projections in your retirement years.
- Ideal asset allocation for capital growth and income needs taking into account your preference for, or aversion to, risk.
- Recommended investment strategies and asset management.
- Taxation profile, including inheritance taxes and capital gains taxes.
- Estate planning and trusts.
- Provision for long-term care and nursing homes if required.

Be prepared to pay a fee for such a report. This will range from about £250 plus VAT to over £1,000 plus VAT, depending upon the complexity of your circumstances.

## STRATEGY #536
## Get the business to pay for your retirement countdown financial plan

If part of general pensions advice, there should be no benefits in kind taxation to pay by the individual. It would be better if the pension fund itself pays for the generation of the retirement report as there is no employer/employee relationship between a member of the pension fund and the trustees of the fund. This is a particularly useful mechanism if there are surpluses in the pension fund.

The business or pension fund can also pay for you and your spouse or partner to receive retirement counselling and attend seminars. Retirement involves certain life changes and these seminars are designed to help you cope with them.

Start your review process or 'countdown' as early as possible – don't leave it until the last minute. Ideally, between two and ten years before retirement, with regular reviews, would be in order. Shortfalls in wealth-creation can then be attended to in time.

---

## STRATEGY #537
## Use the business to accommodate your retirement plans

---

Your business is the generator of personal wealth – whether as an employee or business owner. You are the catalyst. It is up to you to make things happen. After all, you work to eventually retire and pre-planning is essential for this purpose. The more the business can help you along your journey, the easier the path will be. You will see that it is possibly not only for the provision of an adequate pension, but also in other areas where help is obtained, often at no cost to the business.

---

## STRATEGY #538
## On retirement, keep your company car

---

Buying a new car out of your pension cash lump sum can be avoided if the business allows you to keep your present company car (or obtain a new one prior to retirement).

Company cars are usually well maintained. Some are purchased outright by the business; others will be subject to a lease agreement.

The business will have written down the value of the company car over the years in which you had it and could gift the asset to you (you may be liable to some tax as a benefit in kind) or sell it to you at a lower written-down value. The business could even provide a loan (of up to £5,000 to employees – which it could later 'forgive') for you to purchase the vehicle. No NIC is payable on the value of the benefit if you have retired. Alternatively, the business could provide you with the car in retirement at its expense. As you are no longer an employee, there would be no benefits in kind tax to pay. However, the business may not receive tax relief for making the provision.

You could be liable for CGT if the business asset is donated to you as a gift. However, you do have an annual exemption of £6,000 in the 1995/96 tax year.

---

## STRATEGY #539
## Make sure you qualify for retirement reliefs and can defer any chargeable gains

---

Ever heard a business owner say, 'My business is my pension'? We have a saying to match that – 'A widow can't eat shares.'

On retirement from the business, shares can be sold which will attract retirement relief as follows:

Maximum relief is available on the disposal of a business or business assets provided the individual is aged 55 or over (or below the age of 55 where retirement is on the grounds of ill-health) and the business has been conducted for ten years. (Age 50 in 1996/97.)

Reduced relief is available for shorter periods. If you sell your shares in a limited company, then the retirement relief is available to you. If you and your wife retire, then *both* are eligible for the relief. This doubles the benefit for married couples, so long as each qualifies.

Retirement relief is from capital gains tax. In the 1995/96 tax year the first £250,000 is exempt and the next £750,000 is 50% exempt. For example:

Mr Pettigrew is aged 65 and sells the shares in his business in April 1995 for £450,000. He has satisfied the relevant conditions for eight years. The percentage on which he is entitled to relief is 80%.

The chargeable gain is calculated as follows:

|  | £ | £ |
|---|---|---|
| Sale proceeds |  | 450,000 |
| Purchase price including indexation (say) |  | (50,000) |
|  |  | 400,000 |
| **Less** relief at 100% on (£250,000 × 80%) | 200,000 |  |
| relief at 50% on (£400,000 - £200,000) | 100,000 |  |
|  |  | (300,000) |
| Chargeable gain |  | 100,000 |
| **Less** annual exemption |  | (6,000) |
| CGT payable at 40% on |  | 94,000 |
| is |  | 37,600 |

This chargeable amount can be deferred through *investing* it in an unquoted qualifying company and acquiring reinvestment rollover relief.

Note that separate businesses owned successively during the qualifying period may be regarded as the same business in qualifying for retirement relief.

Having established your retirement relief, you must now consider whether to sell your shares or business assets, and who to sell them to. Above all, you must determine whether there is a *market* for your shares or partnership shareholding and at what price.

---

## STRATEGY #540
## Establish a market for your shares or business assets at a fair price

---

The problems facing similar businesses and partnerships and, to a lesser extent, sole traders, is that, although their shareholdings or business assets have an intrinsic value, they are usually highly illiquid or difficult to sell. The most obvious willing buyers are fellow shareholders or partners, but they seldom have sufficient cash at the right time.

In addition, there may be *restrictions* on the sale of shares contained in the memorandum and articles of association of a company and limitations in a partnership agreement. Usually, these stipulate that shares must be offered to existing shareholders or partners first or exclusively. In this case, the alternatives are to sell the whole business or to rely on a dividend policy (which may not be forthcoming in the future).

The business owner may have to create the necessary sales environment through:

- setting up an ESOT (Employee Share Owner Trust) which purchases the shares; *or*
- finding a willing buyer with cash acceptable to the other shareholders; *or*
- assisting purchasers by helping them fund the share purchase. Use of profit-related pay schemes, executive wealth-creation schemes and the like are possibilities.
- Partnerships may need to develop a 'sinking fund' to enable the capital account of the partner to be paid out. Usually, though, the remaining partners are financially burdened in making regular capital payments to the retiring partner. If the retiring partner withdraws his capital account in one go, it may affect the solvency and stability of the partnership.

- Funding can be arranged for incoming new partners to effect the partnership share purchase.

If you are a partner in a business, pay close attention to the terms of the partnership agreement. Often the partner walks away with nothing at retirement, save for his or her own pension funds in lieu of partnership value.

Sufficient time is *essential* to produce the best strategies for how to fund for the purchase of a retiring shareholder's or partner's shares.

## STRATEGY #541
## If your shares are unable to be sold in the future (at retirement) insist on shareholders' or partners' cross option insurances

The worst position would be where you are unable to find a market for your shares at a fair price on retirement, only to have their value disappear altogether on your death. With you gone, the prospects of a continuous dividend policy in favour of your heirs will become more remote and uncertain.

If you left your shares in the business, and the shareholders or partners effected suitable life policies in trust with a double option or cross option agreement, then at least your estate and heirs will benefit from a cash payout in respect of your shares. The necessary cash is then provided at exactly the right time to enable the survivors to purchase your shares at a reasonable price – for cash (see Chapter 11).

## STRATEGY #542
## Use the business to give you and your dependants a pension, even if you haven't funded for one

The rules for companies and partnerships for unfunded pension schemes are different, so each type of business structure is examined separately:

### Company paying an unfunded pension

There are special rules which apply to unfunded pension schemes. If you were taxed under Schedule E, then you would be eligible for such a scheme. There is no requirement that you must also have been a member of an approved scheme. If the company has not had time to either set up an approved scheme or to fund an unapproved scheme, it may pay benefits out of current income or investments to you.

As far as the company is concerned, there is no charge to tax on any reserves set up to provide for your future benefits. When the benefits are actually paid to you, then the company will get tax relief, but not before then.

There are no set limits on the amount of benefits which may be provided to you, and you will be taxed on the pension received as earned income. If you receive a lump sum from an unapproved scheme, it will also be taxed as earned income.

There are variations in structure and some unfunded pre-retirement benefit schemes do exist which can assist in wealth-creation. However, in this case we are concerned with the individual who has little or no retirement funding, where the company can pay a pension or lump sum without having funded for it.

## Partnerships

Where the retiring partner has made no pension provision, the partners can make a pension and lump sum payment to him, his widow or dependants.

Under ICTA 1988, s 674 (1)(a), 683 (1)(a), where the income arising under the settlement consists of annual payments made under a partnership agreement to, or for the benefit of, a former partner or the widow or dependants of a deceased partner, then this settlement is excluded from being treated as that of the partners from a higher-rate tax charge. The pension or annuity payable will be treated as earned income of the recipient [ICTA 1988, section 626].

The partners will have the amount payable as a tax deduction to them equally. This type of unfunded pension may be an interesting way of repaying a retiring partner's capital account in instalments, whilst providing tax reliefs for doing so to the other partners.

It is essential that this mechanism of paying an unfunded pension to a retiring partner be mentioned in the partnership agreement. This type of arrangement should not be substituted for the more tax-efficient approved pension route but is available where little or no pension funding has occurred.

---

## STRATEGY #543
## Getting the best deal from your business's pension scheme

---

Pensions are a complicated subject and in this chapter we are only concerned with strategies on retirement. Pension funding and understanding the pension scheme are covered in Chapters 8 and 20.

Different business structures qualify for different kinds of pension schemes. Some types are interchangeable – for example, companies *without* an occupational pension scheme, partnerships and the self-employed may all have personal pension arrangements (PPPs); any employer may have an occupational pension scheme; the self-employed may only have personal pensions; and partners may have personal pensions as well as being members of an SSAS (Small Self-administered Scheme with less than 12 members).

The options open to those about to retire are as follows:

### a. Occupational Pension Schemes

These are either money purchase schemes (defined contribution schemes) or final salary schemes (defined benefit schemes) where the retirement benefits are determined as a percentage or fraction of the salary of the employee at retirement.

Approved occupational pension schemes must allow for pension benefits to be payable on retirement at any age between 50 and 75. Your scheme rules will set the retirement date. About 60% of all private and public pension schemes have age 65 as normal pension age for males and females; 25% have age 60, with most of the remainder between ages 61 and 64 (NAPF annual survey of schemes 1993).

Occupational pension schemes have maximum permitted benefits calculated on the basis of years' eligibility in the scheme and the employees' final remuneration.

The maximum benefits which are given are then followed by the appropriate strategy, as follows:

1. A pension of no more than $\frac{2}{3}$ of 'final remuneration' or final salary.

---

### STRATEGY #544
**Check the rules to see if the value of your employee benefits count towards 'final remuneration' as well as bonuses and commissions**

---

2. The maximum amount of final salary is capped in 1995/96 at £78,600. You cannot have a pension of more than ⅔ of this amount, i.e. £52,400 per annum. It must take you at least 20 years to get to this level.

---

### STRATEGY #545
**If your salary is in excess of the 'cap', enquire about unlimited unapproved pension benefits known as FURBS. These can be paid on top of your pension benefits**

---

3. You may commute part of your pension benefits for a tax-free cash lump sum. The maximum lump sum is 1.5 × your final salary (³⁄₈₀ of final salary for each year of service up to 40 years maximum service or 2.25 × the pension before computation, if greater).

---

### STRATEGY #546
**Always take the maximum tax-free cash lump sum. This gives you greater flexibility for investments or annuity income using a purchased life annuity which is more tax-efficient**

---

4. A spouse or dependant pension of up to ⅔ of the maximum pension to which the deceased would have been entitled at his or her normal retirement date. The same arrangement is possible on death *after* retirement.

## STRATEGY #547
Check the pension scheme rules to see if an unmarried partner qualifies, or a divorced spouse. If this applies to you, make sure your pension benefits go where they are directed. Get the trustees to accept your wishes

It is important that you do this, because a divorced former spouse will never become your widow(er). You could lose very valuable pension benefits for your family.

## STRATEGY #548
Set up a discretionary trust to receive your death benefits. The 'dead settlor' provisions under section 547 of ICTA 1988 should apply allowing your beneficiaries to receive tax-free income for life from an offshore bond purchased by your trustees

A lump sum of up to four times final salary, plus a refund of the employee's personal contributions, can be paid on the death of an employee in service.

5. On divorce, the courts can now order a split of your pension benefits at retirement. This could seriously affect your wealth-creation plans.

## STRATEGY #549
On divorce, proper pension planning is necessary to minimise the loss of pension benefits

6. If you have a Free Standing Additional Voluntary Contribution Scheme (FSAVC), then its benefits *must* be aggregated with the benefits in the employer's main scheme to ensure that you remain within the limits. No cash lump sum may be paid from an FSAVC.

**STRATEGY #550**
Use your FSAVC to boost the tax-free lump sum benefits from your employer's scheme. Make sure your employer's scheme allows for this

**STRATEGY #551**
Check that your FSAVC is not overfunded. You could pay up to 48% if a higher-rated taxpayer as the excess will be taxed and the balance returned to you. Alternatively, increase your pay

7. Because of the general inflexibility surrounding occupational pension schemes and their rules, there are few areas to squeeze out additional benefits. The major determinant is 'years' service', better known as 'N'. The smaller 'N' is, the lower your pension will be. If you can get more 'N' years' service allocated to you, the bigger your pension will be.

**STRATEGY #552**
Check with your pension scheme rules to determine whether additional years' service or more 'N' can be purchased or given to you. Some schemes may deem eligibility in previous pension funds as qualifying for this as 'back service'

8. Although occupational schemes pay a set and rigid pension based on years' service and 'final remuneration', the company should examine whether it is receiving value for money. The actual pension is payable from a variety of possible sources – selling investments to purchase an annuity; from investment income; from corporate income; from employees' contributions and so on.

---

**STRATEGY #553**

**Generate additional income in the pension fund itself through a review of how pensions and lump sums are paid. Actuarial savings made may mean a lower funding contribution – money which could be applied to other benefits**

---

## 2. Personal Pension Schemes (PPPs)

These are 'money purchase' schemes with defined contributions. The final benefits are made up from contributions paid and invested, thus creating the pension fund. Prior to 30 June 1988, the self-employed and those in non-pensionable employment could contribute to a retirement annuity contract (section 226 contract) and where different strategies are required for those with section 226 plans, these will be given.

1. At retirement, the pension is payable from age 50, but must be taken by age 75 for PPPs and from age 60 for retirement annuities. Certain occupations (boxers, jockeys, cricketers, etc) can retire earlier, or ill-health grounds may have a pension payable before age 50. However, the annuity must be purchased by age 75.

---

**STRATEGY #554**

**Decide on your retirement date and plan accordingly. You do not have to retire from work in order to take your pension benefits. In fact, it may pay you to contribute to your scheme as long as possible. There is no point in taking additional income if earning at your highest levels – it only increases the tax you pay**

---

2. New rules introduced in 1995 (Finance Act 1995) allow you to defer the purchase of an annuity from a PPP until age 75 *and* elect to take income withdrawals from your accumulated fund. (The new rules on annuity deferral do not apply to section 226 contracts.)

> **STRATEGY #555**
> **Keep the growth in your fund for as long as possible. There is no growth in an annuity (with limited riskier exceptions) and your pension investment accumulates free of all taxes – the best growth medium there is**

3. Flexibility allows you to balance and adjust your income flows from personal pensions through flexible retirement and phased retirement applications.

> **STRATEGY #556**
> **Wait for as long as possible before taking your annuity benefits. There are two reasons for this. Firstly, annuity rates may be low and could be expected to go higher; secondly, you achieve a higher annuity rate the older you are**

4. The annuity itself comes in different forms. It can be guaranteed or non-guaranteed, be unit linked or a fixed sum; can escalate or provide a level pension benefit. The annuity payable is just another term for the pension which you receive. If it comes from a pension fund, it is fully taxable in your hands. This is known as a compulsory purchase annuity (CPA).

> **STRATEGY #557**
> **Proper annuity planning can save you thousands of pounds. It is in your own interests to have the various options outlined in a retirement planning report from your retirement planner**

5. There is no point in building up your valuable pension fund only to lose your wealth through poor exercise of your options. The greater the level of guarantee provided, the less annuity you get to take home.

> ## STRATEGY #558
> **Keep up to date with annuity options and trends. Get regular updates from Annuity Direct in London (0171 375 1175) or their outside London number (01423 525566)**

The following example illustrates how guarantees and escalations can reduce the annual annuity relieved.

For a male age 60, female age 58, with fund value £200,000:

|  | Annual annuity | % of Fund |
|---|---|---|
| No guarantee single life level | 37,000 | 18.5 |
| Joint life, ⅔ pension guaranteed 5 years (payable monthly in arrears) level | 19,800 | 9.9 |
| - escalating by 3% | 15,116 | 7.7 |
| - escalating by 5% | 12,202 | 6.1 |
| - escalating by RPI | 11,792 | 5.9 |

Thus, having escalating annuities, or joint life annuities means that more than ⅔ in value of the top nil guarantee rate annuity is lost forever. Would you rather have £37,000 or £11,792 a year on retirement? Proper planning can get you the higher income.

## Determination of life expectancy

It is important at this stage to determine your average life expectancy. The following table is abbreviated and is taken from the *English Life Tables No. 14* published by HMSO. This is drawn from the average mortality experience of England and Wales in 1980–1982.

## EXPECTATIONS OF LIFE TABLE

| Age | Males | Females | Age | Males | Females |
|---|---|---|---|---|---|
| 50 | 24.264 | 29.39 | 76 | 7.275 | 9.622 |
| 51 | 23.411 | 28.5 | 77 | 6.872 | 9.059 |
| 52 | 22.571 | 27.618 | 78 | 6.489 | 8.516 |
| 53 | 21.744 | 26.744 | 79 | 6.126 | 7.994 |
| 54 | 20.932 | 25.88 | 80 | 5.782 | 7.495 |
| 55 | 20.135 | 25.025 | 81 | 5.458 | 7.02 |
| 56 | 19.353 | 24.178 | 82 | 5.152 | 6.57 |
| 57 | 18.586 | 23.342 | 83 | 4.865 | 6.146 |
| 58 | 17.836 | 22.515 | 84 | 4.596 | 5.749 |
| 59 | 17.101 | 21.698 | 85 | 4.345 | 5.381 |
| 60 | 16.383 | 20.89 | 86 | 4.112 | 5.042 |
| 61 | 15.681 | 20.093 | 87 | 3.895 | 4.731 |
| 62 | 14.995 | 19.307 | 88 | 3.693 | 4.446 |
| 63 | 14.326 | 18.53 | 89 | 3.506 | 4.186 |
| 64 | 13.672 | 17.765 | 90 | 3.331 | 3.949 |
| 65 | 13.036 | 17.01 | 91 | 3.167 | 3.733 |
| 66 | 12.417 | 16.266 | 92 | 3.012 | 3.534 |
| 67 | 11.815 | 15.533 | 93 | 2.863 | 3.352 |
| 68 | 11.232 | 14.813 | 94 | 2.718 | 3.182 |
| 69 | 10.668 | 14.106 | 95 | 2.574 | 3.02 |
| 70 | 10.123 | 13.414 | 96 | 2.431 | 2.864 |
| 71 | 9.587 | 12.737 | 97 | 2.288 | 2.706 |
| 72 | 9.092 | 12.077 | 98 | 2.145 | 2.545 |
| 73 | 8.607 | 11.435 | 99 | 2.004 | 2.38 |
| 74 | 8.143 | 10.811 | 100 | 1.865 | 2.21 |
| 75 | 7.699 | 10.207 | 110 | – | 0.755 |

The following table shows the *joint life expectation* of two people (a man and a woman) at various age combinations. This is drawn from the average mortality experience of England and Wales in the years 1980–1982. The columns show the period for which both lives may be expected to survive on average, and which ends on the death of the first of the two to die. (*Source:* OPCS, *English Life Tables No. 14* published by HMSO.)

## JOINT LIFE EXPECTATION OF MALES AND FEMALES

| Age of woman | Age of man | | | | | | | | | | | | | | |
|---|---|---|---|---|---|---|---|---|---|---|---|---|---|---|---|
| | 20 | 25 | 30 | 35 | 40 | 45 | 50 | 55 | 60 | 65 | 70 | 75 | 80 | 85 | 90 |
| 20 | 47.98 | 44.71 | 40.97 | 36.87 | 32.58 | 28.24 | 23.99 | 19.97 | 16.29 | 12.98 | 10.09 | 7.69 | 5.78 | 4.35 | |
| 25 | 45.97 | 43.26 | 39.97 | 36.22 | 32.17 | 27.99 | 23.85 | 19.89 | 16.25 | 12.96 | 10.08 | 7.68 | 5.78 | 4.35 | 3.35 |
| 30 | 43.37 | 41.25 | 38.52 | 35.23 | 31.52 | 27.58 | 23.6 | 19.75 | 16.17 | 12.92 | 10.06 | 7.67 | 5.77 | 4.35 | 3.35 |
| 35 | 40.21 | 38.67 | 36.53 | 33.8 | 30.55 | 26.95 | 23.21 | 19.51 | 16.03 | 12.84 | 10.02 | 7.65 | 5.76 | 4.34 | 3.34 |
| 40 | 36.59 | 35.55 | 33.99 | 31.86 | 29.16 | 26.01 | 22.6 | 19.14 | 15.8 | 12.71 | 9.95 | 7.61 | 5.74 | 4.33 | 3.34 |
| 45 | 32.67 | 32.01 | 30.95 | 29.39 | 27.29 | 24.68 | 21.71 | 18.57 | 15.45 | 12.5 | 9.83 | 7.54 | 5.7 | 4.31 | 3.33 |
| 50 | 28.6 | 28.22 | 27.54 | 26.48 | 24.95 | 22.93 | 20.48 | 17.76 | 14.94 | 12.2 | 9.65 | 7.44 | 5.65 | 4.28 | 3.31 |
| 55 | 24.55 | 24.33 | 23.93 | 23.25 | 22.21 | 20.75 | 18.86 | 16.64 | 14.22 | 11.75 | 9.39 | 7.29 | 5.57 | 4.23 | 3.28 |
| 60 | 20.6 | 20.49 | 20.27 | 19.86 | 19.2 | 18.21 | 16.86 | 15.17 | 13.22 | 11.12 | 9.01 | 7.08 | 5.44 | 4.17 | 3.24 |
| 65 | 16.83 | 16.78 | 16.67 | 16.44 | 16.04 | 15.42 | 14.52 | 13.34 | 11.89 | 10.23 | 8.46 | 6.75 | 5.26 | 4.06 | 3.18 |
| 70 | 13.31 | 13.29 | 13.23 | 13.11 | 12.89 | 12.53 | 11.98 | 11.21 | 10.23 | 9.02 | 7.66 | 6.25 | 4.96 | 3.89 | 3.08 |
| 75 | 10.15 | 10.14 | 10.11 | 10.06 | 9.94 | 9.74 | 9.43 | 8.97 | 8.36 | 7.57 | 6.61 | 5.56 | 4.52 | 3.62 | 2.91 |
| 80 | | 7.46 | 7.45 | 7.43 | 7.37 | 7.27 | 7.1 | 6.84 | 6.5 | 6.02 | 5.41 | 4.69 | 3.94 | 3.24 | 2.66 |
| 85 | | | 5.37 | 5.35 | 5.33 | 5.27 | 5.19 | 5.05 | 4.86 | 4.59 | 4.23 | 3.77 | 3.27 | 2.77 | 2.34 |
| 90 | | | | 3.95 | 3.93 | 3.91 | 3.86 | 3.78 | 3.68 | 3.52 | 3.3 | 3.02 | 2.68 | 2.33 | 2.02 |

By using the two tables, you will be able to ascertain your average life expectancy and for how long your pension can be expected to pay out to you.

If in *ill-health*, you can expect a *higher* annuity rate. Not many people know this and lose a considerable amount of benefit as a result. The annuity provider is essentially taking a gamble on how long you will live. Annuity rates are adjusted accordingly. From our tables, you will see that at age 75, males will live on average for another 7.699 years; females for 10.207 years. However, a serious illness could severely shorten your life span. Better annuity rates are also available for smokers.

---

### STRATEGY #559
### Get yourself underwritten for higher annuity rates if in ill-health. This is not automatic and you must apply for it

---

A recent case was about to pay a pension in retirement of £9,800 p.a. After underwriting, this was increased to £33,400 p.a. as the client had developed cancer.

Annuity benefits can be expensive and are usually designed to protect income flows for a period. The addition of an escalation by 5% can reduce the initial level of benefit (or cost) 33.5%. Having a widow's benefit costs 15% of the value of your pension and guarantees cost from 1.5% of the value up to 10% or more. The only thing is – no one, other than the annuity provider, benefits if you die too soon. In some countries, like South Africa, any excess benefits from annuities supported by your pension fund are payable to your heirs. Not so in the UK. The following strategy will show you how to conserve your wealth – even after you've gone.

---

### STRATEGY #560
**Take a single life annuity with no guarantee. Insure the value of your entire pension fund without evidence of health (or be underwritten)**

---

On your death, the full *original* proceeds pays out free of all taxes (including IHT) to your spouse or nominated beneficiary in trust. This is the ultimate in flexibility. The cost of the premiums comes from doing away with joint lifetime and other guarantees, plus the better rates from the open market option.

---

### STRATEGY #561
**The quickest way to lose wealth is to have a joint and survivor annuity which is guaranteed. Your strategy is not to take one unless absolutely desperate to join 95% of the retiring population who will opt for one because they do not know any better**

---

The problem is – once you elect your annuity, you are locked in for life. There is no going back. Because the annuity provider must guarantee a pension payable for two lifetimes (yours and your partner's), the rate offered to you will be the lowest possible one. The second problem is – once you elect your joint and survivor annuity and your spouse dies *before* you, you are then locked into the selected lower joint rate forever. By insuring your fund, you should be no worse off in *income terms* than had you selected the joint and survivor annuity. However, your flexibility to create new lump sums and increase your income has increased by 100%.

---

### STRATEGY #562
### Shop around for the best annuity deals in retirement – you can increase your income by over 30%

---

All personal pension plans and retirement annuities may use the Open Market Option (OMO) to get a better rate. You do not need to purchase your pension where you built up your pension fund. Rates are on average 15% higher than what your current provider is offering – but instances of over 60% better annuities have occurred in the past. Retirement annuities utilising the OMO have the effect of restricting the size of the lump sum to that for personal pension plans.

Some providers are better at building pensions, others are better at providing annuities.

- A *lump sum* may be taken from a personal pension plan which is tax-free. This is up to 25% of the value of the fund (excluding any part of the fund built up with DSS contributions usually). For a retirement annuity, the maximum lump sum cash amount can equal three times the annual annuity payable after the cash has been taken (subject to a maximum cash lump sum of £150,000 per contract if effected after 17 March 1987).

---

### STRATEGY #563
### Always take the tax-free cash lump sum. It gives greater flexibility for investment purposes and if a further annuity is required, one can be bought with the tax-free cash, giving additional tax reliefs (the capital element of a PLA – Purchased Life Annuity – is not taxed)

---

You will have used the business to accumulate wealth in different forms, ranging from adding value to your shares to accelerated building of pension benefits. It is not enough to merely accumulate assets. One must also plan for maximum retention and keeping more of what you have. By using these strategies you will have learned how to increase income and capital values in retirement years.

## Key points summary

- The objective is to get the most from retirement plans using business retirement planning strategies.

- One must not only look at pension planning but a full spectrum of ways to build a retirement portfolio – from being given the company car to providing marketable private company shares.

- A full retirement planning 'countdown' report, paid for by the business, is not only advisable, but necessary. The field is vast and complex and professional advice is required for 'fine tuning'.

- Flexible retirement planning, maximising fund growth and annuity deferral options, plus strategies to pass your full pension fund to future generations, are core features of this chapter.

# EPILOGUE

*No great thing is created suddenly, any more than a bunch of grapes or a fig. If you tell me that you desire a fig, I answer you that there must be time. Let it first blossom, then bear fruit, then ripen.*
**Epictetus**

A strategy we were never taught in school was how to build wealth successfully. As you expect to spend the rest of your life in the future, you will want to make sure that the future is adequately planned for.

*Wealth Strategies for Your Business* has been written to encourage business owners to look beyond the balance sheet, to undertake a voyage of discovery into what is, for them, uncharted waters and to realise that wealth can be built even where there are no profits and economic conditions are dreadful.

As I write, it has been reported in *The Times* that the number of new businesses being launched is at its lowest level for almost a decade. Yet still 170,000 businesses were created in the first six months of 1995. For the small to medium-sized business sector, profit margins have more than doubled, albeit from a low base, rising from 1.8% on average to 3.8%.

At the same time, borrowings have dropped from 51.3% of funds employed to about 35%, whilst returns to shareholders rose by 81% That's good news – in fact, better than most of us thought.

It shows that wealth can be built under the best or worst or economic conditions, including recession, inflation or depression. There are more than three million businesses in the United Kingdom. Those with fewer than 20 employees account for 19 out of 20 companies. Only 100,000 businesses have turnovers of more than £1 million.

It is to this majority of smaller businesses that this book is aimed – to those entrepreneurs who provide employment, who take big risks using their own wealth to back their ideas and aspirations, who live and die in and for their businesses. Many of them have tasted financial success, others still yearn for it. Financial success is having the money to do the things you want to do, when you want to do them, and to enjoy doing them.

Successful people want to be in control of their own lives. They are winners, not losers. The thought of giving up has no appeal to them; they only make adjustments or fine-tune whatever they are doing and then do it. Winners are doers. They like freedom. They enjoy independence. They want and have sufficient money to have freedom of choice to decide, to sit back and reflect, to consider, to ponder and to make positive decisions. Money buys freedom to choose to do things which other people cannot do. Isn't it strange that the more you have, the more successful you are said to be?

This book is about the accumulation of wealth through the money-producing engine room of the business. It is designed to show how the business could become more efficient and caring if it wanted to; how to prevent money from leaving the business by the bucketful; how to capitalise on tax shelters and tax-reducing strategies, and how to grow wealth when you have it. Keeping wealth is as important as making it. Your whole working life will have been a pointless exercise in wealth-creation if you lose most of it on retirement or death.

You will succeed by applying one strategy at a time and then building on what you have accomplished to reach new heights. Go back and improve on what you have done before. Keep building. Build the business, build your personal wealth in and outside the business. Experience the rewards of life which success brings. You can do it. Just apply *Wealth Strategies for Your Business*. Good luck.

Tony Granger

# BIBLIOGRAPHY

*Allied Dunbar Tax Handbook 1995–96*, A Foreman (Pearson Professional Limited).

*Baffled by Balance Sheets?*, William Lee Johnson (Kogan Page).

*Beat the Competition with Barter*, Buzz Remde and Nick Lindesay-Bethune (Harriman House Publishing Ltd, 1994).

*British Master Tax Guide*, 13th Edition (CCH Editions Ltd).

*Capital Barter Corporation Limited Readers' Guide*, Ivor Tucker and Trish Wales (CBC London).

*Check Your Tax and Moneyfacts*, 1995/96 edition, Graham M Kitchen, FCA (W Foulsham & Co Ltd).

*Corporate Financial Strategy*, 1994 reprint, Keith Ward (Butterworth-Heinemann Ltd).

*Current Tax Developments 1993/94 and 1994/95* (Pannell Kerr Forster, Chartered Accountants).

*Law for the Small Business*, 6th Edition, Patricia Clayton (Kogan Page, 1988).

*Making Money Made Simple!*, Noel Whittaker and James Mackay (New Holland [Publishers] Ltd, 1991).

*Managing to Survive*, John Harvey-Jones (Mandarin, 1994).

*Pensions Pocket Book 1995* (NJL Publications Limited in association with Bacon and Woodrow).

*Personal Tax and Financial Planning 1995* (Price Waterhouse, Chartered Accountants).

*Principles of Corporate Finance*, 4th Edition, Brealey and Myers (McGraw-Hill).

*Sales Promotion*, Julian Cummins (Kogan Page, 1989).

*Setting Business Strategy Seminar* (Brian Tracy Learning Systems, Dundee).

*Taxation – A Guide to Theory and Practice in the UK*, David A Williams (Hodder and Stoughton, 1992).

*The Concise Guide to Interpreting Accounts*, J D Blake (Van Nostrand Reinhold, 1989).

*The Equitable Guide to Investment and Savings*, Lorna Bourke (Bloomsbury, 1993).

*The Marketing Book*, 2nd Edition, Michael J Baker (ed) (Butterworth-Heinemann for the Chartered Institute of Marketing, 1991).

*The 7 Habits of Highly Effective People*, Stephen R Covey (Simon and Schuster, 1989).

*The Task of Marketing Management*, GHG Lucas (ed) (J L Van Schaik, 1983).

*Tolley's Benefits-in-Kind Handbook 1994* (Tolley Publishing Co Ltd).

*Tolley's Employment Handbook*, 7th Edition, Elizabeth Shade and Nigel Giffin (Tolley Publishing Co Ltd, 1991).

*Tolley's Social Security and State Benefits*, Jim Matthewman (Tolley Publishing Co Ltd, 1992 et seq.).

*Tolley's Tax Guide 1995–96*, 13th Edition, Arnold Homer, FCA ATII, and Rita Burrows, MBA, ACIS, ATII (Tolley Publishing Co Ltd).

*Unlimited Power*, Anthony Robbins (Simon and Schuster Ltd, 1988).

*Wealth Without Risk for Canadians*, 2nd Edition, Charles J Givens (Stoddart Publishing Co Ltd).

*Which? Way to Save Tax*, 2nd Edition (Consumers Association).

# ABOUT THE AUTHOR

Tony Granger has a background in law, commerce and financial services and has been helping businesses and the people in them for over 15 years.

He introduced the concept of corporate benefit audits and the inter-linking of individual benefit structures to corporate ones for maximum wealth-creation in the UK. Tony has also developed innovative cost-reduction techniques, especially in the bulk purchase of employee benefits and affinity schemes, for UK businesses.

Latterly he brought out the first Inland Revenue approved Enterprise Investment Scheme (EIS) Fund to raise capital for businesses and now co-ordinates a portfolio of smaller companies and private equity investors for the Independent Financial Partnership Limited of Harrogate, North Yorkshire.

As a highly-qualified independent financial adviser, he has a large client base of individuals and businesses, and specialises in corporate financing and restructuring, as well as advising on higher-risk invest-ments. He is an international speaker on individual and corporate financial planning issues, and a past president of the Institute of Life and Pensions Advisers of South Africa, as well as a member of the Institute of Financial Planning of the United Kingdom, amongst others.

His many publications include a guide to financial services for solic-itors and accountants and a guide to venture capital trusts and enterprise investment schemes. He recently wrote the UK version of *Wealth Without Risk* for Charles J Givens of the USA, which gave him the idea of writing a book on wealth-creation for business owners in the smaller business market.

Currently advising businesses on strategies from raising capital suc-cessfully to getting profits out of the business effectively, he still finds time to develop new financial products for businesses and write infor-mative newsletters, as well as to address seminars on business and financial issues.

---

For more information on how to attend a seminar on wealth-creation strategies for your business in your area, contact
The Independent Financial Partnership Limited
01423 523311

# INDEX

personal pension plan, 101, 105, 107
perspectives, 99-101
protect assets, 453
reach £1m, 287
reduce taxes, 235, 287, 289, 314, 320
SSAS, 290, 471
school fees, 439
Section 32 plan, 101, 103
strategies, Ch. 8, 105, 112
tax transitional rules, 218
People, cost, 403
in business, 404-10
increase profits, 401
Investors In, 409
successful, 483
worth, 402
PEPS, 113, 114, 264, 289, 390
Performance, reward, 199
Permanent Health Insurance (PHI), 124, 126, 128, 131, 141, 159, 161, 162
company owned, 165
costs, 166
group PHI, 168
keyman PHI, 166, 167
partners, 165, 166
Personal allowances, 319, 333
Personal guarantees, 76, 191, 197
Premiums, tax deductible, 144
Price cutting, 190
Private medicine, 131, 161
Profit related pay (PRP), 48, 49, 55, 81, 82, 116, 126, 177, 262, 267, 280, 281, 290, 468
Profits, definition, 6
distribution, 314
effect of costs, 42
increase, 11, 18, 134, 401
policy, 225
retained, 25, 334
strategies, 322
taking, 313

trading, 270
Protection benefits, 126

Ratio analysis, 36, 37
Recreational assets, 303, 310
Redundancy, claim, 137
payments, 50, 150, 189
Refunds, claim, 218, 219
Reinvestment reliefs, 398, 442
Remortgage home, 196
Remuneration, costs, 124
packages, 125, 263
pay policy, 122, 124
strategies, Ch. 9
Retained reserves, 78, 225
Retirement, annuities, 115, 475-481
avoid tax, 392
countdown, 119, 462-5
date, 113, 474
divorced spouse, 473
expectation of life, 477-9
investments, 286
investors' dilemmas, 462
keep car, 466
lump sums, 472, 481
market for shares, 468
maximise, 288
pay off debts, 392
plan, 285
planning strategies, 461-482
PPP reliefs, 289
relief, 215, 390, 391, 455, 467
review, 463-465
sell business, 393
tax free lump sums, 290
written report, 465, 476
unfunded pensions, 469
use the business, 466
Review, pensions, 105
Risk, awareness, 14, 34
business, 20
of investigation, 256
preferences, 14

Salary sacrifice, 240
Sales, increasing, 43, 84
Savings, business, 129

coverages, 131
School fees, 246
scholarships, 248, 440
strategies, 437-442
subsidy, 267
Security, personal assets, 24
Self assessment, 213, 227
reduce profits, 210
self employed, 213
transitional rules, 217
Self-employed, insurance, 151
pension, 101
pension term cover, 156
perspectives, 315
self assessment, 213
strategies, 394
vulnerable, 149
Sensitivity analysis, 33, 190, 203
SERPS, 101
Shares, death, 397
market for, 267
partnerships, 267
schemes, 127
sell, CGT, 334
retirement, 155
Shareholders, agreement, 129, Ch. 11, 396
protection, 129, 153
strategies, 396
Sick pay, 157, 162
benefits, 167
policy, 160
save costs, 160-166
statutory, 158
SIPP, 107, 394
Spouse, build wealth, 180
critical illness cover, 168
contract, 172, 180
deduct housekeeping, 172
employed, 109, 211
employee benefits, 179, 244
in business, 319
income protection, 168
investments, 390
partnership, 179
pension, 177
protect assets, 382
save NIC, 173-175